SHAKESPEARE

A Critical Study of His Mind and Art

SHAKESPEARE

A Critical Study of His Mind and Art

EDWARD DOWDEN, LL.D.
Late Professor of English Literature
in the University of Dublin and Late Vice-President of
'The New Shakespeare Society'

ATLANTIC
PUBLISHERS & DISTRIBUTORS (P) LTD

Published by
ATLANTIC
PUBLISHERS & DISTRIBUTORS (P) LTD
7/22, Ansari Road, Darya Ganj,
New Delhi-110002
Phones : +91-11-40775252, 23273880, 23275880, 23280451
Fax : +91-11-23285873
Web : www.atlanticbooks.com
E-mail : orders@atlanticbooks.com

Branch Office
5, Nallathambi Street, Wallajah Road,
Chennai-600002
Phones : +91-44-64611085, 32413319
E-mail : chennai@atlanticbooks.com

Printed in India at Nice Printing Press, A-33/3A, Site-IV, Industrial Area, Sahibabad, Ghaziabad, U.P.

Preface to the Third Edition

In the present edition I have made such corrections as appeared needful, and have brought my statements on some doubtful points into harmony with the latest results of Shakesperian scholarship.

I wish to insist upon the statement made on pp. 211-12 that *Julius Caesar* lies in point of time beside *Hamlet.* Both are tragedies of thought rather than of passion; both present in their chief characters, the spectacle of noble natures which fail through some weakness or deficiency rather than through crime; upon Brutus as upon Hamlet a burden is laid which he is not able to bear; neither Brutus nor Hamlet is fitted for action, yet both are called to act in dangerous and difficult affairs. *Julius Caesar* was probably complete before *Hamlet* assumed its latest form, perhaps before *Hamlet* was written. Still,—giving the reader a caution as I did in the case of *The Tempest*—I am not unwilling to speak of *Hamlet* as the second of Shakespeare's tragedies. *Hamlet* seems to have its roots so deep in Shakespeare's nature, it was so much a subject of special predilection, it is so closely connected with older dramatic work. We acquire the same feeling with reference to *Hamlet* which we have for Goethe's *Faust*—that it has to do with almost the whole of the deeper part of the poet's life up to the date of its creation.

After Shakespeare had written these two tragedies, or while he was writing them, he continued to write comedy. But the genial spirit of comedy was deserting him. *Twelfth Night* resumes all the admirable humorous characteristics of the group of comedies which it completes. Then the change comes; *All's Well That Ends Well* is grave and earnest; *Measure for Measure* is dark and bitter. In the first edition of this work I did not venture to attempt an interpretation of *Troilus and Cressida.* I now believe this strange and difficult play was a last attempt to continue comedy made when Shakespeare had ceased to be able to smile genially, and when he must be either ironical, or else take a deep, passionate and tragical view of life.

I have elsewhere written as follows:

> *Troilus and Cressida* appeared in two quarto editions in the year 1609; in the title page of the earlier of the two it is stated to have been acted at the Globe; the later contains a singular preface in which the play is spoken of as 'never stal'd with the stage, never clapper-claw'd with the palmes of the vulgar,' and as having been published against the will of 'the grand possessors.' Perhaps the play was printed at first for the use of the theatre, and with the intention of being published after being represented, and that the printers, against the known wish of the proprietors of Shakespeare's manuscript, anticipated the first representation and issued the Quarto with the attractive announcement that it was an absolute novelty. The editors of the Folio, after having decided that *Troilus and Cressida* should follow *Romeo and Juliet* among the Tragedies, changed their minds, apparently uncertain how the play should be classed, and placed it between the Histories and Tragedies; this led to the cancelling of a leaf, and the filling up of a blank space left by the alteration, with the Prologue to *Troilus and Cressida*—a prologue which is believed by several critics not to have come from Shakespeare's hand.
>
> There is extreme uncertainty with respect to the date of the play. Dekker and Chettle were engaged in 1599 upon a play on this subject, and from an entry in the Stationers' Register on 7th Feb. 1602-03 it appears that a *Troilus and Cressida* had been acted by Shakespeare's company, the Lord Chamberlain's Servants. Was this Shakespeare's play? We are thrown back upon internal evidence to decide the question, and the internal evidence is itself of a conflicting kind, and has led to opposite conclusions. The massive worldly wisdom of Ulysses argues it is supposed in favour of a late date, and the general tone of the play has been compared with that of *Timon of Athens.* The fact that it

does not contain a single weak-ending and only six light-endings is however almost decisive evidence against our placing it after either *Timon* or *Macbeth*, and the other metrical characteristics are considered, by Hertzberg, the most careful student of this class of evidence in the case of the present play, to point to a date about 1603. Other authorities place it as late as 1608 or 1609; while a third theory (that of Verplanck and Grant White) attempts to solve the difficulties by supposing that it was first written in 1603 and revised and enlarged shortly before the publication of the Quarto. Parts of the play—notably the last battle of Hector—appear not to be by Shakespeare. The interpretation of the play itself is as difficult as the ascertainment of the external facts of its history. With what intention, and in what spirit did Shakespeare write this strange comedy? All the Greek heroes who fought against Troy are pitilessly exposed to ridicule, Helen and Cressida are light, sensual and heartless, for whose sake it seems infatuated folly to strike a blow; Troilus is an enthusiastic young fool; and even Hector, though valiant and generous, spends his life in a cause which he knows to be unprofitable if not evil. All this is seen and said by Thersites, whose mind is made up of the scum of the foulness of human life. But can Shakespeare's view of things have been the same as that of Thersites?

The central theme, the young love and faith of Troilus given to one who was false and fickle, and his discovery of his error, lends its colour to the whole play. It is the comedy of disillusion. And as Troilus passed through the illusion of his first love for woman, so by middle life the world itself often appears like one that has not kept her promises, and who is a poor deceiver. We come to see the seamy side of life; and from this mood of disillusion it is a deliverance to pass on even to a dark and tragic view of life, to which beauty and virtue reappear even though human weakness or human vice may do them bitter wrong. Now such a mood of contemptuous depreciation of life may have come over Shakespeare, and spoilt him, at that time, for a writer of comedy. But for Isabella we should find the coming on of this mood in *Measure for Measure;* there is perhaps a touch of it in *Hamlet.* At this time *Troilus and Cressida* may have been written, and then Shakespeare rousing himself to a deeper inquest into things may have passed on to his great series of tragedies.

Let us call this then the comedy of disillusion, and certainly wherever we place it we must notice a striking resemblance in its spirit and structure to *Timon of Athens.* Timon has a lax benevolence and shallow trust in the goodness of men; he is undeceived and bitterly turns away from the whole human race in a rage of disappointment. In the same play Alcibiades is in like manner wronged by the world; but he takes his injuries firmly like a man of action and experience and sets about the subduing of his base antagonists. Apemantus again is the dog-like reviler of men, knowing their baseness and base himself. Here, Troilus, the noble green-goose, goes through his youthful agony of ascertaining the unworthiness of her to whom he had given his faith and hope; but he is made of a stronger and more energetic fibre than Timon, and he comes out of his trial a man, no longer a boy, somewhat harder perhaps than before, but strung up for sustained and determined action. He is completely delivered from Cressida and from Pandar, and by Hector's death supplied with a motive for the utmost exertion of his heroic powers. Ulysses,—the antithesis of Troilus,—is the much-experienced man of the world, possessed of its highest and broadest wisdom, which yet always remains worldly wisdom and never rises into the spiritual contemplation of a Prospero. He sees all the unworthiness of human life, but will use it for high worldly ends; the spirit of irreverence and insubordination in the camp he would restrain by the politic machinery of what he calls 'degree'—I. i. 75-136. Cressida he reads at a glance, seeing to the bottom of her sensual shallow nature, and he assists at the disillusioning of the young Prince, whose nobleness is apparent to him from the first. Thersites also sees through the illusions of the world, but his very incapacity to have ever been deceived is a sign of the ignoble nature of the wretch. He feeds and grows strong upon garbage; physical nastinesses and moral sores are the luxuries of his imagination. The other characters, the brute warrior Ajax, the insolent self-worshipper Achilles, Hector, heroic but too careless how and when he expends his heroic strength, are of minor importance. As the blindness of youthful love is shown in Troilus, so old age in its least venerable form, given up to a gratification of sensuality by proxy, is exposed to derision in Pandar. The materials for Troilus and Cressida were found by Shakespeare in Chaucer's *Troilus and Cressida,* Caxton's translation from the French, *Recuyles, or Destruction of Troy,* perhaps also Lydgate's *Troye Boke.* Thersites, he probably found in Book II of Chapman's *Homer.* Shakespeare's conception of Cressida and of Pandar differs widely from Chaucer's; in Shakespeare's hands in accordance with the general design of the drama, Cressida and her uncle grow base and contemptible. Some critics have supposed that the love-story was written at a much earlier date than the part which treats of Ulysses; but we have seen that the contrasted characters of Troilus and Ulysses are both essential parts of the conception of the drama, and were created as counterparts.

The following table presents the plays in a series of groups which succeed one another in chronological order. The position of three or four plays of secondary importance may be doubtful; and I claim no certainty for the order of the plays within the groups; but I offer the arrangement of groups with great confidence as to its general correctness. It will be observed that in some cases one group overlaps in point of time that which follows it. To keep the comedies together I have placed "Middle Tragedy" after the third division of what I have named "Later Comedy;" it will suffice if the reader bear in mind that as a fact the comedy overlaps the succeeding group of tragedies.

1. PRE-SHAKESPEARIAN GROUP
(Touched by Shakespeare.)
Titus Andronicus (1588-90)
1 *Henry VI* (1590-91)

2. EARLY COMEDY
Love's Labour's Lost (1590)
Comedy of Errors (1591)
Two Gentlemen of Verona (1592-93)
Midsummer Night's Dream (1593-94)

3. MARLOWE-SHAKESPEARE GROUP
EARLY HISTORY
2 & 3 *Henry VI* (1591-92)
Richard III (1593)

4. EARLY TRAGEDY
Romeo and Juliet (? two dates, 1591, 1597)

5. MIDDLE HISTORY
Richard II (1594)
King John (1595)

6. MIDDLE COMEDY
Merchant of Venice (1596)

7. LATER HISTORY
History and Comedy united.
1 & 2 *Henry IV* (1597-98)
Henry V (1599)

8. LATER COMEDY
(a) Rough and boisterous comedy
Taming of the Shrew (? 1597)
Merry Wives (? 1598)
(b) Joyous, refined, romantic
Much Ado about Nothing (1598)
As You Like It (1599)
Twelfth Night (1600-01)
(c) Serious, dark, ironical
All's Well (? 1601-02)
Measure for Measure (1603)
Troilus and Cressida (? 1603; revised 1607 ?)

9. MIDDLE TRAGEDY
Julius Cæsar (1601)
Hamlet (1602)

10. LATER TRAGEDY
Othello (1604)
Lear (1605)
Macbeth (1606)
Antony and Cleopatra (1607)
Coriolanus (1608)
Timon (1607-08)

11. ROMANCES
Pericles (1608)
Cymbeline (1609)
Tempest (1610)
Winter's Tale (1610-11)

12. FRAGMENTS
Two Noble Kinsmen (1612)
Henry VIII (1612-13)

POEMS
Venus and Adonis (? 1592)
Lucrece (1593-94)
Sonnets (? 1595-1605)

"The student will observe in this arrangement, early, middle, and later Comedy; early, middle, and later History; and early, middle, and later Tragedy. Not only is it well to view the entire body of Shakespeare's plays in the order of their chronological succession, but also to trace in chronological order the three separate lines of Comedy, History, and Tragedy. The group named Romances connect themselves, of course, with the Comedies; but there is a grave element in them which is connected with the Tragedies which preceded them. It has been noticed that the Romances have in common the incidents of reunions, reconciliations, and the recovery of lost children. Shakespeare, though so remarkable for his power of creating character, is not distinguished among dramatists for his power of inventing incident. Having found a situation which interested his imagination, or was successful on the stage, he introduced it again and again, with variations. Thus, in the Early Comedies, mistakes of identity, disguises, errors, and bewilderments, in various forms, recur as a source of merriment and material for adventure. In the Later Comedies, again, it is quite remarkable how Shakespeare (generally in the portions of these plays which are due to his own invention) repeats, with variations, the incident of a trick or fraud practised upon one who is a self-lover, and its consequences, grave or gay. Thus, Falstaff is fatuous enough to believe that two English matrons are dying of love for him, and is made the victim of their merry tricks. Malvolio is made an ass of by the mischievous Maria taking advantage of his solemn self-esteem; Beatrice and Benedick are cunningly entrapped, through their good-natured vanity, into love for which they had been already predisposed; the boastful Parolles is deceived, flouted, and disgraced by his fellow-soldiers; and (Shakespeare's mood growing earnest, and his thoughts being set upon deep questions of character) Angelo, the self-deceiver, by the craft of the Duke, is discovered painfully to the eyes of others and to his own heart."

For the index which adds to the usefulness of the present edition I have to thank my friend Mr Arthur E. Love of Trinity College, Dublin.

It has been a happiness to me to find that what I have written on Shakespeare has been approved by distinguished Shakespeare scholars in England, in Germany, in France, and in America. I do not thank my critics for their generous recognition of whatever may deserve commendation in my work; I may, however, at least express the sense of encouragement derived from what they have said. One of the earliest voices which spoke a word of emphatic approval of this book is now silent in death, and I cannot but desire to associate, at least by my grateful recollection, this Study of Shakespeare with the honoured name of its reviewer in *The Academy,* the late Mr Richard Simpson.

Preface to the First Edition

The attempt made in this volume to connect the study of Shakespeare's works with an inquiry after the personality of the writer, and to observe, as far as is possible, in its several stages the growth of his intellect and character from youth to full maturity, distinguishes the work from the greater number of preceding criticisms of Shakespeare. A sense of hazard and difficulty necessarily accompanies the attempt to pass through the creations of a great dramatic poet to the mind of the creator. Still no one, I suppose, would maintain that a product of mind, so large and manifold as the writings of Shakespeare, can fail in some measure to reveal its origin and cause.

The reader must not fall into the error of supposing that I endeavour to identify Shakespeare with any one of his dramatic personages. The complex nature of the poet contained a love-idealist like Romeo—(students of the Sonnets will not find it difficult to admit the possibility of this); it contained a speculative intellect like that of Hamlet. But the complete Shakespeare was unlike Romeo, and unlike Hamlet. Still it is evident not from one play, but from many, that the struggle between "blood" and "judgment" was a great affair of Shakespeare's life; and in all his later works we observe the effort to control a wistful curiosity about the mysteries of human existence. And, therefore, I say, a potential Romeo, and a potential Hamlet, taking these names as representative of certain spiritual tendencies or habits, existed in Shakespeare. Nor do I identify Shakespeare with Prospero; although Shakespeare's temper in the plays of the last period is the temper of Prospero. It would not be easy to picture to ourselves the great magician waited on by such ministering spirits as Sir John Falstaff, Sir Toby Belch, and the Nurse of Juliet.

In order to get substantial ground to go upon I have thought it necessary to form acquaintance with a considerable body of recent Shakespeare scholarship, both English and continental. But I avoid the discussion of purely scholastic questions. To approach Shakespeare on the human side is the object of this book; but I believe that Shakespeare is not to be approached on any side through dilettantism.

I have carefully acknowledged my obligations to preceding writers. In working out the general design and main features of this study, I was able to obtain little help; but in details I obtained much. My references express, I may say, considerably more than my actual debt; for in those instances in which I found that my thought had been anticipated, and well expressed elsewhere, I have noted the coincidence. Doubtless many instances of such coincidence remain unobserved by me. Since I wrote the chapter in which *The Tempest* is considered, I have read for the first time Lloyd's essay upon the play, and I have found some striking and satisfactory points of agreement between myself and that good critic.

In all essentials I have adhered to the chronological method of studying Shakespeare's writings. But it seemed pedantry to sacrifice certain advantages of contrast and comparison to a procedure in every instance, from play to play, according to dates. Thus, in the chapter on the English Historical Plays I have, for convenience of illustration, treated *Henry VI* after King *John* and before *Richard III.* In the opening of the eighth chapter I have explained what I believe to be the right manner of using the chronological method. I have called *The Tempest* Shakespeare's last play, but I am quite willing to grant that *A Winter's Tale, Henry VIII* and perhaps *Cymbeline*, may actually have succeeded *The Tempest.* For the purpose of such a study as the present, if it be admitted that these plays belong to one and the same period,—the final period of the growth of Shakespeare's art,—it matters little how the plays succeeded one another within that period.

I refer in one passage to *Henry VIII,* Act iv, Scene 2, as if written by Shakespeare. The scene was, I believe, conceived by Shakespeare, and carried out in the spirit of his design by Fletcher.

About half of this volume was read in the form of lectures ("Saturday Lectures in connection with Alexandra College, Dublin"), in the Museum Buildings, Trinity College, Dublin, during the spring of the year 1874.

In some instances I have referred to, and quoted from papers by the Rev. F.G. Fleay as read at meetings of "The New Shakespeare Society," but which have not received the final corrections of their author.

In seeing the volume through the press, I received valuable suggestions and corrections from Mr Harold Littledale, the editor, for "The New Shakespeare Society," of "The Two Noble Kinsmen," for which I thank him.

I have to thank the Director of "The New Shakespeare Society," Mr F.J. Furnivall, for permission to print the "Trial Table of the order of Shakespeare's Plays," which appears in his introduction to the new edition of Shakespeare Commentaries by Gervinus.

Trial Table of the Order of Shakespeare's Plays

[This, like all other tables, must be lookt on as merely tentative, and open to modification for any good reasons. But if only it comes near the truth, then reading the plays in its order will the sooner enable the student to find out its mistakes. (M. stands for "mentioned by Francis Meres in his *Palladis Tamia,* 1598.")]

In his Introductory Essays to *Shakespeare's Dramatische Werke* (German Shakespeare Society) Prof. Hertzberg dates *Titus* 1587-89, *Love's Labour's Lost,* 1592, *Comedy of Errors* about New Year's Day 1591, *Two Gentlemen* 1592, *All's Well* 1603, *Troilus and Cressida* 1603, and *Cymbeline* 1611.

	Supposed Date	Earliest Allusion	Date of Publication
FIRST PERIOD			
Venus and Adonis	1585-87		1593
Titus Andronicus toucht up	(?) 1588	1594 M	[(?) 1594] 1600
Love's Labour's Lost	1588-89	1598 M	1598 (amended)
Love's Labour's Wonne	]	1598 M	
Comedy of Errors	1589-91	1598 M	1623
Midsummer Night's Dream (? two dates)	1590-91	1598 M	1600

Trial Table of the Order of Shakespeare's—Continued

	Supposed Date	Earliest Allusion	Date of Publication
Two Gentlemen of Verona	1590-92	1598 M	1623
(?) 1 *Henry VI* toucht up	(?) 1590-92		1623
(?) *Troilus and Cressida*, begun		1594	
(?) *Lucrece*			1594
Romeo and Juliet	(?) 1591-93	1595 M	1597
(?) *A Lover's Complaint*			
Richard II.	1593-94	(?) 1595 M	1597
Richard III.	1594	(?) 1595 M	1597
2 & 3 *Henry VI* re-cast	(?) 1594-95		1623
John	1595	1598 M	1623
Second Period			
Merchant of Venice	(?) 1596	1598 M	1600†
Taming of the Shrew, part	(?) 1596-97		1623*‖
1 *Henry IV*	1596-97‡	1598 M	1598
2 *Henry IV*	1597-98‡	1598 M	1600
Merry Wives	1598-99	1602	1602
Henry V	1599‡	1599	1600
Much Ado	1599-1600‡	1600	1600
As you Like it	1600‡	1600	1623§
Twelfth Night	1601‡	1602	1623
All's Well (? *L's. L. Wonne* re-cast)	1601-02		1623
Sonnets	(?) 1592-1602	1598 M	1609
Third Period			
Hamlet	1602-03‡	(?)	1603*
Measure for Measure	(?) 1603		1623
Julius Cæsar	(?) 1601-03	(?)	1623
Othello	(?) 1604	1610	1622
Macbeth	1605-06‡	1610	1623
Lear	1605-06‡	1606	1608*
Troilus & Cressida (?) completed	1606-07	1609	1609
Antony and Cleopatra	1606-07	1608 (?)	1623
Coriolanus	(?) 1607-08		1623
Timon, part	1607-09		1623
Fourth Period			
Pericles, part	1608‡	1608	1609*
Two Noble Kinsmen	1609		1634
Tempest	1610	? 1614	1623
Cymbeline	1610-12		1623
Winter's Tale	(?) 1611	1611	1623
Henry VIII, part.	1613‡	1613 (?)	1623

* Enterd 1 year before at Stationers' Hall.

† Enterd 2 years before at Stationers' Hall.

‡ May be lookt-on as fairly certain.

§ Enterd in the Stationers' Registers in 1600.

‖ 'The Taming of a Shrew' was publisht in 1594.

Contents

1

Shakespeare and the Elizabethan Age

In these chapters an attempt will be made to present a view or aspect of a great poet, and the first word must explain precisely what such a view or aspect is worth, what it professes to be, and what it disclaims. Dr Newman, in his "Grammar of Assent," has distinguished two modes of apprehending propositions. There is what he calls the real apprehension of a proposition, and there is the notional apprehension. In real apprehension there is the perception of some actual, concrete, individual object, either with the eye or some bodily sense, or with the mind's eye—memory, or imagination. But our minds are not so constructed as to be able to receive and retain only an exact image of each of the objects that comes before us one by one, in and for itself. On the contrary, we compare and contrast. We see at once "that man is like man, yet unlike; and unlike a horse, a tree, a mountain, or a monument. And in consequence we are ever grouping and discriminating, measuring and sounding, framing cross classes, and cross divisions, and thereby rising from particulars to generals, that is, from images to notions [...]. 'Man' is no longer what he really is, an individual presented to us by our senses, but as we read him in the light of those comparisons and contrasts which we have made him suggest to us. He is attenuated into an aspect, or relegated to his place in a classification. Thus his appellation is made to suggest, not the real being which he is in this or that specimen of himself, but a definition." Thus individual propositions about the concrete, in the mind of a thinker whose intellect works in the way of notional apprehension, "almost cease to be, and are diluted or starved into abstract notions. The events of history and the characters who figure in it lose their individuality."

Now it is not such an aspect, such a view of Shakespeare which it is here attempted to present. To come into close and living relation with the individuality of a poet must be the chief end of our study—to receive from his nature the peculiar impulse and impression which he, best of all, can give. We must not attenuate Shakespeare to an aspect, or reduce him to a definition, or deprive him of individuality, or make of him a mere notion. Yet also no experiment will here be made to bring Shakespeare before the reader as he spoke, and walked, as he jested in his tavern, or meditated in his solitude. It is a real apprehension of Shakespeare's character and genius which is desired, but not such an apprehension as mere observation of the externals of the man, of his life or of his poetry, would be likely to produce. I wish rather to attain to some central principles of life in him which animate and control the rest, for such there are existent in every man whose life is life in any true sense of the word, and not a mere affair of chance, of impulse, of moods, and of accidents.

In such a study as this we endeavour to pass through the creation of the artist to the mind of the creator: but it by no means prevents our returning to view the work of art simply as such, apart from the artist, and as such to receive delight from it. Nay, in the end it augments our delight by enabling us to discover a mass of fact which would otherwise be overlooked. To enjoy the beauty of a landscape it is not necessary to understand the nature and arrangement of the rocks which underlie or rise up from the soil. While studying the stratification of those rocks we absolutely lose sight of the beauty of the landscape. Nevertheless, a larger mass of pleasure is in the end possessed by one who adds to his instinctive spontaneous feeling of delight, a knowledge of the geology of the country. In like manner, while the study of anatomy is quite distinct from the pleasure which the sight of a beautiful human body gives, yet, in the end, the sculptor who adds to his instinctive, spontaneous delight in the beauty of moulded form and moving limb, a knowledge of human anatomy, receives a mass of pleasure greater than that of one who is unacquainted with the facts of structure and function. There is an obvious cause of this. The geologist and the anatomist *see more*, and see a new class of phenomena, which produce new delights. The lines of force in a landscape, to which an ordinary observer is entirely insensible, come out to the instructed eye, and give it thrills of strong emotion, like those which we receive from the athletes or the gods of Michael Angelo. The lines of force are drawn in the granite and the sandstone differently, and hence an endless variety of delights corresponding to the infinite variety of the disposition of its rock-forces by Nature. We do not only understand better what is before us; we enjoy it more. We are not attenuating it to an aspect, or inobservant of its individuality; we are, on the contrary, penetrating to the centre of that individuality. It is generally not until the dominant lines of force are clearly perceived that we can group in just proportions the minor details which investigation presents to our notice.

One who stands in the Sistine Chapel at Rome, and looks up to its ceiling, must in due time become aware of his own spirit as if it were some over-burdened caryatid, sustaining the weight of the thought of Michael Angelo. The first effort—and it is no trivial effort—must be to raise oneself to the height of the great argument. Merely to conceive prophet, or sibyl, primitive man or the awful demiurge, as placed before one's eyes, is an exercise which demands concentration of self, and abandonment of the world,—an exercise which strains and exhausts the imagination. To ascend from this to a comprehension of the total product,—to feel the stupendous life which animates not alone each single figure, rapt or brooding, but which circles through them all, which plays from each to the other, and forms the one vital soul that lies behind this manifold creation—to achieve this is something rarer and more difficult. But there is yet a higher ascension possible. These vast creations, and much beside these, St Peter's at Rome, the David at Florence, the Slaves of the Louvre, the Last Judgment, the Moses, the Tombs of the Medici, the Poems for Vittoria Colonna,—all these are less than Michael Angelo. These were the projections of a single mind. There is something higher and more wonderful than St Peter's, or the Last Judgment—namely, the *mind* which flung these creations into the world. And yet, it is when we make the effort which demands our most concentrated and most sustained energy,—it is when we strive to come into presence of the living mind of the creator, that the sense of struggle and effort is relieved. We are no longer surrounded by a mere world of thoughts and imaginations which, in an almost selfish way, we labour to appropriate and possess. We are in company with a man; and a sense of real human sympathy and fellowship rises within us. Virtue goes out of him. We are conscious of his strength communicating itself to us. We may not overmaster him, and pluck out the heart of his mystery; yet it is good to remain in his companionship. There is something in this invigorating struggle with a nature greater than one's own which unavoidably puts on in one's imagination, the shape of the Hebrew story of Peniel. We wrestle with an unknown man until the breaking of the day. We say, "Tell me, I pray thee, thy name?" and he will not tell it. But though we cannot compel him to reveal his secret, we wrestle with him still. We say, "I will not let thee go, except thou bless me." And the blessing is obtained.

If to lay hold of Michael Angelo and to strive with him be the most strenuous feat achievable by the critical imagination in the world of plastic art, to deal with Shakespeare requires more endurance, a firmer nerve, and a finer cunning. The great ideal artist, a Milton, a Michael Angelo, a Dante, betrays himself in spite of the haughtiest reserve. But Shakespeare, if an idealist, was also above all else a realist in art, and lurks almost impregnably behind his work. "The secrets of nature have not more gift in taciturnity."* And yet some few of the secrets of nature can be wrested from her. But Shakespeare possessed that most baffling of self-defences—*humour*. Just when we have laid hold of him, he eludes us, and we hear only distant ironical laughter. What is to be done? How shall a dramatist—a dramatist possessed of humour—be cheated of his privacy? How shall his reserve be over-mastered? How shall we

* *Troilus and Cressida*, Act iv, Scene 2.

interrogate him? Is there any magic word which will compel him to put off disguise, and declare himself in his true shape?

If we could watch his writings closely, and observe their growth, the laws of that growth would be referable to the nature of the man, and to the nature of his environment. And we might even be able to refer to one and the other of these two factors producing a common resultant, that which is specially due to each. Fortunately the succession of Shakespeare's writings (although it is probable that neither external nor internal evidence will ever suffice to make the chronology certain and precise), is sufficiently ascertained to enable us to study the main features of the growth of Shakespeare as an artist and as a man. We do not now place *A Midsummer Night's Dream* and *The Tempest* side by side as Shakespeare's plays of fairyland. We know that a long interval of time lies between the two, and that if they resemble one another in superficial or accidental circumstances, they must differ to the whole extent of the difference between the youthful Shakespeare, and the mature, experienced, fully-developed man. Much is due to the industry of Malone; much to the ingenuity and industry of recent Shakespeare scholars who, in the changes which took place in the poet's manner of writing verse, have found an index, trustworthy in the main, to the true chronology of the plays.*

* Mr Spedding, in his article, "Who wrote *Henry VIII*?" (*Gentleman's Magazine*, August 1850) first applied quantitative criticism of verse peculiarities to the study of Shakespeare's writings. Mr Charles Bathurst, in "Remarks on the Differences of Shakespeare's Versification in Different Periods of His Life" (London, 1857), called attention to the change "from broken to interrupted verse" which took place as Shakespeare advanced in his dramatic career; and observed also the increase in the use of double-endings in his later plays. Professor Craik, in his "English of Shakespeare," and Professor J.K. Ingram, in a lecture upon Shakespeare published in "Afternoon Lectures" (Bell and Daldy, 1863), again called attention to these peculiarities of versification as affording evidence for the ascertainment of the chronology of the plays. Finally, about the same time in England and in Germany, two investigators—Rev. F.G. Fleay and Professor Hertzberg—began to apply "quantitative criticism" of the characteristics of verse to the determination of the dates of plays. The test on which Hertzberg chiefly relies is the feminine (double) ending; he gives the percentage of such endings in seventeen plays, and believes

It will be well first to stand away from Shakespeare, and to view him as one element in a world larger than himself. In order that an organism—plant or animal—should exist at all, there must be a certain correspondence between the organism and its environment. If it be found to thrive and flourish, we infer that such correspondence is considerable. Now we know something of the Elizabethan period, and we know that Shakespeare was a man who prospered in that period. In that special environment Shakespeare throve: he put forth his blossoms and bore fruit. And in the smaller matter of material success he flourished, also. In an Elizabethan atmosphere he reached his full stature, and became not only great and wise, but famous, rich, and happy. Can we discover any significance in these facts ? We are told that Shakespeare "was not of an age, but for all time." That assertion misleads us; and indeed in the same poem to the memory of his friend from which these words are taken, Ben Jonson apostrophises his great rival as "Soul of the Age." Shakespeare was for all time by virtue of certain powers and perceptions, but he also belonged especially to an age, his own age, the age of Spenser, Raleigh, Jonson, Bacon, Burleigh, Hooker,—a Protestant age, a monarchical age, an age eminently positive and practical. A man does not attain to the universal by abandoning the particular, nor to the everlasting by an endeavour to overleap the limitations of time and place. The abiding reality exists not somewhere apart in the air, but under certain temporary and local forms of thought, feeling, and endeavour. We come most deeply into communion with the permanent facts and forces of human nature and human life, by accepting first of all this fact,—that a definite

that the percentage indicates their chronological order. See the preface to *Cymbeline* in the German Shakespeare Society's edition of Tieck's and Schlegel's translation. Mr Fleay's results, independently ascertained, were published subsequently to Hertzberg's. See Trans. New Sh. Soc., and *Macmillan's Magazine*, Sept. 1874. In 1873 Mr Furnivall, in founding the New Shakespeare Society,—before he was aware that Mr Fleay's work was in progress,—insisted on the importance of metrical tests for determining the chronology, and gave the proportion of stopt to unstopt lines in three early and three late plays. The latest contribution to the subject is Professor Ingram's valuable paper read before the New Sh. Soc. on the "Weak-ending" Test.

point of observation and sympathy, not a vague nowhere, has been assigned to each of us.

What is the ethical significance of that literary movement to which Shakespeare belonged, and of which he was a part—the Elizabethan drama? The question seems at first improper. There is perhaps nobody of literature which has less of an express tendency for the intellect than the drama of the age of Elizabeth. It is the outcome of a rich and manifold life; it is full of a sense of enjoyment, and overflowing with energy; but it is for the most part absolutely devoid of a conscious purpose. The chief play-wright of the movement declared that the end of playing, "both at the first and now, was and is to hold as 'twere the mirror up to nature." A mirror has no tendency. The questions we ask about it are, "Does this mirror reflect clearly and faithfully?" and "In what direction is it turned?" Capacity for perceiving, for enjoying, and for reproducing facts, and facts of as great variety as possible,—this was the qualification of a dramatist in the days of Elizabeth. The facts were those of human passion, and human activity. He needed not, as each of our poets at the present time needs, to have a doctrine, or a revelation, or an interpretation. The mere fact was enough without any theory about the fact; and this fact men saw more in its totality, more in the round, because they approached it in the spirit of frank enjoyment. It was not for them attenuated into an aspect, or relegated to a class.

In the Renaissance and Reformation period life had grown a real thing,—this life on earth for three score years and ten. The terror and sadness of the Middle Ages, the abandonment of earthly joy, the wistfulness and pathos of spiritual desire, and, on the other hand, the scepticism, irony, and sensuality under the ban were things which, as dominant forms of human life, had passed away. The highest mediaeval spirits were those which had felt with most intensity that we are strangers and pilgrims here on earth, that we have no abiding place among human loves and human sorrows, that life is of little worth except with reference to infinite, invisible antecedents and issues in other worlds. With all his tender affinities to the brotherhood of elemental powers, and of animals, Saint Francis felt allied to these as brethren only because they had ceased to be rivals for his heart with the supreme lover, Jesus. The deepest religious voice of the Middle Ages couples in a single breath the words *de imitatione Christi* and *de contemptu omnium vanitatum mundi.* It is the ascetic quester, Galahad, with vision undimmed by any mist of earthly passion, who beholds the mystical Grail. Angelico paints paradise, and, because the earth can afford no equal beauty, then paradise again; below the glory of seraphim and cherubim appear the homely faces of priest and monk, transported into the pellucid and changeless atmosphere of heaven, for these men had abandoned earth, and may therefore inherit perpetual blessedness. Dante—filled with keen political passion as he was—finds his subjects of highest imaginative interest not in the life of Florence, Pisa, and Verona, but in circles of Hell, and the mount of Purgatory, and the rose of beatified spirits. Human love ceases to be adequate for the needs of his adult heart; the woman who was dearest to him ceases to be woman, and is sublimed into the supernatural wisdom of theology. While the world was thus given over to Satan, those who were lacking in the spiritual passion, and who could not abandon this world, closed a bargain with the evil One. Together with the world and the flesh they accepted the devil, as in the legend Faustus does, and as many as one did in fact. Our imagination can hardly find a place for Shakespeare in any part of the Middle Ages. Either they would transform him, or he would confound and disorganise them. With his ever present sense of truth, his realisation of fact, and especially of that great fact, a moral order of the universe, we cannot think of Shakespeare among the men of pleasure, scepticism, and irony; he could not stay his energy or his humour with the shallow lubricities of Boccaccio. Neither can we picture to ourselves an ascetic Shakespeare, suppressing his desire of knowledge, transforming his hearty sense of natural enjoyment into curiosities of mystic joy, exhaling his strength in sighs after an "Urbs beata Ierusalem," or in tender lamentation over the vanity of human love and human grief.

But in the Renaissance and Reformation period, instead of substituting supernatural powers, and persons, and events for the natural facts of the world, men recurred to those facts, and found in them inspiration and sustenance for heart, and intellect, and conscience. Of paradise men knew somewhat less than Angelico had known, or Dante; but they saw that this earth is good. Physical nature was not damnable; the outlying regions of the earth were not all tenanted by vampires and devils. Sir John Mandeville brought back stories of obscure valleys communicating with hell, and haunted by homicidal demons; Raleigh brought back the tobacco plant and the potato. In the college of his new Atlantis Bacon erects a statue to the inventor of sugar. Dreams of unexplored regions excited the imagination of Spaniard and Englishman in the later Renaissance; but it was of El Dorado they dreamed, with its gold-roofed city, and auriferous sands. Hardy men went forth to establish plantations and possess the earth. And as these were eager to acquire power over the physical world by extending in the Indies and America the dominion of civilised man, others were no less eagerly engaged in endeavouring to extend, by means of scientific discovery, the dominion of man over all forces and provinces of nature. The student of science was not now a magician, a dealer in the black art, in miracles of the diabolic kind; he pleaded in the courts, he held a seat in parliament, he became Lord Chancellor of England. It was ascertained that heaven was not constructed of a series of spheres moving over and around the earth, but that the earth was truly *in* heaven. This is typical of the moral discovery of the time. Men found that the earth is in heaven, that God is not above nature, touching it only through rare preternatural points of contact,—rather that He is not far from every one of us, that human life is sacred, and time a fragment of eternity.*

* See the excellent opening chapters of "Shakespeare als Protestant, Politiker, Psycholog, und Dichter," by Dr Eduard Vehse. "Shakespeare, der ungelehrte, unstudirte Dichter ist der erste, in welchem sich der moderne Geist, der von der Welt weiss, der die gesammte Wirklichkeit zu begreifen sucht, energisch zusammenfasst. Dieser moderne Geist ist der gerade Gegensatz des mittelalterlichen Geistes; er erfasst die Welt und namentlich die innere Welt als ein Stück des Himmels, und das Leben als einen Theil der Ewigkeit." vol. i, p. 62.

Catholicism had endeavoured to sanctify things secular by virtue proceeding towards them from special ecclesiastical persons, and places and acts. The modern spirit, of which Protestantism is a part, revealed in the total life of men a deeper and truer sanctity than can be conferred by touches of any wand of ecclesiastical magic. The burden of the curse was lightened. Knowledge was good, and men set about increasing the store of knowledge by interrogation of nature, and by research into the life of mankind as preserved in ancient literatures. Visible pomp was a thing which the eye might frankly enjoy; men tried to make life splendid. Raleigh rode by the queen in silver armour; the Jesuit Drexelius estimated the value of the shoes worn by this minion of the English Cleopatra at six thousand six hundred gold pieces. The essays "Of Building" and "Of Gardens," by Bacon, show how this superb mundane ritualism had a charm for his imagination. Beauty was now confessed to be good; not the beauty of paradise which Angelico painted, but that of Lionardo's Monna Lisa, and Raffaele's Fornarina, and of the daughters of Palma Vecchio. The earth and those excellent creatures, man and woman, walking upon it, formed a spectacle worth a painter's soul. One's country was for the present not the heavenly Jerusalem, but a certain defined portion of this habitable globe; and patriotism became a virtue, and queen-worship a piece of religion. Conscience was a faithful witness; an actual sense of sin, and an actual need of righteousness were individual concerns, belonging to the inmost self of each human being, and not to be dealt with by ecclesiastical mechanism, by sale of indulgence, or dispensation of a Pope. Woman was neither a satanic bait to catch the soul of man, nor was she the supernatural object of mediaeval chivalric devotion; she was no miracle, yet not less nor other than that endlessly interesting thing—woman. Love, friendship, marriage, the ties of parent and child, jealousy, ambition, hatred, revenge, loyalty, devotion, mercy,—these were not insignificant affairs because belonging to a world which passes away; human life being of importance, these, the blessings and curses of human life, were important also. Heaven may be very real; we have a good hope that it is so; meanwhile here is our earth, a substantial, indubitable fact.

The self-conscious ethics of the Elizabethan period find an imaginative utterance in Spenser's *Faerie Queene*. Spenser's view of human life is grave and earnest; it is that of a knightly encounter with principalities and powers of evil. Yet Spenser is neither mediaeval nor essentially Puritan; the design of the *Faerie Queene* is in harmony with the general Elizabethan movement. The problem which the poet sets himself to consider is not that of our great English prose allegory,—"The Pilgrim's Progress"—how the soul of man may escape from earth to heaven. Nor is the quest of a mystical Grail a central point in this epic of Arthur. The general end of Spenser's poem is "to fashion a gentleman or noble person in virtuous and gentle discipline." A grand self-culture is that about which Spenser is concerned; not as with Bunyan the escape of the soul to heaven; not the attainment of supernatural grace through a point of mystical contact, like the vision which was granted to the virgin knight of the mediaeval allegory. Self-culture, the formation of a complete character for the uses of earth, and afterwards, if need be, for the uses of heaven—this was subject sufficient for the twenty-four books designed to form the epic of the age of Elizabeth. And the means of that self-culture are of the active kind, namely warfare,—warfare not for its own sake, but for the generous accomplishment of unselfish ends. Godliness, self-mastery, chastity, fraternity, justice, courtesy, constancy—each of these is an element in the ideal of human character conceived by the poet; not an ascetic, not a mediaeval ideal. If we are to give a name to that ideal we must call it Magnificence, Great-doing. Penitential discipline and heavenly contemplation are recognised by Spenser as needful to the perfecting of the Godward side of man's nature, and as preparing him for strenuous encounter with evil; yet it is characteristic that even Heavenly Contemplation in Spenser's allegory cannot forget the importance of those wonderful things of earth,—London and the Queen.

Nor is each of Spenser's knights (although upon his own strength and skill assisted by divine grace depends the issue of his strife), a solitary knight-errant. The poet is not without a sense of the corporate life of humanity. As the virtues are linked one to another by a golden chain, so is each noble nature bound to his fellows. Arthur is the succourer of all; all are the servants of Gloriana. Spenser would seem to have longed for some new order of lofty, corporate life, a later Round Table, suitable to the Elizabethan age. If it were a dream, more fitted for Faery Land than for England of the sixteenth century, we may perhaps pardon Spenser for belief in incalculable possibilities of virtue; for he had known Sidney, and the character of Sidney seems forever to have lived with him inspiring him with inextinguishable faith in man. With national life Spenser owned a sympathy which we do not expect to find in the mediaeval romances of Arthur, written before England had acquired an independent national character, nor in Bunyan's allegory, which does not concern itself with affairs of earthly polity, and which came into existence at a period of national depression, a time when the political enemies of England were her religious allies. But in the days of Elizabeth the nation had sprung up to a consciousness of new strength and vitality, and its political and religious antagonists, Spain and the Papacy, were identical. Faery Land with Spenser is indeed no dream world; it lies in no distant latitude. His epic abounds with contemporary political and religious feeling. The combat with Orgoglio, the stripping of Duessa, the death of Kirkrapine could have been written only by an Englishman and a Protestant possessed by no half-hearted hatred towards Spain and the Papal power. Spenser's views on Irish politics, which interested him so nearly, are to be discovered in the Legend of Arthegall with hardly less clearness than in his prose dialogue upon the Present State of Ireland.

Further, in his material life, Spenser appears to have had a sufficient hold upon positive fact. During the same year, in which, for the second time, he became a lover, the year during which he wooed his Elizabeth, and recorded his despairs and raptures in the Italian love-philosophy of the *Amoretti,* the piping and pastoral Colin Clout exhibited suit for three ploughlands, parcels of Shanballymore, and was alleged to have "converted a great deal of corn" elsewhere "to his proper use." Neither love nor poetry made him insensible to the substantial though minor fact of ploughlands of Shanballymore.

With measureless dominion in Faery Land he yet did not disdain a slice of the forfeited estate of the Earl of Desmond. Some powerful hostility hindered his court-preferment; and the grievance finds a place in Spenser's verse. His own material life he endeavoured, not altogether successfully, to render solid and prosperous. The intention of his great poetical achievement is one which, while in a high sense religious, is at the same time eminently positive. A complete development of noble human character for active uses, not a cloistered virtue, is that which Spenser looked upon as most needed for God and man. Such a design is in harmony with the spirit of England in the days of Elizabeth. To be great and to do great things seemed better than to enter the Celestial City, and forget the City of Destruction; better than to receive in ecstasy the vision of a divine mystery, or to be fed with miraculous food. In Spenser these ethics of the Elizabethan age arrived at a self-conscious existence.

Let us, remaining at the same point of view, glance now at Bacon and the scientific movement. Bacon and Shakespeare stand far apart. In moral character and in gifts of intellect and soul we should find little resemblance between them. While Bacon's sense of the presence of physical law in the universe was for his time extraordinarily developed, he seems practically to have acted upon the theory that the moral laws of the world are not inexorable, but rather by tactics and dexterity may be cleverly evaded. Their supremacy was acknowledged by Shakespeare in the minutest as well as in the greatest concerns of human life. Bacon's superb intellect was neither disturbed nor impelled by the promptings of his heart. Of perfect friendship or of perfect love he may, without reluctance, be pronounced incapable. Shakespeare yielded his whole being to boundless and measureless devotion. Bacon's ethical writings sparkle with a frosty brilliance of fancy, playing over the worldly maxims which constituted his wisdom for the conduct of life. Shakespeare reaches to the ultimate truths of human life and character through a supreme and indivisible energy of love, imagination, and thought. Yet Bacon and Shakespeare belonged to one great movement of humanity. The whole endeavour of

Bacon in science is to attain the fact, and to ascend from particular facts to general. He turned away with utter dissatisfaction from the speculating *in vacuo* of the middle ages. His intellect demanded positive knowledge; he could not feed upon the wind. From the tradition of philosophy and from authority he reverted to nature. Between faith and reason Bacon set a great and impassable gulf. Theology is something too high for human intellect to discuss. Bacon is profoundly deferential to theology, because, as one cannot help suspecting, he was profoundly indifferent about it. The schoolmen for the service of faith had summoned human reason to their aid, and Reason, the ally, had in time proved a dangerous antagonist. Bacon, in the interest of science, dismissed faith to the unexceptionable province of supernatural truths. To him a dogma of theology was equally credible whether it possessed an appearance of reasonableness or appeared absurd. The total force of intellect he reserved for subjugating to the understanding the world of positive fact.

As the matter with which Bacon's philosophy concerns itself is positive, so its end is pre-eminently practical. The knowledge he chiefly valued was that which promised to extend the dominion of man over nature, and thus to enrich man's life. His conception of human welfare was large and magnificent; yet it was wanting in some spiritual elements which had not been lost sight of in earlier and darker times. To human welfare, thus conceived in a way somewhat materialistic, science is to minister. And the instruments of science by which it attains this end are the purely natural instruments of observation, experiment, and inference. Devotion to the fact, a return from the supernatural to the strictly natural and human, with a practical, mundane object—these are the characteristics of the Elizabethan movement in science.*

Let us now turn to the religious movement in England. That movement cannot be said to have had, like the Reformation

* Mr Spedding's estimate of Bacon differs much from that given above; and Mr Spedding has the best right of any living person to speak of Bacon. One must, however, remain faithful to one's own impression of facts, even when that impression is founded on partial (yet not wholly insufficient) knowledge.

movement in Germany, a central point of vitality and sustenance in the agony of an individual conscience. Nor was it guided like the movement in France by a supreme organising power—theological and political, capable of large, if somewhat too logically rigid, ideal conceptions. The dogma of Anglicanism is not like Calvinistic dogma, the expression and development of an idea; it becomes intelligible only through recollection of a series of historical events,—the balance of parties, compromises with this side and with that, the exigencies of times and seasons. But if England had neither a Luther nor a Calvin, she had Cranmer and Hooker. The religious revolution of France in the sixteenth century, like the political revolution of 1789, though it sent a strong wave of moral feeling through Europe, failed to sustain itself. Its uncompromising ideality kept it too much out of relation with the vital, concrete, and ever-altering facts of human society. The English reformation on the other hand, if less presentable in logical formulae to the intellect, was, like English political freedom as compared with French liberty, equality, and fraternity, much more of a practical success.

Cosmopolitan the English Reformation was not; it was a growth of the soil, and cannot be transplanted; this is its note of inferiority, and equally its characteristic excellence. By combined firmness and easiness of temper, by concessions and compromises, by unweariable good sense, a reformed church was brought into existence,—a manufacture rather than a creation,—in which the average man might find average piety, average rationality, and an average amount of soothing appeal to the senses; while rarer spirits could frame out of the moderation of the Anglican ritual and Anglican devotional temper, a refined type of piety, free from extravagance, delicate and pure, offending like the cathedrals of England neither by rigidity on the one hand, not by flamboyant fervours on the other, the type of piety realized in a distinguished degree by George Herbert, by Ken, by Keble. In his Ecclesiastical Sonnets Wordsworth speaks of the ritual and liturgy of the Church of England as affording material and scope for "the intensities of hope and fear," and for "passionate exercise of lofty thoughts." In the preface to *The Christian Year* the moderation, the soothing influence of the devotional services of the church are noticed. Wordsworth, even when the flood of spiritual light and strength which encompassed his youth and early manhood had ebbed, remained Wordsworth still; and from beyond the little neatly-ordered enclosure of Anglicanism voices still came to him of mountain winds and of "mighty waters rolling evermore." Keble, who was born and bred in the Anglican paddock, understood its limitations better, and wrote the true poetry of his communion—a poetry free from all risk of being over poetical. Dante is the poet of Catholicism; Milton is the poet of Puritanism; the poet of Anglicanism is Keble.

Much in the ecclesiastical history of our country was due to Cranmer. Had that unworthy right hand of his been less sensitive or less pliable, the Church of England might have been a more heroic witness for truth (sometimes a noble failure serves the world as faithfully as does a distinguished success), but it could hardly have become a national institution with roots which ramify through every layer of society. And Hooker,—in what lies the special greatness of Hooker? Is not his special quality a majestic common sense?* "If we are to fix on any fundamental position," writes the Dean of St Paul's, "as the key of Hooker's method of arguing, I should look for it in his doctrine, so pertinaciously urged, and always implied, of the concurrence and cooperation, each in its due place, of all possible means of knowledge for man's direction." Puritanism appealed, against reason to the letter of Scripture, and sacrificed fact to theory. The Renaissance philosophers appealed from authority to human reason alone. Hooker, while assigning the ultimate, judicial position to reason, will not deny its place to either Scripture or to the Church, or to tradition. He is an embodiment of the ecclesiastical wisdom of England. While providing the Church, as the Dean of St Paul's has said, with a broad, intelligible theory, Hooker saves this theory from rigidity, and merely ideal constructiveness, by rooting it in his rich feeling for the concrete fact. Characteristically English the work of Hooker will always remain by its lying close to reality, by its

* I am not sure whether Mr Matthew Arnold has not applied this expression "majestic common sense" to Hooker.

practical tendency, by its moderation, by its large good-sense. More massive Hooker's spirituality becomes, because it includes a noble realization of positive fact.

Now the same soil that produced Bacon and Hooker produced Shakespeare; the same environment fostered the growth of all three. Can we discover anything possessed in common by the scientific movement, the ecclesiastical movement, and the drama of the period? That which appears to be common to all is *a rich feeling for positive, concrete fact.* The facts with which the drama concerns itself are those of human character in its living play. And assuredly, whatever be its imperfection, its crudeness, its extravagance, no other body of literature has amassed in equal fulness and equal variety a store of concrete facts concerning human character and human life; assuredly not the drama of Æschylus and Sophocles, not the drama of Calderon and Lope de Vega, not the drama of Corneille and Racine. These give us views of human life and select portions of it for artistic handling. The Elizabethan drama gives us the stuff of life itself, the coarse with the fine, the mean with the heroic, the humorous and grotesque with the tragic and the terrible. The personages of the drama—if we except those of Marlowe—"are not symbols of any absolute or ideal type [...]. The human being is not defined by its most prominent faculty, nor life by its most potent manifestation. The beings themselves, life itself, are brought before us on the scene, and that with a reality, truth, and perfection the highest ever attained by man."*

Poetry in this Elizabethan period is put upon a purely human basis. No fate broods over the actions of men, and the history of families; the only fatality is the fatality of character.†

---

* Joseph Mazzini, *Critical and Literary Writings*, vol. ii, pp. 133-34. On what follows Mazzini writes, "In Shakespeare, and this is a real progress (as compared with Æschylus), liberty does exist. The act of a single day, or it may be of an hour, has thrown an entire life under the dominion of necessity, but in that day or hour the man was free, and arbiter of his own future."—p. 135.

† Shakespeare stellte zuerst seine Stücke auf ganz rein menschlichen Boden [...]. Wie eines Menschen Gemüth ist, so ist auch sein Schicksal [...]. Alles, was äusserlich geschieht, ist bei Shakespeare durch ein Inneres bedingt."—E. Vehse, *Shakespeare als Protestant, &c.*, vol. i, pp. 57-58.

Luck, an outstanding element, helping to determine the lives of mortals, and not reducible to known law, luck good and bad, Shakespeare readily admits; but luck is strictly a thing in the course of nature. The divinity which shapes our ends works efficiently, but secretly. Men's lives in the drama of Shakespeare are not disorganised and denaturalised by irruptions of the miraculous. The one standing miracle is the world itself. That power and virtue which can achieve wonders, which can do higher things than all feats of grotesque magic recorded in the Legend, is simply a noble or beautiful soul of man or woman. If we recognise in a moral order of the world a divine presence, then the divine presence is never absent from the Shakespearian world. For such sacred thaumaturgy as that of Calderon's *Autos* we shall in vain seek in the drama of England.*

A vigorous, mundane vitality—this constitutes the basis of the Elizabethan drama. Vigour reveals on the one hand the tragedy of life. Love and hatred, joy and sorrow, life and death being very real to a vigorous nature, tragedy becomes possible. To one who exists languidly from day to day, neither can the cross and passion of any human heart be intelligible, nor the solemn intensities of joy, the glorious resurrection and ascension of a life and soul. The heart must be all alive and sensitive before the imagination can conceive, with swift assurance, and no hesitation or error, extremes of rapture and of pain. The stupendous mass of Lear's agony, and the spasms of anguish which make Othello writhe in body as in mind, fell within the compass of the same imagination that included at the other extremity the trembling expectation of Troilus, before the entrance of Cressida,†—into which the dramatist enters so

* It is remarkable that the peculiar merit of Calderon recognised by Shelley in his Defence of Poetry,—a merit which Shelley cannot attribute to the Elizabethan dramatists,—should be his endeavour to connect art with religion.

† *Troilus.*—I am giddy; expectation whirls me round.
The imaginary relish is so sweet
That it enchants my sense; what will it be,
When that the watery palate tastes indeed
Love's thrice repured nectar? Death, I fear me,
Swooning destruction, or some joy too fine,
Too subtle-potent, tuned too sharp in sweetness,

profoundly, while at the same time he holds himself ironically aloof,—the fulness of satisfied need when Posthumus embraces Imogen:

> Hang there like fruit, my soul,
> Till the tree die!

and the rapture (almost transcending the bounds of consciousness) of Pericles upon the recovery of his long-lost Marina:

> O Helicanus, strike me, honour'd sir;
> Give me a gash, put me to present pain;
> Lest this great sea of joys rushing upon me
> O'erbear the shores of my mortality,
> And drown me with their sweetness.

On the other hand this same vigour enables men to perceive and enjoy the comedy of life; for vigour enjoys folly; when it laughs, like Shakespeare's Valentine, "it laughs like a cock." One who is thoroughly in earnest is not afraid to laugh; he knows that he may safely have his laugh out, and that it will not disturb the solid relations of things. It is only when we are half in earnest that we cherish our seriousness, and tremble lest the dignity of our griefs or joys should be impaired. And accordingly when great tragedies can be written joyous comedies can be written also. But when life grows base or trivial, when great tragedy ceases (as in the period of the Restoration), when false heroics, and showy sentimentality take the place of tragic passion, then the laughter of men becomes brutal and joyless,—the crackling of thorns under a pot.

This vigorous vitality which underlies the Elizabethan drama is essentially mundane. To it all that is upon this earth is real; and it does not concern itself greatly about the reality of other things. Of heaven or hell it has no power to sing. It finds such and such facts here and now, and does not invent or discover

---

> For the capacity of my ruder powers:
> I fear it much: and I do fear besides,
> That I shall lose distinction in my joys;
> As doth a battle, when they charge on heaps
> The enemy flying.—Act iii, Scene 2.

supernatural causes to explain the facts. It pursues man to the moment of death, but it pursues him no farther. If it confesses "the burden of the mystery" of human life it does not attempt to lighten that burden by any "Thus saith the Lord," which cannot be verified or attested by actual experience. If it contains a divine element, the divine is to be looked for *in* the human, not apart from the human. It knows eternity only through time which is a part of eternity.*

Without an ethical tendency, then, the Elizabethan drama yet produces an ethical effect. A faithful presentation of the

* The following passage adds to what has been written above, and illustrates it. "The feeling which we commonly call pathos seems, when one analyses it, to arise out of a perception of grand incongruities—filling a place in one class of our ideas corresponding to that in another in which the sense of the ludicrous is placed by Locke. And this pathos was attained by mediaeval asceticism through its habit of dwarfing into insignificance the earthly life and its belongings, and setting the meanness and wretchedness which it attributed to it, in contrast to the far-off vision of glory and greatness [...]. Another sort of pathos—the Pagan— [...] results from a full realising of the joy and the beauty of the earth, and the nobleness of men's lives on it, and from seeing a grand inexplicableness in the incongruity between the brightness of these and the darkness which lies at either end of them—the infinite contradiction between actual greatness and the apparent nothingness of its whence and whither—the mystery of strong and beautiful impulses finding no adequate outcome now, nor promise of ever finding it hereafter—human passion kindling into light and glow, only to burn itself out into ashes—the struggle kept up by the will of successive generations against Fate, ever beginning and ever ending in defeat, to recommence as vainly as before—the never-answered, why? uttered unceasingly in myriad tones from out all human life. The poetry of the Greeks gained from the contemplation of these things a pathos which, however gladly a Christian poet may forego such gain for his art, was in its sadness inexpressibly beautiful. The Iliad had a deep under-current of it even in the midst of all its healthy childlike objectivity, and it was ever present amongst the great tragedian's introspective analysings of humanity. High art of later times has, for the most part, retained this Pagan beauty. Though there is no reason to think that there was any Paganism in Shakespeare's creed, yet we cannot help feeling that, whether the cause is to be sought in his individual genius, or in Renaissance influences, the spirit of his art is in many respects Pagan. In his great tragedies he traces the workings of noble or lovely human characters on to the point—and no further—where they disappear into the darkness of death, and ends with a look *back*, never on towards anything beyond. His sternly truthful realism will

facts of the world does not leave us indifferent to good and evil, but rather rouses within us, more than all maxims and all preaching can, an inextinguishable loyalty to good. It is any falsifying of those facts, whether the falsification be that of the sensualist or of the purist, whether it be a lie told to seduce us to vice, or to bribe us to virtue,—it is this which may possibly lead us aside from directness, simplicity, and uprightness of action. Is the Elizabethan drama religious! No, if religion be something which stands over and above human life, luring it away from earth: no, if the highest acts of religion be an access to the Divine presence through special ecclesiastical rites, and places, and persons. Yes, if the facts of the world be themselves sacred,—parts of a divine order of things, and interpenetrated by that Supreme Reality, apprehended yet unknowable, of which the worlds of matter and of mind are a manifestation.

To many, at the present time, the sanity and the strength of Shakespeare would assuredly be an influence that might well be called religious. The Elizabethan drama is thoroughly free from lassitude, and from that lethargy of heart, which most of us have felt at one time or another. Those whose lot falls in a period of doubt and spiritual alteration, between the ebb and the flow, in the welter and wash of the waves, are,—because they lack the joyous energy of a faith—peculiarly subject to this mood of barren lethargy. And it is not alone in the mystic, spiritual life of the soul that we may suffer from coldness or aridity. There are seasons when a sterile world-weariness is induced by the superficial barrenness of life. The persons we

---

not, of course, allow him to attempt a shallow poetical justice, and mete out to each of his men and women the portion of earthly good which might seem their due; and his artistic instincts—positive rather than speculative—prefer the majesty and infinite sadness of unexplainedness to any attempt to look on towards a future solution of hard riddles in human fates."—E.D. West (in the first of two articles on "Browning as a Preacher": *The Dark Blue Magazine*, October and November 1871). This passage may be borne in mind to illustrate the view taken of the great tragedies of Shakespeare in a subsequent chapter of this volume. See also on the agnosticism of Shakespeare—Mr Ruskin's lecture, "The Mystery of Life and Its Arts" in Afternoon Lectures (Dublin: M'Gee, 1869), pp. 110-11.

know seem to shrivel up and become wizened and grotesque. The places we have loved transform themselves into ugly little prisons. The ideals for which we lived appear absurd patterns, insignificant arabesques, devoid of idea and of beauty. Our own heart is a most impertinent and unprofitable handful of dust. It is well if some supreme joy or sorrow which has overtaken us save us from possible recurrence of this mood of weary cynicism. But humbler means at times have served. The tear shed over a tale of Marmontel by one who recorded his malady and his recovery, has occasioned certain smiles on critical lips.* A true physician of the soul discerns that such a tear is not despicable, but significant as the beads of perspiration which tell that the crisis of a fever is favourably passed. To this mood of barren world-weariness the Elizabethan drama comes with no direct teaching, but with the vision of life. Even though death end all, these things at least *are*—beauty and force, purity, sin, and love, and anguish and joy. These things are, and therefore life cannot be a little idle whirl of dust. We are shown the strong man taken in the toils, the sinner sinking farther and farther away from light and reality and the substantial life of things into the dubious and the dusk, the pure heart all vital, and confident, and joyous; we are shown the glad, vicarious sacrifice of soul for soul, the malign activity of evil, the vindication of right by the true justiciary; we are shown the good common things of the world, and the good things that are rare; the love of parents and children, the comradeship of young men, the exquisite vivacity, courage, and high-spirited intellect of noble girlhood, the devotion of man and woman to man and woman. The vision of life rises before us; and we know that the vision represents a reality. These things, then, being actual, how poor and shallow a trick of the heart is cynicism!

Two views of the character of Shakespeare have been offered for our acceptance; we are expected to make a choice between the two. According to one of these views Shakespeare stands before us a cheerful, self-possessed, and prudent man, who conducted his life with sound worldly judgment; and he wrote

---

* J.S. Mill's *Autobiography*, pp. 140-41.

plays, about which he did not greatly care; acquired property, about which he cared much; retired to Stratford, and attaining the end of his ambition, became a wealthy and respectable burgess of his native town, bore the arms of a gentleman, married his two daughters with prudence, and died with the happy consciousness of having gained a creditable and substantial position in the world. The other view of Shakespeare's character has been recently presented by M. Taine with his unflagging brilliancy and energy. According to this second conception Shakespeare was a man of almost superhuman passions, extreme in joy and pain, impetuous in his transports, disorderly in his conduct, heedless of conscience, but sensitive to every touch of pleasure, a man of inordinate, extravagant genius.

It is impossible to accept either of these representations of Shakespeare as a complete statement of the fact. Certain it is, however, that a portion of truth is contained in the first of these two Shakespeare theories. There can be no doubt that Shakespeare considered it worth his while to be prudent, industrious, and economical. He would appear to have had a very sufficient sense of life, and in particular of his own life, as real, and of this earth as a possession. He had seen his father sinking deeper and deeper into pecuniary embarrassment, and dropping away from the good position which he had held amongst his fellow townsmen. Shakespeare had married at eighteen years of age; he was at the age of twenty-one the father of a son, and of two daughters; a reckless, improvident life became more than ever undesirable. He took the means which gave him the best chance of attaining worldly prosperity; he made himself useful in every possible way to his dramatic company. While others, Greene, and Peele, and Marlowe, had squandered their strength in the turbulent life of London, Shakespeare husbanded his strength. The theatrical life did not bring satisfaction to him; he felt that his moral being suffered loss while he spent himself upon the miscellaneous activities forced upon him by his position and profession; he was made for a higher, purer life of more continuous progress towards all that is excellent, and he felt painfully that his nature was being subdued to what it worked in, as the dyer's hand receives its stain.* Nevertheless he did not, in the fashion of idealists, hastily abandon the life which seemed to entail a certain spiritual loss; he recognised the reality of external, objective duties and claims, duties to his father, to his family, to his own future self; he accepted the logic of facts; he compelled the lower and provisional life of player and playwright to become the servant of his higher life, as far as circumstances permitted; and he carefully and steadily applied himself to effecting his deliverance from that provisional life at the earliest suitable period; but not before that period had arrived. And afterwards when Shakespeare had become a prosperous country gentleman, he did not endeavour to cut himself loose from his past life which had served him, and the associates who had been his friends and helpers; the Stratford gentleman who might write himself Armigero "in any bill, warrant, quittance, or obligation," was not so enamoured of this distinction as to be ashamed of the days when he lived by public means; he remembers in his will among the rural esquires and gentry, "My Fellowes, John Hemynges, Richard Burbage, and Henry Cundell."

Thus all through his life we observe in Shakespeare a sufficient recognition of external fact, external claims, and obligations. Hence worldly prosperity could not be a matter which would ever seem unimportant to Shakespeare. In 1604, when he was a wealthy man, William Shakespeare brought an action against Philip Rogers, in the Court of Stratford, for £1, 15s. 10d., being the price of malt sold and delivered to him at different times. The incident is characteristic. Shakespeare evidently could estimate the precise value for this temporal life (though possibly not for eternity), of £1, 15s. 10d.; and in addition to this he bore down with unfaltering insistence on the positive fact that the right place out of all the universe for the said £1, 15s. 10d. to occupy, lay in the pocket of William Shakespeare.

Practical, positive, and alive to material interests, Shakespeare unquestionably was. But there is another side to his character. About the same time that he brought his action

---

* *Sonnets,* cxi.

against Philip Rogers for the price of malt, the poet was engaged upon his *Othello* and his *Lear.* Is it conceivable that Shakespeare thought more of his pounds than of his plays? Strongly as he felt the fact about the little sum of money which he sought to recover, is it not beyond possibility of doubt that his whole nature was immeasurably more kindled, aroused, and swayed by the vision of Lear upon the heath, of Othello taken in the snake-like folds of Iago's cunning, and by the inscrutable mysteries respecting human life which these suggested? It is highly important to fix our attention on what is positive, practical, and finite in Shakespeare's art, as well as in Shakespeare's life. But if the poet was of his own age, he was also "for all time." He does not merely endeavour to compass and comprehend the knowable; he broods with a passionate intensity over that which cannot be known. And again, he not only studies self-control; he could depict, and we cannot doubt that he knew by personal experience absolute abandonment and self-surrender. The infinite of meditation, the infinite of passion, both these lay within the range of Shakespeare's experience and Shakespeare's art. He does not, indeed, come forward with explanations of the mysteries of existence; perhaps because he felt more than other men their mysteriousness. Many of us seem to think it the all-essential thing to be provided with answers to the difficult questions which the world propounds, no matter how little the answers be to these great questions. Shakespeare seems to have considered it more important to put the questions greatly, to feel the supreme problems.

Thus Shakespeare, like nature and like the vision of human life itself, if he does not furnish us with a doctrine, has the power to free, arouse, dilate. Again and again we fall back into our little creed or our little theory. Shakespeare delivers us; under his influence we come anew into the presence of stupendous mysteries, and, instead of our little piece of comfort, and support, and contentment, we receive the gift of solemn awe, and bow the head in reverential silence. These questions are not stated by Shakespeare as intellectual problems. He states them poignantly, for the emotions and for the imagination.

And it is by virtue of his very knowledge that he comes face to face with the mystery of the unknown. Because he had sent down his plummet farther into the depths than other men, he knew better than others how fathomless for human thought those depths remain. "Un génie," Victor Hugo has said, "est un promontoire dans l'infini." This promontory which we name Shakespeare stretching out long and sharp has before it measureless sea and the mass of threatening cloud; behind it the habitable globe, illuminated, and alive with moving figures of man and woman.

Our conclusion, therefore, is that Shakespeare lived and moved in two worlds—one limited, practical, positive; the other a world opening into two infinites, an infinite of thought, and an infinite of passion. He did not suppress either life to the advantage of the other; but he adjusted them, and by stern and persistent resolution held them in the necessary adjustment. In the year 1602 Shakespeare bought for the sum of three hundred and twenty pounds, one hundred and seven acres of arable land in the parish of Old Stratford. It was in the same year (if the chronology of Delius be accepted as correct) that Shakespeare, in the person of his Hamlet, musing on a skull, was tracing out the relations of a buyer of land to the soil in a somewhat singular fashion. "This fellow might be in's time a great buyer of land, with his statutes, his recognizances, his fines, his double vouchers, his recoveries; is this the fine of his fines, and the recovery of his recoveries, to have his fine pate full of fine dirt?" The courtier Osric, who has "much land and fertile," is described by the Prince (who could be contented in a nutshell, but that he has bad dreams) as "spacious in the possession of dirt." Yet this dirt Shakespeare used to serve his needs.

How shall a man live sanely in presence of the small daily facts of life (which are also not small but great), and in presence of the vast mystery of death? How shall he proportion his interests between the bright illuminated spot of the known, and the dim, environing unknown which possesses such strong attraction for the soul? How shall he restrain and attach his desires to the little objects which claim each its definite share of the heart, while the heart longs to abandon itself to some one thing with measureless devotion? Shakespeare's attainment of sanity and self-control was not that of a day or of a year, it was the attainment of his life. Now he was tempted by his speculative intellect and imagination to lose all clear perception of his limited and finite life; and again he was tempted to resign the conduct of his being by the promptings of a passionate heart. He is inexorable in his plays to all rebels against the fact; because he was conscious of the strongest temptation to become himself a rebel. He cannot forgive an idealist, because in spite of his practical and positive nature he was (let the Sonnets witness) an idealist himself. His series of dramatic writings is one long study of self-control.

And Shakespeare, we have good reason to believe, did at last attain to the serene self-possession which he had sought with such persistent effort. He feared that he might become (in spite of Mercutio's jests) a Romeo; he feared that he might falter from his strong self-maintenance into a Hamlet; he suffered grievous wrong and he resolved that he would not be a Timon. He ended by becoming Duke Prospero. Admired Miranda—truly "a thread of his own life"—he made over to the young gallant Ferdinand—(and yet was there not a touch of sadness in resigning to a somewhat shallow-souled Fletcher the art he loved?). He broke his magic staff; he drowned his book deeper than ever plummet sounded; he went back, serenely looking down upon all of human life, yet refusing his share in none of it, to his Dukedom at Stratford resolved to do Duke's work, such as it is, well; yet Prospero must forever have remained somewhat apart and distinguished from other Dukes, and Warwickshire magnificoes, by virtue of the enchanted island, and the marvellous years of mageship.

It has been asked whether Shakespeare was a Protestant or a Catholic, and he has been proved to belong to each communion to the satisfaction of contending theological zealots. Shakespeare's poetry, resting upon a purely human basis, is not a rendering into art of the dogmas of either Catholicism or Protestantism. Shakespeare himself, a great artistic nature, framed for manifold joy and pain, may, like other artists, have had no faculty for the attainment of certitude upon extra-mundane and superhuman matters; of concrete moral facts he had the clearest perception, but we do not find that he was interested, at least as an artist, in truths or alleged truths which transcend the limits of human experience. That the world suggests inquiries which cannot be answered,—that mysteries confront and baffle us,—that around our knowledge lies ignorance, around our light, darkness, this to Shakespeare seemed a fact containing within it a profound significance, which might almost be named religious. But studiously as Shakespeare abstains from embodying theological dogma in his art, and tolerant as his spirit is, it is certain that the spirit of Protestantism,—of Protestantism considered as portion of a great movement of humanity,—animates and breathes through his writings. Unless he had stood in antagonism to his time, it could not be otherwise. Shakespeare's creed is not a series of abstract statements of truth, but a body of concrete impulses, tendencies, and habits. The spirit of his faith is not to be ascertained by bringing together little sentences from the utterances of this one of his *aramatis personae* and of that. By such a method he might be proved (as Birch tried to prove Shakespeare), an atheist.* The faith by which Shakespeare lived, is rather to be discovered by noting the total issue and resultant of his art towards the fostering and sustenance of a certain type of human character. It may be asserted, without hesitation, that the Protestant type of character, and the Protestant polity in state and nation, is that which has received impulse and vigour from the mind of the greatest of English poets. Energy, devotion to the fact, self-government, tolerance, a disbelief in minute apparatus for the improvement of human character, an indifference to externals in comparison with that which is of the invisible life, and a resolution to judge all things from a

* "Inquiry into the Philosophy and Religion of Shakespeare," 1848. This is also too much the method (leading, however, to a very different result), of Flathe in the laborious chapter "Die Anschauungen Shakespeare's über sein Selbst, &c.," which opens the first volume of "Shakespeare in seiner Wirklichkeit." On this subject see Vehse's book already referred to; the last of Kreyssig's lectures in his smaller work, *Shakespeare-Fragen*, and Rümelin *Shakespeare-Studien*, pp. 207-15 (second edition).

purely human standpoint, these grow upon us as habits of thought and feeling, as long as Shakespeare remains an influence with us in the building up of character. Such habits of thought and feeling are those which belong more especially to the Protestant ideal of manhood.*

Is Shakespeare a religious poet? An answer has been given to this question by Mr Walter Bagehot, which contains the essential truth. "If this world is not all evil, he who has understood and painted it best, must probably have some good. If the underlying and almighty essence of this world be good, then it is likely that the writer who most deeply approached to that essence will be himself good. There is a religion of week-days as well as of Sundays, a religion of 'cakes and ale' as well as of pews and altar cloths. This England lay before Shakespeare as it lies before us all, with its green fields, and its long hedgerows, and its many trees, and its great towns, and its endless hamlets, and its motley society, and its long history, and its bold exploits, and its gathering power; and he saw that they were good. To him perhaps more than to any one else has it been given to see that they were a great unity, a great religious object; that if you could only descend to the inner life, to the deep things, to the secret principles of its noble vigour, to the essence of character [...] we might, so far as we are capable of so doing, understand the nature which God has made. Let us then think of him, not as a teacher of dry dogmas, or a sayer of hard sayings, but as:

A priest to us all
Of the wonder and bloom of the world,—

a teacher of the hearts of men and women."†

---

* See on this subject the able reply to Rio by Michael Bernays in *Jahrbuch der Deutschen Shakespeare-Gesellschaft,* vol. i, pp. 220-99. A minute but perhaps significant piece of evidence has been noticed recently by H. von Friesen. In *Romeo and Juliet,* Act iv, Scene 1, we read, "Or shall I come to you at evening mass?" No Catholic, observes H. von Friesen, could have spoken of "evening mass."—"Altengland and William Shakespeare (1874)," pp. 286-87. Staunton had previously noticed the difficulty. But see the paper on this passage by the late Mr R. Simpson, in "Transactions of New Shakespeare Society, 1875-76."

† Estimates of some Englishmen and Scotchmen, by Walter Bagehot, p. 270.

It is impossible, however, that the sixteenth or the seventeenth century should set a limit to the nineteenth. The voyaging spirit of man cannot remain within the enclosure of any one age or any single mind. We need to supplement the noble positivism of Shakespeare with an element not easy to describe or define, but none-the-less actual, which the present century has demanded as essential to its spiritual life and well-being, and with its spiritual teachers—Wordsworth, Coleridge, Shelley, Newman, Maurice, Carlyle, Browning, Whitman (a strange and apparently motley assemblage!) have supplied and are still supplying. The scientific movement of the present century is not more unquestionably a fact, than this is a fact. In the meantime to enter with strong and undisturbed comprehension into Shakespeare, let us endeavour to hold ourselves strenuously at the Shakespearian standpoint, and view the universe from thence. We shall afterwards go our way, as seems best; bearing with us Shakespeare's gift. And Shakespeare has no better gift to bestow than the strength and courage to pursue our own path, through pain or through joy, with vigour and resolution.

2

THE GROWTH OF SHAKESPEARE'S MIND AND ART

In the preceding chapter a brief and partial study was attempted of Shakespeare the man, and Shakespeare the artist, considered as one element in the great intellectual and spiritual movement of the Elizabethan period. The organism,—a dramatic poet,—we endeavoured to view in connection with its environment. Now we proceed to observe, in some few of its stages of progress, the growth of that organism. Shakespeare in 1590, Shakespeare in 1600, and Shakespeare in 1610, was one and the same living entity; but the adolescent Shakespeare differed from the adult, and again from Shakespeare in the supremacy of his ripened manhood, as much as the slender stem, graceful and pliant, spreading its first leaves to the sunshine of May, differs from the moving expanse of greenery, visible a century later, which is hard to comprehend and probe with the eye in its infinite details, multitudinous and yet one, receiving through its sensitive surfaces the gifts of light and dew, of noonday and of night, grasping the earth with inextricable living knots, not unpossessed of haunts of shadow and secrecy, instinct with ample mysterious murmurs,—the tree which has a history, and bears in wrinkled bark and wrenched bough memorials of time and change, of hardship, and drought, and storm. The poet Gray in a well-known passage, invented a piece of beautiful mythology, according to which the infant Shakespeare is represented as receiving gifts from the great Dispensatress:

> Far from the son and summer gale
> In thy green lap was Nature's darling laid,
> What time, where lucid Avon stayed,

To him the mighty Mother did unveil
Her awful face; the dauntless Child
Stretched forth his little arms and smiled;
This pencil take, she said, whose colours clear
Richly paint the vernal year,
Thine too these golden keys, immortal Boy!
This can unlock the gates of Joy,
Of Horror that, and thrilling Fears,
Or ope the sacred fount of sympathetic Tears.

But the mighty Mother, more studious of the welfare of her charge, in fact gave her gifts only as they could be used. Those keys she did not entrust to Shakespeare until, by manifold experience, by consolidating of intellect, imagination and passions, and by the growth of self-control, he had become fitted to confront the dreadful, actual presences of human anguish and of human joy.

Everything takes up its place more rightly in a spacious world, accurately observed, than in the narrow world of the mere idealist. In bare acquisition of observed fact Shakespeare marvellously increased from year to year. He grew in wisdom and in knowledge (such an admission does not wrong the divinity of genius), not less but more than other men. Quite a little library exists, illustrating the minute acquaintance of Shakespeare with this branch of information, and with that: "The Legal Acquirements of Shakespeare," "Shakespeare's Knowledge and use of the Bible," "Shakespeare's Delineations of Insanity," "The Rural Life of Shakespeare," "Shakespeare's Garden," "The Ornithology of Shakespeare," "The Insects mentioned by Shakespeare," and such like. Conjectural enquiry, which attempts to determine whether Shakespeare was an attorney's clerk, or whether he was a soldier, whether Shakespeare was ever in Italy, or whether he was in Germany, or whether he was in Scotland; enquiry such as this may lead to no very certain result, with respect to the particular matter in question. But one thing which such special critical studies as these establish, is the enormous receptivity of the poet. This vast and varied mass of information he assimilated and made his own. And such store of information came to Shakespeare only by the way, as an addition to the more important possession of knowledge about human character and human life which forms the proper body of fact needful for dramatic art. In proportion as an animal is of great size, the masses of nutriment which he procures are large. "The Arctic whale gulps in whole shoals of acalephae and molluscs."

But it was not alone, or chiefly through mass of acquisition that Shakespeare became great. He was not merely a centre for the drifting capital of knowledge. Each faculty expanded, and became more energetic, while at the same time the structural arrangement of the man's whole nature became more complex and involved. His power of thought increased steadily as years went by, both in sure grasp of the known, and in brooding intensity of gaze upon the unknown. His emotions instead of losing their energy and subtilty as youth deepened into manhood, instead of becoming dulled and crusted over by contact with the world, became (as is the case with all the greatest men and women), by contact with the world swifter and of more ample volume. As Shakespeare penetrated farther and farther into the actual facts of our life, he found in those facts more to rouse and kindle and sustain the heart; he discovered more awful and mysterious darkness, and also more intense and lovelier light. And it is clearly ascertainable from his plays and poems, that Shakespeare's *will* grew with advancing age, beyond measure, calmer, and more strong. Each formidable temptation he succeeded, before he was done with it, in subduing, at least so far as to preclude a fatal result. In the end he obtained serene and indefeasible possession of himself. He still remained indeed baffled before the mystery of life and death; but he had gained vigour to cope with fate; he could "accept all things not understood." And during these years, while each faculty was augmenting its proper life, the vital play of one faculty into and through the other, became more swift, subtile, and penetrating. In Shakespeare's earlier writings, we can observe him setting his wit to work, or his fancy to work; now he is clever and intellectual, and again he is tender and enthusiastic. But in his later style, imagination and thought, wisdom, and mirth, and charity, experience and surmise play into and through one another, until frequently the significance of a passage becomes obscured by its manifold vitality. The murmur of an embryo thought or feeling already obscurely mingles with the murmurs of the parent life in which it is enveloped.*

Now, what does extraordinary growth imply?† It implies capacity for obtaining the materials of growth; in this case materials for the growth of intellect, of imagination, of the will, of the emotions. It means, therefore, capacity of seeing many facts, of meditating, of feeling deeply, and of controlling such feeling. It implies the avoidance of injuries which interfere with growth, escape from enemies which bring life to a sudden end; and therefore strength, and skill, and prudence in dealing with the world. It implies a power in the organism of fitting its movements to meet numerous external co-existences and sequences. In a word, we are brought back once again to Shakespeare's resolute fidelity to the fact. By virtue of this his life became a success, as far as success is permitted to such a creature as man in such a world as the present.

It seems much that the needy youth who left his native town probably under pressure of poverty, should at the age of thirty-three have become possessor of New Place at Stratford, and from year to year have added to his worldly dignity and wealth. Such material advancement argues a power of understanding, and adapting oneself to the facts of the material world. But that was not the chief success in the life of Shakespeare. When Wordsworth thought of "mighty poets in their misery dead," when in sudden mood of dejection he murmured to himself:

> We poets in our youth begin in gladness,
> But thereof comes in the end despondency and madness,

he thought of Chatterton and of Burns, not of Shakespeare. The

* See the valuable criticism of Shakespeare's style as contrasted with Fletcher's in "A letter on Shakespeare's Authorship of 'The Two Noble Kinsmen,'" 1833 (by Mr Spalding), pp. 13-18. The criticism applies with special propriety to Shakespeare's later style.

† In my answer to this question, I borrow several expressions from Herbert Spencer's Biology.

early contemporaries of Shakespeare—Marlowe and Greene—one of them a man of splendid genius, failed as Chatterton failed. It must have appeared to Shakespeare (who well enough understood honest frolic) a poor affair, a flimsy kind of idealism—this reckless knocking of a man's head against the solid laws of the universe. The protest against fact, against our subjection to law made by such men as Marlowe and Greene, was a vulgar and superficial protest. Shakespeare could get no delight from the insanity of sowing wild oats. His insanity was of a far graver and more terrible kind. It assumed two forms—the Romeo form and the Hamlet form—abandonment to passion, abandonment to brooding thought—two diseases of youth, each fatal in its own way; two forms of the one supreme crime in Shakespeare's eyes, want of fidelity to the fact. The noble practical energy of Shakespeare was tempted to self-betrayal on the one hand by the supremacy of blind desire; on the other hand, by the sapping in of thought upon the will and active powers. The struggle between self-will and reason, between "blood" and "judgment," appears in all his writings to be ever in the background, a theme ready at any moment, if permitted, to become prominent. And Shakespeare's profoundest and most sympathetic psychological study—Hamlet—represents in detail the other chief temptation to which he was, it would seem, subjected. In all the later plays his eye is intently fixed upon the deep insoluble questions suggested by human character and destiny, fixed with a brooding wistfulness, which yet, we perceive, he became, as years went on, more and more able to control.

Shakespeare's central self pronounced in favour of sanity—in favour of seeing things as they are, and shaping life accordingly. He bought up houses and lands in Stratford, and so made a protest superficial, indeed, yet real, against the Romeo and the Hamlet within him. But the idealist within him made Shakespeare at all times far other than a mere country magnate or wealthy burgher. It remained, after all, *nearly* the deepest part of him:

> *Hamlet.* Is not parchment made of sheep-skins?
> *Horatio.* Ay, my lord, and of calf-skins too.

> *Hamlet.* They are sheep and calves which seek out assurance in that.

And Prospero declares the end of the whole matter:

> We are such stuff
> As dreams are made on, and our little life
> Is rounded with a sleep.

Shakespeare's devotion to material interests was the least part of the protest made against his temptation to extravagance of soul. There are more important facts than those of the material life. Shakespeare cast his plummet into the sea of human sorrow, and wrong, and loss. He studied evil. He would let none of that dark side of life escape from him. He denied none of the bitterness, the sins, the calamity of the world. He looked steadily at Cordelia strangled in the arms of Lear; and he summoned up a strenuous fortitude, a stoical submission to make endurable such a spectacle. But at the same time he retained his loyalty to good; over against Edmund and the monstrous sisters he saw the invincible loyalty of a Kent, the practical genius of an Edgar in the service of good, and the redeeming ardour of a Cordelia. Rescuing his soul from all bitterness, he arrived finally at a temper strong and self-possessed as that of stoicism, yet free from the stoical attitude of defiance; a temper liberal, gracious, charitable, a tender yet strenuous calm.

The *Venus and Adonis* is styled by its author in the dedication to the Earl of Southampton, "the first heir of my invention." Gervinus believes that the poem may have been written before the poet left Stratford. Although possibly separated by a considerable interval from its companion poem *The Rape of Lucrece* (1594), the two may be regarded as essentially one in kind.* The speciality of these poems as

* Mr Furnivall notes in the *Venus and Adonis* the following pictures from Shakespeare's youthful life at Stratford,—the horse (*l.* 260-318); the hare-hunt (*l.* 763-68); the overflowing Avon (72); the two silver doves (366); the milch doe and fawn in some brake in Charlecote Park (875-76); the red morn (453); the hush of the wind before it rains (458); the many clouds consulting for foul weather (972); the night-owl (531); the lark (853). The *Lucrece,* he adds, "must have been written some time after the *Venus,* as

portions of Shakespeare's art has perhaps not been sufficiently observed.* Each is an artistic *study;* and they form, as has been just observed, companion studies—one of female lust and boyish coldness, the other of male lust and womanly chastity. Coleridge noticed "the utter aloofness of the poet's own feelings from those of which he is at once the painter and the analyst;" but it can hardly be admitted that this aloofness of the poet's own feelings proceeds from a dramatic abandonment of self. The subjects of these two poems did not call and choose their poet, they did not possess him and compel him to render them into art. Rather, the poet expressly made choice of the subjects, and deliberately set himself down before each to accomplish an exhaustive study of it.

If the Venus and Adonis sonnets in "The Passionate Pilgrim" be by Shakespeare, it would seem that he had been trying various poetical exercises on this theme. And for a young writer of the Renaissance, the subject of Shakespeare's earliest poem was a splendid one,—as voluptuous and unspiritual as that of a classical picture by Titian. It included two figures containing inexhaustible pasture for the fleshly eye, and delicacies and dainties for the sensuous imagination of the Renaissance,—the enamoured Queen of Beauty, and the beautiful, disdainful boy. It afforded occasion for endless exercises and variations on the themes,—Beauty, Lust, and Death. In holding the subject before his imagination Shakespeare is perfectly cool and collected. He has made choice of the subject, and he is interested in doing his duty by it in the most thorough way a young poet can, but he remains unimpassioned,—intent wholly upon getting down the right colours and lines upon his canvas. Observe his determination to put in accurately the details of each object; to omit nothing. Poor Wat, the hare, is described in a dozen stanzas. Another series of stanzas describes the stallion; all his points are enumerated:

---

its proportion of unstopt lines is 1 in 10.81 (171 such lines to the poem's *l.* 1855) against the *Venus's* 1 in 25.40 (47 run-on lines in 1, 194)." Preface by F.J. Furnivall to *Shakespeare Commentaries* by Gervinus (ed. 1874).

* Coleridge touches upon the fact, and it is noted by Lloyd.

Round-hoof'd, short-jointed, fetlocks shag and long,
Broad breast, full eye, small head and nostril wide,
High crest, short ears, straight legs and passing strong,
Thin mane, thick tail, broad buttock, tender hide.

This passage of poetry has been admired: but is it poetry or a paragraph from an advertisement of a horse sale? It is part of Shakespeare's study of an animal, and he does his work thoroughly. In like manner he does not shrink from faithfully putting down each one of the amorous provocations and urgencies of Venus. The complete series of manoeuvres must be detailed.

In *Lucrece* the action is delayed and delayed that every minute particular may be described, every minor incident recorded. In the newness of her suffering and shame Lucrece finds time for an elaborate *tirade* appropriate to the theme "Night," another to that of "Time," another to that of "Opportunity." Each topic is exhausted. Then studiously a new incident is introduced, and its significance for the emotions is drained to the last drop in a new tirade. We nowhere else discover Shakespeare so evidently engaged upon his work. Afterwards he puts a stress upon his verses to compel them to contain the hidden wealth of his thought and imagination. Here he displays at large such wealth as he possesses; he will have none of it half seen. The descriptions and declamations are undramatic, but they shew us the materials laid out in detail from which dramatic poetry originates. Having drawn so carefully from models, the time comes when he can trust himself to draw from memory, and he possesses marvellous freedom of hand, because his previous studies have been so laborious. It was the same hand that drew the stallion in *Venus and Adonis*, which afterwards drew with infallible touch, as though they were alive, the dogs of Theseus:

My hounds are bred out of the Spartan kind
So flew'd, so sanded, and their heads are hung
With ears that sweep away the morning dew;
Crook-kneed, and dew-lapped like Thessalian bulls;
Slow in pursuit; but match'd in mouth like bells,
Each under each. A cry more tuneable

Was never holla'd to, nor cheer'd with horn
In Crete, in Sparta, nor in Thessaly.*

When these poems were written Shakespeare was cautiously feeling his way. Large, slow-growing natures, gifted with a sense of concrete fact and with humour, ordinarily possess no great self-confidence in youth. An idealist, like Milton, may resolve in early manhood that he will achieve a great epic poem, and in old age may turn into fact the ideas of his youth. An idealist, like Marlowe, may begin his career with a splendid youthful audacity, a stupendous "Tamburlaine." A man of the kind to which Shakespeare belonged, although very resolute, and determined, if possible, to succeed, requires the evidence of objective facts to give him self-confidence. His special virtue lies in a peculiarly pregnant and rich relation with the actual world, and such relation commonly establishes itself by a gradual process. Accordingly, instead of flinging abroad into the world while still a stripling some unprecedented creation, as Marlowe

---

* The comparison of these two passages is from Hazlitt, whose unfavourable criticism of Shakespeare's poems expresses well one side of the truth. "The two poems of *Venus and Adonis*, and of *Tarquin and Lucrece*, appear to us like a couple of ice-houses. They are about as hard, as glittering, and as cold. The author seems all the time to be thinking of his verses, and not of his subject—not of what his characters would feel, but of what he shall say; and as it must happen in all such cases he always puts into their mouths those things which they would be the last to think of, and which it shows the greatest ingenuity in him to find out. The whole is laboured up-hill work. The poet is perpetually singling out the difficulties of the art to make an exhibition of his strength and skill in wrestling with them. He is making perpetual trials of them as if his mastery over them were doubted [...]. A beautiful thought is sure to be lost in an endless commentary upon it [...]. There is besides a strange attempt to substitute the language of painting for that of poetry, to make us *see* their feelings in the faces of the persons." Characters of Shakespeare's Plays (ed. 1818), pp. 348-49. Coleridge's much more favourable criticism will be found in *Biographia Literaria*, vol. ii, chap. ii (ed. 1847). The peculiarity of the poems last noticed in the extract from Hazlitt is ingeniously accounted for by Coleridge. "The great instinct which impelled the poet to the drama was secretly working in him, prompting him [...] to provide a substitute for that visual language, that constant intervention and running comment by tone, look, and gesture, which in his dramatic works he was entitled to expect from the players," pp. 18-19.

did, or as Victor Hugo did, and securing thereby the position of a leader of an insurgent school, Shakespeare began, if not timidly, at least cautiously and tentatively. He undertakes work of any and every description, and tries and tests himself upon all. He is therefore a valued person in his theatrical company, ready to turn his hand to anything helpful, a Jack of all trades, a "Johannes factotum;" he is obliging and free from self-assertion; he is waiting his time; he is not yet sure of himself; he finds it the sensible thing not to profess singularity. "Divers of worship" report his "uprightness of dealing;" he is "excellent in the quality he professes;"* his demeanour is civil; he is recognized even already as haying a "facetious grace in writing."† Let us not suppose because Shakespeare declines to assault the real world, and the world of imagination, and take them by violence, that he is therefore a person of slight force of character. He is determined to master both these worlds if possible. He approaches them with a facile and engaging air; by and by his grasp upon facts will tighten. From Marlowe and from Milton half of the world escapes. Shakespeare will lay hold of it in its totality, and once that he has laid hold of it, will never let it go.

This is the period of Shakespeare's tentative dramatic efforts. Among these, notwithstanding strong external evidence,—the testimony of Meres, and the fact that Heminge and Condell included the play in the first folio,—it is difficult to admit Titus Andronicus. That tragedy belongs to the pre-Shakespearian school of bloody dramas. If any portions of it be from Shakespeare's hand, it has at least this interest—it shows that there was a period of Shakespeare's authorship when the poet had not yet discovered himself, a period when he yielded to the popular influences of the day and hour; this much interest and no more. That Shakespeare himself entered with passion or

* On the special use of the word "quality" for the stage-player's profession see a note by Hermann Kurz in his article "Shakespeare der Schauspieler." *Shakespeare Jahrbuch,* Vol. vi, pp. 317-18.

† Chettle'a Kind Heart's Dream, 1592. But see Mr Howard Staunton'a letter, in *The Athenaeum,* Feb. 7th, 1874, Mr Simpson'a article, "Shakespeare Allusion Books." *The Academy,* April 11, 1874; and Dr Ingleby'a preface to "Shakespeare Allusion Books," published for the New Shakespeare Society.

energy into the literary movement which the Spanish Tragedy of Kyd may be taken to represent, his other early writings forbid us to believe. The supposed *Sturm und Drang* period of Shakespeare's artistic career exists only in the imagination of his German critics. The early years of Shakespeare's authorship were years of bright and tender play of fancy and of feeling. If an epoch of storm and stress at any time arrived, it was when Shakespeare's genius had reached its full maturity, and Lear was the product of that epoch. But *then,* if the storm and stress were prolonged and urgent, Shakespeare possessed sufficient power of endurance, and had obtained sufficient grasp of the strong sure roots of life to save him from being borne away into the chaos or in any direction across the borders of the ordered realm of art. Upon the whole, *Titus Andronicus* may be disregarded. Even if it were a work of Shakespeare we should still call it un-Shakespearian. "Shakespeare's tragedy," Gerald Massey has truly said, "is the tragedy of Terror; this is the tragedy of Horror [...]. It reeks blood, it smells of blood, we almost feel that we have handled blood—it is so gross. The mental stain is not whitened by Shakespeare's sweet springs of pity; the horror is not hallowed by that appalling sublimity with which he invested his chosen ministers of death. It is tragedy only in the coarsest material relationships."*

Of Pericles the portion written by Shakespeare—the lovely little romance which Mr Fleay has separated from the coarse work of Rowley and Wilkins, and named "Marina,"—belongs to the period of Shakespeare's maturity, after 1600. Rowley's work "is always detached and splits off from his coadjutors with a clean cleavage. In Fletcher's *Maid of the Mill* the work of the two men might be published as two separate plays."† Similarly

* Shakespeare's Sonnets and his Private Friends, p. 581. Kreyssig, who accepts *Titus Andronicus* as an early work of Shakespeare, gives an elaborate study of the play. For matters of external evidence, &c., consult the article by H. Kurz in *Shakespeare Jahrbuch*, vol. v; and on characteristics of metre, the preface by Hertzberg in *Schlegel's and Tieck's translation*, edited by members of the German Shakespeare Society. See also Mr Albert Cohn's "Shakespeare in Germany." p. cxii.

† Transactions of the New Shakespeare Society, part i. On the play of *Pericles*, by the Rev. F.G. Fleay.

in the play *A Cure for a Cuckold,* the work of Rowley splits off from that of Webster, leaving the little drama which Mr Gosse claims the honour of having delivered out of the compound manufacture of the two authors, and which he has gracefully entitled *Love's Graduate.**

Setting aside *Titus Andronicus* and *Marina,* four dramatic experiments by Shakespeare remain, each in a different manner from the rest. First, a portion at least of the second and third parts of *King Henry VI*—English historical drama.† *The Two Gentlemen of Verona,* a comedy of graceful mirth and sprightly and tender feeling, with the interest of love predominant; *Love's Labour's Lost,* a comedy of dialogue, a piece of airy satire, with an underlying serious intention; the *Comedy of Errors,* a comedy of incident, of almost farcical adventure—the sole attempt of Shakespeare at imitation of the comic drama of ancient Rome. In this play Shakespeare gaily confronts improbabilities, and requires the spectator to accept them. He adds to the twins Antipholus the twins Dromio. If we are in for improbability, let us at least be repaid for it by fun, and have that in abundance. Let the incredible become a twofold incredibility, and it is none the worse.‡ We may conclude that, while Shakespeare was ready to try his hand upon a farcical subject, a single experiment

* *Fraser's Magazine,* May 1874. "John Webster," by Edmund W. Gosse.

† In Mr R. Grant White's Essay upon the authorship of *Henry VI,* he argues that the early *Contention* and the *True Tragedie* contain portions by Shakespeare, afterwards transferred to his *Henry VI,* Parts II and III; and that the remaining portions are by Marlowe, Greene, and Peele. But see note, p. 73.

‡ The source of this comedy is usually said to be a translation of the Menoechmi of Plautus, by W. Warner. Hertzberg, in his preface to the play in the German Shakespeare Society's edition of *Schlegel's and Tieck's* translation, carefully distinguishes the characters and incidents which Shakespeare did *not* owe to the Menoechmi. In the article "Zwei neuentdeckte Shakespearequellen" (*Die Literatur,* January 16, 1874), the writer, Dr Paul Wislicenus, points out another source in the Amphitruo. His supposition that the incident of the storm in the *Comedy of Errors* is derived from the storm in *Pericles,* must be set aside as untenable. Shakespeare's acquaintance with the Amphitruo may have been made, in the first instance, through the rude English imitation of Plautus' comedy, *Jack Juggler.*

satisfied him that this was not his province; for to such subjects he never returned.

During the years in which the poet was experimenting in history, comedy, and farce, that about which he was most of all secretly concerned was a tragedy—a tragedy of a kind altogether different from *Titus Andronicus*, and the group of bloody plays to which it belongs. Such a graceful piece of comedy as *The Two Gentlemen of Verona* did not profoundly engage his imagination. If the fifth act came from Shakespeare's pen as it now stands, we must believe that he handed over his play to the actors while a portion of it still remained only a hasty sketch, the *denouement* being left for future working out.* But the designed tragedy seems to have been the great affair of his literary career at this period. It is the opinion of Dyce, of Grant White, and of others, that Shakespeare began to work upon *Romeo and Juliet* not later than about 1591; that is, according to the commonly received chronology, almost at the moment when he began to write for the stage; and that having occupied him for a series of years, the tragedy assumed its present form about 1595-97. If this be the case, and if, as there is reason to believe, Shakespeare was also during many years interested in the subject of Hamlet, we discover a fact, which is characteristic

* Hertzberg is of opinion that either the play was re-handled and cut down by some Elizabethan playwright, or our text was imperfectly made up from copies of the parts of the several actors. If either of these hypotheses be correct, we are not in possession of Shakespeare's complete play. The words addressed by Valentine to Proteus (Act v, Scene 4), "All that is mine in Sylvia I give thee," cannot be an interpolation, for they are needed to account for Julia's fainting. Were they spoken by Valentine to test the loyalty of his professedly repentant friend? And is there a gap here, originally occupied by speeches of Proteus and Sylvia? See Hertzberg's preface in the German Shakespeare Society's edition of Schlegel's and Tieck's translation. Hertzberg (relying partly on metrical evidence) assigns a later place to *The Two Gentlemen of Verona* in the succession of Shakespeare's plays than that usually assigned by critics. I remain unconvinced by the arguments for lateness of date. See on this subject a lecture by Mr Hales reported in *The Academy*, January 31, 1874, and Mr Furnivall's criticism of the paper by Rev. F.G. Fleay in Transactions of the New Shakespeare Society, 1874. Having made out the group of Shakespeare's early comedies, it does not greatly matter, for the purposes of the present study, in what order the plays followed one another within the group; but I incline towards placing *A Midsummer Night's Dream* last.

of the poet; that he accepted the knowledge that his powers were undeveloped, and acted upon it, waiting with his two chosen subjects—the story of the star-crossed lovers, and the story of the man summoned to action whose will was sapped—until he believed himself competent to do justice to his conceptions. What a contrast is presented by this waiting of genius, this patience "until the golden couplets are disclosed," to the feverish eagerness of Marlowe to appease his ambition, and unburden himself of the pressure of his imagination.

As characteristic of these early plays, we may notice,* (i) frequency of rhyme, in various arrangements: *(a)* rhymed couplets, (*b*) rhymed quatrains, (*c*) the sextain, consisting of an alternately rhyming quatrain, followed by a couplet (the arrangement of the last six lines of Shakespeare's sonnets); (ii) occurrence of rhymed doggrel verse in two forms: *(a)* very short lines, and *(b)* very long lines; (iii) comparative infrequency of the feminine (or double) ending; (iv) comparative infrequency of the weak-ending; (v) comparative infrequency of the unstopped line; (vi) regular internal structure of the line; extra syllables seldom packed into the verse; (vii) frequency of classical allusions; (viii) frequency of puns and conceits; (ix) wit and imagery drawn out in detail to the point of exhaustion; (x) clowns who are, by comparison with the later comic characters, outstanding persons in the play told off specially for clownage; (xi) the presence of termagant or shrewish women; (xii) soliloquies addressed rather to the audience (to explain the business of the piece or the motives of the actors), than to the speaker's self; (xiii) symmetry in the grouping of persons.

To illustrate the last of these characteristics—and each *of* the above mentioned characteristics might readily be illustrated at length—we may observe the arrangement of *dramatis personae* in *The Two Gentlemen of Verona.* Porteus the fickle is set over against Valentine the faithful;† Sylvia, the bright and

* See on this subject a lecture by Mr Hales, reported in *The Academy,* January 17th, 1874.

† When Mr Hales said, "Even Proteus" name is a sign of early work—the riper Shakespeare does not like significant names," he forgot Perdita, Marina, Miranda.

intellectual, is set over against Julia, the ardent and tender; Launce, the humourist, is set over against Speed, the wit. So, in *Love's Labour's Lost,* the king and his three fellow students balance the Princess and her three ladies. The arrangement is too geometrical; the groups are obviously artificial, not organic and vital. This indicates a certain want of confidence on the part of the poet; he fears the weight of too much liberty. He cannot yet feel that his structure is secure without a system of mechanism to support the structure. He endeavours to attain unity of effect-less by the inspiration of a common life than by the disposition of parts. He finds he can bring forward his forces, in turn, one after another, more readily when they are numbered and marshalled in definite order. In the opening scene of his earliest tragedy, two Capulet men-servants are first introduced, next two Montague men-servants, then Benvolio on the Montague side, then Tybalt on the Capulet side, then on each side citizens, then old Capulet and Lady Capulet, then Montague and Lady Montague—finally, as keystone to bind all together, the prince. In the plays which belong to Shakespeare's period of mastership, he can dispense with such artifice. In these later plays unity is present through the virtue of one living force which animates the whole. The unity is not merely structural, but vital. And, therefore, the poet has no apprehension that the minor centres of development, in his creation, will suddenly become insubordinate. Assured that the organism is living, he fearlessly lets it develop itself in its proper mode, unicentral (as *Macbeth*), or multicentral (as *King Lear*). In the early plays structure determines function; in the later plays organisation is preceded by life.*

* Hebler in his ingenious and delightfully brief analyses of fourteen comedies of Shakespeare endeavours to point out a curiously symmetrical arrangement in the structure and action of several, as well late as early. I give a few examples, abbreviating Hebler yet further. *Two Gentlemen,* a loyal friend and lover set over against a disloyal. *Merry Wives,* an old sinner flouted and disappointed; and a young pair of lovers whose roguery is successful. *Measure for Measure,* Angelo condemns Claudio to death for consummating his marriage without church rites; by stratagem he is himself placed in an identical position of guilt. *Comedy of Errors,* the twins Dromio and their story repeat the twins Antipholus and theirs. *Much Ado,* two lovers (Beatrice and Benedict), are brought together by

The growth of Shakespeare's freedom, as an artist, was really identical with his passing under the influence of a higher law. This statement which applies to the structure of his plays, applies in like manner to the altering character of his versification. For in truth, such an apparently mechanical thing as the stopping of a passage of verse is not mechanical, but in its essence spiritual. At first when we resolve to live a life somewhat higher than the common life of vulgar accident, we do well to put ourselves under a system of rules and precepts; through strict observance of these we shall secure in a certain degree the ideality our life has need of. But in due time we fling away our manuals, our codes of spiritual drill, our little rules and restrictions. A deeper order takes authority over our being, and resumes in itself the narrower order; the rhythm of our life acquires a larger harmony, a movement free and yet sure as that of nature. In like manner, a thought at first endeavours to secure ideality for its life by adherence to a system of narrow rule. This is the explanation of the early manner of all great writers of verse, all great painters, and musicians, as compared with their later manner. Their style becomes free and daring, because the great facts of the world have now taken hold of them, and because their subjection to highest law is at length complete. They and their work are as free as the winds, or as the growing grass, or as the waves, or the drift of clouds, or the motion of the stars. As free; that is to say in complete, noble, and glad subjection.

Love's Labour's Lost, if we do not assign that place to *The Two Gentlemen of Verona*, is the first independent, wholly

---

an honest fraud; two lovers (Claudio and Hero), are separated by a criminal fraud. *A Midsummer Night's Dream*, the love of Theseus and Hippolyta—its course running smooth; and the troubled course of love of the human mortals, of Oberon and Titania, and (as comic contrast), of Pyramus and Thisbe. *All's Well*, a young nobleman misled by a false friend to whom he cleaves, and from whom he is separated at length; and led aright by a true wife whom he deserts, and to whom he is united at length (The friend, I add, is all words without deeds,—Parolles. The wife is deeds without words). See the interesting passage from Vischer, with reference to the double action of Shakespeare's comedies, quoted by Hebler. Aufsätze über Shakespeare, pp. 198-99.

original work of Shakespeare. Mr Charles Knight named it *The Comedy of Affectations*, and that title aptly interprets one intention of the play. It is a satirical extravaganza embodying Shakespeare's criticism upon contemporary fashions and foibles in speech, in manners, and in literature. This probably more than any other of the plays of Shakespeare suffers through lapse of time. Fantastical speech, pedantic learning, extravagant love-hyperbole, frigid fervours in poetry, against each of these, with the brightness and vivacity of youth, confident in the success of its cause, Shakespeare directs the light artillery of his wit. Being young and clever, he is absolutely devoid of respect for nonsense, whether it be dainty, affected nonsense, or grave unconscious nonsense.

But over and above this, there is a serious intention in the play. It is a protest against youthful schemes of shaping life according to notions rather than according to reality, a protest against idealizing away the facts of life. The play is chiefly interesting as containing Shakespeare's confession of faith with respect to the true principles of self-culture. The King of Navarre and his young lords had resolved for a definite period of time to circumscribe their beings and their lives with a little code of rules. They had designed to enclose a little favoured park in which ideas should rule to the exclusion of the blind and rude forces of nature. They were pleased to rearrange human character and human life, so that it might accord with their idealistic scheme of self-development. The court was to be a little Academe; no woman was to be looked at for the space of three years; food and sleep were to be placed under precise regulation. And the result is, what? That human nature refuses to be dealt with in this fashion of arbitrary selection and rejection. The youthful idealists had supposed that they would form a little group of select and refined ascetics of knowledge and culture; it was quickly proved that they were men. The play is Shakespeare's declaration in favour of the fact as it is. Here, he says, we are with such and such appetites and passions. Let us in any scheme of self-development get *that* fact acknowledged at all events. Otherwise, we shall quickly enough betray ourselves as arrant fools, fit to be flouted by women, and needing to learn from them a portion of their directness, practicality, and good sense.

And yet the Princess, and Rosaline, and Maria, have not the entire advantage on their side. It is well to be practical; but to be practical, and also to have a capacity for ideas is better. Berowne, the exponent of Shakespeare's own thought, who entered into the youthful, idealistic project of his friends with a satisfactory assurance that the time would come when the entire dream-structure would tumble ridiculously about the ears of them all,—Berowne is yet a larger nature than the Princess or Rosaline. *His* good sense is the good sense of a thinker and of a man of action. When he is most flouted and bemocked, we yet acknowledge him victorious and the master; and Rosaline will confess the fact by and by.

In the midst of merriment and nonsense comes a sudden and grievous incursion of fact full of pain. The father of the Princess is dead. All the world is not mirth—"this side is Hiems, Winter, this Ver, the Spring." The lovers must part—"Jack hath not his Jill," and to engrave the lesson deeply, which each heart needs, the king and two of his companions are dismissed for a twelvemonth to learn the difference between reality and unreality, while Berowne, who has known the mirth of the world, must also make acquaintance with its sorrow, must visit the speechless sick and try to win "the pained impotent to smile."

Let us get hold of the realities of human nature and human life, Shakespeare would say, and let us found upon these realities, and not upon the mist or the air, our schemes of individual and social advancement. Not that Shakespeare is hostile to culture; but he knows that a perfect education must include the culture, through actual experience, of the senses and of the affections. Long after this play was written, Shakespeare imagined Perdita, his shepherdess-princess, possessed of all the grace and refinement of perfect breeding with all the innocence and native liberty of rustic girlhood. Perdita refuses to admit into her garden the party-coloured flowers that had been artificially produced, "streaked gillyvors, which some call nature's bastards." But into Polixenes' mouth Shakespeare puts an unanswerable defence of culture, so that to make good her decision there remains to Perdita only an exquisite instinct of unreasoning sincerity, or a graceful wilfulness which refuses to be convinced:

Pol. Wherefore, gentle maiden,
Do you neglect them?

Per. For I have heard it said,
There is an art which, in their piedness, shares
With great creating nature.

Pol. Say, there be;
Yet nature is made better by no mean
But nature makes that mean; so over that art*
Which you say adds to nature, is an art
That nature makes. You see, sweet maid, we marry
A gentler scion to the wildest stock,
And make conceive a bark of baser kind
By bud of nobler race; this is an art
Which does mend nature, change it rather, but
The art itself is nature.

Per. So it is.

Pol. Then make your garden rich in gillyvors
And do not call them bastards.

Per. I'll not put
The dibble in earth to set one slip of them.

Shakespeare's view of human culture and human life admitted no essential opposition between Perdita's instinct of sincerity, and the maturer wisdom of Polixenes.

In the second act of the *Comedy of Errors* (scene ii) occurs the following dialogue:

Luciana. Dromio, go bid the servants spread for dinner.

Dro. S. O, for my beads! I cross me for a sinner.
This is the fairy-land: O spite of spites!
We talk with goblins, owls, and sprites:
If we obey them not, this will ensue,—
They'll suck our breath or pinch us black and blue.

---

* Professor Craik conjectured—"*even* that art."

Luc.	Why prat'st thou to thyself and answer'st not?
	Dromio, thou drone, thou snail, thou slug, thou sot!
Dro. S.	I am transformed, master, am I not?
Aut. S.	I think thou art, in mind, and so am I.
Dro. S.	Nay, master, both in mind and in my shape.
Aut. S.	Thou hast thine own form.
Dro. S.	No, I am an ape.
Luc.	If thou art changed to aught 'tis to an ass.

When Shakespeare wrote thus of fairy-land, of the pranks of Robin Goodfellow, and of the transformation of a man to an ass, can it be doubted that he had in his thoughts *A Midsummer Night's Dream*? The play was perhaps so named because it is a dream-play, the fantastic adventures of a night, and because it was first represented in midsummer—the midsummer, perhaps, of 1594. The imagined season of the action of the play is the beginning of May, for according to the magnificent piece of mediaeval-classical mythology embodied here, and in the Knight's *Tale of Chaucer*, and again in the *Two Noble Kinsmen* of Shakespeare and Fletcher, this was the month of Theseus' marriage with his Amazonian bride.* In like manner the play of *Twelfth Night* received its name probably because it was first enacted at that season of festivity, and as if to declare more emphatically that it shall be nameless, Shakespeare adds a second title *Twelfth Night, or What you will,* that is (for we need seek no deeper significance)—*Twelfth Night,* or anything you like to call it. *A Midsummer Night's Dream* was written on the occasion of the marriage of some noble couple—possibly for the marriage of the poet's patron Southampton with Elizabeth Vernon, as Mr Gerald Massey supposes; possibly at an earlier date to do honour to the marriage of the Earl of Essex with Lady Sidney.†

* Titania says to Oberon, *Act* ii, *Scene* 1,

> And never since the middle summer's spring
> Met we on hill, in dale, forest, or mead, &c.

Perhaps a night in early May might be considered a night in the spring of midsummer.

† Mr Massey is obliged to entertain the supposition that the play was written some time before the marriage actually took place (1598) "at a period when it may have been thought the Queen's consent could be

The central figure of the play is that of Theseus. There is no figure in the early drama of Shakespeare so magnificent. His are the large hands that have helped to shape the world. His utterance is the rich-toned speech of one who is master of events—who has never known a shrill or eager feeling. His nuptial day is at hand; and while the other lovers are agitated, bewildered, incensed, Theseus, who does not think of himself as a lover but rather as a beneficent conqueror, remains in calm possession of his joy. Theseus, a grand ideal figure, is to be studied as Shakespeare's conception of the heroic man of action in his hour of enjoyment and of leisure. With a splendid capacity for enjoyment, gracious to all, ennobled by the glory, implied rather than explicit, of great foregone achievement, he stands as centre of the poem, giving their true proportions to the fairy tribe upon the one hand, and upon the other to the "human mortals." The heroic men of action, Theseus, Henry V, Hector, —are supremely admired by Shakespeare. Yet it is observable that as the total Shakespeare is superior to Romeo, the man given over to passion, and to Hamlet, the man given over to thought, so the Hamlet and the Romeo within him give Shakespeare an infinite advantage over even the most heroic men of action. He admires these men of action supremely, but he admires them from an outside point of view. "These fellows of infinite tongue," says Henry, wooing the French princess, "that can rhyme themselves into ladies' favours, they do always reason themselves out again. What! a speaker is but a prater, a

---

obtained [...]. I have ventured the date of 1595." Shakespeare Sonnets and his Private Friends, p. 481. Professor Karl Elze's theory maintained in a highly ingenious paper in *Shakespeare Jahrbuch*, vol. iii, that the play was written for the marriage of the young Earl of Essex, would throw back the date to 1590, a good deal too early believe. Prof. Elze has, however, much to say in favour of this opinion. See also the excellent article by Hermann Kurz in *Shakespeare-Jahrbuch*, vol. iv. Illustrations of the Fairy Mythology of *A Midsummer Night's Dream* will be found in the volume by Halliwell bearing that name, issued by the Shakespeare Society (1845), and also in *Shakespeare-Forschungen*, ii, *Nachklänge Germanischer Mythe*, by Benno Tschischwitz (1868). Mr Halpin's exceedingly ingenious study of Oberon's Vision interprets that celebrated passage as having reference to Leicester's intrigue with Lettice, daughter of Sir Francis Knollys, and wife of Walter Devereux, Earl of Essex.

rhyme is but a ballad." It is into Theseus' mouth that Shakespeare puts the words which class together "the lunatic, the lover, and the poet" as of imagination all compact. That is the touch, which shows how Shakespeare stood off from Theseus, did not identify himself with this grand ideal (which he admired so truly), and admitted to himself a secret superiority of his own soul over that of this noble master of the world.

Comments by Shakespeare upon his own art are not so numerous that we can afford to overlook them. It must here be noted that Shakespeare makes the "palpable gross" interlude of the Athenian mechanicals serve as an indirect apology for his own necessarily imperfect attempt to represent fairy-land, and the majestic world of heroic life. Maginn writes, "When Hippolyta speaks scornfully of the tragedy in which Bottom holds so conspicuous a part, Theseus answers that the best of this kind" [scenic performances] "are but shadows, and the worst no worse, if imagination amend them. She answers" [for Hippolyta has none of Theseus' indulgence towards inefficiency, but rather a woman's intolerance of the absurd], "that it must be *your* imagination then, not *theirs.* He retorts with a joke on the vanity of actors, and the conversation is immediately changed. The meaning of the Duke is that, however we may laugh at the silliness of Bottom and his companions in their ridiculous play, the author labours under no more than the common calamity of dramatists. They are all but dealers in shadowy representations of life, and if the worst among them can set the mind of the spectator at work, he is equal to the best."*

Maginn has missed the more important significance of the passage. Its dramatic appropriateness is the essential point to observe. To Theseus, the great man of action, the worst and the best of these shadowy representations are all one. He graciously lends himself to be amused, and will not give unmannerly rebuff to the painstaking craftsmen who have so laboriously done their best to please him. But Shakespeare's mind by no means goes along with the utterance of Theseus in this instance

* Shakespeare Papers, p. 119.

any more than when he places in a single group the lover, the lunatic, and the poet. With one principle enounced by the duke, however, Shakespeare evidently does agree, namely, that it is the business of the dramatist to set the spectator's imagination to work, that the dramatist must rather appeal to the mind's eye than to the eye of sense, and that the co-operation of the spectator with the poet is necessary. For the method of Bottom and his company is precisely the reverse, as Gervinus has observed, of Shakespeare's own method. They are determined to leave nothing to be supplied by the imagination. Wall must be plaistered; Moonshine must carry lanthorn and bush. And when Hippolyta, again becoming impatient of absurdity, exclaims, "I am aweary of this moon! would he would change!" Shakespeare further insists on his piece of dramatic criticism by urging, through the duke's mouth, the absolute necessity of the man in the moon being *within* his lanthorn. Shakespeare as much as says, "If you do not approve my dramatic method of presenting fairy land and the heroic world, here is a specimen of the rival method. You think my fairy-world might be amended. Well, amend it with your own imagination. I can do no more unless I adopt the artistic ideas of these Athenian handicraftsmen."*

It is a delightful example of Shakespeare's impartiality that he can represent Theseus with so much genuine enthusiasm. Mr Matthew Arnold has named our aristocrats with their hardy, efficient manners, their addiction to field sports, and their hatred of ideas, "the Barbarians." Theseus is a splendid and gracious aristocrat, perhaps not without a touch of the Barbarian in him. He would have found Hamlet a wholly unintelligible person, who, in possession of his own thoughts, could be contented in a nutshell. When Shakespeare wrote *The Two Gentlemen of Verona*, in which, with little dramatic propriety, the Duke of Milan celebrates "the force of heaven-bred poesy,"

* On Shakespeare's studies of chivalric mediaeval poetry see some interesting pages in Mr Spalding's "Letter on Shakespeare's authorship of the *Two Noble Kinsmen*," pp. 67-75; the article "Chaucer and Shakespeare" in the *Quarterly Review*, January 1873; and Hertzberg's learned discussion of the sources of the Troilus story in *Shakespeare-Jahrbuch* vol. vi.

we may reasonably suppose that the poet might not have been quite just to one who was indifferent to art. But now his self-mastery has increased, and therefore with unfeigned satisfaction he presents Theseus, the master of the world, who, having beauty and heroic strength in actual possession does not need to summon them to occupy his imagination—the great chieftain to whom art is a very small concern of life, fit for a leisure hour between battle and battle. Theseus, who has nothing antique or Grecian about him, is an idealized study from the life. Perhaps he is idealized Essex, perhaps idealized Southampton. Perhaps some night a dramatic company was ordered to perform in presence of a great Elizabethan noble—we know not whom—who needed to entertain his guests, and there, in a moment of fine imaginative vision, the poet discovered Theseus.

A Midsummer Night's Dream is, as its name implies, a phantasmagory; a mask of shadows full of marvel, surprises, splendour, and grotesqueness. But during the same years in which Shakespeare was writing his comedies, and while he was engaged upon his first great tragedy, he continued also steadily at work upon his series of English historical plays. The culture afforded to Shakespeare by the writing of these plays was highly important at that precise period of his career. The substantial matter, upon which he was engaged, served to extend and consolidate that relation which was establishing itself slowly but surely between the imagination of the dramatist and the actual world. The tough clay of historical fact did not take artistic shape too readily, and his hands were strengthened by the labour of moulding it into form. In treating historical subjects, moreover, unrealities of every kind must be sternly set aside; no graceful poetical phrasing, no delicate conceits, no quips and cranks of wit, Shakespeare perceived, would compensate here for want of fidelity to the essential truth of things. Then, again, if in writing *Romeo and Juliet* Shakespeare ran a certain risk of abandoning his genius over much to lyrical intensity, the culture afforded by the historical dramas acted as a safeguard. If in his early comedies Shakespeare relied upon symmetry of arrangement for securing unity of design, here such symmetry was obviously unattainable, and he must look for a deeper ground of unity.

But the most important influence exercised by his dramatic studies in English history upon the mind of Shakespeare was that they engaged his imagination in an inquiry into the sources of power and of weakness, of success and of failure in a man's dealing with the positive, social world. They kept constantly before Shakespeare's mind the problem, "How is a man to obtain a mastery of the actual world, and in what ways may he fail of such mastery?" This was a subject in which Shakespeare had a personal interest, for he was himself resolved, as far as in him lay, not to fail in this material life of ours, but rather, if possible, to be for his own needs a master of events. The portraits of English kings from King John to King Henry V are a series of studies of weakness and of strength for the attaining of kingly ends. To fail is the supreme sin. Worse almost than criminality is weakness, except that crime besides being crime, is itself a certain kind of weakness. Henry VI is a timid saint; it were better that he had been a man. Does his timid saintliness serve him in the place of energy of thought and will, or secure him from a miserable overthrow? It is important to observe the fundamental difference which exists between the series of English historical plays and the great series of tragedies, beginning with *Hamlet*, ending with *Timon of Athens*, in which Shakespeare embodied his ripest experience of life. In the historical plays the question which inevitably comes forward again and again is this, "By what means shall a man attain the noblest practical success in the objective world?" In the great tragedies the problem is a spiritual one. It is still the problem of failure and success. But in these tragedies success means not any practical achievement in the world, but the perfected life of the soul; and failure means the ruin of the life of a soul through passion or weakness, through calamity or crime.

The historical plays lead up to Henry V, in the chronological succession of Shakespeare's plays the last of the series. The tragedies lead up to *The Tempest*, which closes Shakespeare's entire career as dramatist. Gervinus has spoken of King Henry V as if he were Shakespeare's ideal of highest manhood, and other critics have assented to this opinion. It is an opinion which, stated in an unqualified way, must be set aside as not warranted by the facts of Shakespeare's dramas. But it is clear and unquestionable that King Henry V is Shakespeare's ideal of the *practical* heroic character. He is the king who will not fail. He will not fail as the saintly Henry VI failed, nor as Richard II failed, a hectic, self-indulgent nature, a mockery king of pageantry, and sentiment, and rhetoric; nor will he only partially succeed by prudential devices, and stratagems, and crimes, like his father, "great Bolingbroke." The success of Henry V will be sound throughout, and it will be complete. With his glorious practical virtues, his courage, his integrity, his unfaltering justice, his hearty English warmth, his modesty, his love of plainness rather than of pageantry, his joyous temper, his business-like English piety, Henry is indeed the ideal of the king who must attain a success complete, and thoroughly real and sound.

But is this practical, positive, efficient character, with his soldier-like piety and his jolly fashion of wooing, is this the highest ideal of our supreme poet? Is this the highest ideal of Shakespeare, who lived, and moved, and had his being not alone in the world of limitation, of tangible, positive fact, but also in a world of the soul, a world opening into two endless vistas, the vista of meditation and the vista of passion. Assuredly it is not so. We turn to the great tragedies, and what do we there discover? In these Shakespeare is engaged in a series of studies not concerning success in the mastery of events and things, but concerning the higher success and the more awful failure which appear in the exaltation or the ruin of a soul. This with Shakespeare is the true theme of tragedy. Having exhibited various calamity overtaking the being and essential life of man, calamity commonly arising from flaws of character which disclose themselves and become formidable in the test of circumstances, having shown in Macbeth, in Antony, in Othello, in Coriolanus the ruin of character in greater or less degree, Shakespeare represented absolute, overwhelming, irretrievable ruin in *Timon of Athens*, a play written, probably not long before the *Tempest*. And, after exhibiting the absolute ruin of a life and of a soul, Shakespeare closed the wonderful series of his dramatic writings by exhibiting the noblest elevation of character, the most admirable attainment of heart, of intellect, of will, which our present life admits, in the person of Prospero. What more was left for Shakespeare to say? Is it so very strange that he accepted as a good possession the calm energy of his Stratford life, having at last wholly liberated his mind?

Shakespeare, when he had completed his English historical plays, needed rest for his imagination; and in such a mood, craving refreshment and recreation, be wrote his play of *As You Like It.* To understand the spirit of this play, we must bear in mind that it was written immediately after Shakespeare's great series of histories, ending with Henry V (1599), and before he began the great series of tragedies. Shakespeare turned with a sense of relief, and a long easeful sigh, from the oppressive subjects of history, so grave, so real, so massive, and found rest and freedom and pleasure in escape from courts and camps to the Forest of Arden:

> Who doth ambition shun,
> And loves to live i' the sun,
> Come hither, come hither, come hither.

In somewhat the same spirit needing relief for an overstrained imagination he wrote his other pastoral drama, *The Winter's Tale,* immediately or almost immediately after *Timon of Athens.* In each case he chose a graceful story in great part made ready to his hand, from among the prose writings of his early contemporaries, Thomas Lodge and Robert Greene. Like the banished Duke, Shakespeare himself found the forest life of Arden more sweet than that of painted pomp; a life "exempt from public haunt," in a quiet retreat, where for turbulent citizens, the deer, "poor dappled fools," are the only native burghers.

The play has been represented by one of its recent editors as an early attempt made by the poet to control the dark spirit of melancholy in himself "by thinking it away." The characters of the banished Duke, of Orlando, of Rosalind are described as three gradations of cheerfulness in adversity, with Jacques placed over against them in designed contrast.* But no real adversity

---

* *As You Like It,* edited by the Rev. C.E. Moberly (1872), pp. 7-9.

has come to any one of them. Shakespeare, when he put into the Duke's mouth the words, "Sweet are the uses of adversity," knew something of deeper affliction than a life in the golden leisure of Arden. Of real melancholy there is none in the play; for the melancholy of Jacques is not grave and earnest, but sentimental, a self-indulgent humour, a petted foible of character, melancholy prepense and cultivated; "it is a melancholy of mine own, compounded of many simples, extracted from many objects; and indeed the sundry contemplation of my travels, in which my often rumination wraps me in a most humorous sadness." The Duke declares that Jacques has been "a libertine as sensual as the brutish sting itself;" but the Duke is unable to understand such a character as that of Jacques.* Jacques has been no more than a curious experimenter in libertinism, for the sake of adding an experience of madness and folly to the store of various superficial experiences which constitute his unpractical foolery of wisdom. The haunts of sin have been visited as a part of his travel. By and by he will go to the usurping Duke who has put on a religious life, because:

> Out of these convertites
> There is much matter to be heard and learned.

Jacques died, we know not how, or when, or where; but he came to life again a century later, and appeared in the world as an English clergyman; we need stand in no doubt as to his character, for we all know him under his later name of Lawrence Sterne. Mr Yorick made a mistake about his family tree; he came not out of the play of *Hamlet*, but out of *As You Like It*. In Arden he wept and moralised over the wounded deer; and at Namport his tears and sentiment gushed forth for the dead donkey. Jacques knows no bonds that unite him to any living thing. He lives upon novel, curious, and delicate sensations. He seeks the delicious *imprévu* so loved and studiously sought for by that perfected French egoist, Henri Beyle. "A fool! a fool! I

* The Duke accordingly repels Jacques. *Jacques*—"I have been all this day to avoid him; he is too disputable for my company; I think of as many matters as he, but I give heaven thanks and make no boast of them."

met a fool i' the forest!"—and in the delight of coming upon this exquisite surprise, Jacques laughs like chanticleer:

> Sans intermission
> An hour by his dia—

His whole life is unsubstantial and unreal; a curiosity of dainty mockery. To him "all the world's a stage, and all the men and women merely players;" to him sentiment stands in place of passion; an aesthetic, amateurish experience of various modes of life stands in place of practical wisdom; and words, in place of deeds.

"He fatigues me," wrote our earnest and sensitive Thackeray of the Jacques of English literature, "with his perpetual disquiet and his uneasy appeals to my risible or sentimental faculties. He is always looking in my face, watching his effect, uncertain whether I think him an impostor or not; posture-making, coaxing, and imploring me. 'See what sensibility I have—own now that I'm very clever—do cry now, you can't resist this.'" Yes; for Jacques was at his best in the Forest of Arden, and was a little spoiled by preaching weekly sermons, and by writing so long a caprice as his Tristram Shandy. Shakespeare has given us just enough of Jacques; and not too much; and in his undogmatic, artistic, tender, playful, and yet earnest manner upon Jacques Shakespeare has pronounced judgment. Falstaff supposed that by infinite play of wit, and inexhaustible resource of a genius creative of splendid mendacity, he could coruscate away the facts of life, and always remain master of the situation by giving it a clever turn in the idea, or by playing over it with an arabesque of arch waggery:

> I know thee not, old man; fall to thy prayers;
> How ill white hairs become a fool and jester!

That was the terrible incursion of fact; such words as these, coming from the lips of a man who had an unerring perception, and an unfaltering grasp of the fact, were more than words,—they were a deed, which Falstaff the unsubduable, with all his wit, could not coruscate away. "By my troth, he'll yield the crow a pudding one of these days; the king has kill'd his heart." Jacques in his own way supposes that he can dispense with realities. The world, not as it is, but as it mirrors itself in his own mind, which gives to each object a humorous distortion, this is what alone interests Jacques. Shakespeare would say to us, "This egoistic, contemplative, unreal manner of treating life is only a delicate kind of foolery. Real knowledge of life can never be acquired by the curious seeker for experiences." But this Shakespeare says in his non-hortatory, undogmatic way.

Upon the whole, *As You Like It* is the sweetest and happiest of all Shakespeare's comedies. No one suffers; no one lives an eager intense life; there is no tragic interest in it as there is in *The Merchant of Venice*, as there is in *Much Ado about Nothing*. It is mirthful, but the mirth is sprightly, graceful, exquisite; there is none of the rollicking fun of a Sir Toby here; the songs are not "coziers' catches" shouted in the night time, "without any mitigation or remorse of voice," but the solos and duets of pages in the wild-wood, or the noisier chorus of foresters. The wit of Touchstone is not mere clownage, nor has it any indirect serious significances; it is a dainty kind of absurdity worthy to hold comparison with the melancholy of Jacques. And Orlando in the beauty and strength of early manhood, and Rosalind:

> A gallant curtle-axe upon her thigh,
> A boar-spear in her hand,

and the bright, tender, loyal womanhood within—are figures which quicken and restore our spirits, as music does, which is neither noisy nor superficial, and yet which knows little of the deep passion and sorrow of the world.

Shakespeare, when he wrote this idyllic play, was himself in his Forest of Arden. He had ended one great ambition—the historical plays—and not yet commenced his tragedies. It was a resting-place. He sends his imagination into the woods to find repose. Instead of the courts and camps of England, and the embattled plains of France, here was this woodland scene, where the palm-tree, the lioness, and the serpent are to be found; possessed of a flora and fauna that flourish in spite of physical geographers. There is an open-air feeling throughout the play. The dialogue, as has been observed, catches freedom and freshness from the atmosphere. "Never is the scene within-doors, except when something discordant is introduced to heighten as it were the harmony."* After the trumpet-tones of *Henry V* comes the sweet pastoral strain, so bright, so tender. Must it not be all in keeping? Shakespeare was not trying to control his melancholy. When he needed to do that, Shakespeare confronted his melancholy very passionately, and looked it full in the face. Here he needed refreshment, a sunlight tempered by forest-boughs, a breeze upon his forehead, a stream murmuring in his ears.†

Of the group of comedies which belong to this period the two latest in date are probably *Measure for Measure* and *All's Well That Ends Well.* When the former of these plays was written Shakespeare was evidently bidding farewell to mirth; its significance is grave and earnest; the humorous scenes would be altogether repulsive were it not that they are needed to present without disguise or extenuation the world of moral licence and corruption out of and above which rise the virginal strength and severity and beauty of Isabella. At the entrance to the dark and dangerous tragic world into which Shakespeare was now about to pass stand the figures of Isabella and of Helena,—one the embodiment of conscience, the other the embodiment of will. Isabella is the only one of Shakespeare's women whose heart and eyes are fixed upon an impersonal ideal, to whom something abstract is more, in the ardour and energy of her youth, than any human personality. Out of this Vienna in which:

Corruption boils and bubbles
Till it o'errun the stew,

---

* C.A. Brown, *Shakespeare's Autobiographical Poems*, p. 283.

† Hebler writes of *As You Like It*,—"Es ist eine Waldcur für Hofleute, die zum Glück mit heutigen Bad-oder Luftcuren das gemein hat, dass viele Gesunde dabei sind. So vor Allen Orlando und Rosalinde, für welche beide die Cur keine andere Bedeutung hat, als ihre Liebe auf die lieblichste Weise zur Erscheinung and Reife zu bringen, während das vorübergehend Bedenkliche ihrer Lage den Alles, selbst die Liebe noch, verschönenden Götterfunken des Humors hervorlockt. Daneben der Contrast der blossen lieben Natur in dem Schäferpäärchen, und die heitere Parodie des idyllischen Hoflebens in der Heirath des Narren mit einem Landmädchen, während der Blasirte (Jacques) auch der frischesten Natur seine eigene Farbe ankränkelt"—Aufsätze über Shakespeare, p. 195.

emerges this pure zeal, this rectitude of will, this virgin sanctity. Isabella's saintliness is not of the passive, timorous, or merely meditative kind. It is an active pursuit of holiness through exercise and discipline. She knows nothing of a Manichean hatred of the body; the life runs strongly and gladly in her veins; simply her soul is set upon things belonging to the soul, and uses the body for its own purposes. And that the life of the soul may be invigorated she would bring every unruly thought into captivity, "having in a readiness to revenge all disobedience":

Isab. And have you nuns no farther privileges?
Tran. Are these not large enough?
Isab. Yes, truly. I speak not as desiring more;
But rather wishing a more strict restraint
Upon the sisterhood.

This severity of Isabella proceeds from no real turning away on her part from the joys and hopes of womanhood; her brother, her schoolfellow Julia, the memory of her father, are precious to her; her severity is only a portion of the vital energy of her heart; living actively she must live purely; and to her the cloister is looked upon as the place where her energy can spend itself in stern efforts towards ideal objects. Bodily suffering is bodily suffering to Isabella, whose "cheek-roses" proclaim her physical health and vigour; but bodily suffering is swallowed up in the joy of quickened spiritual existence:

Were I under the terms of death
The impression of keen whips I'd wear as rubies,
And strip myself to death, as to a bed
That longing have been sick for ere I'd yield
My body up to shame.

And as she had strength to accept pain and death for herself rather than dishonour, so she can resolutely accept pain and death for those who are dearest to her. When Claudio falters back dismayed from the immediate prospect of the grave, Isabella utters her piteous "Alas, alas!" to perceive the tenderness and timorousness of his spirit; but when he faintly invites her to yield herself to shame for his sake, she severs herself with indignation, not from her brother, not from Claudio, but from this disgrace of manhood in her brother's form—this treason against fidelity of the heart:

> O, you beast!
> O, faithless coward! O, dishonest wretch!
> Wilt thou be made a man out of my vice?
> . . . .
> Take my defiance!
> Die; perish!

Isabella does not return to the sisterhood of Saint Clare. Putting aside from her the dress of religion, and the strict conventual rule, she accepts her place as Duchess of Vienna. In this there is no dropping away, through love of pleasure or through supineness, from her ideal; it is entirely meet and right. She has learned that in the world may be found a discipline more strict, more awful than the discipline of the convent; she has learned that the world has need of her; her life is still a consecrated life; the vital energy of her heart can exert and augment itself through glad and faithful wifehood, and through noble station more fully than in seclusion. To preside over this polluted and feculent Vienna is the office and charge of Isabella, "a thing ensky'd and sainted":

> Spirits are not finely touched
> But to fine issues; nor Nature never lends
> The smallest scruple of her excellence,
> But, like a thrifty goddess, she determines
> Herself the glory of a creditor,—
> Both thanks and use.*

In *All's Well That Ends Well,* a subject of extreme difficulty, when regarded on the ethical side, was treated by Shakespeare with a full consciousness of its difficulty.† A woman who seeks

* *Measure for Measure, Act* i, *Scene* 1.

† Years wide apart have been assigned for the date of *All's Well That Ends Well.* Mr Fleay believes that it was written at two different periods, and that the play contains early and later work, which he endeavours to separate. His date for the completed play is 1602. H. von Friesen is also of opinion that this is one of Shakespeare's earliest plays, and was afterwards rehandled. See *Shakespeare Jahrbuch,* vol. ii, pp. 48-54. So also Gervinus. (H. von Friesen observes resemblances of style to the

her husband, and gains him against his will; who afterwards by a fraud—a fraud however pious—defeats his intention of estranging her, and becomes the mother of his child; such a personage it would seem a sufficiently difficult task to render attractive or admirable. Yet Helena has been named by Coleridge "the loveliest of Shakespeare's characters." Possibly Coleridge recognised in Helena the single quality which, if brought to bear upon himself by one to whom he yielded love and worship, would have given definiteness and energy to his somewhat vague and incoherent life. For sake of this one thing Shakespeare was interested in the story, and so admirable did it seem to him, that he could not choose but endeavour to make beautiful and noble the entire character and action of Helena. This one thing is the energy, the leap-up, the direct advance of the *will* of Helena, her prompt, unerroneous tendency towards the right and efficient *deed.* She does not display herself through her words; she does not, except on rarest occasions, allow her feelings to expand and deploy themselves; her entire force of character is concentrated in what she does. And therefore we see her quite as much indirectly, through the effect which she has produced upon other persons of the drama, as through self-confession or immediate presentation of her character.

Duke's speeches in *Measure for Measure*; and Prof. Karl Elze points out various parallels to passages in *Hamlet. Shakespeare Jahrbuch,* vii, pp. 235-36.) Delius, whose opinion on such a matter must be regarded as weighty, pronounces the style and the verse *throughout* to be different in their characteristic peculiarities from those of Shakespeare's early plays. Professor Hertzberg assigns the date 1603; and he expressly denies that an early and later style are observable in the play. "Man muss eingestehen dass die metrischen wie stilistischen Eigenthümlichkeiten sich gleichmässig auf das ganze Gedicht erstrecken und es durchaus als aus einem Guss gearbeitet erscheinen lassen. Wenn also diese Characterzüge einer späteren Periode, aus einer zweiten 'Textesrecension' entsprungen sein sollten, so müsste man annehmen, dass der Dichter mit Absicht von Anfang bis zu Ende seinen klaren Ausdruck angedunkelt, den einfachen Satzbau verwickelt und die regelmässigen und glatten Verse anomal und holprig gemacht habe. Dies kann Niemand annehmen." Hertzberg rejects the opinion that *All's Well* is the play (in an earlier form) mentioned by Meres as "Love's Labour's Won." Hertzberg contends that *Love's Labour's Won* was the *Taming of the Shrew.* Kreyssig connects *All's Well,*—the subdual of husband by wife,—with the Shrew,—the subdual of wife by husband.

A motto for the play may be found in the words uttered with pious astonishment by the clown, when his mistress bids him to begone, "That man should be at woman's command and yet no hurt done." Helena is the providence of the play; and there is "no hurt done," but rather healing—healing of the body of the French King, healing of the spirit of the man she loves.* For Bertram, when the story begins, though endowed with beauty and bravery and the advantages (and disadvantages), of rank, is in character, in heart, in will, a crude, ungracious boy. Helena loves him, and sets him, in her love, above herself, the poor physician's daughter, out of her sphere:

> 'Twere all one
> That I should love a bright, particular star
> And think to wed it, he is so above me.

She loves him thus, but (if love can be conceived as distinct from liking) she does not wholly like him. She admits to herself that in worship of Bertram there is a certain fatuousness:

> Now he's gone, and my idolatrous fancy
> Must sanctify his reliques.

She sees from the first that the friend of his choice, the French captain, is "a notorious liar," "solely a coward," "a great way fool"; she trembles for what Bertram may learn at the court:

> God send him well!
> The court's a learning place; and he is one—
> *Parol.* What one i' faith?
> *Hel.* That I wish well.

Yet she sees in Bertram a potential nobleness, waiting to be evoked. And her will leaps forward to help him. Now she loves him,—loves him with devotion which comes from a consciousness that she can confer much; and she will form him so that one day she shall like him also:

> *Hel.* 'Tis pity.
> *Parol.* What's pity?

---

* "Nicht nur am Könige, sondern auch an Bertram vollbringt sie eine glückliche Heilung." Professor Karl Elze. *Shakespeare Jahrbuch*, vol. vii, p. 222.

Hel. That wishing well had not a body in't,
Which might be felt; that we, the poorer born,
Whose baser stars do shut us up in wishes,
Might with effects of them follow our friends,
And shew what we alone must think.

But the "wishing well" of such a woman as Helena has indeed a sensible and apprehensible body in it. With a sacred boldness she assumes a command over Bertram's fate and her own. She cannot believe in the piety of resignation, or passiveness, in the religious duty of letting things drift; rather, she finds in the love which prompts her a true mandate from above, and a veritable providential power:

Our remedies oft in ourselves do lie
Which we ascribe to heaven: the fated sky
Gives us free scope, only doth backward pull
Our slow designs when we ourselves are dull.
What power is it that mounts my love so high?

Helena goes forth, encouraged by her mistress, the mother of the man she seeks to win; goes forth to gain her husband, to allay her own need of service to him, to impose herself on Bertram as the blessing that he requires. All this Helena does openly, with perfect courage. She does not conceal her love from the Countess; she does not for a moment dream of stealing after Bertram in man's attire. It is the most impulsively or the most delicately, and exquisitely feminine of Shakespeare's women whom he delights to disguise in the "garnish of a boy,"—Julia with her hair knit up "in twenty odd-conceited true-love knots," Rosalind, the gallant curtle-axe upon her thigh, Viola, the sweet-voiced in whom "all is semblative a woman's part," Jessica, for whose transformation Cupid himself would blush, Portia, the wise young judge, so poignantly feminine in her gifts of intellect and heart, Imogen, who steps into the cavern's mouth with the advanced sword in a slender and trembling hand. In Helena there is so much solidity and strength of character that we feel she would be enfeebled by any male disguise which might complicate the impression produced by her plain womanhood. There could be no charm in presenting as a pretender to male courage one who was actually courageous as a man.

But throughout, while Helena is abundantly courageous, Shakespeare intends that she shall at no moment appear unwomanly. In offering herself to Bertram, she first discloses her real feeling by words addressed to one of the young lords, from among whom it is granted her to choose a husband:

> Be not afraid that I your hand should take;
> I'll never do you wrong for your own sake.

Only with Bertram she would venture on the bold experiment of wronging him for his own sake. The experiment, indeed, does not at first seem to succeed. Helena is wedded to Bertram; she has laid her will without reserve in her husband's hands; she had desired to surrender all to him, for his good, and she has surrendered all. But Bertram does not find this providential superintendence of his affairs of the heart, altogether to his taste; and in company with Paroller he flies from his wife's presence to the Italian war. Upon reading the concise and cruel letter in which Bertram has declared the finality of his separation from her, Helena does not faint, nor does she break forth into bitter lamentation. "This is a dreadful sentence," "'Tis bitter,"— thus, pruning her words, Helena controls "the thoughts which swell and throng" over her, until they condense themselves into one strong purpose. She will leave her mother, leave her home, and when she is gone and forgotten, Bertram will return from hardship and danger. But she would fain see him, and if anything can still be done, she will do that thing.

The mode by which Helena succeeds in accomplishing the conditions upon which Bertram has promised to acknowledge her as his wife, seems indeed hardly to possess any moral force, any validity for the heart or the conscience. It can only be said in explanation, that to Helena an infinite virtue and significance resides in a *deed;* out of a word or out of a feeling she does not hope for measureless good to come; but out of a deed what may not come? That Bertram should actually have received her as his wife, actually, though unwittingly, that he should indeed be father of the child she bears him; these are facts, accomplished things, which must work out some real advantage. And now Bertram has learnt his need of self-distrust, perhaps has learnt true modesty. His friend (who was all vain words apart from deeds), has been unmasked, and pitilessly exposed. May not Bertram now be capable of estimating the worth of things and of persons more justly? Helena, in taking the place of Diana, in beguiling her husband into at least material virtue, is still "doing him wrong, for his own sake." The man is "at woman's command," and there is "no hurt done."

Even at the last Bertram's attainment is but small; he is still no more than a potential piece of worthy manhood. We cannot suppose that Shakespeare has represented him thus without a purpose. Does not the poet wish us to feel that although much remains to be wrought in Bertram, his welfare is now assured? The courageous title of the play *All's Well That Ends Well*, is like an utterance of the heart of Helena, who has strength and endurance to attain the end, and who will measure things, not by the pains and trials of the way, not by the dubious and difficult means, but by that end, by the accomplished issue. We need not, therefore, concern ourselves any longer about Bertram; he is safe in the hands of Helena; she will fashion him as he should be fashioned; Bertram is at length delivered from the snares and delusions which beset his years of haughty ignorance and dulness of the heart; he is doubly won by Helena; therefore he cannot wander far, therefore he cannot finally be lost.*

The changes of type which took place in the prominent female characters of Shakespeare's plays as the poet passed from youth to manhood, and from early manhood to riper maturity, would form an interesting subject for detailed study. The emotional women of the early plays, if not turbulent and aggressive, are still deficient in delicacy of heart, in refinement of instinct, impulse, and habit. The intellectual women, who

---

* On this play consult Professor Karl Elze's article in *Shakespeare Jahrbuch*, vol. vii, and preface by Hertzberg in the German Shakespeare Society's edition of *Schlegel's and Tieck's Translation of Shakespeare*, vol. xi. Hertzberg maintains that love of Lafeu'a daughter is a motive of Bertram's rejection of Helena. But see Elze's reply in the above mentioned article, p. 226.

stand by the side of these, are bright and clever, but over-confident, forward, or defiant. In the early historical plays appear terrible female forms,—women whose ambitions have been foiled, whose hearts have been torn and crushed, who are filled with fierce sorrow, passionate indignation, a thirst for revenge. Such are the Duchess of Gloster, Margaret of Anjou, Queen Elinor, Constance. As comedy succeeds comedy, the female characters become more complex, more subtile, more exquisite. Rosaline's flouting of Berowne, becomes Rosalind's arch mockery of Orlando, or the sportive contests of Beatrice with Benedict. In Portia of *The Merchant of Venice* intellect and emotions play into one another with exquisite swiftness, brightness, and vital warmth.

Just at the close of the period which gave birth to Shakespeare's most joyous comedies, and at the entrance to the tragic period, appear types of female character which are distinguished by some single element of peculiar strength, Helena, Isabella, Portia of Julius Caesar (type of perfect womanly heroism, yet environed by the weakness of her sex); and over against these are studies of feminine incapacity or ignobleness—Ophelia, Gertrude, Cressida. It is as if Shakespeare at this time needed some one strong, outstanding excellence to grasp and steady himself by, and had lost his delight in the even harmony of character which suits us, and brings us joy when we make no single, urgent, and peculiar demand for help. Next follow the tragic figures—Desdemona, the invincible loyalty of wifehood; Cordelia, the invincible filial loyalty; sacrificial lives, which are offered up, and which sanctify the earth, lives which fall in the strife with evil, and which falling achieve their victories of love. And as these make the world beautiful and sacred, even while they leave it strange and sorrowful, so over against them appear the destroyers of life—Lady Macbeth, and the monsters Goneril, Regan.

Finally, in Shakespeare's latest plays appear upon the one hand the figures of the great sufferers—calm, self-possessed, much enduring, free from self-partiality, unjust resentment, and the passion of revenge—Queen Katharine, Hermione; and on the other hand are exquisite girlish figures, children who have known no sorrow, over whom is shed a magical beauty, an ideal light, while above them Shakespeare is seen, as it were, bowing tenderly—Miranda, Perdita. How great a distance has been traversed! Instead of the terrible Margaret of Anjou we have here Queen Katharine. Shakespeare in his early period would have found cold, and without suitability for the purposes of art, Katharine's patience, reserve, and equilibrium of soul. Instead of Rosaline here is Perdita. A death-bed glorious with a vision of angels, and the exquisite dawn of a young girl's life, these are the two last themes on which the imagination of the poet cared to dwell affectionately and long.

Here for the present we may pause. We have glanced at the growth of Shakespeare's mind and art as far onward as the opening of the period of the great tragedies. What Shakespeare gained of insight and of strength during that period a subsequent chapter will attempt to tell.*

* I am unwilling to offer any criticism of the play of *Troylus and Cressida* until I see my way more clearly through certain difficulties respecting its date and its ethical significance. Mr Fleay believes that three stories can be distinguished—(1) Troylus and Cressida; (2) Hector; (3) Ajax, Ulysses, and the Greek Camp; and that these stories were written at different periods. (See Transactions of the New Shakespeare Society.) Mr Furnivall says: "that there are two parts, an early and a late, I do not doubt." Hertzberg assigns the date 1603. See his valuable Preface in the German Shakespeare Society's edition of *Tieck's and Schlegel's Translation of Shakespeare*, vol. xi, and on the sources of the play his article in *Shakespeare Jahrbuch*, vol. vi; also in vol. iii the article by Karl Eitner. Hertzberg believes that the play remained unprinted and unacted until 1609. Ulrici's article on Troilus and Cressida in *Shakespeare Jahrbuch*, vol. ix, make it clear that the play belongs rather to comedy than tragedy. This article may be consulted (as well as Hertzberg's preface) on the questions raised by the concluding lines of the difficult epilogue by Pandarus.

So far was written in 1875; but since then I have come to understand in some degree, I believe, the significance of this difficult play. See *ante*, preface to the third edition.

3

THE FIRST AND THE SECOND TRAGEDY: *ROMEO AND JULIET; HAMLET*

During the first ten years of Shakespeare's dramatic career he wrote quickly, producing (if we suppose that he commenced authorship in 1590 at the age of twenty-six), on an average, about two plays in each year. These eighteen or twenty plays written between 1590 and 1600, include some eight or nine comedies, and the whole of the great series of English historical dramas, which, when *Henry V* was written, Shakespeare probably looked upon as complete. To this field he did not return, except in one instance when it would seem that a portion of a play on the subject of Henry VIII was written, and while still incomplete was handed over on some special occasion to the dramatist Fletcher to expand from three acts into five. In the first decade of Shakespeare's authorship (if we set aside *Titus Andronicus* as the work of an unknown writer), a single tragedy appears,—*Romeo and Juliet.* This play is believed to have engaged Shakespeare's attention during a number of years. Dissatisfied probably with the first form which it assumed, Shakespeare worked upon the play again, rewriting and enlarging it.* But it is not unlikely that even then he considered

* The opinion of Mr Richard Grant White deserves to be stated. It is "That the *Romeo and Juliet* which has come down to us (for there may have been an antecedent play upon the same story), was first written [in 1591], by two or more playwrights, of whom Shakespeare was one; that subsequently [in 1596], Shakespeare re-wrote this old play, of which he was part author, making his principal changes in the passages which were contributed by his co-labourers." Mr R.G. White believes the first quarto of *Romeo and Juliet* to be an imperfect and garbled copy, obtained

his powers to be insufficiently matured for the great dealing as artist with human life and passion, which tragedy demands; for, having written *Romeo and Juliet*, Shakespeare returned to the histories, in which, doubtless, he was aware that he was receiving the best possible culture for future tragedy; and he wrote the little group of comedies in which Shakespearian mirth obtains its highest and most complete expression. Then, after an interval of about five years, a second tragedy, *Hamlet*, was produced. Over *Hamlet*, as over *Romeo and Juliet*, it is supposed that Shakespeare laboured long and carefully. Like *Romeo and Juliet* the play exists in two forms, and there is reason to believe that in the earlier form in each instance we possess an imperfect report of Shakespeare's first treatment of his theme.*

It may be thought paradoxical to infer from the absence of tragedy in the earlier years of Shakespeare's dramatic career, that he looked upon the writing of tragedy as his chief vocation as author; yet the inference is not unconfirmed by facts in Shakespeare's subsequent career. Almost from the first it would appear that he had before him the design of *Romeo and Juliet*. When after five or six years it was actually accomplished, there still appeared in the play unmistakable marks of immature judgment. Shakespeare accordingly, who in his histories had abundance of work planned out for him, wisely abstained for some time further from writing tragedy. But as soon as *Hamlet* was completed, and it became a demonstrated fact to the poet that he had attained his full maturity, and was master of his craft, then he no longer hesitated or delayed, and year by year from 1602 to 1612 he added to the great roll of his tragedies, accomplishing in those years by sustained energy of heart and

---

by the aid of a reporter, of Shakespeare's new work, the defects of which were supplied partly by some versemongers of the day, and partly from the old play in the composition of which Shakespeare was one of two or more co-labourers.

* The editors of the Cambridge Shakespeare believe that there was an old play on the subject of Hamlet, "some portions of which are still preserved in the quarto of 1603." For various bits of evidence (some good, some bad), to prove that the text of this quarto was obtained orally, and not directly from a manuscript, see Tschischwitz's *Shakespeare-Forschungen I. Hamlet*, pp. 10-14.

imagination as marvellous a feat of authorship as the world has seen.

When Shakespeare began to write for the stage, as was noticed in the preceding chapter, he was by no means misled by self-confidence. He began cautiously and tentatively, feeling his way. And there was one cause which might reasonably make him timid in the direction of tragedy. Shakespeare, at the age of twenty-six, was not afraid to compete with contemporary writers in comedy and history. He co-operated, it may be, in the writing of historical plays, *The First Part of the Contention*, and *The True Tragedie of Richard Duke of Yorke*, at an early age, and afterwards by revision and addition made these plays still more his own.* But the department of tragedy was dominated by a writer of superb genius, Christopher Marlowe. Shakespeare, whose powers ripened slowly, may at the time when he wrote *The Comedy of Errors*, and *Love's Labour's Lost*, have well hesitated to dispute with Marlowe his special province. Imitators and disciples had crowded around the master. All the vices of his style had been exaggerated. Shakespeare saw one thing clearly, that if the time ever came when he would write tragedy, the tragedy must be of a kind altogether different from that created upon Marlowe's method,—the method of idealising passions on a gigantic scale. To add to the pieces of the school of Marlowe a rhapsody of blood commingled with nonsense was impossible for Shakespeare, who was never altogether wanting in a sane judgment, and a lively sense of the absurd.

Thus it came about that Shakespeare at nearly forty years of age was the author of but two or three tragedies. Of these, *Romeo and Juliet* may be looked upon as the work of the artist's adolescence; and *Hamlet* as the evidence that he had become adult, and in this supreme department master of his craft. To add to the interest of these plays as subjects of Shakespearian

---

* The latest study of 2 and 3 *Henry VI* and the relation of these to *The Contention* and *True Tragedie* is the admirably careful essay by Miss Jane Lee, "Transactions of the New Shakespeare Society 1875-76." The opinion arrived at by Miss Lee is that in 2 and 3 *Henry VI* Shakespeare and Marlowe are revisers of work by Marlowe, Greene and perhaps Peele.

study, each, as was observed above, exists in two very different forms; and from these something may be learnt as to the poet's method of rehandling his own work. In the case of *Romeo and Juliet*, we possess the English original, a poem by Arthur Brooke, upon which Shakespeare founded his drama, and which in many particulars he minutely followed. It is therefore possible in the case of this play, to investigate with peculiar advantage Shakespeare's method of treating his original.

The first two tragedies having been so carefully and deliberately thought out, having been looked upon by their author as of chief importance among his writings, we might anticipate that the second could hardly have been written without conscious reference to the first. In his early tentative plays Shakespeare made trial of various styles; he broke out now on this side, now on that, in directions which were wide apart; now he was engaged upon a history, now upon a comedy of incident, almost a farce; now a comedy of dialogue; and again a comedy of tender and graceful sentiment. He evidently had resolved that he would not repeat himself, that he would not allow his invention to come under control of any one of its own creatures. Too often a distinguished literary success is the prelude to literary failure. The artist in fainter colours, and with a more uncertain outline repeats his admired figures and situations. Shakespeare instinctively and by resolve put himself into relation with facts of the most diverse kinds, and preferred a comparatively slow attainment of a comprehension of life to a narrow intensity of individuality. The broad history of the nation interested him; but also, the passion of love and death in two young hearts; he could laugh brightly, and mock the affectations and fashionable follies of his day; but he must also stand before the tomb of the Capulets possessed by a sense of mystery, and that strenuous pain, in which something else than mere sorrow is predominant.

Now when writing *Hamlet*, his second tragedy, Shakespeare, we must needs believe, determined that he would break away from the influence of his first tragedy, *Romeo and Juliet*. *Romeo and Juliet* is steeped in passion; *Hamlet* is steeped in meditation. Contrast the hero of the one play, the man of the South, with the chief figure of the other, the Teuton, the man of the North. Contrast Hamlet's friend and comforter, Horatio, possessed of grave strength, self-government, and balance of character, with Romeo's friend, Mercutio, all brilliance, intellect, wit, and effervescent animal spirits. Contrast the gay festival in Capulet's house with the brutal drinking of the Danish king and courtiers. Contrast the moonlit night in the garden, while the nightingale's song is panting forth from the pomegranate tree, with the silence, the nipping and eager air of the platform of Elsinore, the beetling height to seaward, and the form of terror which stalked before the sentinels. Contrast the perfect love of Juliet and her Romeo, with the piteous foiled desire for love in Hamlet and Ophelia. Contrast the passionate seizure upon death, as her immediate and highest need, of the Italian wife, with the misadventure of the crazed Ophelia, so pitiful, so accidental, so un-heroic, ending in "muddy death." Yet, with all their points of contrast, there is one central point of affinity between the plays. Like Mr Browning's Paracelsus and his Sordello, the poems are companion poems, while they are set over one against the other; they are contrasted but complementary.* Hamlet resembles Romeo in his inability to maintain the will in a fruitful relation with facts, and with the real world. Neither is a ruler of events. Luck is for ever against Romeo; the stars are inauspicious to him, and to such men the stars will always be inauspicious, as to a Henry V they will always prove auxiliary. With Hamlet to resolve is to stand at gaze before an action, and to become incapable of achieving it. The necessary coupling between the purpose and the deed has been fatally dissolved. There is this central point in common between Hamlet and Romeo—the will in each is sapped; but in each it is sapped by a totally different disease of soul.†

* See the writer's lecture on the poetry of Mr Tennyson and Mr Browning: *Afternoon Lectures*, vol. v, p. 178.

† "Romeo is Hamlet in love. There is the same rich exuberance of passion and sentiment in the one, that there is of thought and sentiment in the other. Both are absent and self-involved; both live out of themselves in a world of imagination."—Hazlitt, *Characters of Shakespeare's Plays*, p. 177 (ed. 1818).

The external atmosphere of the tragedy of *Romeo and Juliet,* its Italian colour and warmth, have been so finely felt by M. Philarète Chasles that his words deserve to be a portion of every criticism of that play.—"Who does not recall those lovely summer nights, in which the forces of nature seem eager for development, and constrained to remain in drowsy languor—a mingling of intense heat, superabundant energy, impetuous power, and silent freshness?

"The nightingale sings in the depths of the woods. The flower-cups are half-closed. A pale lustre is shed over the foliage of the forests, and upon the brow of the hills. The deep repose conceals, we are aware, a procreant force; the melancholy reserve of nature is the mask of a passionate emotion. Under the paleness and the coolness of the night you divine restrained ardours, and flowers which brood in silence, impatient to shine forth.

"Such is the peculiar atmosphere with which Shakespeare has enveloped one of his most wonderful creations—*Romeo and Juliet.*

"Not only the substance, but the forms of the language come from the South. Italy was the inventor of the tale: she drew it from her national memorials, her old family-feuds, her annals filled with amorous and bloody intrigues. In its lyric accent, its blindness of passion, its blossoming and abundant vitality, in the brilliant imagery, in the bold composition, no one can fail to recognise Italy. Romeo utters himself like a sonnet of Petrarch, with the same refined choice, and the same antitheses; there is the same grace and the same pleasure in versifying passion in allegorical stanzas. Juliet, too, is wholly the woman of Italy; with small gift of forethought, and absolutely ingenuous in her *abandon,* she is at once vehement and pure."*

The season is midsummer. It wants a fortnight and odd days of Lammastide (August 1st). Wilhelm Schlegel, and after him Hazlitt, have spoken as if the atmosphere of the play were that of a southern spring.† Such a criticism indicates a want of

* Études sur W. Shakespeare, Marie Stuart, et L'Arétin, pp. 141-42.

† So also Flathe, *Shakespeare,* &c. Part ii, p. 188.

sensibility to the tone and colouring of the piece. The mid-July heat broods over the five tragic days of the story. The mad blood is stirring in men's veins during these hot summer days.* There is a thunderous feeling in the moral element. The summer was needed also that the nights and mornings might quickly meet. The nights are those luminous nights from which the daylight seems never wholly to depart, nights through which the warmth of day still hangs over the trees and flowers.

It is worth-while to pause and note Shakespeare's method of treating external nature as the *milieu* or enveloping medium of human passion; while sometimes, in addition, between external nature and human passion Shakespeare reveals acute points of special contact. We recall in *King Lear* the long and terrible day which begins at moonset before the dawn, when Kent is put in the stocks, and which ends with the storm upon the heath. The agony is intensified by the stretch of time, strained with passion and events, until the time tingles and is intense; it culminates in the night of furious wind and spouting rain, of lightning and of thunder, when the roots of nature seem shaken in the same upheaval of things which makes a daughter cruel. We remember how Duncan breathed a delicate air when he entered under the martlet-haunted portals of Macbeth, as though nature insinuated into Duncan's senses a treacherous presentiment of peace and security; and there followed upon this the night when the earth was feverous and the air was filled with lamentings and strange screams of death. We remember that other night of tempest and prodigy which preceded the fall of Julius Caesar, when Cassius, catching exhilaration and energy from the mutiny in the heaven, walked about the streets unbraced, "submitting him unto the perilous night." Then in contrast with these we think of the lyric love of Lorenzo and Jessica under the star-sown sky, every orb of which sings in its motion like an angel "still quiring to the young-eyed cherubims;" we think of the Forest of Arden, with its tempered light and shade, its streams where the deer comes to drink, and green

---

* *Benvolio.*—"For now these hot days is the mad blood stirring." See the extract from Dr Theodor Sträter in H.H. Furness's *Variorum Edition of Romeo and Juliet*, pp. 461-62.

haunts in which adversity grows sweet; we think of the mountain country of Wales, and the salutations to the heaven of the royal youths whom Cymbeline had lost. The air which surrounds the island of Prospero is one of enchantment fit to breathe upon marvel and beauty:

> The isle is full of noises
> Sounds and sweet airs that give delight and hurt not.

In the play of *Pericles* we are for ever in presence of the waters furious or serene, and their voices of tumult or of calm are for ever mingling with the human voices, with the sorrow of the bereaved father, and the magical singing of the sea-pure and sea-sensitive Marina. Once again, in Timon, we are in presence of the sea,—but it is not the stormy waters of Pericles that we gaze at; it is not the yellow sands of Prospero's island, where the sea-nymphs dance, and curtsy, and take hands; in Timon it is neither the strength nor the beauty of the waves we are made to feel:

> Timon hath made his everlasting mansion
> Upon the beachèd verge of the salt flood;
> Who once a day with his embossed froth
> The turbulent surge shall cover.

We see the cold white lip of the wave curling over, and curling over again, with bitter monotony upon the sand; and it is there, touched by the salt and pitiless edge of the sea, that the corpse of the desperate man must lie abandoned.

Romeo is not the determiner of events in the play. He does not stand prominently forward, a single figure in the first scene, as does Marlowe's Barabas, and Shakespeare's Richard III, soliloquising about his own persons and his plans. The first scene of the play prepares a place for Romeo, it presents the moral environment of the hero, it exhibits the feud of the houses which determines the lovers' fate, although they for a brief space forget these grim realities in the rapture of their joy. The strife of the houses Capulet and Montague appears in this first scene in its trivial, ludicrous aspect; threatening, however, in a moment to become earnest and formidable. The serving men Gregory and Samson biting thumbs at the serving-men

Abraham and Balthasar,—this is the obverse of the tragic show. Turn to the other side, and what do we see? The dead bodies of young and beautiful human creatures, of Tybalt and Paris, of Juliet and Romeo, the bloody harvest of the strife. This first scene, half ludicrous, but wholly grave, was written not without a reference to the final scene. The bandying of vulgar wit between the servants must not hide from us a certain grim irony which underlies the opening of the play. Here the two old rivals meet; they will meet again. And the prince appears in the last scene as in the first. Then old Capulet and Montague will be pacified; then they will consent to let their desolated lives decline to the grave in quietness. Meanwhile serving-men with a sense of personal dignity must bite their thumbs, and other incidents may happen.

Few critics of the play have omitted to call attention to the fact that Shakespeare represents Romeo as already in love before he gives his heart to Juliet, in love with the pale-cheeked, dark-eyed, disdainful Rosaline. "If we are right," Coleridge wrote, "[...] in pronouncing this one of Shakespeare's early dramas, it affords a strong instance of the fineness of his insight into the nature of the passions, that Romeo is introduced already love-bewildered." The circumstance is not of Shakespeare's invention. He has retained it from Brooke's poem; but that he thought fit to retain the circumstance, fearlessly declaring that Romeo's supreme love is not his first love, is noteworthy. The contrast in the mind of the earlier poet between Rosaline, who:

> From her youth was fostered evermore
> With vertues foode, and taught in schole, of wisdomes skilfull lore,

and Juliet, who yields to her passion, and by it is destroyed, was a contrast which Shakespeare rejected as a piece of formal and barren morality. Of what character is the love of Romeo for Rosaline? Romeo's is not an active practical nature like Henry V; neither is he great by intellect, a thinker in any high sense of the word. But if he lives and moves and has his being neither heroically in the objective world of action, like Henry V, nor in the world of the mind like Hamlet, all the more he lives, moves, and has his being in the world of mere emotion. To him emotion which enriches and exalts itself with the imagination, emotion apart from thought, and apart from action, is an end in itself. Therefore it delights him to hover over his own sentiment, to brood upon it, to feed upon it richly. Romeo must needs steep his whole nature in feeling, and, if Juliet does not appear, he must love Rosaline.

Nevertheless the love of Rosaline cannot be to Romeo as is the love of Juliet. It is a law in moral dynamics, too little recognised, that the breadth, and height, and permanence of a feeling depend in a certain degree at least upon the actual force of its external cause. No ardour of self-protection, no abandonment prepense, no self-sustained energy, can create and shape a passion of equal volume, and possessing a like certainty and directness of advance with a passion shaped, determined, and for ever re-invigorated by positive, objective fact. Shakespeare had become assured that the facts of the world are worthy to command our highest ardour, our most resolute action, our most solemn awe, and that the more we penetrate into fact the more will our nature be quickened, enriched, and exalted. The play of *Romeo and Juliet* exhibits to us the deliverance of a man from dream into reality. In Romeo's love of Rosaline we find represented the dream-life as yet undisturbed, the abandonment to emotion for emotion's sake. Romeo nurses his love; he sheds tears; he cultivates solitude; he utters his groans in the hearing of the comfortable friar; he stimulates his fancy with the sought-out phrases, the curious antitheses of the amorous dialect of the period:*

> Why, then, O brawling love! Oloving hate!
> O anything, of nothing first create!
> O heavy lightness! Serious vanity!
> Mis-shapen chaos of well-seeming forms!
> Feather of lead, bright smoke, cold fire, sick health!

He broods upon the luxury of his sorrow. And then Romeo meets Juliet. Juliet is an actual force beyond and above himself,

* Mrs Jameson has noticed that in *All's Well That Ends Well* Helena mockingly reproduces this style of amorous antitheses (Act i, Sc. I, II. 180-89). Helena, who lives so effectively in the world of fact, is contemptuous towards all unreality and affectation.

a veritable fact of the world. Nevertheless there remains a certain clinging self-consciousness, an absence of perfect simplicity and directness even in Romeo's very real love of Juliet. This is placed by Shakespeare in designed contrast with the singleness of Juliet's nature, her direct unerroneous passion which goes straight to its object, and never broods upon itself. It is Romeo who says in the garden scene:

> How silver-sweet sound lovers' tongues by night,
> Like softest music to attending ears.

He has overheard the voice of Juliet, and he cannot answer her call until he has drained the sweetness of the sound. He is one of those men to whom the emotional atmosphere which is given out by the real object, and which surrounds it like a luminous mist, is more important than the reality itself. As he turns slowly away, loath to leave, Romeo exclaims:

> Love goes toward love, as school-boys from their books,
> But love from love, towards school with heavy looks.

But Juliet's first thought is of the danger to which Romeo is exposed in her father's grounds. It is Juliet who will not allow the utterance of any oath because the whole reality of that night's event, terrible in its joy, has flashed upon her, and she, who lives in no golden haze of luxurious feeling, is aroused and alarmed by the sudden shock of too much happiness. It is Juliet who uses direct and simple words:

> Farewell compliment!
> Dost thou love me? I know thou wilt say "Ay,"
> And I will take thy word.

She has declared that her bounty is measureless, that her love is infinite, when a sudden prosaic interruption occurs; the nurse calls within, Juliet leaves the window, and Romeo is left alone. Is this new joy a dream?

> O blessed, blessed night! I am afeard,
> Being in night, all this is but a dream,
> Too flattering-sweet to be substantial.

But Juliet hastily reappears with words upon her lips which make it evident that it is no dream of joy in which she lives:

Three words, dear Romeo, and good night indeed.
If that thy bent of love be honourable,
Thy purpose marriage, send me word to-morrow,
By one that I'll procure to come to thee,
Where, and what time thou wilt perform the rite,
And all my fortunes at thy foot I'll lay,
And follow thee, my lord, throughout the world.

The wholeness and crystalline purity of Juliet's passion is flawed by no double self. She is all and entire in each act of her soul. While Romeo, on the contrary, is as yet but half delivered from self-consciousness.

If Shakespeare ventured upon any generalization about women, it was perhaps this—that the natures of women are usually made up of fewer elements than those of men, but that those elements are ordinarily in juster poise, more fully organized, more coherent and compact; and that, consequently, prompt and efficient action is more a woman's gift than a man's. "Man delights not me, nor woman neither," confessed Hamlet; and the courtiers declare they smiled to think if he delighted not in man, what lenten entertainment *the players* would receive from him. *The players*—for the drama is founded on mere delight in human personality. Man delighted Shakespeare, and woman also; but the chief problems of life seemed to lurk for Shakespeare in the souls and in the lives of men, and therefore he was more profoundly interested in the natures of men than in those of women. His great tragedies are not Cordelia, Desdemona, Ophelia, Volumnia; but Lear, Othello, Hamlet, Coriolanus. Shakespeare's men have a history, moral growth or moral decay; his women act and are acted upon, but seldom grow and are transformed. We get from Shakespeare no histories of a woman's soul like the history of Romola, or of Maggie Tulliver, or of Dorothea Brooke; none—unless, perhaps, that of Cleopatra—at all so carefully studied and curiously detailed as may be found in the novels of Goethe. Shakespeare creates his women by a single strong or exquisite inspiration; but he studies his mean. His witty women are not a complex of all various qualities like Falstaff; his wicked women are simply wicked like Goneril and Regan, not an inscrutable mystery of iniquity like Iago; his women of intellect are bright, are effective with ideas which they use as the means of action or of enjoyment, but among them there is not a female Hamlet.*

Yet the women of Shakespeare have almost always the advantage of his men. Although their natures are made up of fewer elements, yet because those elements are quite vital and coherent, his women are in the highest degree direct in feeling and efficient in action. All the half-organised power of men is not a match for their directness and efficiency. Portia in the *Merchant of Venice* can bring all her wits at a moment's notice into play; every faculty is instinct with a single and indivisible energy; set over against the great masculine force of Shylock she proves more than a match for him. In Helena (*All's Well That Ends Well*) there is perfect rectitude of intellect and will, and a solid unity of character which enables her to shape events as she has decided it is well they should be shaped, and secures her from all distraction and all illusion. She imposes herself as a blessing upon the high-born youth, who, for his part, had been sufficiently blind and dull; at length he perceives that while he stumbled and seemed to go astray, Helena was the providence which forced him to stumble into security, and strength, and the abiding-place of love. Volumnia, by the unfaltering insistence of her single moral motive subdues Coriolanus. Macbeth is brave and cowardly, sceptical and superstitious, loyal and treacherous, ambitious and capable of service, at once restrained and stimulated by his imagination.

* See on this subject Mrs Jameson's *Characteristics of Women*, Introduction; also a remarkable passage in Mr Ruskin's *Sesame and Lilies*, pp. 126-31. Rümelin maintains that in consequence of his position as player, Shakespeare was excluded from the acquaintance of women of fine culture and character, and therefore drew upon his fancy for his female portraits. At the same time Shakespeare shared with Goethe, Petrarch, Raphael, Dante, Rousseau, Jean Paul (a strange assemblage!) a mystical veneration for the feminine element of humanity as the higher and more divine. For a comparison of Shakespeare with Goethe in this respect, see *Rümelin Shakespeare Studien*, pp. 288-92. It is clever and superficial, like much of the "realistic criticism" of Rümelin. Leo's "Shakespeare's Frauen-Ideale" is a somewhat misleading title. In the few pages on Shakespeare's women (pp. 35-44), there is contained little that is new or valuable.

Lady Macbeth is terribly efficient; at one time a will strung tense, at another a conscience strung tense; possessed of only that active kind of imagination which masters practical difficulties. She has violently wrenched her nature; and the wrench is fatal. But Macbeth can live on, sinking farther and farther from reality and strength and joy, dropping away into the shadow, undergoing gradual extinction, decay, and disintegration of his moral being; never a sudden and absolute ruin.

Juliet at once takes the lead. It is she who proposes and urges on the sudden marriage. She is impatient for complete self-surrender, eager that the deed should become perfect and irreversible. When, after the death of Tybalt, Romeo learns from the lips of the Friar that he has been condemned to banishment he is utterly unmanned. He abandons himself to helpless and hopeless despair. He turns the tender emotion upon himself, and extracts all the misery which is contained in that one word "banished." He throws himself upon the ground and grovels pitifully in the abjectness of his dismay. His will is unable to deal with his own emotions so as to subdue or control them. Upon the next day, after her casting away of her own kindred, after her parting with her husband, Juliet comes to the same cell of Friar Laurence, her face pale and traces of tears upon it which she cannot hide. Paris, the lover whom her father and mother have designed for Juliet, is there. She meets him with gay words, gallantly concealing the heart which is eager and trembling, and upheld from desperation only by a high-strung fortitude. Then when the door is shut her heart relieves itself, and she urges the Friar, with passionate energy, to devise forthwith a remedy for the evil that has befallen.

In her home Juliet is now without adviser or sustainer; a girl of fourteen years, she stands the centre of a circle of power which is tyrannous, and pledged to crush her resistance; old Capulet (the Capulets are a fiery self-willed race, unlike the milder Montagues) has vehemently urged upon her the marriage with Count Paris. She turns her pale face upon her father, and addresses him appealingly:*

* Shakespeare, as Mr Clark notices, contrives to bring before us the paleness

Good father, I beseech you on my knees
Hear me with patience but to speak a word.

She turns to her mother,—the proud Italian matron, still young, who had not married for love, whose hatred is cold and deadly, and whose relation with the child, who is dear to her, is pathetically imperfect:*

Is there no pity sitting in the clouds,
That sees into the bottom of my grief?
O sweet my mother, cast me not away!
Delay this marriage for a month, a week.

Last she looks for support to her Nurse, turning in that dreadful moment with the instinct of childhood to the woman on whose breast she had lain, and uttering words of desperate and simple earnestness:

O God! O nurse! how shall this be prevented?
. . . .
Some comfort, nurse.

The same unfaltering severity with which a surgeon operates is shown by Shakespeare in his fidelity here to the nurse's character. The gross and wanton heart, while the sun of prosperity is full, blossoms into broad vulgarity; and the raillery of Mercutio deals with it sufficiently. Now in the hour of trial her grossness rises to the dignity of a crime. "The Count is a

---

of Juliet's face in this great crisis of her life, dramatically, by means of old Capulet's vituperative terms:

Out you green-sickness carrion! out you baggage!
You tallow face!

* Shakespeare reduces Juliet's age from the sixteen years of Brooke's poem to fourteen. He loved the years of budding womanhood—Miranda is fifteen years of age, Marina fourteen. Lady Capulet says to Juliet:

By my count
I was your mother much upon these years
That you are now a maid. Act i, Scene 3.

Therefore she is perhaps under thirty years of age. But it is thirty years since old Capulet last went masking (Act i, Scene 5). Observe Lady Capulet's manner of speech with her husband in Act iv, Scene 4, and note her announcement (intended to gratify Juliet) that she will despatch a messenger to Mantua to poison Rameo. Act iii, Scene 5.

lovely gentleman; Romeo's a dishclout to him; the second match excels the first; or if it does not, Juliet's first is dead, or as good as dead, being away from her." "This moment," Mrs Jameson has finely said, "reveals Juliet to herself. She does not break into upbraidings; it is no moment for anger; it is incredulous amazement, succeeded by the extremity of scorn and abhorrence, which takes possession of her mind. She assumes at once and asserts all her own superiority, and rises to majesty in the strength of her despair." Here Juliet enters into her solitude.*

The Friar has given Juliet a phial containing a strange, untried mixture, and she is alone in her chamber. Juliet's soliloquy ends with one of those triumphant touches by which Shakespeare glorified that which he appropriated from his originals. In Brooke's poem, Juliet swallows the sleeping-potion hastily lest her courage should fail. "Shakespeare," Coleridge wrote, "provides for the finest decencies. It would have been too bold a thing for a girl of fifteen;—but she swallows the draught in a fit of fright." This deprives Juliet of all that is most characteristic in the act. In the night and the solitude, with a desperate deed to do, her imagination is intensely and morbidly excited. All the hideous secrets of the tomb appear before her. Suddenly in her disordered vision the figure of the murdered Tybalt rises, and is manifestly in pursuit of some one. Of whom? Not of Juliet, but of her lover who had slain him. A moment before Juliet had shrunk with horror from the thought of confronting Tybalt in the vault of the Capulets. But now Romeo is in danger. All fear deserts her. To stand by Romeo's side is her one necessity. With a confused sense that this draught will somehow place her close to the murderous Tybalt,

* "The nurse has a certain vulgarised air of rank and refinement, as if, priding herself on the confidence of her superiors, she had caught and assimilated their manners to her own vulgar nature. In this mixture of refinement and vulgarity both elements are made the worse for being together [...]. She abounds, however, in serviceable qualities." Hudson, *Shakespeare's Life, Art and Characters*, vol. ii, pp. 214-15. Mrs Jameson observes justly that the sweetness and dignity of Juliet's character could hardly have been preserved inviolate if Shakespeare had placed her in connection with any common-place dramatic waiting-woman.

and close to Romeo whom she would save, calling aloud to Tybalt to delay one moment,—"Stay, Tybalt, stay!"—she drains the phial, not "in a fit of fright," but with the words "Romeo! I come; this do I drink to thee."

The brooding nature of Romeo, which cherishes emotion, and lives in it, is made salient by contrast with Mercutio, who is all wit, and intellect, and vivacity, an uncontrollable play of gleaming and glancing life. Upon the morning after the betrothal with Juliet, a meeting happens between Romeo and Mercutio. Previously, while lover of Rosaline, Romeo had cultivated a lover-like melancholy. But now, partly because his blood runs gladly, partly because the union of soul with Juliet has made the whole world more real and substantial, and things have grown too solid and lasting to be disturbed by a laugh, Romeo can contend in jest with Mercutio himself, and stretch his wit of cheveril "from an inch narrow to an ell broad." Mercutio and the nurse are Shakespeare's creations in this play. For the character of the former he had but a slight hint in the poem of Arthur Brooke. There we read of Mercutio as a courtier who was bold among the bashful maidens as a lion among lambs, and we are told that he had an "ice-cold hand." Putting together these two suggestions, discovering a significance in them, and animating them with the breath of his own life, Shakespeare created the brilliant figure which lights up the first half of *Romeo and Juliet,* and disappears when the colours become all too grave and sombre.

Romeo has accepted the great bond of love. Mercutio, with his ice-cold hand, the lion among maidens, chooses above all things a defiant liberty, a liberty of speech, gaily at war with the proprieties, an airy freedom of fancy, a careless and masterful courage in dealing with life, as though it were a matter of slight importance. He will not attach himself to either of the houses. He is invited by Capulet to the banquet; but he goes to the banquet in company with Romeo and the Montagues. He can do generous and disinterested things; but he will not submit to the trammels of being recognised as generous. He dies maintaining his freedom, and defying death with a jest. To be made worm's meat of so stupidly, by a villain that fights by the book of arithmetic, and through Romeo's awkwardness, is enough to make a man impatient. "A plague o' both your houses!" The death of Mercutio is like the removal of a shifting breadth of sunlight, which sparkles on the sea; now the clouds close in upon one another, and the stress of the gale begins.*

The moment that Romeo receives the false tidings of Juliet's death, is the moment of his assuming full manhood. Now, for the first time, he is completely delivered from the life of dream, completely adult, and able to act with an initiative in his own will, and with manly determination. Accordingly, he now speaks with masculine directness, and energy:

Is it even so? Then I defy you, stars!

Yes; he is now master of events; the stars cannot alter his course:

Thou know'st my lodgings: get me ink and paper,
And hire post-horses; I will hence to-night.
Bal. I do beseech you, sir, have patience.
Your looks are pale and wild, and do import
Some misadventure.
Rom. Tush! thou art deceiv'd
Leave me, and do the thing I bid thee do.
Hast thou no letters to me from the Friar?
Bal. No, my good lord.
Rom. No matter; get thee gone,
And hire those horses; I'll be with thee straight.

"Nothing," as Maginn has observed, "can be more quiet than his final determination:

Well, Juliet, I will lie with thee to-night.

It is plain Juliet [...]. There is nothing about 'Cupid's arrow,' or 'Dian's wit;' no honeyed word escapes his lips, nor again does any accent of despair. His mind is so made up; the whole course of the short remainder of his life so unalterably fixed

* The German Professor sometimes does not quite keep pace with Shakespeare, and is heard stumbling heavily behind him. Gervinus thus describes Mercutio: "A man without culture, coarse and rude, ugly, a scornful ridiculer of all sensibility and love."

that it is perfectly useless to think more about it."* These words because they are the simplest are amongst the most memorable that Romeo utters. Is this indeed the same Romeo who sighed, and wept, and spoke sonnet-wise, and penned himself in his chamber, shutting the daylight out for love of Rosaline? Now passion, imagination, and will, are fused together, and Romeo who was weak has at length become strong.

In two noteworthy particulars Shakespeare has varied from his original. He has compressed the action from some months into four or five days.† Thus precipitancy is added to the course

---

* Shakespeare Papers, p. 99.

† The following passage quoted by H.H. Furness (*Variorum Romeo and Juliet*, pp. 226-27), from Mr Clarke may be serviceable as giving some of the notes of time which occur in this play, "In Scene 1, the Prince desires Capulet to go with him at once, and Montague to come to him, 'this afternoon.' In Scene 2, Capulet speaks of Montague being 'bound' as well as himself, which indicates that the Prince's charge has just been given to both of them, and shortly after speaks of the festival at his house 'this night.' At this festival Romeo sees Juliet when she speaks of sending to him 'to-morrow,' and on that 'morrow' the lovers are united by Friar Laurence. Act iii opens with the scene where Tybalt kills Mercutio, and during which scene Romeo's words, 'Tybalt, that *an hour* hath been my kinsman' show that the then time is the afternoon of the same day. The Friar, at the close of Scene 3 of that Act bids Romeo good night;" and in the next scene, Paris, in reply to Capulet's inquiry, 'What day is this?' replies, *'Monday*, my lord.' This, by the way, denotes that the 'old accustomed feast' of the Capulets, according to a usual practice in Catholic countries, was celebrated on a Sunday evening. In Scene 5 of Act iii comes the parting of the lovers at the dawn of Tuesday, and when at the close of the scene, Juliet says she shall repair to Friar Laurence's cell. *Act* iv commences with her appearance there, thus carrying on the action during the same day, Tuesday. But the effect of long time is introduced by the mention of *'evening mass,'* and by the Friar's detailed directions and reference to 'to-morrow's night;' so that when the mind has been prepared by the change of scene, by Capulet's anxious preparations for the wedding, and by Juliet's return to filial submission, there seems no violence done to the imagination by Lady Capulet's remarking, ''Tis now near night' [...]. Juliet retires to her own room with the intention of selecting wedding attire for the next morning, which her father has said shall be that of the marriage, anticipating it by a whole day— Wednesday instead of Thursday." The sleeping-potion is expected by the Friar to operate during two and forty hours, Act iv, Scene 1. Juliet drinks it upon Tuesday night, or rather in the night hours of Wednesday morning—delaying as long as she dare. On the night of Thursday she

of events and passions. Shakespeare has also made the catastrophe more calamitous than it is in Brooke's poem. It was his invention to bring Paris across Romeo in the church-yard. Paris comes to strew his flowers, uttering in a rhymed sextain, (such as might have fallen from Romeo's lips in the first Act) his pretty lamentation. Romeo goes resolutely forward to death. He is no longer "young Romeo," but adult, and Paris is the boy. He speaks with the gentleness, and with the authority of one who knows what life and death are of one who has gained the superior position of those who are about to die over those who still may live:

> Good, gentle youth, tempt not a desperate man.
> Fly hence and leave me; think upon these gone;
> Let them affright thee. I beseech thee, youth,
> Put not another sin upon my head,
> By urging me to fury.

He would save Paris if that might be. But Paris still crosses Romeo, and he must needs be dealt with:

> Wilt thou provoke me? then have at thee, boy!

Romeo has now a definite object; he has a deed to do, and he will not brook obstacles.*

Friar Laurence remains to furnish the Prince with an explanation of the events. It is impossible to agree with those critics, among others Gervinus, who represent the Friar as a kind of chorus expressing Shakespeare's own ethical ideas, and his opinions respecting the characters and action. It is not Shakespeare's practice to expound the moralities of his artistic creations; nor does he ever by means of a chorus stand above and outside the men and women of his plays, who are bone of his bone and flesh of his flesh. The nearest approach perhaps to

---

awakens in the tomb and dies. Maginn believed that there must be some mistake in the reading "two and forty hours;" but there is no need to suppose this. The play, as Maginn observes, is dated by Shakespeare throughout with a most exact attention to hours.

* In the first quarto Benvolio dies. Montague, Act v Scene 3, announces the death of his wife,—the quarto adds the line, "And young Benvolio is deceased too."

a chorus, is to be found in the person of Enobarbus in Antony and Cleopatra. Hamlet commissions Horatio to report him and his cause aright to the unsatisfied; and Horatio placing the bodies of the dead upon a stage is about, in judicial manner, to declare the causes of things; but Shakespeare declines to put on record for us the explanations made by Horatio. No! Friar Laurence also is moving in the cloud, and misled by error as well as the rest. Shakespeare has never made the moderate, self-possessed, sedate person, a final or absolute judge of the impulsive and the passionate; the one sees a side of truth which is unseen by the other; but to neither is the whole truth visible. The Friar had supposed that by virtue of his prudence, his moderation, his sage counsels, his amiable sophistries, he could guide these two young, passionate lives, and do away the old tradition of enmity between the houses. There in the tomb of the Capulets is the return brought in by his investment of kindly scheming. Shakespeare did not believe that the highest wisdom of human life was acquirable by mild, monastic meditation, and by gathering of simples in the coolness of the dawn. Friar Laurence too, old man, had his lesson to learn.

In accordance with his view that the Friar represents the chorus in this tragedy, Gervinus discovers as the leading idea of the piece a lesson of moderation; the poet makes his confession that "excess in any enjoyment, however pure in itself, transforms its sweet into bitterness, that devotion to any single feeling, however noble, bespeaks its ascendancy; that this ascendancy moves the man and woman out of their natural spheres."* It is somewhat hard upon Shakespeare to suppose that he secreted in each of his dramas a central idea for a German critic to discover. But if there be a central idea in *Romeo and Juliet* can this be it? What! did Shakespeare then mean that Romeo and Juliet loved too well? That all would have been better if they had surrendered their lives each to the other less rapturously, less absolutely? At what precise point ought a discreet regard for another human soul to check itself and say, "Thus far towards

* *Shakespeare Commentaries*, by Gervinus, translated by F.E. Bunnett. 1863, Vol. i, p. 293.

complete union will I advance, but here it is prudent to stop?" Or are not Romeo's words at least as true as the Friar's?

> Come what sorrow can,
> It cannot countervail the exchange of joy
> That one short minute gives me in her sight.
> Do thou but close our hands with holy words,
> Then love-devouring Death do what he dare,
> It is enough I may but call her mine.

Doubtless, also, Cordelia misunderstood the true nature of the filial relation; upon perceiving a possibility of defeat, she ought to have retreated to the safe coast of France. Portia upon hearing that the enemies of Brutus were making head, weakly "fell distract," and swallowed fire, not having learned that a well-balanced heart bestows upon a husband only a regulated moderation of love; Shakespeare, by the example of Portia, would teach us that a penalty is paid for excess of wifely loyalty! No; this method of judging characters and actions by gross awards of pleasure and pain as measured by the senses does not interpret the ethics or the art of Shakespeare, or of any great poet. Shakespeare was aware that every strong emotion which exalts and quickens the inner life of man at the same time exposes the outer life of accident and circumstance to increased risk. But the theme of tragedy, as conceived by the poet, is not material prosperity or failure; it is spiritual; fulfilment or failure of a destiny higher than that which is related to the art of getting on in life. To die under certain conditions may be a higher rapture than to live.

Shakespeare did not intend that the feeling evoked by the last scene of this tragedy of *Romeo and Juliet* should be one of hopeless sorrow or despair in presence of failure, ruin, and miserable collapse.* Juliet and Romeo, to whom Verona has

---

* Kreyssig writes with reference to this tragedy: "Nicht zufällig ist die ideale, leidenschaftliche Jugendliebe in Sage und Gedicht aller Völker die Schwester des Leides. Sie hat ihren Lohn in sich selbst. Das Leben hat ihr Nichts weiter zu bieten."—Shakespeare Fragen, p. 120. In the *Shakespeare Jahrbuch*, vol. ix, p. 328, will be found a notice of a study of Romeo and Juliet (Leipzic, 1874) by the celebrated author of the "Philosophie des Unbewussten," E. von Hartmann. He pronounces that the love between

been a harsh step mother, have accomplished their lives. They loved perfectly. Romeo had attained to manhood. Juliet had suddenly blossomed into heroic womanhood. Through her, and through anguish and joy, her lover had emerged from the life of dream into the waking life of truth. Juliet had saved his soul; she had rescued him from abandonment to spurious feeling, from abandonment to morbid self-consciousness, and the enervating luxury of emotion for emotion's sake. What more was needed? And as secondary to all this, the enmity of the houses is appeased? Montague will raise in pure gold the statue of true and faithful Juliet; Capulet will place Romeo by her side. Their lives are accomplished; they go to take up their place in the large history of the world, which contains many such things. Shakespeare in this last scene carries forward our imagination from the horror of the tomb to the better life of man, when such love as that of Juliet and Romeo will be publicly honoured, and remembered by a memorial all gold.*

Juliet and Romeo is not the deep, spiritual, German ideal of love, but a sensuous play of passionate fancy. (Did not this latest leader of German thought previously teach that love at its best and truest is an illusion imposed upon the individual by the Unconscious Somewhat which displays itself through nature and man, an illusion which serves the important purpose of securing the continuance of the species?) To such criticism the true answer was given long since by Franz Horn,—"Shakespeare knows nothing, and chooses to know nothing, of that false division of love into spiritual and sensual; or rather, he knows of it only when he purposely takes notice of it, that is, when he wishes to depict affectation striving after a misconceived platonism; or on the other hand, when he portrays a coarse, brutish, merely earthly passion." (Translated in Furness's *Romeo and Juliet*, p. 446.) Contrast Juliet with Cressida; or Goethe's Mignon with his Philina. See *Shakespeare Jahrbuch*, vol. vii, p. 16; and Mrs Jameson's *Characteristics of Woman*, especially the passage in which she comments upon Juliet's soliloquy, "Gallop apace."

* Among the critics of this play, one of the most intelligently appreciative is George Fletcher in his Studies of Shakespeare, 1847. Fletcher's interpretation of Juliet's soliloquy before she drinks the sleeping-potion differs from that given above; and I will not assert that Fletcher may not be right, pp. 349-55. It may be worth-while to add a note on the chief critical crux of the play, "Runnawayes Eyes," Act iii, Scene 2, l. 6. The notes on this passage in Mr Furness's edition of the play fill nearly thirty closely printed pages. "Die Zeit ist unendlich lang," said Goethe. I add my stone to this cairn, under which the meaning lies buried. In *The*

II

When *Hamlet* was written Shakespeare had passed through his years of apprenticeship, and become a master-dramatist. In point of style the play stands midway between his early and his latest works. The studious superintendence of the poet over the development of his thought and imaginings, very apparent in Shakespeare's early writings, now conceals itself; but the action of imagination and thought has not yet become embarrassing in its swiftness and multiplicity of direction.* Rapid dialogue in verse, admirable for its combination of verisimilitude with artistic metrical effects occurs in the scene in which Hamlet questions his friends respecting the appearance of the ghost (Act i, Scene 2); the soliloquies of Hamlet are excellent examples of the slow, dwelling verse which Shakespeare appropriates to the utterance of thought in solitude; and nowhere did

---

Merchant of Venice, Act ii, Scene 6, there is an echo of the sense and of the language of this passage which confirms the reading *Runnawayes.* Gratiano and Salarino have spoken of the eagerness of lovers out-running time. This set Shakespeare thinking of the passage in *Romeo and Juliet.* Jessica, in her boy's disguise, says—

Love is blind, and lovers cannot see
The pretty follies that themselves commit.
. . . .
Lorenzo.— But come at once;
For the *close night* doth play the *runaway.*

Compare the first ten lines of Juliet's soliloquy; and observe the echo o sense and speech.

* The characteristics of Shakespeare's latest style are described by Mr Spedding in the following masterly piece of criticism: "The opening of [Henry VIII] [...] seemed to have the full stamp of Shakespeare, in his latest manner; the same close-packed expression; the same life, and reality, and freshness; the same rapid and abrupt turnings of thought, so quick that language can hardly follow fast enough; the same impatient activity of intellect and fancy, which having once disclosed an idea, cannot wait to work it orderly out; the same daring confidence in the resources of language, which plunges headlong into a sentence without knowing how it is to come forth; the same careless metre which disdains to produce its harmonious effects by the ordinary devices, yet is evidently subject to a master of harmony; the same entire freedom from book-language and commonplace."—On the several shares of Shakespeare and Fletcher in the play of *Henry VIII*, by James Spedding; reprinted in Transactions of the New Shakespeare Society from *The Gentleman's Magazine* for August 1850.

Shakespeare write a nobler piece of prose than the speech in which Hamlet describes to Rosencrantz and Guildenstern his melancholy. But such particulars as these do not constitute the chief evidence which proves that the poet had now attained maturity. The mystery, the baffling, vital obscurity of the play, and in particular of the character of its chief person, make it evident that Shakespeare had left far behind him that early stage of development when an artist obtrudes his intentions, or distrusting his own ability to keep sight of one uniform design, deliberately and with effort holds that design persistently before him. When Shakespeare completed *Hamlet* he must have trusted himself and trusted his audience; he trusts himself to enter into relation with his subject, highly complex as that subject was, in a pure, emotional manner. *Hamlet* might so easily have been manufactured into an enigma, or a puzzle; and then the puzzle, if sufficient pains were bestowed, could be completely taken to pieces and explained. But Shakespeare created it a mystery, and therefore it is for ever suggestive; for ever suggestive, and never wholly explicable.

It must not be supposed, then, that any *idea,* any magic phrase will solve the difficulties presented by the play, or suddenly illuminate everything in it which is obscure. The obscurity itself is a vital part of the work of art which deals not with a problem, but with a life; and in that life, the history of a soul which moved through shadowy borderlands between the night and day, there is much (as in many a life that is real) to elude and baffle enquiry. It is a remarkable circumstance that while the length of the play in the second quarto considerably exceeds its length in the earlier form of 1603, and thus materials for the interpretation of Shakespeare's purpose in the play are offered in greater abundance, the obscurity does not diminish, but, on the contrary, deepens, and if some questions appear to be solved, other questions in greater number spring into existence.

We may at once set aside as misdirected a certain class of *Hamlet* interpretations, those which would transform this tragedy of an individual life into a dramatic study of some general social phenomenon, or of some period in the history of civilization. A writer, who has applied an admirable genius for criticism, comprehensive and penetrative, to the study of this play,* describes it as Shakespeare's artistic presentation of a phenomenon recurrent in the world with the regularity of a law of nature, the phenomenon of revolutions. Hamlet cannot escape from the world which surrounds him. In the wreck of a society, which is rotten to the core, he goes down; with the accession of Fortinbras a new and sounder era opens. We must not allow any theory, however ingenious, to divert our attention from fixing itself on this fact, that Hamlet is the central point of the play of *Hamlet*. It is not the general cataclysm in which a decayed order of things is swept away to give place to new rough material; it is not the downfall of the Danish monarchy, and of a corrupt society, together with the accession of a new dynasty and of a hardier civilization that chiefly interested Shakespeare. The vital heart of the tragedy of Hamlet cannot be an idea; neither can it be a fragment of political philosophy. Out of Shakespeare's profound sympathy with an individual soul and a personal life, the wonderful creation came into being.

It is true, however, as the critic referred to maintains, that the weakness of Hamlet is not to be wholly set down to his own account. The world is against him. There is no such thing as naked manhood. Shakespeare, who felt so truly the significance of external nature as the environing medium of human passion, understood also that no man is independent of the social and moral conditions under which he lives and acts. Goethe in the celebrated criticism upon this play contained in his *Wilhelm Meister* has only offered a half interpretation of its difficulties; and subsequent criticism, under the influence of Goethe, has exhibited a tendency too exclusively subjective. "To me," wrote Goethe, "it is clear that Shakespeare meant [...] to represent the effects of a great action laid upon a soul unfit for the performance of it. In this view the whole piece seems to be composed. There is an oak tree planted in a costly jar, which should have borne pleasant flowers in its bosom: the roots expand, the jar is shivered."

* H.A. Werner. Ueber das Dunkel in der Hamlet-Tragödie. Jahrbuch der Deutschen Shakespeare-Gesellschaft, vol. v, pp. 37-81.

This is one half of the truth; but only one half. In several of the tragedies of Shakespeare the tragic disturbance of character and life is caused by the subjection of the chief person of the drama to some dominant passion, essentially antipathetic to his nature, though proceeding from some inherent weakness or imperfection,—a passion from which the victim cannot deliver himself, and which finally works out his destruction. Thus Othello, whose nature is instinctively trustful and confiding, with a noble child-like trust, a man:

> Of a free and open nature
> That thinks men honest that but seem to be so,

a man "not easily jealous," Othello is inoculated with the poison of jealousy and suspicion, and the poison maddens and destroys him. Macbeth, made for subordination, is the victim of a terrible and unnatural ambition. Lear, ignorant of true love, yet with a supreme need of loving and of being loved, is compelled to hatred, and drives from his presence the one being who could have satisfied the hunger of his heart. Timon, who would fain indulge an universal, lax benevolence is transformed to a revolter from humanity; "I am Misanthropos and hate mankind." We may reasonably conjecture that the Hamlet of the old play,—a play at least as old as that group of bloody tragedies inspired by the earlier works of Marlowe,—was actually what Shakespeare's Hamlet, with a bitter pleasure in misrepresenting his own nature, describes himself as being, "very proud, revengeful, ambitious." This revengeful Hamlet of the old play exhibited, we may suppose, a close kinship to the Hamlet of the French novelist, Belleforest, and of the English "Historie,"—the Hamlet who in the banquet-hall burns to death his uncle's courtiers, whom he had previously stupefied with strong drink. But Shakespeare, in accordance with his dramatic method, and his interest as artist in complex rather than simple phenomena of human passion and experience, when re-creating the character of the Danish Prince, fashions him as a man to whom persistent action, and in an especial degree the duty of deliberate revenge is peculiarly antipathetic. Under the pitiless burden imposed upon him Hamlet trembles, totters, falls. Thus far Goethe is right.

But the tragic *nodus* in Shakespeare's first tragedy—*Romeo and Juliet*—was not wholly of a subjective character. The two lovers are in harmony with one another, and with the purest and highest impulses of their own hearts. The discord comes from the outer world: they are a pair of "star-crossed lovers." Their love is enveloped in the hatred of the houses. Their life had grown upon a larger life, a tradition and inheritance of hostility and crime; against this they rebelled, and the larger life subdued them. The world fought against Romeo and Juliet, and they fell in the unequal strife. Now Goethe failed to observe, or did not observe sufficiently, that this is also the case with Hamlet:

> The time is out of joint: O cursed spite,
> That ever I was born to set it right.

Hamlet is called upon to assert moral order in a world of moral confusion and obscurity. He has not an open plain or a hillside on which to fight his battle; but a place dangerous and misleading, with dim and winding ways. He is made for honesty, and he is compelled to use the weapons of his adversaries, compelled to practise a shifting and subtle stratagem; thus he comes to waste himself in ingenuity, and crafty device. All the strength which he possesses would have become organised and available had his world been one of honesty, of happiness, of human love. But a world of deceit, of espionage, of selfishness surrounds him; his idealism, at thirty years of age, almost takes the form of pessimism; his life and his heart become sterile; he loses the energy which sound and joyous feeling supplies; and in the widespreading waste of corruption which lies around him, he is tempted to understand and detest things, rather than accomplish some limited practical service. In the unweeded garden of the world, why should he task his life to uproot a single weed?

If Goethe's study of the play, admirable as it was, misled criticism in one way by directing attention too exclusively upon the inner nature of Hamlet, the studies by Schlegel and by Coleridge tended to mislead criticism in another, by attaching an exaggerated importance to one element of Hamlet's character. "The whole," wrote Schlegel, "is intended to show that a calculating consideration, which exhausts all the relations and possible consequences of a deed, must cripple the power of acting." It is true that Hamlet's power of acting was crippled by his habit of "thinking too precisely on the event;" and it is true, as Coleridge said, that in Hamlet we see "a great, an almost enormous intellectual activity, and a proportionate aversion to real action consequent upon it." But Hamlet is not merely or chiefly intellectual; the emotional side of his character is quite as important as the intellectual; his malady is as deep-seated in his sensibilities and in his heart as it is in the brain. If all his feelings translate themselves into thoughts, it is no less true that all his thoughts are impregnated with feeling. To represent Hamlet as a man of preponderating power of reflection, and to disregard his craving, sensitive heart is to make the whole play incoherent and unintelligible.*

It is Hamlet's intellect, however, together with his deep and abiding sense of the moral qualities of things, which distinguishes him, upon the glance of a moment, from the hero of Shakespeare's first tragedy, Romeo. If Romeo fail to retain a sense of fact and of the real world because the fact, as it were, melts away and disappears in a solvent of delicious emotion, Hamlet equally loses a sense of fact because with him each object and event transforms and expands itself into an idea. When the play opens he has reached the age of thirty years,—the age, it has been said, when the ideality of youth ought to become one with and inform the practical tendencies of manhood,—and he has received culture of every kind except the culture of active life. During the reign of the strong-willed elder Hamlet there was no call to action for his meditative son. He has slipped on into years of full manhood still a haunter of the university, a student of philosophies, an amateur in art, a ponderer on the things of life and death, who has never formed a resolution or executed a deed.

This long course of thinking, apart from action, has destroyed Hamlet's very capacity for belief; since in belief there exists a certain element contributed by the will. Hamlet cannot adjust the infinite part of him to the finite; the one invades the

* See W. Oehlmann's article Die Gemüthsseite des Hamlet—Characters in *Jahrbuch der Deutschen Shakespeare-Gesellschaft*, vol. iii, p. 208.

other and infects it; or rather the finite dislimns and dissolves, and leaves him only in presence of the idea. He cannot make real to himself the actual world, even while he supposes himself a materialist; he cannot steadily keep alive within himself a sense of the importance of any positive, limited thing,—a deed for example. Things in their actual, phenomenal aspect flit before him as transitory, accidental and unreal. And the absolute truth of things is so hard to attain and only, if at all, is to be attained in the *mind.* Accordingly Hamlet can lay hold of nothing with calm, resolved energy; he cannot even retain a thought in indefeasible possession. Thus all through the play he wavers between materialism and spiritualism, between belief in immortality and disbelief, between reliance upon providence and a bowing under fate.* In presence of the ghost a sense of his own spiritual existence, and the immortal life of the soul grows strong within him. In presence of spirit he is himself a spirit:

> I do not set my life at a pin's fee;
> And for my soul, what can it do to that,
> Being a thing immortal as itself?

When left to his private thoughts he wavers uncertainly to and fro; death is a sleep, a sleep, it may be, troubled with dreams. In the graveyard, in the presence of human dust, the base affinities of our bodily nature prove irresistibly attractive to the curiosity of Hamlet's imagination; and he cannot choose but pursue the history of human dust through all its series of hideous metamorphoses. Thus, as Romeo's emotions, while he lived in abandonment to the life of feeling for feeling's sake, are not genuine emotions, so Hamlet's thoughts, while he is given over to the life of brooding meditation, are hardly even so much as real thoughts; but are rather phantom ideas which dissolve, reform, and dissolve again, changing forever with every wind of circumstance. He is incapable of certitude.

---

* In *Shakespeare-Forschungen I Hamlet,* by Benno Tschischwitz (Halle, 1868), the author endeavours to prove that Shakespeare was acquainted with the philosophy of Bruno, and embodied portions of it in the play of *Hamlet.* Giordano Bruno lived in London from the year 1583 to 1586, where he seems to have received the patronage of Sir P. Sidney, Lord Buckhurst, and the Earl of Leicester. He became professor at Wittenberg.

When Hamlet first stands before us, his father has been two months dead; his mother has been for a month the wife of Claudius. He is solitary in the midst of the court. A mass of sorrow, and of wounded feeling, of shame and of disgust has been thrown back upon him; and this secretion of feeling which obtains no vent is busy in producing a widespreading, morbid humour. The misery of self-suppression leaves him in a state of weak and intense irritability. Every word uttered pricks him, and he is longing to be alone. A little bitterness escapes in his brief acrid answers to the king, and when his mother, in her insensibility to true feeling, chances upon the word "seems" his irritation breaks forth, and after his fashion (that of one who relieves himself by speech rather than by deeds) he unpacks his heart in words. The queen who is soft and sensual, a lover of ease, withal a little sentimental, and therefore incapable of genuine passion, does not resent the outbreak of her strange son; and Hamlet, somewhat ashamed of his demonstration, which has the look of a display of superior feeling, endures in silence his uncle's tedious moralizing on the duties of mourners. Then with grave courtesy he yields to his mother's request that he should renounce his intention of returning to Wittenberg:

> I shall in all my best obey you, madam.

What matters it whether he go or stay! Life is all so flat, stale, and unprofitable, that the difference between Wittenberg and Elsinore cannot be worth contending for.* But when at length he is alone, Hamlet feels himself enfranchised,—free to shed abroad his sorrow, to gaze intensely and mournfully upon his own aridity of spirit, and to compensate in the idea, for the expenditure of kindness in act made on his mother's behalf. A frail mother, an incestuous mother, a mother endowed with less discourse of reason than the beasts! He has satisfied the queen with an act; and action, this way or that, is profoundly insignificant to Hamlet. But in his mind she shall get no

---

* Observe the contrast between Hamlet and Laertes. The latter wrings by laboursome petition leave from his father to return to Paris. Laertes had come from Paris to the coronation; Horatio, from Wittenberg to the late king's funeral.

advantage of him. He will see her as she is, and if he is gracious to her in his deeds, he will, in his thoughts, be stern and inexorable.

In this scene we make acquaintance with two important persons in Hamlet's world. "Something is rotten in the state of Denmark," exclaimed Marcellus. Rather all is rotten—the whole head is sick and the whole heart faint. On the throne, the heart of the living organism of a state, reigns the appearance of a king; but under this kingly appearance is hidden a wretched, corrupt, and cowardly soul, a poisoner of the true king and of true kingship, incestuous, gross and wanton, a fierce drinker, a palterer with his conscience, and as Hamlet vehemently urging the fact describes him "a vice of kings," "a villain and a cut-purse," "a paddock, a bat, a gib." Such is kingship in Denmark.

And the queen, Hamlet's mother, one of the two women from whom Hamlet must infer what womanhood is, what is she? For thirty years she had given the appearance, the *simulacrum* of true love to her husband, one on whom:

> Every god did seem to set his seal
> To give the world assurance of a man,

one who even in the place of penance still retains his solicitude for her; and this show of thirty years' love had proved to be without reality or root in her being; it had been no more than a sinking down upon the accidental things of life, its comforts and pleasures; her husband had passed out of her existence like any other casual object; during all those years of blameless wifehood she had never once conceived the possibility of a love which is founded upon the essential, not the accidental elements of life; she had never once known what is the bond of life to life, and of soul to soul. The timid, self-indulgent, sensuous, sentimental queen is as remote from true woman's virtue as Claudius is from the virtues of royal manhood.

The third scene of the first act introduces another group of personages, distinguished figures of the Danish Court. Laertes is the cultured young gentleman of the period.* He is

* Gervinus has described Hamlet as a man of a civilized period standing in the centre of a heroic age of rough manners and physical daring.—

accomplished, chivalric, gallant; but the accomplishments are superficial, the chivalry theatrical, the gallantry of a showy kind. He is master of events up to a certain point, because he sees their coarse, gaudy, superficial significance. It is his part to do fine things and make fine speeches; to enter the king's presence gallantly demanding atonement for his father's murder; to leap into his sister's grave and utter a theatrical rant of sorrow. Hamlet sees in his own cause an image of that of Laertes. Each has lost a father by foul means, and Laertes delays not to seek revenge. But Shakespeare does not make the contrast between Hamlet and Laertes favourable to the latter. No overweight of thought, no susceptibility of conscience retard the action of the young gallant. He readily falls in with the king's scheme of assassination, and adds his private contribution of villainy—the venom on his rapier's point. Laertes has been no student of philosophic Wittenberg.* The French capital, "so dear to the average, sensual man," is Laertes' school of education. What lessons he learnt there we may conjecture from the conversation of Polonius with his servant Reynaldo.

Laertes' little sister, Ophelia, is loved by the Lord Hamlet What is Ophelia? Can she contribute to the deliverance of Hamlet from his sad life of brooding thought, from his weakness and his melancholy? Juliet had delivered Romeo from his dream of self-conscious egoistic feeling into the reality of anguish and of joy. What can Ophelia do? Nothing. She is a tender little fragile soul, who might have grown to her slight perfection in some neat garden-plat of life. Hamlet falls into the too frequent error of supposing that a man gains rest and composure through the presence of a nature weak, gentle, and clinging; and that the very incapacity of such a nature to share the troubles of heart and brain which beset one must be a source of refreshment

---

Shakespeare Commentaries, vol. ii, p. 161. No piece of criticism could fall more wide of the mark. The age of Claudius, Polonius, Laertes, Osric, and of the students of philosophy at Wittenberg is an age complex and refined, and in all things the reverse of heroic. See Kreyssig, *Vorlesungen über Shakespeare*, vol. ii, p. 222. (ed. 1862.)

* Shakespeare remembered Luther, thinks Gervinus. He had Giordano Bruno in his mind, says Tschischwitz. The University was famous: Giordano Bruno names it the Athens of Germany.

and repose. And so it is, for moments, when the pathos of slender joy, unaware of the great interests and sorrows of the world, touches us. But a strong nature was what Hamlet really needed. All the comfort he ever got in life came from one who was "more an antique Roman than a Dane," his friend Horatio. If he had found one who to Horatio's fortitude, his passive strength, had added ardour and enthusiasm, Hamlet's melancholy must have vanished away; he would have been lifted up into the light and strength of the good facts of the world, and then he could not have faltered upon his way.

As things were Hamlet quickly learned, and the knowledge embittered him, that Ophelia could neither receive great gifts of soul, nor in return render equivalent gifts. There is an exchange of little tokens between the lovers, but of the large exchange of soul there is none, and Hamlet in his bitter mood can truthfully exclaim, "I never gave you aught." Hamlet was conscious of no constraining power to prevent him, when he thought of his mother's frailty, from extending his words to her whole sex, "Frailty, thy name is woman." Had a noble nature stood in Ophelia's place to utter such words would have been treason against his inmost consciousness. Let the reader contrast Juliet's commanding energy of feeling, of imagination, of will with Ophelia's timidity and self-distrust, the incapable sweetness and gentleness of her heart, her docility to all lawful guardians and governors. Juliet throws off father, mother, and nurse, and stands in solitary strength of love, she always uses the directest word, always counsels the bravest action. In his later plays Shakespeare can still be seen to rejoice and expand in presence of the courage of true love. Desdemona:

> A maiden never bold;
> Of spirit so still and quiet that her motion
> Blush'd at herself,

standing by Othello's side can confront her indignant father, with the Duke and magnificoes. Imogen, for Posthumus' sake, can shoot against the king her shafts of indignant scorn, so keen and exquisite, yet heavily timbered enough to wing forward through the wind of Cymbeline's anger. But Ophelia is decorous and timid, with no initiative in her own heart; unimaginative; choosing her phrases with a sense of maidenly propriety:

> He hath, my lord, of late made many tenders
> Of his affection to me.

And Polonius inquires, "Do you believe his tenders, as you call them?" "I do not know, my lord, what I should think." It may be that her brother and father are right; that the "holy vows" of Hamlet on which she, poor little soul, had relied, are but "springes to catch woodcocks." In her madness, the impression made upon her by the words of Polonius and Laertes, which she had until then concealed, finds utterance: "She says she hears there's tricks i' the world." Juliet resolved her doubts, not by consulting old Capulet or her nurse, but by pressing forward to perfect knowledge of the heart of Romeo, and by occupying that heart with a purity of passion only less than her own. Ophelia, when her father directs her to distrust the man she loves, to deny him her presence, to repel his letters, has only her meek, little submission to utter, "I shall obey, my lord."

The comic element in this scene is present, but is not obtruded. Shakespeare, "der feine Shakespeare, der Schalk,"* smiles visibly, but restrains himself from downright laughter. Laertes has read his moral lecture to Ophelia, and she in turn ventures upon a gentle, little piece of sisterly advice. Laertes suddenly discovers that he ought to be aboard his ship: "I stay too long." Ophelia "is giving the conversation a needless and inconvenient turn; [...] for sisters to lecture brothers is an inversion of the natural order of things."† But at this moment the venerable chamberlain appears. Laertes, who was supposed to have gone, is caught. There is only one mode of escape from the imminent scolding—to kneel and ask a second blessing. What matter that it has all been said once before? Start the old man on his hobby of uttering wisdom, and off he will go:

> A double blessing is a double grace;
> Occasion smiles upon a second leave.

---

* F. Th. Vischer, in *Jahrbuch der Deutschen Shakespeare-Gesellschaft*, vol. ii, p. 149.

† C.E. Moberly, Rugby edition of *Hamlet*, p. 21.

The advice of Polonius is a cento of quotations from Lyly's "Euphues."* Its significance must be looked for less in the matter than in the sententious manner. Polonius has been wise with the little wisdom of worldly prudence. He has been a master of indirect means of getting at the truth, "windlaces and assays of bias." In the shallow lore of life he has been learned. Of true wisdom he has never had a gleam. And what Shakespeare wishes to signify in this speech is that wisdom of Polonius' kind consists of a set of maxims; all such wisdom might be set down for the headlines of copybooks. That is to say, his wisdom is not the outflow of a rich or deep nature, but the little, accumulated hoard of a long and superficial experience. This is what the sententious manner signifies. And very rightly Shakespeare has put into Polonius' mouth the noble lines:

> To thine own self be true,
> And it must follow as the night the day
> Thou canst not then be false to any man.

Yes; Polonius has got one great truth among his copybook maxims, but it comes in as a little bit of hard, un-vital wisdom like the rest. "*Dress well, don't lend or borrow money; to thine own self be true.*"†

But to appreciate and enjoy fully the Chamberlain's morality, we must observe him in the first scene of the second act. Reynaldo is despatched as a spy upon the conduct of the son on whom the paternal blessing had been so tenderly bestowed.

---

* Mr W.L. Rushton, in his *Shakespeare's Euphuism*, pp. 44-47 (London, 1871), places side by side the precepts of Polonius and of Euphues. "*Pol.* Give thy thoughts no tongue. *Euph.* Be not lavish of thy tongue. *Pol.* Do not dull thy palm, &c. *Euph.* Every one that shaketh thee by the hand is not joined to thee in heart. *Pol.* Beware of entrance to a quarrel, &c. *Euph.* Be not quarrellous for every light occasion. *Pol.* Give every man thine ear, but few thy voice. *Euph.* It shall be there better to hear what they say, than to speak what thou thinkest." Both Polonius and Euphues speak of the advice given as "these few precepts."

† Compare and contrast with the advice of Polonius the parting words of the Countess to Bertram—(*All's Well That Ends Well*, Act i, Scene 1) Observe how the speech of the Countess opens and ends with motherly passion of fear and pride, in which lies enclosed her little effort at moral precept.

Polonius does not expect morality of an ideal kind from the boy. As is natural, Laertes in Paris will sow his wild oats. If he come back the accomplished cavalier, skilful in manage of his horse, a master of fencing, able to finger a lute, Polonius will treasure up in his heart, not discontented, the knowledge of his son's "wild slips and sallies."*

Meanwhile Hamlet, in the midst of his sterile world-weariness, has received a shock, but not the shock of joy. His father's spirit is abroad. With Horatio and Marcellus, Hamlet on the platform at night is awaiting the appearance of the ghost. The sounds of Claudius' revelry reach their ears. Hamlet is started upon a series of reflections suggested by the Danish drinking customs; his surroundings disappear; he has ceased to remember the purpose with which he has come hither; he is lost in his own thoughts. The Ghost is present before Hamlet is aware; it is Horatio who interrupts his meditation, and rouses him to behold the apparition. No sooner has Hamlet heard the word "Murder" upon his father's lips than he is addrest to "sweep to his revenge,"—in the idea:

With wings as swift
As meditation or the thoughts of love.

He will change his entire mental stock and store; he will forget his arts and his philosophies; he will retain no thought save of his murdered father. And when the ghost departs he draws—"not his sword, but his notebook."† There at least he can get it down in black and white that the smiling Claudius is a villain, can put that fact beyond the reach of doubt or vicissitude; for subjective impressions, Hamlet is too well aware, do not retain the certitude which during one vivid moment seemed to

* The last words of Polonius to Reynaldo are—"And let him [Laertes] ply his music." On these words Vischer observes—"Die paar Wörtchen erst enthalten den ganzen Schlüssel; der Sohn darf spielen, trinken, raufen, fluchen, zanken, in saubre Häuser, "*videlicet* Bordelle" gehen, wenn er nur Musik treibt; ächte Cavalierserziehung!" Die realistische Shakespeare-Kritik und Hamlet, von. F. Th. Vischer in *Jahrbuch der deutschen Shakespeare-Gesellschaft*, vol. ii, p. 149.

† W. Oehlmann, *Jahrbuch der Deutschen Shakespeare-Gesellschaft*, vol. iii, p. 211.

characterise them. He will henceforth remember nothing but the ghost, and to assure himself of *that,* he sets down his father's parting words, "Adieu, adieu! remember me." That is to say, "he puts a knot upon his handkerchief."* He is conscious that he is not made for the world of action; that the fact is always in process of gliding away from him and being replaced by an idea. And he is resolved to guard against this in the present instance.

It is now in a sudden inspiration of excited feeling that Hamlet conceives the possibility of his assuming an antic disposition. What is Hamlet's purpose in this? He finds that he is involuntarily conducting himself in a wild and unintelligible fashion. He has escaped "from his own feelings of the overwhelming and supernatural by a wild transition to the Judicrous,—a sort of cunning bravado, bordering on the flights of delirium." His mind struggles "to resume its accustomed course, and effect a dominion over the awful shapes and sounds that have usurped its sovereignty."† He assumes madness as a means of concealing his actual disturbance of mind. His over-excitability may betray him; but if it be a received opinion that his mind is unhinged, such an access of over-excitement will pass unobserved and unstudied. At this moment Hamlet's immediate need is to calm himself, to escape into solitude, there to recover self-mastery, and come to a clear understanding of the altered state of things. In the light of the court he is persecuted by the eyes of the curious and the suspicious; he is "too much i' the sun." To be in presence of all, and yet to be hidden,—to be intelligible to himself, and a perplexity to others,

* Hebler, *Aufsätze über Shakespeare* (Bern, 1865), p. 138.

† The first quotation is from S.T. Coleridge; the second from an essay by Hartley Coleridge, "On the Character of Hamlet." *Essays and Marginalia,* vol. i, pp. 151-71. An earlier writer than S.T. Coleridge had well said, "Hamlet was fully sensible how strange those involuntary improprieties must appear to others: he was conscious he could not suppress them: he knew he was surrounded with spies; and he was justly apprehensive lest his suspicions or purposes should be discovered. But how are these consequences to be prevented? By counterfeiting an insanity which in part exists."—Richardson's *Essays on Shakespeare's Dramatic Characters* (1786), p. 163.

to be within reach of everyone, and to be himself inaccessible, that would be an enviable position! Madness possesses exquisite immunities and privileges. From the safe vantage of unintelligibility he can delight himself by uttering his whole mind and sending forth his words among the words of others, with their meaning disguised, as he himself must be, clothed in an antic garb of parable, dark sayings which speak the truth in a mystery.

Hamlet does not assume madness to conceal any plan of revenge. He possesses no such plan. And as far as his active powers are concerned, the assumed madness is a misfortune. Instead of assisting him to achieve anything, it is one of the causes which tend to retard his action. For now, instead of forcing himself upon the world, and compelling it to accept a mandate of his will, he can enjoy the delight of a mere observer and critic; an observer and critic both of himself and of others. He can understand and mock; whereas he ought to set himself sternly to his piece of work. He utters himself henceforth at large, because he is unintelligible. He does not aim at producing any effect with his speech, except in the instance of his appeal to Gertude's conscience. His words are not deeds. They are uttered self-indulgently to please the intellectual or artistic part of him, or to gratify his passing mood of melancholy, of irritation or of scorn. He bewilders Polonius with mockery, which effects nothing, but which bitterly delights Hamlet by its subtlety and cleverness. He speaks with singular openness to his courtier friends, because they filled with thoughts of worldly advancement and ambition, read all his meanings upside down, and the heart of his mystery is absolutely inaccessible to their shallow wits. When he describes to them his melancholy he is in truth speaking in solitude to himself. Nothing is easier than to throw them off the scent. "A knavish speech sleeps in a foolish ear." The exquisite cleverness of his mimetics and his mockery is some compensation to Hamlet for his inaction; this intellectual versatility, this agility flatters his consciousness; and it is only on occasions that he is compelled to observe into what a swoon or syncope his will has fallen.

Yet it has been truly said that only one who feels Hamlet's

strength should venture to speak of Hamlet's weakness. That in spite of difficulties without, and inward difficulties, he still clings to his terrible duty,—letting it go indeed for a time, but returning to it again, and in the end accomplishing it—implies strength. He is not incapable of vigorous action,—if only he be allowed no chance of thinking the fact away into an idea. He is the first to board the pirate; he stabs Polonius through the arras; he suddenly alters the sealed commission, and sends his schoolfellows to the English headsman; he finally executes justice upon the king. But all his action is sudden and fragmentary; it is not continuous and coherent. His violent excitability exhausts him; after the night of encounter with the ghost a fit of abject despondency, we may be certain, ensued, which had begun to set in when the words were uttered:

> The time is out of joint; O, cursed spite
> That ever I was born to set it right.

After he has slain Polonius, he weeps; after his struggle with Laertes in Ophelia's grave a mood of depression ensues:

> Thus awhile the fit will work on him,
> Anon as patient as the female dove,
> When that her golden couplets art disclosed,
> His silence will sit drooping.

His feelings are not under control. They quickly fatigue themselves, like a dog who now hurries before his master, and now drops behind, but will not advance steadily.*

At the moment when Polonius has dismissed Reynaldo, Ophelia comes running to her father, "Alas, my lord, I have been so affrighted!" Such is the piteously inadequate response of Ophelia to Hamlet's mute confession of his sorrow. His letters have been repelled; her presence has been denied to him. Hamlet resolves that he will see her, and hear her speak. He goes, profoundly agitated, in the disordered attire which is now nothing unusual with him, and which constitutes part of Hamlet's "transformation." He is not in the mood to consider very attentively particulars of the toilet. He discovers Ophelia

* The illustration is Hebler's.

sewing in her closet. He stands unable to speak, holding her hand, gazing in her face, trying to discover if there be in her any virtue or strength, anything which can give a shadow of hope that the widening gulf between them is not quite impassable. He endeavours to make a new study of her soul through her eyes. And in her eyes he reads—*fright.* The most piteous part of the incident is that Ophelia is wholly blameless. She is shocked, bewildered, alarmed, anxious to run away, and get under the protection of her father. No wonder Hamlet cannot utter a word! No wonder that his gesture expresses absolute confirmation of his unhappy fears, utter despair of finding virtue in her! A sigh rises from the depths of his spirit. He feels that all is over. He knows how strange and remote his voice would sound. And as Hamlet can feel nothing without generalising he recognises in this failure of heart to answer heart a type of one great sorrow of the world.

Polonius receives from the docile Ophelia the letters of Hamlet. She does not shrink from betraying the secrets of his weakness and his melancholy confided to her. The oddest of the letters, that which seemed most incoherent, is carried off to be read aloud to the king,—Ophelia consenting. What is the purport of this letter? Was it meant as a kind of test? Did Hamlet wish to ascertain whether Ophelia would be puzzled by the superficial oddity of it, or would penetrate to the grief and the love which lay beneath it? "He that hath ears to hear let him hear"—upon this principle Hamlet constantly act. He is content that the feeble-hearted and dull witted should find him a puzzle and an offence.

The Prince comes by reading. Polonius accosts him, assuming that Hamlet is downright mad. Hamlet's irony here consists in his adoption and exaggeration of the ideas of Polonius. "You have immured your daughter; you have repelled my letters, and denied me sight of her; O wise old man! for woman's virtue is the frailest of things, and there is no male creature who is not a corrupter of virtue. If the most glorious and vivifying thing in the universe, the sun, will breed maggots out of carrion, truly Prince Hamlet may be suspected! Beware of your daughter; Friend look to 't." And then, in more direct fashion, Hamlet breaks forth into a satire on old men with their weak hams and most plentiful lack of wit. Polonius retires bewildered, and two new persecutors appear.

In Goethe's novel, *Wilhelm Meister*, the hero, when adapting the play of Hamlet to the German stage, alters it in certain particulars. Serlo, the manager of the theatre, suggests that Rosencrantz and Guildenstern should be "compressed into one." "Heaven keep me from all such curtailments," exclaims Wilhelm; "they destroy at once the sense and the effect. What these two persons are and do, it is impossible to represent by one. In such small matters, we discover Shakespeare's greatness. These soft approaches, this smirking and bowing, this assenting, wheedling, flattering, this whisking agility, this wagging of the tail, this allness and emptiness, this legal knavery, this ineptitude and insipidity, how can they be expressed by a single man? There ought to be at least a dozen of these people if they could be had; for it is only in society that they are anything; they *are* society itself, and Shakespeare showed no little wisdom and discernment in bringing in a pair of them." What Goethe admirably expresses, Shakespeare "der Schalk," has perhaps hinted in the address of the king and queen to the pair of courtiers:

> *King.* Thanks, Rosencrantz and gentle Guildenstern.
> *Queen.* Thanks, Guildenstern and gentle Rosencrantz.

That is, "six to one, and half a dozen to the other." With no tie of friendship, or capacity for true human comradeship, the companions hunt in a couple; and they go with the same indistinguishable smirking and bowing to their fate in England. There is grim irony in this ending of the courtiers' history. "They were lovely, and pleasant in their lives" after the taste of Claudius' court, "and in their death they were not divided."

In the first scene of the third act Ophelia is stationed as a decoy to expose to her father and the king, the disease of the man she loves. It will assist, she is assured, to bring about Hamlet's restoration; and Ophelia is docile, and does not question her instructors. A book of devotions is placed in her hand.* Hamlet comes by, brooding upon suicide, upon the manifold ills of the world, and his own weakness. He sees Ophelia, so lovely, so child-like, so innocent, praying. She is for a moment something better and more beautiful than woman, something "afar from the sphere of his sorrow;" and he involuntarily exclaims:

> Nymph, in thy orisons
> Be all my sins remembered.

But Ophelia plays her part with a manner that betrays her. Observe the four rhymed lines, ending with the little set sentence (which looks as if prepared beforehand):

> For to the noble mind
> Rich gifts wax poor when givers prove unkind.

And then, upon the spot, the Prince's presents are produced. How could Hamlet, endowed with swift penetration as he is, fail to detect the fraud? He had unmasked Rosencrantz and Guildenstern, and thereby his suspicions had been quickened. And as for a moment he had been touched and exalted by the presence of Ophelia's innocence and piety, he is now proportionately indignant.

One of the deepest characteristics of Hamlet's nature, is a longing for sincerity, for truth in mind and manners, an aversion from all that is false, affected or exaggerated.† Ophelia is joined with the rest of them; she is an impostor, a spy; incapable of truth, of honour, of love. Have they desired to observe an outbreak of his insanity? He will give it to them with a vengeance.

---

* Polonius (giving the book), says:

> Read on this book;
> That show of such an *exercise* may colour
> Your loneliness. We are oft to blame in this,—
> 'Tis too much proved—that with devotion's visage,
> And pious action, we do sugar o'er
> The devil himself.

Hamlet seeing her at prayer exclaims,

> Nymph, in thy *orisons*
> Be all my sins remembered.

† False, as the bearing of Rosencrantz and Guildenstern; affected as the manner of Osric; exaggerated, as Laertes' theatrical rant in Ophelia.

With an almost savage zeal, which is underneath nothing but bitter pain, he pounces upon Ophelia's deceit. "Ha, ha, are you honest?" His cruelty is that of an idealist, who cannot precisely measure the effect of his words upon his hearer, but who requires to liberate his mind. And again Hamlet plays bitterly at approving of the principles and conduct of Polonius in the matter of his relations with Ophelia: "You have been secluded from that dangerous corrupter of youth, Prince Hamlet; you love to devote yourself to prayer and solitude. Most wise and right! I am all that your father has represented me, and worse—very proud, revengeful, ambitious [all that Hamlet was *not*]. And yet there *is* in the world such a thing as calumny; it may happen to touch your self some day. You who are so fair and frail, so pious in appearance, so false in deed, do you look on us *men* as dangerous to virtue? *I* have heard a little of women's doings too; keep your precious virtue, if you can, and let us male monsters be. Get thee to a nunnery!" And to complete the startling effect of this outbreak of insanity, solicited by his persecutors, he sends a shaft after the Chamberlain, and a shaft after the King:

> *Ham.* Where's your father?
> *Oph.* [*Coming out with her docile little lie*] At home, my lord.
> *Ham.* Let the doors be shut upon him, that he may play the fool nowhere but in 's own house.

This for Polonius; and for the King with menacing emphasis the words are uttered, "I say we will have no more marriages: those that are married already, all but one, shall live; the rest shall keep as they are. To a nunnery, go!"

Hamlet bursts out of the lobby with a triumphant and yet bitter sense of having turned the tables upon his tormentors. He has thrown into sudden confusion the ranks of the enemy. Ophelia remains to weep. In the pauses of Hamlet's cruel invective, she had uttered her piteous, little appeals to heaven: "Heavenly powers, restore him!" "O help him, you sweet heavens!" When he abruptly departs, the poor girl's sorrow overflows. In her lament, Hamlet's noble reason, which is overthrown, somehow gets mixed up with the elegance of his costume, which has suffered equal ruin. He who was the "glass of fashion," noticed by every one, "the observed of all observers," is a hopeless lunatic. She has no bitter thought about her lover. She is "of ladies most deject and wretched;" all her emotion is helpless tenderness and sorrow. Her grief is as deep as her soul is deep.

Hamlet now binds himself more closely than ever to Horatio. This friend and fellow-scholar is the one sterling thing in the rotten state of Denmark. There is a touching devotion shown by Hamlet to Horatio in the meeting which follows the scene in the lobby with Ophelia; a devotion which is the overflow of gratitude for the comfort and refuge he finds with his friend after the recent proof of the incapacity and want of integrity in the woman he had loved. Horatio's equanimity, his evenness of temper, is like solid land to Hamlet after the tossings and tumult of his own heart. The Prince apologises with beautiful delicacy for seeming to flatter Horatio. It is not flattery; what can he expect from a man so poor? It is genuine delight in the sanity, the strength, the constancy of Horatio's character. Yet all the while Shakespeare compels us to feel that it is Hamlet with his manifold weakness, and ill-commingled blood and judgment, who is the rarer nature of the two; and that Horatio is made to be his helpmate, recognising in service his highest duty.

There is no Friar Laurence in this play. To him the Catholic children of Verona carried their troubles, and received from their father comfort and counsel. Hamlet is hardly the man to seek for wisdom or for succour from a priest. Let them resolve his doubts about the soul, about immortality, about God first. But Shakespeare has taken care to show us in the effete society of Denmark, where everything needs renewing, what religion is. To Ophelia's funeral the Church reluctantly sends her representative. All that the occasion suggests of harsh, formal, and essentially inhuman dogmatics, is uttered by the Priest. The distracted girl has by untimely accident met her death; and therefore, instead of charitable prayers,

> Shards, flints, and pebbles should be thrown on her.

These are the sacred words of truth, of peace, of consolation which Religion has to whisper to wounded hearts!

We should profane the service of the dead,
To sing a requiem and such rest to her
As to peace-parted souls.

This is the religion which helps to make Claudius a palterer with his conscience, and Hamlet an aimless wanderer after truth. Better consort in Denmark with players than with priests!*

When the play is about to be enacted Hamlet declines a seat near his mother, because he wishes to occupy a position from which he can scrutinize the king's countenance. He is now fully roused, every nerve high-strung. Just at present Ophelia is nothing to him. If he says anything to her it will be for the sake of staying his own heart in its tremulous intensity, and getting through the eager moments of suspense. It will be something issuing from the bitter upper surface of his soul—a bitter jest most likely. Hamlet derives an acrid pleasure from perplexing and embarrassing Polonius, and Rosencrantz, and Guildenstern. Now it pleases him to embarrass Ophelia with half-ambiguous obscenities. These are the electrical sparks which scintillate and snap while the current is streaming to its receptacle. With Ophelia, who cherished the proprieties as though they constituted the moral law, Hamlet finds himself tempted to be intolerably improper. Ophelia understands his words, and ventures to deliver a gentle reprimand. "You are naught, you are naught; I'll mark the play." But Hamlet continues his persecution. All this comes from the superficial part of Hamlet; as one toys with some trifle while a doom is impending. His passion is concentrated in watching the countenance of the king.†

This is the night of Hamlet's triumph. The king's guilt is unkennelled; Hamlet disposes of one after another of his tormentors; he has superabundant energy; he takes each in turn, and is equal to all. And yet Hamlet is for ever walking over the ice; his power of self-control is never quite to be trusted.

* H.A. Werner, *Jahrbuch der Deutschen Shakespeare-Gesellschaft*, vol. v, p. 56.

† On the speech of "some dozen or sixteen lines" which Hamlet inserts in the play, see the discussion by Prof. Seeley, Mr Malleson and others, "New Shak. Soc. Trans. 1874."

The success of his device for ascertaining the guilt of Claudius is followed by the same mood of wild excitement which followed the encounter with his father's spirit; again he seems incoherently, extravagantly gay; again his words are "wild and whirling words."* And as on that occasion Hamlet had felt the need of calming himself, and in his somewhat fantastic way had expressed that need, "For my own poor part, look you, I'll go pray," so now he calls for music, "Come, some music; come the recorders!" But he is haunted by the irrepressible Rosencrantz and Guildenstern. With them Hamlet is now severely and imperiously courteous, now enigmatical, now ironical. At last, when he advances to interpret his parable of the recorders, he becomes terribly direct and frank. The courtiers are silenced; they have not the spirit even to mutter a lie. And having disposed of them, Hamlet takes in hand Polonius. He is assuming the offensive with his foes. He steps forward to assist the old chamberlain to expose his folly; he lends him a hand to render himself contemptible. Next Hamlet hastens to his mother's closet.† He has words that must be spoken. He has a great essay to make towards the deliverance of a human soul from the bondage of corruption. The slaughter of Polonius appears to him a trivial incident by the way; it does not affect him until he has spent his powers in the effort to uplift his mother's weak soul, and breathe into it strength and courage and constancy. Then in the exhaustion which succeeds his effort, his tears flow fast.

In the dawn of the following morning Hamlet is despatched to England. From this time forward he acts, if not with continuity and with a plan, at least with energy. He has fallen in love with

---

* On the line "A very, very—pajock," see the article on Shakespeare in *Edinburgh Review*, October 1872, pp. 361-62.

† Of the speech in presence of the praying Claudius, Richardson had said what S.T. Coleridge, in other words, repeated, "I venture to affirm that these are not Hamlet's real sentiments." Notice that the ghost appears precisely at the point where Hamlet's words respecting Claudius are most vituperative. Hamlet is immediately sensible that he is weakening his heart with words, and has neglected deeds. The air, which had been so heated, seems to grow icy, and the temperature of Hamlet's passion suddenly falls—to rise again by-and-by.

action; but the action is sudden, convulsive, and interrupted. He is abandoning himself more than previously to his chances of achieving things; and thinks less of forming any consistent scheme. The death of Polonius was accidental, and Hamlet recognised, or tried to recognise in it (since in his own will the deed had no origin) the pleasure of heaven:

> I do repent: but heaven hath pleased it so,
> To punish me with this, and this with me,
> That I must be their scourge and minister.

When about to depart for England, Hamlet accepts the necessity with as resolute a spirit as may be, believing, or trying to believe, that he and his concerns are in the hand of God.

> *Ham.* For England!
> *King.* Ay, Hamlet.
> *Ham.* Good.
> *King.* So is it, if thou knew'st our purposes.
> *Ham. I see a cherub that sees them.*

That is, My times are in God's hand. Again, when he reflects that acting upon a sudden impulse, in which there was nothing voluntary (for the deed was accomplished before he had conceived what it was), he had sent his two schoolfellows to death, Hamlet's thoughts go on to discover the divine purpose in the event:

> Let us know
> Our indiscretion sometimes serves us well,
> When our deep plots do pall; and that should teach us
> There's a divinity that shapes our ends,
> Rough-hew them how we will.

Horatio. That is most certain.

Once more, when Horatio bids the prince yield to the secret misgiving which troubled his heart before he went to the trial of skill with Laertes, Hamlet puts aside his friend's advice with the words, "We defy augury; there's a special providence in the fall of a sparrow. If it be now, 'tis not to come; if it be not to come, it will be now; if it be not now, yet it will come; the readiness is all."

Does Shakespeare accept the interpretation of events which Hamlet is led to adopt? No; the providence in which Shakespeare believed is a moral order which includes man's highest exercise of foresight, energy, and resolution. The disposition of Hamlet to reduce to a minimum the share which man's conscious will and foresight have in the disposing of events, and to enlarge the sphere of the action of powers outside the will has a dramatic, not a theological significance. Helena, who clearly sees what she resolves to do, and accomplishes neither less nor more than she has resolved, professes a different creed:

> Our remedies oft in ourselves do lie,
> Which we ascribe to heaven; the fated sky
> Gives us free scope, only doth backward pull
> Our slow designs when we ourselves are dull.*

Horatio, a believer in the "divinity that shapes our ends," by his promised explanation of the events, delivers us from the transcendental optimism of Hamlet, and restores the purely human way of viewing things:

> Give order that these bodies
> High on a stage be placed to the view;
> And let me speak to the yet unknowing world
> How these things came about: so shall you hear
> Of carnal, bloody, and unnatural acts,
> Of accidental judgments, casual slaughters,
> Of deaths put on by cunning and forced cause,
> And in this upshot purposes mistook,
> Fall'n on the inventors' heads: all this can I
> Truly deliver.

The arrival of Fortinbras contributes also to the restoration of a practical and positive feeling. With none of the rare qualities of the Danish Prince, he excels him in plain grasp of ordinary fact. Shakespeare knows that the success of these men who are limited, definite, positive, will do no dishonour to the failure of the rarer natures, to whom the problem of living is more embarrassing, and for whom the tests of the world are stricter and more delicate. Shakespeare "beats triumphant marches"

* *All's Well That Ends Well,* Act i, Sc. 1.

not for successful persons alone, but also "for conquered and slain persons."

Does Hamlet finally attain deliverance from his disease of will? Shakespeare has left the answer to that question doubtful. Probably if anything could supply the link which was wanting between the purpose and the deed, it was the achievement of some supreme action. The last moments of Hamlet's life are well spent, and for energy and foresight are the noblest moments of his existence; he snatches the poisoned bowl from Horatio, and saves his friend; he gives his dying voice for Fortinbras, and saves his country. The rest is silence:

> Had I but time—as this fell sergeant, death,
> Is strict in his arrest—O, I could tell you.

But he has not told. Let us not too readily assume that we "know the stops" of Hamlet, that we can "pluck out the heart of his mystery."

One thing, however, we *do* know—that the man who wrote the play of *Hamlet* had obtained a thorough comprehension of Hamlet's malady. And assured, as we are by abundant evidence, that Shakespeare transformed with energetic will his knowledge into fact, we may be confident that when *Hamlet* was written, Shakespeare had gained a further stage in his culture of self-control, and that he had become not only adult as an author, but had entered upon the full maturity of his manhood.*

---

* To refer even to the best portion of the immense Hamlet-literature would require considerable space. I believe my study of the play is indebted chiefly to the article by H.A. Werner in *Jahrbuch der Deutschen Shakespeare-Gesellschaft*, vol. v, and to an essay by my friend, J. Todhunter, M.D., read before the Dublin University Shakespeare Society. The doctors of the insane have been studious of the state of Hamlet's mind—Doctors Ray, Kellogg, Conolly, Bucknill. They are unanimous in wishing to put Hamlet under judicious medical treatment; but they find it harder than Polonius did to hit upon a definition of madness:

> For to define true madness
> What is't but to be nothing else but mad?

The critics are nearly equally divided in their estimates of Ophelia. Flathe is extravagantly hostile to the Polonius family. Mr Ruskin (Sesame and Lilies) may be mentioned among English writers as forming no favourable estimate of Ophelia; and against Mrs Jameson's authority, we may set the authority of a lady writer in *Jahrbuch der Deutschen Shakespeare-Gesellschaft*, vol. ii, pp. 16-36. Vischer chivalrously defends Ophelia, and Hebler coincides. The study of Hamlet, by Benno Tschischwitz, is learned and ingenious. H. von Friesen's *Briefe über Shakespeare's Hamlet* contains much more than its name implies, and is indeed a study of the entire development of Shakespeare. Sir Edward Strachey's *Shakespeare's Hamlet*, 1848, interprets the play throughout in a different sense from the interpretation attempted in this chapter. See especially what is called "Hamlet's final discovery," pp. 91-93.

Werder's *Vorlesungen über Shakespeare's Hamlet*, 1875, presents with remarkable force the view that Hamlet's was *not* a weak nature. Mr Frank Marshall's *A Study of Hamlet* if less brilliant is, I think, more sound. Last must be mentioned Mr Furness's magnificent Variorum edition of the play in two volumes, 1877.

4

The English Historical Plays

The historical plays of Shakespeare may be approached from many sides. It would be interesting to endeavour to ascertain from them what was Shakespeare's political creed.* It would be interesting to compare his method as artist when handling historical matter with that of some other great dramatist,—with that of Schiller when writing *Wallenstein*, or Goethe when writing *Egmont*, or Victor Hugo when writing *Cromwell*. Shakespeare's opinions, however, and Shakespeare's method as artist are less than Shakespeare himself. It is the man we are still seeking to discover—behind his works, behind his opinions, behind his artistic process. Shakespeare's life, we must believe, ran on below his art, and was to himself of deeper import than his work as artist. Not perhaps his material life, though to this also he contrived to make his art contribute, but the life of his inmost being. To him art was not, as it has been to some poets and painters and musicians, a temple-worship; a devotion of self, a surrender which is at once blissful and pathetic to some presence greater and nobler than oneself. Of such pathos we discover none in Shakespeare's life. He possessed his art, and

* See on this subject Shakespeare-Forschungen by Benno Tschischwitz, III—Shakespeare's Staat und Königthum. The writer dwells on the moral and religious character of the relation between king and people as conceived by Shakespeare. He says well, "Für Shakespeare nämlich ist das Königthum durchaus nicht die *gekrönte Spitze einer Pyramide*, sondern der lebendige Mittelpunkt eines organischen Ganzen, nach welchem zu das Gesammtleben des Organismus pulsirt," p. 84. See the subsequent chapter in this volume upon "The Roman Plays," pp. 276-338.

was not possessed by it. With him poetry was not, as it was with Keats, or as it was with Shelley, a passion from which deliverance was impossible. Shakespeare delivered himself from his life as artist with quiet determination, and found it well to enjoy his store of worldly success, and learn to possess his soul among the fields and streams of Stratford, before there came an end of all. The main question therefore which it is desirable to put in the case of the historical plays now to be considered is this—What was Shakespeare gaining for himself of wisdom or of strength while these were the organs through which his faculties of thought and imagination nourished themselves, inhaling and exhaling their breath of life? That Shakespeare should have accomplished so great an achievement towards the interpreting of history is much,—that he should have grasped in thought the national life of England during a century and upwards, in her periods of disaster and collapse, of civil embroilment, and of heroic union and exaltation,—this is much. But that by his study of history Shakespeare should have built up his own moral nature, and have fortified himself for the conduct of life, was, we may surmise, to Shakespeare the chief outcome of his toil.

And certainly not the least remarkable thing about these historical plays is that while each is an effort so earnest to realise objective fact, at the same time they disclose so much of the writer's personality. Even Shakespeare cannot transcend himself. Facts must group and organise themselves before they become available for the service of art; and for each artist they group themselves around his strongest feelings and most cherished convictions respecting human life. If by favourable chance hands at work among confused slips of ancient parchment were to lay hold of the inventory of Shakespeare's goods and chattels, if it were ascertained what household stuff the poet had gathered around him at Stratford, the information would be eagerly welcomed as throwing light upon the obscure story of his worldly career. But here in these historical plays and in all his plays, are documents written over everywhere with facts about Shakespeare. The facts are there,—must be there. What is required to ascertain them can be nothing but eyes to which those facts will disclose themselves.

If the outline of Shakespeare's character sketched in these pages be at all a genuine likeness, we shall not think of him merely or chiefly as the gay, genial quick-witted haunter of the Mermaid, careering in light defiance around the bulk of Ben Jonson's mind; we shall not remember him as the Shakespeare about whose deer-stealing expeditions in the country, and less innocent adventures in town, stories of dubious authority have come down to us. We shall rather think of him as a man possessing immense potential strength, but aware of certain weaknesses of his own nature; resolved therefore to be stern with himself and to master those weaknesses; resolved to realise all that potential strength which lay within him. That his sensitiveness to pleasure and to pain was of extraordinary range and delicacy we are certain; we are certain also that he determined he would not leave himself to be the plaything, the thrall or the victim of that sensitiveness. We are accustomed to speak of the tenderness, the infinite tolerance of the genius of Shakespeare. The impartial student must surely be no less impressed by the unyielding justice of Shakespeare, his stern fidelity to fact; and by the large demands he makes upon human character. By much of our passionate intolerance founded upon prejudice, and personal or class-feeling, Shakespeare remained wholly untouched. When we come to Shakespeare and miss our own little bitterness and violences, and find him so large and human, we naturally describe him as tolerant. Shakespeare's tolerance, however, is nothing else but justice, and even his humour, the humour of a man framed for abundant joy and sorrow, has in it something of severity; because he employs it to recover himself from the narrowing intensity of his enthusiasms, and to restore him to the level of everyday fact. In the characters of the weak or the wicked whom he condemns, Shakespeare denies no beautiful or tender trait; but he condemns them without reprieve.

The characters in the historical plays are conceived chiefly with reference to action. The world represented in these plays is not so much the world of feeling or of thought, as the limited world of the practicable. In the great tragedies we are concerned more with what man *is* than with what he *does*. At the close of each tragedy we are left with a sense of measureless failure, or with the stern joy of absolute and concluded attainment. There is something infinite in thought and emotion. We do not think so far, and then stop; beyond the known our thoughts must travel until they are confronted by the unknowable. We do not love, we do not suffer so much and no more; our love is without limitation, and our anguish and our joy cannot be weighed in the balances of earth. But our deeds are definite. And each man when tested by deeds can be brought to a positive standard. The question in this case is not, What has been the life of your soul, what have you thought and suffered and enjoyed? The question is, What have you done? And accordingly in the historical plays we are conscious of a certain limitation, a certain measuring of men by positive achievements and results:

> Action is transitory—a step, a blow,
> The motion of a muscle—this way or that—
> 'Tis done; and in the after-vacancy
> We wonder at ourselves like men betrayed:
> Suffering is permanent, obscure, and dark,
> And has the nature of infinity.

The histories, like the tragedies, are for the reader a school of discipline; but the issues with which they deal are not the infinite issues of life and death; the impression each leaves at the close is not an impression of measureless pathos, or of pain dissolved in perfect joy. They deal with the finite issues of failure or success in the achieving of practical ends; and the feeling which they leave with us is that of a wholesome, mundane pity and terror, or a sane and strong mundane satisfaction.

But if the historical plays cannot compete with the tragedies in depth of spiritual significance, they compensate in some measure for this, as Gervinus has observed, by their breadth and comprehensiveness. The life of man, good or evil, is not seen in its infinite significance for the individual, but its consequences are shown in a definite series of events, as a sanative virtue in society, or as a spreading infection. The mystery of evil is not here an awful shadow, before which we stand appalled, striving to accept the darkness which is not understood for the light's sake, which authenticates and justifies itself. Evil in the historical plays is wrong-doing, which is followed by inevitable retribution. Sir Walter Raleigh, in the preface to the *History of World*, has traced in a remarkable passage, written possibly to vindicate his own orthodoxy, the justice of God in the lives of English Kings, "Whatsoever a man soweth, that shall he also reap." "The sins of the fathers shall be visited upon the children to the third and fourth generation;" these are the texts of Raleigh's theology of history. Going over the same period of history, Shakespeare, with an unfaltering hand, exposes the consequences of weakness, of error, and of crime. Our greatest living novelist has insisted with dreadful emphasis upon the irreparable, irreversible issue still developing itself, of every base or evil deed. Shakespeare denies fact as little as George Eliot. But he shows us also how the sources of good are incalculable; he shows us how the consequences of ill deeds may at a later time be caught up by a flood of blessing, and may really be borne away for ever into oblivion. It is indeed demonstrably true that the power which survives an evil act can be subdued or transformed only at the expense of so much of the virtuous force of the world. Still it is well to be assured that evil even at the expense of good *can* be subdued; such an assurance buoys us above despair. In the stern justice of George Eliot there is a certain idealism which proceeds from a desire for scientific rigour, definiteness, and certitude. Shakespeare, possessing himself of the concrete facts of the world with a larger grasp, shows us the mingled web of good and evil, as it actually is; and to draw the threads asunder, and observe each one apart from the rest is hardly less difficult to accomplish in Shakespeare's world of imagination than in that of the veritable life of man.

Setting aside *Henry VIII*, a play written probably for some special occasion, or upon some special occasion handed over to the dramatist Fletcher to complete; setting aside also the somewhat slight sketch of Edward IV, which appears in *King Henry VI*, Part iii, and in the opening scenes of *King Richard III*, six full-length portraits of kings of England have been left by Shakespeare. These six fall into two groups of three each,—one group consisting of studies of kingly weakness, the other group of studies of kingly strength. In the one group stand King John, King Richard II, and King Henry VI, in the other King Henry IV, King Henry V, and King Richard III. John is the royal criminal, weak in his criminality; Henry VI is the royal saint, weak in his saintliness. The feebleness of Richard II cannot be characterised in a word; he is a graceful, sentimental monarch. Richard III, in the other group, is a royal criminal, strong in his crime. Henry IV, the usurping Bolingbroke, is strong by a fine craft in dealing with events, by resolution and policy, by equal caution and daring. The strength of Henry V is that of plain heroic magnitude, thoroughly sound and substantial, founded upon the eternal verities. Here, then, we may recognise the one dominant subject of the histories, *viz.*, how a man may fail, and how a man may succeed in attaining a practical mastery of the world. These plays are, as Schlegel has named them, a "mirror for kings;" and the characters of these plays all lead up to Henry V, the man framed for the most noble and joyous mastery of things.

I

In *King John* the hour of utmost ebb in the national life of England is investigated by the imagination of the poet. The king reigns neither by warrant of a just title, nor, like Bolingbroke, by warrant of the right of the strongest. He knows that his house is founded upon the sand; he knows that he has no justice of God and no virtue of man on which to rely. Therefore he assumes an air of authority and regal grandeur. But within all is rottenness and shame. Unlike the bold usurper Richard, John endeavours to turn away his eyes from facts of which he is yet aware; he dare not gaze into his own wretched and cowardly soul. When threatened by France with war, and now alone with his mother, John exclaims, making an effort to fortify his heart:

> Our strong possession and our right for us.

But Elinor, with a woman's courage and directness, forbids the unavailing self-deceit:

> Your strong possession much more than your right,
> Or else it must go wrong with you and me.

King Richard, when be would make away with the young princes, summons Tyrrel to his presence, and enquires with cynical indifference to human sentiment:

> Dar'st thou resolve to kill a friend of mine?

and when Tyrrel accepts the commission, Richard, in a moment of undisguised exultation, breaks forth with "Thou sing'st sweet music!" John would inspire Hubert with his murderous purpose rather like some vague influence than like a personal will, obscurely as some pale mist works which creeps across the fields, and leaves blight behind it in the sunshine. He trembles lest he should have said too much; he trembles lest he should not have said enough; at last the nearer fear prevails, and the words "death," "a grave," form themselves upon his lips. Having touched a spring which will produce assassination he furtively withdraws himself from the mechanism of crime. It suits the king's interest afterwards that Arthur should be living, and John adds to his crime the baseness of a miserable attempt by chicanery and timorous sophisms to transfer the responsibility of murder from himself to his instrument and accomplice. He would fain darken the eyes of his conscience and of his understanding.

The show of kingly strength and dignity in which John is clothed in the earlier scenes of the play, must therefore be recognised (although Shakespeare does not obtrude the fact), as no more than a poor pretence of true regal strength and honour. The fact, only hinted in these earlier scenes, becomes afterwards all the more impressive, when the time comes to show this dastard king, who had been so great in the barter of territory, in the sale of cities, in the sacrifice of love and marriage-truth to policy; now changing from pale to red in the presence of his own nobles, now vainly trying to tread back the path of crime, now incapable of enduring the physical suffering of the hour of death. Sensible that he is a king with no inward strength of justice or of virtue, John endeavours to buttress up his power with external supports; against the advice of his nobles he celebrates a second coronation, only forthwith to remove the crown from his head and place it in the hands of an Italian priest. Pandulph "of fair Millaine cardinal," who possesses the astuteness and skill to direct the various conflicting forces of the time to his own advantage, Pandulph is the *de facto* master of England, and as he pleases makes peace or announces war.

The country, as in periods of doubt and danger, was "possessed with rumours, full of idle dreams." Peter of Pomfret had announced that before Ascension day at noon the king should deliver up his crown. John submits to the degradation demanded of him, and has the incredible baseness to be pleased that he has done so of his own free will:

> Is this Ascension-day? did not the prophet
> Say that before Ascension-day at noon
> My crown I should give off? Even so I have.
> I did suppose it should be on constraint;
> But, heaven be thank'd! it is but voluntary.

After this we are not surprised that when the Bastard endeavours to rouse him to manliness and resolution:

> Away and glister like the god of war
> When he intendeth to become the field,

John is not ashamed to announce the "happy peace" which he has made with the Papal legate, on whom he relies for protection against the invaders of England. Faulconbridge still urges the duty of an effort at self-defence, for the sake of honour, and of safety, and the King, incapable of accepting his own responsibilities and privileges, hands over the care of England to his illegitimate nephew, "Have thou the ordering of this present time."

There is little in the play of *King John* which strengthens or gladdens the heart. In the tug of selfish power, hither and thither, amid the struggle of kingly greeds, and priestly pride, amid the sales of cities, the loveless marriage of princes, the rumours and confusion of the people, a pathetic beauty illumines the boyish figure of Arthur, so gracious, so passive, untouched by the adult rapacities and crimes of the others:

> Good, my mother, peace!
> I would that I were low laid in my grave;
> I am not worth this coil that's made for me.

The voice of maternal passion, a woman's voice impotent and shrill, among the unheeding male forces, goes up also from the play. There is the pity of stern, armed men for the ruin of a child's life. These, and the boisterous but genuine and hearty patriotism of Faulconbridge, are the only presences of human virtue or beauty which are to be perceived in the degenerate world depicted by Shakespeare. And the end, like what preceded it, is miserable. The King lies poisoned, overmastered by mere physical agony, agony which leaves little room for any pangs of conscience, were the palsied moral nature of the criminal capable of such nobler suffering:

> I am a scribbled form, drawn with a pen
> Upon a parchment, and against this fire
> Do I shrink up.

II

Whether any portions of the first part of *Henry VI* be from the hand of Shakespeare, and if there be, what those portions are, need not be here investigated. The play belongs, in the main, to the pre-Shakespearian school. Shakespeare finds his own genius for the dramatic rendering of history for the first time distinctly in the second and third parts of *Henry VI*. The writer of the first part does not stand above the characters which he creates; he is violently prejudiced against some, and he feels a lyrical delight in singing the praises of others. But in the treatment of the characters of the King, of Gloster, of York, of Richard, in the later parts of the trilogy the Shakespearian impartiality and irony are clearly discernible. Shakespeare does not hate King Henry; he is as favourably disposed to him as is possible; but he says, with the same clear and definite expression in which the historical fact uttered itself, that this saint of a feeble type upon the throne of England was a curse to the land and to the time only less than a royal criminal as weak as Henry would have been.

The heroic days of the fifth Henry, when the play opens, belong to the past; but their memory survives in the hearts and in the vigorous muscles of the great lords and earls who surround the king. He only, who most should have treasured and augmented his inheritance of glory and of power, is insensible to the large responsibilities and privileges of his place. He is cold in great affairs; his supreme concern is to remain blameless. Free from all greeds and ambitions, he yet is possessed by egoism, the egoism of timid saintliness. His virtue is negative, because there is no vigorous basis of manhood within him out of which heroic saintliness might develop itself. For fear of what is wrong, he shrinks from what is right. This is not the virtue ascribed to the nearest followers of "the Faithful and True" who in his righteousness doth judge and make war. Henry is passive in the presence of evil, and weeps. He would keep his garments clean; but the garments of God's soldier-saints, who do not fear the soils of struggle, gleam with a higher, intenser purity. "His eyes were as a flame of fire, and on his head were many crowns; [...]. And the armies which were in heaven followed him upon white horses, clothed in fine linen, white and clean." These soldiers in heaven have their representatives in earth; and Henry was not one of these. Zeal must come before charity, and then when charity comes it will appear as a self-denial.* But Henry knows nothing of zeal; and he is amiable, not charitable.

There is something of irony in the scene with which the second part of *Henry VI* opens. Suffolk, the Lancelot of this tragedy, has brought from France the Princess Margaret, and the joy of the blameless king upon receiving, at the cost of two hard-won provinces, this terrible wife, who will "dandle him like a baby," has in it something pitiable, something pathetic, and something ludicrous. The relations of the King to Margaret throughout the play are delicately and profoundly conceived. He clings to her as to something stronger than himself; he dreads her as a boy might dread some formidable master:

> *Exeter.* Here comes the Queen, whose looks betray her anger: I'll steal away.
>
> *Henry.* And so will I.

Yet through his own freedom from passion, he derives a sense of superiority to his wife; and after she has dashed him all over

---

* J.H. Newman, *Verses on Various Occasions,* p. 60.

with the spray of her violent anger and her scorn, Henry may be seen mildly wiping away the drops, insufferably placable, offering excuses for the vituperation and the insults which he has received:

> Poor Queen, how love to me and to her son
> Hath made her break out into terms of rage.

Among his "wolfish Earls" Henry is in constant terror, not of being himself torn to pieces, but of their flying at one another's throats. Violent scenes, disturbing the cloistral peace which it would please him to see reign throughout the universe, are hateful and terrible to Henry. He rides out hawking with his Queen and Suffolk, the Cardinal and Gloster; some of the riders hardly able for an hour to conceal their emulation and their hate. Henry takes a languid interest in the sport, but all occasions supply food for his contemplative piety; he suffers from a certain incontinence of devout feeling, and now the falcons set him moralising:

> But what a point, my lord, your falcon made,
> And what a pitch she flew above the rest!
> To see how God in all his creatures works!

A moment after, and the peers, with Margaret among them, are bandying furious words. Henry's anguish is extreme, but he hopes that something may be done by a few moral reflections suitable to the occasion:

> I pr'ythee, peace,
> Good Queen, and whet not on these furious peers,
> For blessed are the peacemakers on earth.
> *Cardinal.* Let me be blessed for the peace I make
> Against this proud Protector with my sword.

The angry colloquy is presently silenced by the cry, "A miracle! a miracle!" and the impostor Simcox and his wife appear. Henry, with his fatuous proclivity towards the edifying, rejoices in this manifestation of God's grace in the restoration to sight of a man born blind:

> Great is his comfort in this earthly vale,
> Although by his sight his sin be multiplied;

(That is to say, "If we had the good fortune to be deprived of all our senses and appetites, we should have a fair chance of being quite spotless; yet let us thank God for his mysterious goodness to this man!") And once more, when the Protector, by a slight exercise of shrewdness and common sense, has unmasked the rogue, and has had him whipt, extreme is the anguish of the King:

> *K. Hen.* O God! seest Thou this, and bearest so long?
> *Queen.* It made me laugh to see the villain run.

But the feeble saint, who is cast down upon the occurrence of a piece of vulgar knavery, can himself abandon to butchers the noblest life in England. His conscience assures him that Gloster is innocent; he hopes the Duke will be able to clear himself; but Gloster's judges are Suffolk "with his cloudy brow," sharp Buckingham,

> And dogged York, that reaches at the moon.

Henry is not equal to confronting such terrible faces as these; and so trusting to God, who will do all things well, he slinks out of the Parliament shedding tears, and leaves Gloster to his fate:

> My lords, what to your wisdom seemeth best,
> Do, or undo, as if ourself were here.

When Henry hears that his uncle is dead he swoons; he suspects that the noble old man has been foully dealt with; but judgment belongs to God; possibly his suspicion may be a false one; how terrible if he should sully his purity of heart with a false suspicion; may God forgive him if he do so! And thus humouring his timorous, irritable conscience, Henry is incapable of action, and allows things to take their course.

This morbid scrupulosity of conscience which characterizes Henry while he neglects the high duties of his position, sets him speculating uneasily about the validity of his title to the throne—a title which has descended through the great victor of Agincourt from Henry's grandfather. He turns from York to Warwick, from Warwick to Northumberland, uncertain what he ought to think. Clifford boldly cuts the knot; and Henry's courage revives:

> King Henry, be thy title right or wrong,
> Lord Clifford vows to fight in thy defence.

But the king, in the presence of armed force, cannot maintain his resolution, and ends by a compromise, which, upon condition of the forfeiture of his son's rights, will secure peace in *his* days. We sympathize with the indignant Margaret. Yet in Henry's conduct there has been no active selfishness; he has only accepted peace at the price required.

Between York on the one hand, and York's instrument, Jack Cade, on the other, the unhappy king is hard set. Not that it is of himself he chiefly thinks; he suffers on account of the rebels as much as on his own account. He will parley with Cade; still better, he will send "some holy bishop" to entreat with the rebels. York, meanwhile, is approaching, and demands that the king's adviser, Somerset, be removed. Henry, with placid acquiescence, sees Somerset prepared to sacrifice himself, and despatches Buckingham to confer in gentle language with his antagonist. At least the virtue to refrain from disguising, as John disguised, under high-sounding words, the abjectness of his state belongs to Henry:

> I pray thee, Buckingham, go and meet him,
> And ask him what's the reason of these arms.
> Tell him I'll send Duke Edmund to the Tower;
> And, Somerset, we will commit thee hither
> Until his army be dismissed from him.
>
> *Som.* My lord,
> I'll yield myself to prison willingly,
> Or unto death, to do my country good.
>
> *K. Hen.* In any case be not too rough in terms,
> For he is fierce, and cannot brook hard language.
>
> *Buck.* I will, my lord; and doubt not so to deal
> As all things shall redound unto your good.
>
> *K. Hen.* Come, wife, let's in and learn to govern better,
> For yet may England curse my wretched reign.

At length the wretched reign approaches its end. Henry has longed to be a subject, and he is such for some short time before his death. From the battle in which Richard, blood-hound-wise, is pursuing Clifford, Henry withdraws, and, seating himself upon a mole-hill, meditates on the happy life of shepherd-swains, and prays that to whom God wills the victory may fall. He mildly begs the fugitives to take him along with them:

> Nay, take me with thee, good sweet Exeter;
> Not that I fear to stay, but love to go
> Whither the queen intends.

When the keepers make him their prisoner, Henry is sincerely concerned about the purity of conscience of his captors. He enquires, with unfeigned and disinterested anxiety, whether they have taken an oath of allegiance to him. At all events he will not now command them to release him, and so they cannot offend. His own fate does not concern him; he wears his crown *Content;* and he is sure that the new king will execute neither more nor less than God wills.

In prison Henry at last is really happy; now he is responsible for nothing; he enjoys for the first time tranquil solitude; he is a bird who sings in his cage. His latter days he will spend, to the rebuke of sin and the praise of his creator, in devotion. Henry's equanimity is not of the highest kind; he is incapable of commotion. His peace is not that which underlies wholesome agitation, a peace which passes understanding. "Quietness is a grace, not in itself; only when it is grafted on the stem of faith, zeal, self-abasement, and diligence."* If Henry had known the nobleness of true kingship, his content in prison might be admirable; as it is, the beauty of that content does not strike us as of a rich or vivid kind. But the end is come, and that is a gain. Henry has yielded to the house of York, and the evil time is growing shorter. The words of the great Duke of York are confirmed by our sense of fact and right:

> King did I call thee? nay, thou art not king.
>
> . . . . . .
>
> Give place; by heaven thou shalt rule no more
> O'er him whom heaven created for thy ruler.†

* J.H. Newman, *Parochial and Plain Sermons*, vol. v, p. 71.

† Without entering into the controversy as to the authorship of the *First*

III

Certain qualities which make it unique among the dramas of Shakespeare characterize the play of *King Richard III.* Its manner of conceiving and presenting character has a certain resemblance, not elsewhere to be found in Shakespeare's writings, to the ideal manner of Marlowe. As in the plays of Marlowe, there is here one dominant figure distinguished by a few strongly marked and inordinately developed qualities. There is in the characterization no mystery, but much of a daemonic intensity. Certain passages are entirely in the lyrical-dramatic style; an emotion which is one and the same, occupying at the same moment two or three of the personages, and obtaining utterance through them almost simultaneously, or in immediate succession; as a musical motive is interpreted by an orchestra, or taken up singly by successive instruments:

> *Q. Eliz.* Was never widow had so dear a loss!
> *Children.* Were never orphans had so dear a loss!
> *Duckets.* Was never mother had so dear a loss!
> Alas! I am the mother of these griefs.

Mere verisimilitude in the play of *King Richard III* becomes at times subordinate to effects of symphonic orchestration, or of statuesque composition. There is a Blake-like terror and beauty in the scene in which the three women,—queens and a duchess,—seat themselves upon the ground in their desolation and despair, and cry aloud in utter anguish of spirit. First by the mother of two kings, then by Edward's widow, last by the

---

Part of the Contention, and *The True Tragedie* (the old plays corresponding to the second and third parts of King Henry VI), it may be instructive to mention how authorities are divided. In favour of Shakespeare's authorship of these plays, Johnson, Steevens, Knight, Schlegel, Tieck, Ulrici, Delius, Oechelhäuser, H. von Friesen. In favour of Greene's or Marlowe's authorship, Malone, Collier, Dyce, Courtenay, Gervinus, Kreyssig and the French critics. Clark and Wright, Halliwell, Lloyd, and others believe that a portion of Shakespeare's work may be found in these old plays. See the note from which I partly obtain this list of authorities in *Jahrbuch der Deutschen Shakespeare-Gesellschaft*, vol. iii, p. 42. See also in vol. i the article by Ulrici, "Christopher Marlowe und Shakespeare's Verhältniss zu ihm." See the previous notes, p. 56, and pp. 97-98, for the opinions of Mr Grant White, and Miss J. Lee.

terrible Medusa-like Queen Margaret, the same attitude is assumed, and the same grief is poured forth. Misery has made them indifferent to all ceremony of queenship, and for a time to their private differences; they are seated, a rigid yet tumultuously passionate group, in the majesty of mere womanhood and supreme calamity. Readers acquainted with Blake's illustrations to the *Book of Job* will remember what effects, sublime and appalling, the artist produces by animating a group of figures with one common passion, which spontaneously produces in each individual the same extravagant movement of head and limbs.

The daemonic intensity which distinguishes the play proceeds from the character of Richard, as from its source and centre. As with the chief personages of Marlowe's plays, so Richard in this play rather occupies the imagination by audacity and force, than insinuates himself through some subtle solvent, some magic and mystery of art. His character does not grow upon us; from the first it is complete. We are not curious to discover what Richard is, as we are curious to come into presence of the soul of Hamlet. We are in no doubt about Richard; but it yields us a strong sensation to observe him in various circumstances and situations; we are roused and animated by the presence of almost superhuman energy and power, even though that power and that energy be malign.

Coleridge has said of Richard that pride of intellect is his characteristic. This is true, but his dominant characteristic is not intellectual; it is rather a daemonic energy of will. The same cause which produces tempest and shipwreck produces Richard; he is a fierce elemental power raging through the world; but this elemental power is concentrated in a human will. The need of action is with Richard an appetite to which all the other appetites are subordinate. He requires space in the world to bustle in; his will must wreak itself on men and things. All that is done in the play proceeds from Richard; there is, as has been observed by Mr Hudson, no interaction. "The drama is not so much a composition of co-operative characters, mutually developing and developed, as the prolonged yet hurried outcome of a single character, to which the other persons serve but as exponents and conductors; as if he were a volume of electricity disclosing himself by means of others, and quenching their active powers in the very process of doing so."*

Richard, with his distorted and withered body, his arm shrunk like "a blasted sapling," is yet a sublime figure by virtue of his energy of will and tremendous power of intellect. All obstacles give way before him;—the courage of men, and the bitter animosity of women. And Richard has a passionate scorn of men, because they are weaker and more obtuse than he, the deformed outcast of nature. He practices hypocrisy not merely for the sake of success, but because his hypocrisy is a cynical jest, or a gross insult to humanity. The Mayor of London has a *bourgeois* veneration for piety and established forms of religion. Richard advances to meet him reading a book of prayers, and supported on each side by a bishop. The grim joke, the contemptuous insult to the citizen faith in church and king, flatters his malignant sense of power. To cheat a gull, a coarse hypocrisy suffices.†

Towards his tool Buckingham, when occasion suits, Richard can be frankly contemptuous. Buckingham is unable to keep pace with Richard in his headlong career; he falls behind and is scant of breath:

> The deep-revolving, witty Buckingham
> No more shall be the neighbour to my counsel;
> Hath he so long held out with me untired
> And stops he now for breath?

The duke, "his other self, his counsel's consistory, his oracle, his prophet," comes before the king claiming the fulfilment of a promise, that he should receive the Earldom of Hereford. Richard becomes suddenly deaf and, contemptuously disregarding the interpellations of Buckingham, continues his talk on indifferent matters. At length he turns to "his other self":

---

* H.N. Hudson, *Shakespeare, His Life, Art and Characters*, vol. ii, p. 156.

† The plan originates with Buckingham, but Richard plays his part with manifest delight. Shakespeare had no historical authority for the presence of the Bishops. See Skottowe's *Life of Shakespeare*, vol. i, pp. 195-96.

Buck. My lord!
K. Rich. Ay, what's o'clock?
Buck. I am thus bold to put your Grace in mind
Of what you promised me.
K. Rich. Well, but what's o'clock?
Buck. Upon the stroke of ten.
K. Rich. Well, let it strike.
Buck. Why let it strike?
K. Rich. Because that like a Jack thou keep'st the stroke
Betwixt thy begging and my meditation.
I am not in the giving vein to-day.

Richard's cynicism and insolence have in them a kind of grim mirth; such a *bonhomie* as might be met with among the humourists of Pandemonium. His brutality is a manner of joking with a purpose. When his mother, with Queen Elizabeth, comes by "copious in exclaims," ready to "smother her damned son in the breath of bitter words," the mirthful Richard calls for a flourish of trumpets to drown these shrill female voices:

A flourish trumpets! strike alarum, drums!
Let not the heavens hear these tell-tale women
Rail on the Lord's anointed. Strike, I say!

On an occasion when hypocrisy is more serviceable than brutality, Richard kneels to implore his mother's blessing, but has a characteristic word of contemptuous impiety to utter aside:

Duchess. God bless thee and put meekness in thy breast,
Love, charity, obedience, and true duty.
Richard. Amen! and make me die a good old man!
That is the butt-end of a mother's blessing;
I marvel that her grace did leave it out.

He plays his part before his future wife, the Lady Anne, laying open his breast to the sword's point with a malicious confidence. He knows the measure of woman's frailty, and relies on the spiritual force of his audacity and dissimulation to subdue the weak hand, which tries to lift the sword. With no friends to back his suit, with nothing but "the plain devil, and dissembling looks," he wins his bride. The hideous irony of such a courtship, the mockery it implies of human love, is enough to make a man "your only jigmaker," and sends Richard's blood dancing along his veins.

While Richard is plotting for the crown, Lord Hastings threatens to prove an obstacle in the way. What is to be done? Buckingham is dubious and tentative:

> Now, my lord, what shall we do, if we perceive
> Lord Hastings will not yield to our complots?

With sharp detonation, quickly begun and quickly over, Richard's answer is discharged, "Chop off his head, man." There can be no beginning, middle, or end to a deed so simple and so summary. Presently Hastings making sundry small assignations for future days and weeks, goes, a murdered man, to the conference at the Tower. Richard, whose startling figure emerges from the background throughout the play with small regard for verisimilitude and always at the most effective moment, is suddenly on the spot, just as Hastings is about to give his voice in the conference as though he were the representative of the absent Duke. Richard is prepared, when the opportune instant has arrived, to spring a mine under Hastings' feet. But meanwhile a matter of equal importance concerns him,—my Lord of Ely's strawberries: the flavour of Holborn strawberries is exquisite, and the fruit must be sent for. Richard's desire to appear disengaged from sinister thought is less important to note than Richard's need of indulging a cynical contempt of human life. The explosion takes place; Hastings is seized; and the delicacies are reserved until the head of Richard's enemy is off. There is a wantonness of *diablerie* in this incident:

> Talk'st thou to me of *ifs*? Thou art a traitor—
> Off with his head! Now by Saint Paul I swear
> I will not dine until I see the same.*

---

* This scene, including the incident of the dish of strawberries, is from Sir T. More's history. See *Courtenay's Commentaries* on Shakespeare, vol. ii, pp. 84-87.

The fiery energy of Richard is at its simplest, unmingled with irony or dissimulation in great days of military movement and of battle. Then the force within him expends itself in a paroxysm which has all the intensity of ungovernable spasmodic action, and which is yet organised and controlled by his intellect. Then he is engaged at his truest devotions, and numbers his Ave-Maries, not with beads but with ringing strokes upon the helmets of his foes.* He is inspired with "the spleen of fiery dragons;" "a thousand hearts are great within his bosom." On the eve of the battle of Bosworth field, Richard, with uncontrollable eagerness, urges his enquiry into the minutiae of preparation which may ensure success. He lacks his usual alacrity of spirit, yet a dozen subalterns would hardly suffice to receive the orders which he rapidly enunciates. He is upon the wing of "fiery expedition":

I will not sup to-night. Give me some ink and paper.
What, is my beaver easier than it was?
And all my armour laid within my tent?
Catesby. It is, my liege, and all things are in readiness.
K. Rich. Good Norfolk, hie thee to thy charge;
Use careful watch, choose trusty sentinels.
Norfolk. I go, my lord.
K. Rich. Stir with the lark to-morrow, gentle Norfolk.
Norfolk. I warrant you, my lord.
K. Rich. Catesby!
Catesby. My Lord?
K. Rich. Send out a pursuivant at arms
To Stanley's regiment; bid him bring his power
Before sun-rising, lest his son George fall
Into the blind cave of eternal night.
Fill me a bowl of wine. Give me a watch.
[*Exit Catesby.*]
Saddle White Surrey for the field to-morrow.
Look that my staves be sound, and not too heavy,
Ratcliff!

And learning from Ratcliff, that Northumberland and Surrey are alert, giving his last direction that his attendant should

* 3 *Henry VI*, Act ii, Scene 1.

return at midnight to help him to arm, King Richard retires into his tent.

In all his military movements, as in the whole of Richard's career, there is something else than self-seeking. It is true that Richard, like Edmund, like Iago, is solitary; he has no friend, no brother; "I am myself alone;" and all that Richard achieves tends to his own supremacy. Nevertheless, the central characteristic of Richard is not self-seeking or ambition. It is the necessity of releasing and letting loose upon the world the force within him (mere force in which there is nothing moral), the necessity of deploying before himself and others the terrible resources of his will. One human tie Shakespeare attributes to Richard; contemptuous to his mother, indifferent to the life or death of Clarence and Edward, except as their life or death may serve his own attempt upon the crown, cynically loveless towards his feeble and unhappy wife, Richard admires with an enthusiastic admiration his great father:

> Methinks 'tis prize enough to be his son.

And the memory of his father supplies him with a family pride which, however, does not imply attachment or loyalty to any member of his house:

> But I was born so high;
> Our aery buildeth in the cedar's top,
> And dallies with the wind and scorns the sun.

History supplied Shakespeare with the figure of his Richard. He has been accused of darkening the colours and exaggerating the deformity of the character of the historical Richard found in More and Holinshed. The fact is precisely the contrary. The mythic Richard of the historians (and there must have been some appalling fact to originate such a myth) is made somewhat less grim and bloody by the dramatist.* Essentially, however,

* See the detailed study of this play by W. Oechelhäuser in *Jahrbuch der Deutschen Shakespeare-Gesellschaft*, vol. iii, pp. 37-39, and pp. 47, 53. Holinshed's treatment of the character of Richard is hardly in harmony with itself. From the death of Edward IV onwards the Richard of Holinshed resembles Shakespeare's Richard, but possesses fainter traces of humanity. "Wenn hiernach also thatsächlich zwei Holinshed'sche Versionen des Charakters und der Handlungen Richard's vorliegen, so

Shakespeare's Richard is of the diabolical (something more dreadful than the criminal) class. He is not weak, because he is single-hearted in his devotion to evil. Richard does not serve two masters. He is not like John, a dastardly criminal; he is not like Macbeth, joyless and faithless because he has deserted loyalty and honour. He has a fierce joy, and he is an intense believer,—in the creed of hell. And therefore he is strong. He inverts the moral order of things, and tries to live in this inverted system. He does not succeed; he dashes himself to pieces against the laws of the world which he has outraged. Yet, while John is wholly despicable, we cannot refrain from yielding a certain tribute of admiration to the bolder malefactor, who ventures on the daring experiment of choosing evil for his good.

Such an experiment, Shakespeare declares emphatically, as experience and history declare, must in the end fail. The ghosts of the usurper's victims rise between the camps, and are to Richard the Erinnyes, to Richmond inspirers of hope and victorious courage. At length Richard trembles on the brink of annihilation, trembles over the loveless gulf:

> I shall despair; there is no creature loves me;
> And if I die, no soul shall pity me.

But the stir of battle restores him to resolute thoughts, "Come, bustle, bustle, caparison my horse," and he dies in a fierce paroxysm of action. Richmond conquers, and he conquers expressly as the champion and representative of the moral order of the world, which Richard had endeavoured to set aside:

> O Thou, whose captain I account myself,
> Look on my forces with a gracious eye;
> Put in their hands thy bruising irons of wrath,
> That they may crush down with a heavy fall

---

hat Shakespeare allerdings die auf More basirte, also die schwärzere gewählt; über diese ist er aber nicht, wie so vielfack behauptet wird, hinausgegangen, sondern er hat sie sogar gemildert, hat die Fäden, welche das Ungeheuer noch mit der Menschheit verkmipfen, verstärkt, statt sie ganz zu lösen."

> The usurping helmets of our adversaries!
> Make us thy ministers of chastisement,
> That we may praise thee ill thy victory.

The female figures of this play,—Queen Elizabeth, Queen Margaret, the Duchess of York, the Lady Anne; and with these the women of Shakespeare's other historical plays, would form an interesting subject for a separate study. The women of the histories do not attain the best happiness of women. In the rough struggle of interests, of parties, of nations, they are defrauded of their joy, and of its objects. Like Constance, like Elizabeth, like Margaret, like the Queen of the Second Richard, like Katharine of Arragon, they mourn some the loss of children, some of husbands, some of brothers, and all of love. Or else, like Harry Percy's wife (who also lives to lament her husband's death, and to tremble for her father's fate),* they are the wives of men of action to whom they are dear, but "in sort or limitation," dwelling but in the suburbs of their husbands' good-pleasure:

> To keep with you at meals, comfort your bed,
> And talk with you sometimes.

The wooing of the French Katharine by King Henry V is business-like, and soundly affectionate, but by no means of the kind which is most satisfying to the heart of a sensitive or ardent woman. That Shakespeare himself loved in another fashion than that of Hotspur or Henry might be inferred, if no other sufficient evidence were forthcoming, from the admirable mockery of the love given by men of letters, and men of imagination—poets in chief—which he puts into Henry's mouth. "And while thou livest, dear Kate, take a fellow of plain and uncoined constancy; for he perforce must do thee right, because he hath not the gift to woo in other places; for these fellows of infinite tongue, that can rhyme themselves into ladies' favours, they do always reason themselves out again." Was this a skit by Shakespeare against himself, or against an interpretation of himself for which he perceived there was a good deal to be said, from a point of view other than his own? While the poet was

* See the pathetic scene, 2 *Henry IV*, Act ii, Scene 3.

buying up land near Stratford, he could describe his courtier Osric as "very spacious in the possession of dirt." Is this a piece of irony similar in kind?

The figure of Queen Margaret is painfully persistent upon the mind's eye, and tyrannises, almost as much as the figure of King Richard himself, over the imagination. "Although banished upon pain of death, she returns to England to assist at the intestine conflicts of the House of York. Shakespeare personifies in her the ancient Nemesis; he gives her more than human proportions, and represents her as a sort of supernatural apparition. She penetrates freely into the palace of Edward IV, she there breathes forth her hatred in presence of the family of York, and its courtier attendants. No one dreams of arresting her, although she is an exiled woman, and she goes forth, meeting no obstacle, as she had entered. The same magic ring, which on the first occasion opened the doors of the royal mansion, opens them for her once again, when Edward IV is dead, and his sons have been assassinated in the Tower by the order of Richard. She came, the first time, to curse her enemies; she comes now to gather the fruits of her malediction. Like an avenging Fury, or the classical Fate, she has announced to each his doom."*

The play must not be dismissed without one word spoken of King Edward IV. He did not interest the imagination of Shakespeare. Edward is the self-indulgent, luxurious king. The one thing which Shakespeare cared to say about him was, that his pleasant delusion of peacemaking shortly before his death, was a poor and insufficient compensation for a life spent in ease and luxury rather than in laying the hard and strong bases of a substantial peace. A few soft words, and placing of hands in hands will not repair the ravage of fierce years, and the decay of sound human bonds during soft, effeminate years. Just as the peace-making is perfect, Richard is present on the scene:

> There wanteth now our brother Gloster here
> To make the blessed period of our peace.

And Gloster stands before the dying king to announce that

* A. Mézières, *Shakespeare, ses Œuvres et ses Critiques*, p. 139.

Clarence lies murdered in the Tower. This is Shakespeare's comment upon and condemnation of the self-indulgent King.*

IV

The play of *King Richard II* possesses none of the titanic stormy force which breathes through *King Richard III,* but in delicate cunning in the rendering of character it excels the more popular play. The two principal figures in *King Richard II,* that of the king who fell, and that of the king who rose—the usurping Bolingbroke—grow before us insensibly through a series of fine and characteristic strokes. They do not, like the figures in *King Richard III,* forcibly possess themselves of our imagination, but engage it before it is aware, and by degrees advance stronger claims upon us, and make good those claims. It will be worth-while to try to ascertain what Shakespeare looked upon as most significant in the characters of these two royal persons,—the weak king who could not rule, and the strong king who pressed him from his place.

There is a condition of the intellect which we describe by the word "boyishness." The mind in the boyish stage of growth "has no discriminating convictions, and no grasp of consequences." It has not as yet got hold of realities; it is "merely dazzled by phenomena instead of perceiving things as they are." The talk of a person who remains in this sense boyish is often clever, but it is unreal; now he will say brilliant things upon this side of a question, and now upon the opposite side. He has no consistency of view. He is wanting as yet in seriousness of intellect; in the adult mind.† Now if we extend this characteristic of boyishness, from the intellect to the entire character, we may understand much of what Shakespeare meant to represent in the person of Richard II. Not alone his intellect,

---

* Otto Ludwig notices the ideal treatment of time in *King Richard III.* But does it differ from the treatment of time in other historical plays of Shakespeare? "Wie in keinem anderen seiner Stücke die Begebenheiten gewaltsamer zusammengerückt sind, so ist auch in keinem anderen die Zeit so ideal behandelt als hier. Hier giebt es kein Gestern, kein Morgen, keine Uhr, und keinen Kalendar."—*Shakespeare-Studien,* pp. 450-51.

† John Henry Newman, *Idea of a University*—Preface.

but his feelings, live in the world of phenomena, and altogether fail to lay hold of things as they are; they have no consistency and no continuity. His will is entirely unformed; it possesses no authority and no executive power; he is at the mercy of every chance impulse and transitory mood. He has a kind of artistic relation to life, without being an artist. An artist in life seizes upon the stuff of circumstance, and with strenuous will, and strong creative power, shapes some new and noble form of human existence.

Richard, to whom all things are unreal, has a fine feeling for "situations." Without true kingly strength or dignity, he has a fine feeling for the royal situation. Without any making real to himself what God or what death is, he can put himself, if need be, in the appropriate attitude towards God and towards death. Instead of comprehending things as they are, and achieving heroic deeds, he satiates his heart with the grace, the tenderness, the beauty, or the pathos of situations. Life is to Richard a show, a succession of images; and to put himself into accord with the aesthetic requirements of his position is Richard's first necessity. He is equal to playing any part gracefully which he is called upon by circumstances to enact. But when he has exhausted the aesthetic satisfaction to be derived from the situations of his life, he is left with nothing further to do. He is an amateur in living; not an artist.*

Nothing had disturbed the graceful dream of Richard's adolescence. The son of the Black Prince, beautiful in face and form, though now past his youth, a king since boyhood, he has known no antagonism of men or circumstance which might arouse the will. He has an indescribable charm of person and presence; Hotspur remembers him as "Richard, that sweet, lovely rose." But a king who rules a discontented people and

* "Die guten Eigenschaften seiner Natur werden ihm unnütz, ja gefährlich; er gewährt das erschütternde Schauspiel eines beispiellosen, geistigen und gemüthlichen nicht weniger als äusserlichen Bankerutts in Folge des einen Umstandes—dass die Natur ihn mit einem Dilettantencharacter auf eine Stelle berufen, die mehr als jede andere einen Künstler fordert." Kreyssig, *Vorlesungen über Shakespeare* (ed. 1874), vol. i, p. 189. See what follows on Richard's "Dilettantismus."

turbulent nobles needs to be something more than a beautiful blossoming flower. Richard has abandoned his nature to self-indulgence, and therefore the world becomes to him more unreal than ever. He has been surrounded by flatterers, who helped to make his atmosphere a luminous mist, through which the facts of life appeared with all their ragged outlines smoothed away. In the first scene of the play he enacts the part of a king with a fine show of dignity; his bearing is splendid and irreproachable. Mowbray is obstinate, and will not throw down the gage of Bolingbroke; Richard exclaims:

> Rage must be withstood:
> Give me his gage: lions make leopards tame.

But Mowbray retains the gage. "We were not born to sue, but to command," declares Richard with royal majesty; yet he admits that to command exceeds his power. What of that? Has not Richard borne himself splendidly, and uttered himself in a royal metaphor: "Lions make leopards tame?"

At this very moment Bolingbroke, with eye set upon his purpose afar off, has resolutely taken the first step towards attaining it. The challenge of Mowbray conceals a deeper purpose. So little does Bolingbroke really feel of hostility to his antagonist, that one of his first acts, as soon as he is in a position to act with authority, is to declare Mowbray's repeal.* But to stand forward as champion of the wrongs of England, to make himself the eminent justiciary by right of nature, this is the initial step towards future kingship; and Bolingbroke perceives clearly that the fact of Gloster's death may serve as fulcrum for the lever which is to shake the throne of England. Nor is the King quite insensible of the tendency of his cousin's action. Already he begins to quail before his bold antagonist:

> How high a pitch his resolution soars.

Richard tries gracefully to conceal his discomposure, and to deceive Bolingbroke; but he is not, like Richard the hunchback, a daring and efficient hypocrite. He betrays his weakness and

* Kreyssig suggests that this piece of magnanimity was really a piece of fine hypocrisy; Bolingbroke was perhaps aware of Norfolk's death at the time that he gave order for his repeal.

his distrust, administering to the two men decreed to exile an oath which pledges them never to reconcile themselves in their banishment, and never to plot against the king.

Bolingbroke accepts his exile, parts from the English crowd with an air of gracious, condescending familiarity, which flatters (whereas Richard's undignified familiarity only displeases),* and bids farewell to his country as a son bids farewell to the mother with whom his natural loyalty remains, and whom, in due time, he will see again. John of Gaunt is lying on his death-bed. The last of the great race of the time of Edward III, no English spirit will breathe such patriotism as his until the days of Agincourt. With the prophetic inspiration of a dying man he dares to warn his grand-nephew, and to rebuke him for his treason against the ancient honour of England. Richard, who, with his characteristic sensibility of a superficial kind, turns pale as he listens, recovers himself by a transition from overawed alarm to boyish insolence. The white-haired warrior, now a prophet, who lies dying before him, is

> A lunatic, lean-witted fool,
> Presuming on an ague's privilege.

who dares with a frozen admonition to make pale the royal cheek of Richard. The facts are very disagreeable, and why should a king admit into his consciousness an ugly or disagreeable fact?

By and by, being informed that John of Gaunt is dead, Richard has the most graceful and appropriate word ready for so solemn an occasion:

> The ripest fruit first falls, and so doth he;
> His time is spent, our pilgrimage must be.

---

* The skipping King, he ambled up and down
With shallow jesters and rash bavin wits,
Soon kindled and soon burnt; carded his state,
Mingled his royalty with capering fools,

. . . .

Grew a companion to the common streets.

Thus Henry IV describes his predecessor as a lesson to Prince Henry, whose familiarity with his future subjects is neither in his father's manner, nor in that of Richard II.

In which pilgrimage the first step is to seize upon:

> The plate, coin, revenues, and moveables,
> Whereof our uncle Gaunt did stand possessed.

Even York, the temporising York, who would fain be all things to all men if by any means he might save himself, is amazed and ventures to remonstrate against the criminal folly of this act. But Richard, like all self-indulgent natures, has only a half belief in any possible future; he chooses to make the present time easy, and let the future provide for itself; he has been living upon chances too long; he has too long been mortgaging the health of to-morrow for the pleasure of to-day:

> Think what you will, we seize into our hands
> His plate, his goods, his money, and his lands.

But now the tempest begins to sing. Bolingbroke (before he can possibly have heard of his father's death and the seizure by Richard of his own rights and royalties) has equipped an expedition, and is about to land upon the English coast. The King makes a hasty return from his "military promenade" in Ireland.* The first words of each, as he touches his native soil, are characteristic, and were, doubtless, placed by Shakespeare in designed contrast. "*How far is it, my lord, to Berkeley now?*" The banished man has no tender phrases to bestow upon English earth, now that he sets foot upon it once more. All his faculties are firm set, and bent upon achievement. But Richard, who has been absent for a few days in Ireland, enters with all possible zeal into the sentiment of his situation:

> I weep for joy
> To stand upon my kingdom once again.
> Dear earth, I do salute thee with my hand,
> Though rebels wound thee with their horses' hoofs;
> As a long-parted mother with her child
> Plays fondly with her tears and smiles in meeting,
> So weeping, smiling, greet I thee, my earth,
> And do thee favours with my royal hands.

---

* Fr. Kreyssig, *Vorlesungen über Shakespeare*, vol. i, p. 191.

Which sentimental favours form a graceful incident in the play of Richard's life, but can hardly compensate the want of true and manly patriotism. This same earth which Richard caressed with extravagant sensibility was the England which John of Gaunt with strong enthusiasm had apostrophised:

> This blessed plot, this earth, this realm, this England,
> This nurse, this teeming womb of royal kings,
> Fear'd by their breed, and famous for their birth,
> Renowned for their deeds.

It was the England which Richard had alienated from himself and leased out "like to a tenement or pelting farm." What of that, however? Did not Richard address his England with phrases full of tender sensibility, and render her mockery favours with his royal hands?

Bolingbroke has already gained the support of the Welsh. Richard has upon his side powers higher than natural flesh and blood. Shall he not rise like the sun in the eastern sky, and with the majesty of his royal apparition scare away the treasons of the night? Is he not the anointed deputy of God?

> Not all the water in the rough rude sea
> Can wash the balm from an anointed king:
> The breath of worldly men cannot depose
> The deputy elected by the Lord.

Yes; he will rely on God; it is devout; it is not laborious. For every armed man who fights for Bolingbroke:

> God for his Richard hath in heavenly pay
> A glorious angel.

And at this moment Salisbury enters to announce the revolt of Wales. Richard has been slack in action, and arrived a day too late. Remorseless comment upon the rhetorical piety of the King! A company of angels fight upon his side; true, but the sturdy Welshmen stand for Bolingbroke! He is the deputy elected by the Lord; but the Lord's deputy has arrived a day too late!

And now Richard alternates between abject despondency (relieved by accepting all the aesthetic satisfaction derivable from the situation of vanquished king) and an airy, unreal confidence. There is in Richard, as Coleridge has finely observed, "a constant overflow of emotions from a total incapability of controlling them, and thence a waste of that energy, which should have been reserved for actions, in the passion and effort of mere resolves and menaces. The consequence is moral exhaustion and rapid alternations of unmanly despair and ungrounded hope, every feeling being abandoned for its direct opposite upon the pressure of external accident."* A certain unreality infects every motion of Richard; his feelings are but the shadows of true feeling. Now he will be great and a king; now what matters it to lose a kingdom? If Bolingbroke and he alike serve God, Bolingbroke can be no more than his fellow-servant. Now he plays the wanton with his pride, and now with his misery:

> Of comfort no man speak:
> Let's talk of graves, of worms and epitaphs;
> . . . .
> For God's sake, let us sit upon the ground
> And tell sad stories of the death of kings.

At one moment he pictures God mustering armies of pestilence in his clouds to strike the usurper and his descendants; in the next he yields to Bolingbroke's demands, and welcomes his "right noble cousin." He is proud, and he is pious; he is courageous and cowardly; and pride and piety, cowardice and courage, are all the passions of a dream.

Yet Shakespeare has thrown over the figure of Richard a certain atmosphere of charm. If only the world were not a real world, to which serious hearts are due, we could find in Richard some wavering, vague attraction. There is a certain wistfulness about him; without any genuine kingly power, he has a feeling for what kingly power must be; without any veritable religion, he has a pale shadow of religiosity. And few of us have ourselves wholly escaped from unreality. "It takes a long time really to feel and understand things as they are; we learn to do so only gradually."† Into what glimmering limbo will such a soul as that

* *Lectures upon Shakespeare* (ed. 1849), vol. i, p. 178.

† John H. Newman, *Parochial and Plain Sermons.* "Unreal Words," vol. v, p. 43.

of Richard pass when the breath leaves the body? The pains of hell and the joys of heaven belong to those who have serious hearts. Richard has been a graceful phantom. Is there some tenuous, unsubstantial world of spirits reserved for the sentimentalist, the dreamer, and the dilettante? Richard is, as it were, fading out of existence. Bolingbroke seems not only to have robbed him of his authority, but to have encroached upon his very personality, and to have usurped his understanding and his will. Richard is discovering that he is no more than a shadow; the discovery itself has something unreal and shadowy about it. Is not some such fact as this symbolised by the incident of the mirror? Before he quite ceases to be king, Richard, with his taste for "pseudo-poetic pathos,"* would once more look upon the image of his face, and see what wrinkles have been traced upon it by sorrow. And Bolingbroke, suppressing his inward feeling of disdain, directs that the mirror be brought. Richard gazes against it, and finds that sorrow has wrought no change upon the beautiful lips and forehead. And then exclaiming:

> A brittle glory shineth in this face,
> As brittle as the glory is the face,

he dashes the glass against the ground:

> For there it is crack'd in a hundred shivers.
> Mark, silent King, the moral of this sport,
> How soon my sorrow hath destroy'd my face.
> *Boling.* The shadow of your sorrow hath destroy'd
> The shadow of your face.
> *K. Rich.* Say that again.
> The shadow of my sorrow! ha! let's see.

Does Richard, as Professor Flathe (contemptuously dismissing the criticisms of Gervinus and of Kreyssig) maintains, rise morally from his humiliation as a king? Is he heartily sorry for his misdoings? While drinking the wine and eating the bread of sorrow, does he truly and earnestly repent, and intend to lead a new life? The habit of his nature is not so quickly

* Kreyssig.

unlearnt. Richard in prison remains the same person as Richard on the throne. Calamity is no more real to him now than prosperity had been in brighter days. The soliloquy of Richard in Pomfret Castle (Act v, Scene 5) might almost be transferred, as far as tone and manner are concerned, to one other personage in Shakespeare's plays—to Jacques. The curious intellect of Jacques gives him his distinction. He plays his parts for the sake of understanding the world in his way of superficial fool's-wisdom. Richard plays his parts to possess himself of the aesthetic satisfaction of an amateur in life, with a fine feeling for situations. But each lives in the world of shadow, in the world of mockery wisdom, or the world of mockery passion. Mr Hudson is right when he says, "Richard is so steeped in voluptuous habits that he must needs be a voluptuary even in his sorrow, and make a luxury of woe itself; pleasure has so thoroughly mastered his spirit, that he cannot think of bearing pain as a duty or an honour, but merely as a license for the pleasure of maudlin self-compassion; so he hangs over his griefs, hugs them, nurses them, buries himself in them, as if the sweet agony thereof were to him a glad refuge from the stings of self-reproach, or a dear release from the exercise of manly thought."*

Yet to the last a little of real love is reserved by one heart or two for the shadowy, attractive Richard; the love of a wife who is filled with a piteous sense of her husband's mental and moral effacement, seeing her "fair rose wither," and the love of a groom whose loyalty to his master is associated with loyalty to his master's horse, roan Barbary. This incident of roan Barbary is an invention of the poet. Did Shakespeare intend only a little bit of helpless pathos? Or is there a touch of hidden irony here? A poor spark of affection remains for Richard, but it has been kindled half by Richard, and half by Richard's horse. The fancy of the fallen king disports itself for the last time, and hangs its latest wreath around this incident. Then suddenly comes the darkness. Suddenly the hectic passion of Richard flares; he snatches an axe from a servant, and deals about him deadly

* *Shakespeare: His Life Art and Character*, vol. ii, p. 55.

blows. In another moment he is extinct; the graceful futile existence has ceased.

V

Bolingbroke utters few words in the play of *Richard II*; yet we feel that from the first the chief force centres in him. He possesses every element of power except those which are spontaneous and unconscious. He is dauntless, but his courage is under the control of his judgment; it never becomes a glorious martial rage like that of the Greek Achilles, or like that of the English Henry, Bolingbroke's son. He is ambitious, but his ambition is not an inordinate desire to wreak his will upon the world, and expend a fiery energy like that of *Richard III*; it is an ambition which aims at definite ends, and can be held in reserve until these seem attainable. He is studious to obtain the good graces of nobles and of people, and he succeeds because, wedded to his end, he does not become impatient of the means; but he is wholly lacking in genius of the heart; and therefore he obtains the love of no man. He is indeed formidable; his enemies describe England as:

> A bleeding land,
> Gasping for life under great Bolingbroke;

and he is aware of his strength; but there is in his nature no fund of incalculable strength of which he cannot be aware. All his faculties are well-organized, and help one another; he is embarrassed by no throng of conflicting desires or sympathies. He is resolved to win the throne, and has no personal hostility to the king to divide or waste his energies; only a little of contempt. In the deposition scene he gives as little pain as may be to Richard; he controls and checks Northumberland, who irritates and excites the king by requiring him to read the articles of his accusation. Because Bolingbroke is strong, he is not cruel.* He decides when to augment his power by clemency, and when by severity. Aumerle he can pardon, who will live to fight and fall gallantly for Henry's son at Agincourt. He can

* Mézières, Shakespeare ses Œuvres et ses Critiques, p. 205. Kreyssig, *Vorlesungen über Shakespeare*, vol. i, p. 194 (ed. 1874).

dismiss to a dignified retreat the Bishop, who, loyal to the hereditary principle, had pleaded against Henry's title to the throne. But Bushy, Green, and such like caterpillars of the Commonwealth, Henry has sworn to weed and pluck away. And when he pardons Aumerle he sternly decrees to death his own brother-in-law.

The honour of England he cherished not with passionate devotion, but with a strong considerate care, as though it were his own honour. There is nothing infinite in the character of Henry, but his is a strong finite character. When he has attained the object of his ambition he is still aspiring, but he does not aspire towards anything higher and further than that which he had set before him; his ambition is now to hold firmly that which he has energetically grasped. He tries to control England as he controlled roan Barbary:

> Great Bolingbroke,
> Mounted upon a hot and fiery steed,
> Which his aspiring rider seem'd to know,
> With slow but stately pace kept on his course.

"Even in his policy," Mr Hudson has truly said, "there was much of the breadth and largeness which distinguished the statesman from the politician." He can conceive beforehand with practical imaginative faculty the exigencies of a case, and provide for them. Of Richard's hectic fancy (which must not be mistaken for imagination) Henry has none. Nor does he ever unpack his heart with words. Aiming at things, his words are right and efficient without aiming. In the scene of Richard's deposition, while the king is setting his fancy to work in making arabesques out of all the details of the situation, Bolingbroke does not become impatient. The wound which he inflicts on Richard must of course suppurate. "I thought you had been willing to resign." "Are you contented to resign the crown?" With these brief and decisive sentences Henry calmly urges his point. In a later scene, where Aumerle has flung himself before the king and confessed his treason, while York, who speedily transferred all his loyalty from the deposed prince to his successor, pleads eagerly against his son, and the duchess on her knees implores his pardon, Henry allows the passionate flood to foam about his feet. He has resolved upon his part, and knows that in a little while he can allay this tempest. "Rise up, good aunt," "Good aunt, rise up," "Good aunt, stand up,"—these words, uttered in each pause of the passionate appeal, are all that Henry has at first to say; and then the traitor is forgiven, and a loyal subject gained for ever. "I pardon him as God will pardon me;" "With all my heart I pardon him."

Yet the success of Bolingbroke,—although he succeeded to the full measure of his powers and lost no point of advantage by laxness or self-indulgence—was not a complete achievement. When a little before his death his heart was at last set right with his son's heart, he could confess:

God knows, my son,
By what by-paths and indirect crook'd ways
I met this crown, and I myself know well
How troublesome it sat upon my head.
To thee it shall descend with better quiet,
Better opinion, better confirmation.*

By caution and by boldness he had won the crown, and held it resolutely. But his followers fell away; the turbulent nobles of the north were in revolt, and there was a profound suspicion of the policy of the king. One son had reproduced the character of his father without the larger and finer features of that character. The other he could not understand, failing to discern, almost up to the last, the steadfast hidden loyalty and love of that son. It is hard for the free, spontaneous heart to disclose itself to the deliberate and cautious heart, which yet yearns pathetically for a child's affection. There is something piteously undiscerning in the wish of the father of a *Henry V* that he might have been the father of a Hotspur.

Then, too, his life never knew repose and refreshment. The incessant care and labour of his mind went on day after day,

---

* 2 *Henry IV*, Act. iv, Scene 5. Of the King in this scene, Mr Hudson says well, "Though we have indeed his subtle policy, working out like a ruling passion strong in death, still its workings are suffused with gushes of right feeling, enough to show that he was not all politician; that beneath his close-knit prudence there was a soul of moral sense, a kernel of religion." *Shakespeare*: *His Life, Art, and Characters*, vol. ii, p. 71.

night after night. He has no exultant faith in God, no strong reliance upon principles. Every future contingency must be anticipated and provided for by policy. Henry can never rid himself of cares; can never for an hour let things be, and join in the wholesome laughter and frolic of the world. And accordingly, in spite of his energy and strenuous resolution, seasons of exhaustion and depression necessarily come. Sleep forsakes him; he summons his councillors at midnight; he broods over the rank diseases that grow near the heart of his kingdom. He longs inexpressibly to read the secrets of futurity. He can hardly sustain himself from sinking into discouragement and languor:

> O God! that one might read the book of fate,
> And see the revolution of the times
> Make mountains level, and the continent,
> Weary of solid firmness, melt itself
> Into the sea! and, other times, to see
> The beachy girdle of the ocean
> Too wide for Neptune's hips: how chances mock,
> And changes fill the cup of alteration
> With divers liquors? O, if this were seen,
> The happiest youth, viewing his progress through,
> What perils past, what crosses to ensue,
> Would shut the book, and sit him down and die.

But the thought that such things as these are necessities of human life restores Henry to himself. "I am sworn brother, sweet, to grim Necessity," exclaimed King Richard II to his queen, "And he and I will keep a league till death." Henry does not personify Necessity, and greet it with this romantic display of fraternity; but he admits the inevitable fact, and the fact is something to lay hold of firmly, a support and resting place,—something which reanimates him for exertion:

> Are these things then necessities?
> Then let us meet them like necessities;
> And that same word even now cries out on us:
> They say the Bishop and Northumberland
> Are fifty thousand strong.

His faculties are firm-set and re-organised and go to work once more.

VI

Shakespeare has judged Henry IV and pronounced that his life was not a failure; still it was at best a partial success. Shakespeare saw, and he preceded to show to others, that all which Bolingbroke had attained, and almost incalculably greater possession of good things could be attained more joyously, by nobler means. The unmistakable enthusiasm of the poet about his Henry V has induced critics to believe that in him we find Shakespeare's ideal of manhood. He must certainly be regarded as Shakespeare's ideal of manhood in the sphere of practical achievement,—the hero, and central figure therefore of the historical plays.

The fact has been noticed that with respect to Henry's youthful follies, Shakespeare deviated from all authorities known to have been accessible to him. "An extraordinary conversion was generally thought to have fallen upon the Prince on coming to the crown,—insomuch that the old chroniclers could only account for the change by some miracle of grace or touch of supernatural benediction."* Shakespeare, it would seem, engaged now upon historical matter and not the fantastic substance of a comedy, found something incredible in the sudden transformation of a reckless libertine (the Henry described by Caxton, by Fabyan and others) into a character of majestic force, and large practical wisdom. Rather than reproduce this incredible popular tradition concerning Henry, Shakespeare preferred to attempt the difficult task of exhibiting the Prince as a sharer in the wild frolic of youth, while at the same time he was holding himself prepared for the splendid entrance upon his manhood, and stood really aloof in his inmost being from the unworthy life of his associates.

The change which effected itself in the Prince, as represented by Shakespeare, was no miraculous conversion, but merely the transition from boyhood to adult years, and from unchartered freedom to the solemn responsibilities of a great ruler. We must not suppose that Henry formed a deliberate plan for concealing

* Hudson, *Shakespeare: His Life, Art and Characters*, vol. ii, p. 78. See also C. Knight's *Studies of Shakespeare*, B. iv, chap. ii, p. 164.

the strength and splendour of his character, in order afterwards to flash forth upon men's sight and overwhelm and dazzle them. When he soliloquizes (1 *Henry IV,* Act i, Scene 2), having bid farewell to Poins and Falstaff:

> I know you all, and will awhile uphold
> The unyoked humour of your idleness:
> Yet herein will I imitate the sun,
> Who doth permit the base contagious clouds
> To smother up his beauty from the world,
> That, when he please again to be himself,
> Being wanted, he may be more wonder'd at,
> By breaking through the foul and ugly mists
> Of vapours, that did seem to strangle him.

—when Henry soliloquises thus, we are not to suppose that he was quite as wise and diplomatical as he pleased to represent himself, for the time being, to his own heart and conscience.* The Prince entered heartily and without reserve into the fun and frolic of his Eastcheap life; the vigour and the folly of it were delightful; to be clapped on the back, and shouted for as "Hal," was far better than the doffing of caps and crooking of knees, and delicate, unreal phraseology of the court. But Henry, at the same time, kept himself from subjugation to what was really base. He could truthfully stand before his father (1 *Henry IV,* Act iii, Scene 2), and maintain that his nature was substantially sound and untainted, capable of redeeming itself from all past, superficial dishonour.

Has Shakespeare erred? Or is it not possible to take energetic part in a provisional life, which is known to be provisional, while at the same time a man holds his truest self in reserve for the life that is best, and highest, and most real? May not the very consciousness, indeed, that such a life is provisional, enable one to give oneself away to it, satisfying its demands with scrupulous care, or with full and free enjoyment, as a man could not if it were a life which had any chance of engaging his whole personality, and that finally? Is it possible to adjust two

---

* Kreyssig, *Vorlesungen über Shakespeare* (ed. 1874), vol. i, p. 212. R. Genée, *Shakespeare, sein Leben und seine Werke,* p. 202.

states of being, one temporary and provisional, the other absolute and final, and to pass freely out of one into the other? Precisely because the one is perfect and indestructible, it does not fear the counter-life. May there not have been passages in Shakespeare's own experience which authorised him in his attempt to exhibit the successful adjustment of two apparently incoherent lives?*

The central element in the character of Henry is his noble realisation of fact. To Richard II life was a graceful and shadowy ceremony, containing beautiful and pathetic situations. Henry IV saw in the world a substantial reality, and he resolved to obtain mastery over it by courage and by craft. But while Bolingbroke with his caution and his policy, his address and his ambition, penetrated only a little way among the facts of life, his son, with a true genius for the discovery of the noblest facts, and of all facts, came into relation with the central and vital forces of the universe, so that, instead of constructing a strong but careful life for himself, life breathed through him, and blossomed into a glorious enthusiasm of existence. And therefore from all that was unreal, and from all exaggerated egoism, Henry was absolutely delivered. A man who firmly holds, or rather is held by the beneficent forces of the world, whose feet are upon a rock, and whose goings are established, may with confidence abandon much of the prudence, and many of the artificial proprieties of the world. For every unreality Henry exhibits a sovereign disregard—for unreal manners, unreal glory, unreal heroism, unreal piety, unreal warfare, unreal love. The plain fact is so precious it needs no ornament.

From the coldness, the caution, the convention of his father's court (an atmosphere which suited well the temperament of John of Lancaster), Henry escapes to the teeming vitality of the

---

* Rümelin, who argues that Shakespeare wrote to please the *jeunesse dorée* of the period, suggests that the character of the Prince was drawn from that of the Earl of Southampton! The originals of many of Shakespeare's historical personages, Rümelin supposes, sat upon the side-seats of the stage, and are, alas! irrecoverably lost. (With such conjectures must "realist" criticism buttress up its case!) *Shakespeare-Studien* (ed. 1874), p. 127.

London streets, and the tavern where Falstaff is monarch. There, among ostlers, and carriers, and drawers, and merchants, and pilgrims, and loud robustious women, he at least has freedom and frolic. "If it be a sin to covet honour," Henry declares, "I am the most offending soul alive." But the honour that Henry covets is not that which Hotspur is ambitious after:

> By heaven, methinks it were an easy leap
> To pluck bright honour from the pale-faced moon.*

The honour that Henry covets is the achievement of great deeds, not the words of men which vibrate around such deeds. Falstaff, the despiser of honour, labours across the field bearing the body of the fallen Hotspur, the impassioned pursuer of glory, and in his fashion of splendid imposture or stupendous joke, the fat knight claims credit for the achievement of the day's victory. Henry is not concerned on this occasion to put the old sinner to shame. To have added to the deeds of the world a glorious deed is itself the only honour that Henry seeks. Nor is his heroic greatness inconsistent with the admission of very humble incidents of humanity:

> *Prince.* Doth it not show vilely in me to desire small beer?
>
> *Point.* Why, a prince should not be so loosely studied as to remember so weak a composition.
>
> *Prince.* Belike, then, my appetite was not princely got; for by my troth I do now remember the poor creature, small beer. But indeed these humble considerations make me out of love with my greatness.†

Henry with his lank frame, and vigorous muscle (the opposite of the Danish Prince who is "fat and scant of breath"),

---

* 1 *Henry IV*, Act i, Scene 3. Kreyssig contrasts Hotspur's passion for honour with Falstaff's indifference to it. "Can honour set to a leg or an arm? no: or take away the grief of a wound? no." Henry in this matter is equally remote from Falstaff and from Hotspur. *Vorlesungen über Shakespeare*, vol. i, pp. 244-45.

† Jack Cade, in his aspiration after greatness, announces—"I will make it felony to drink small beer. [...] when I am king, as king I will be." Henry's desire would seem then to be inexpressibly humiliating.

is actually wearied to excess and thirsty, and he is by no means afraid to confess the fact; his appetite at least has not been pampered. "Before God, Kate," such is Henry's fashion of wooing, "I cannot look greenly, nor gasp out my eloquence, nor I have no cunning in protestation; only downright oaths, which I never use till urged, nor never break for urging [...]. I speak to thee plain soldier; if thou canst love me for this take me; if not, to say to thee that I shall die is true; but for thy love, by the Lord, no; yet I love thee too."

And as in his love there is a certain substantial homeliness and heartiness, so is there also in his piety. He is not harassed like his son, the saintly Henry, with refinements of scrupulosity, the disease of an irritable conscience, which is delivered from its irritability by no active pursuit of noble ends. Henry has done what is right; he has tried to repair his father's faults; he has built "two chantries, where the sad and solemn priests still sing for Richard's soul." He has done his part by God and man, will not God in like manner stand by him and perform what belongs to God? Henry's freedom from egoism, his modesty his integrity, his joyous humour, his practical piety, his habit of judging things by natural and not artificial standards; all these are various developments of the central element of his character, his noble realisation of fact.

But his realisation of fact produces something more than this integrity, this homely honesty of nature. It breathes through him an enthusiasm which would be intense if it were not so massive. Through his union with the vital strength of the world, he becomes one of the world's most glorious and beneficent forces. From the plain and mirth-creating comrade of his fellow-soldiers he rises into the genius of impassioned battle. From the modest and quiet adviser with his counsellors and prelates, he is transformed, when the occasion requires it, into the terrible administrator of justice. When Henry takes from his father's pillow the crown, and places it upon his own head, the deed is done with no fluttering rapture of attainment. He has entered gravely upon his manhood. He has made very real to himself the long, careful, and joyless life of the father who had won for him this "golden care." His heart is full of tenderness for this sad father, to whom he had been able to bring so little happiness. But now he takes his due, the crown, and the world's whole force shall not wrest it from him:

> Thy due from me
> Is tears and heavy sorrows of the blood,
> Which nature, love, and filial tenderness,
> Shall, O dear father, pay thee plenteously:
> My due from thee is this imperial crown,
> Which, as immediate from thy place and blood,
> Derives itself to me. Lo, here it sits,
> Which God shall guard; and put the world's whole strength
> Into one giant arm, it shall not force
> This lineal honour from me.

Here is no aesthetic feeling for the "situation," only the profoundest and noblest entrance into the fact.

The same noble and disinterested loyalty to the truth of things renders it easy, natural, and indeed inevitable that Henry should confirm in his office the Chief Justice who had formerly executed the law against himself, and equally inevitable that he should disengage himself absolutely from Falstaff and the associates of his provisional life of careless frolic. To such a life an end must come; and as no terms of half-acquaintance are possible with the fat Knight, exorbitant in good fellowship as he is, and inexhaustible in resources, Henry must become to Falstaff an absolute stranger:

> I know thee not, old man: fall to thy prayers:
> How ill white hairs become a fool and jester.

Henry has been stern to his former self, and turned him away for ever; therefore he can be stern to Falstaff. There is no faltering. But at an enforced distance of ten miles from his person (for the fascination of Falstaff can hardly weave a bridge across that interval) Falstaff shall be sufficiently provided for:

> For competence of life I will allow you
> That lack of means enforce you not to evil:
> And as we hear you do reform yourselves,

We will, according to your strengths and qualities,
Give you advancement.*

Shortly before the English army sets sail for France the treason of Cambridge, Scroop, and Grey is disclosed to the King. He does not betray his acquaintance with their designs. Surrounded by traitors, he boldly enters his council chamber at Southampton (the wind is sitting fair, and but one deed remains to do before they go aboard). On the preceding day a man was arrested who had railed against the person of the King. Henry gives orders that he be set at liberty:

We consider
It was excess of wine that set him on;
And on his more advice we pardon him.

But Scroop, and Grey, and Cambridge interpose. It would be true mercy, they insist, to punish such an offender. And then, when they have unawares brought themselves within the range of justice, Henry unfolds their guilt. The wrath of Henry has in it some of that awfulness and terror suggested by the apocalyptic reference to "the wrath of the Lamb." It is the more terrible because it transcends all egoistic feeling. What fills the king with indignation is not so much that his life should have been conspired against by men on whom his bounty has been bestowed without measure, as that they should have revolted against the loyalty of man, weakened the bonds of fellowship, and lowered the high tradition of humanity:

O how hast thou with jealousy infected
The sweetness of affiance! Show men dutiful?
Why so didst thou: seem they grave and learned?
Why so didst thou: come they of noble family?
Why so didst thou: seem they religious?
Why so didst thou: or are they spare in diet,
Free from gross passion, or of mirth or anger,

---

* It is noteworthy that although we meet Sir John so often in 2 *Henry IV*, we find the Prince only on a single occasion in his company: and it would be beyond human nature to deny himself the delight and edification of such a spectacle as the fat Knight cuddling and kissing Doll Tearsheet: Henry *must* go.

Constant in spirit, not swerving with the blood,
Garnish'd and deck'd in modest complement,
Not working with the eye without the ear,
And but in purged judgement trusting neither?
Such and so finely bolted didst thou seem:
And thus thy fall hath left a kind of blot
To mark the full-fraught man and best indued
With some suspicion. I will weep for thee;
For this revolt of thine, methinks, is like
Another fall of man.

No wonder that the terrible moral insistence of these words can subdue consciences made of penetrable stuff; no wonder that such an awful discovery of high realities of life should call forth the loyalty that lurked within a traitor's heart. But though tears escape Henry he cannot relent:

Touching our person seek we no revenge;
But we our kingdom's safety must so tender,
Whose ruin you have sought, that to her laws
We do deliver you. Get you therefore hence,
Poor miserable wretches, to your death,
The taste whereof God of his mercy give
You patience to endure, and true repentance
Of all your dear offences!

And having vindicated the justice of God, and purged his country of treason, Henry sets his face to France with the light of splendid achievement in his eyes.

On the night before the great battle, Henry moves among his soldiers, and passes disguised from sentinel to sentinel. He is not, like his father, exhausted and outworn by the careful construction of a life. If an hour of depression comes upon him, he yet is strong, because he can look through his depression to a strength and virtue outside of and beyond himself. Joy may ebb with him or rise, as it will; the current of his inmost being is fed by a source that springs from the hard rock of life, and is no tidal flow. He accepts his weakness and his weariness as part of the surrender of ease and strength and self which he makes on behalf of England. With a touch of his old love of frolic he enters on the quarrel with Williams, and exchanges gages with the soldier. When morning dawns he looks freshly, and "overbears attaint," with cheerful semblance and sweet majesty:

> A largess universal like the sun
> His liberal eye doth give to every one,
> Thawing cold fear.

With a prayer to God he sets to rights the heavenward side of his nature, and there leaves it. In the battle Henry does not, in the manner of his politic father, send into the field a number of counterfeit Kings to attract away from himself the centre of the war. There is no stratagem at Agincourt; it is "plain shock and even play of battle." If Henry for a moment ceases to be the skilful wielder of resolute strength, it is only when he rises into the genius of the rage of battle:

> I was not angry since I came to France
> Until this instant. Take a trumpet, herald;
> Ride thou unto the horsemen on yon hill:
> If they will fight with us, bid them come down,
> Or void the field; they do offend our sight:
> If they do neither we will come to them,
> And make them skirr away as swift as stones
> Enforced from the old Assyrian slings;
> Besides we'll cut the throats of those we have,
> And not a man of them that we shall take
> Shall taste our mercy.

It is in harmony with the spirit of the play, and with the character of Henry that it should close with no ostentatious heroics, but with the half jocular, whole earnest wooing of the French princess by the English king. With a touch of irony to which one of the critics of the play has called attention,* we are furnished with a hint as to the events which must follow Henry's glorious reign. "Shall not thou and I," exclaims the king in his unconventional manner of winning a bride, "Shall not thou and I, between Saint Denis and Saint George, compound a boy, half

* H.N. Hudson.

French, half English, that shall go to Constantinople and take the Turk by the beard." This boy destined to go to Constantinople and confront the Turk was the helpless Henry the Sixth.

The historical plays are documents written all over with facts about Shakespeare. Some of these facts are now discernible. We have learned something about Shakespeare's convictions as to how the noblest practical success in life may be achieved. We know what Shakespeare would have tried to become himself if there had not been a side of his character which acknowledged closer affinity with Hamlet than with Henry. We can in some measure infer how Shakespeare would endeavour to control, and in what directions he would endeavour to reinforce his own nature while in pursuit of a practical mastery over events and things.

5

Othello, *Macbeth* and *Lear*

If Shakespeare had died at the age of forty, it might have been said, "The world has lost much, but the world's chief poet could hardly have created anything more wonderful than Hamlet." But after *Hamlet* came *King Lear*. *Hamlet* was, in fact, only the point of departure in Shakespeare's immense and final sweep of mind,—that in which he endeavoured to include and comprehend life for the first time adequately. Through *Hamlet*—perhaps also through events in the poet's personal history, which tested his will as Hamlet's will was tested—Shakespeare had been reached and touched by the shadow of some of the deep mysteries of human existence. Somehow a relation between his soul and the dark and terrible forces of the world was established, and to escape from a thorough investigation and sounding of the depths of life was no longer possible. Shakespeare had by this time mastered the world from a practical point of view. He was a prosperous and wealthy man. He had completed his English historical plays, which are concerned with this practical mastery of the world. But all the more because he had resolved his material difficulties was his mind open to the profounder spiritual problems of life. Having completed *Henry V*, for a short period he yielded his imagination and his heart to the brightest and most exuberant enjoyment. Around the year 1600 are grouped some of the most mirthful comedies that Shakespeare ever wrote. Then, a little later, as soon as *Hamlet* is completed, all changes. From 1604 to 1610 a show of tragic figures, like the kings who passed before Macbeth, filled the vision of Shakespeare; until at last the desperate image of Timon rose before him; when, as though unable to endure or to conceive a more lamentable ruin of man, he turned for relief to the pastoral loves of Prince Florizel and Perdita; and as soon as the tone of his mind was restored, gave expression to its ultimate mood of grave serenity in *The Tempest*: and so ended.

During these years the imaginative fervour of Shakespeare was at its highest, and sustained itself without abatement. There was no feverish excitement in his energy, and there was no pause. In some of his earlier years of authorship (if the generally received chronology be accepted) two or even three plays were produced within a twelve-month, of which this or that was afterwards acknowledged by its author to be a hasty piece of work, yet of sufficient substance and merit to deserve re-handling. During a certain brief season it may have been that Shakespeare altogether ceased to write for the stage. But now in unbroken series, year by year, one great tragedy succeeds another. Having created *Othello* surely the eye of a poet's mind would demand quietude, passive acceptance of some calm beauty, a period of restoration. But *Othello* is pursued by *Lear*, *Lear* by *Macbeth*, *Macbeth* by *Antony and Cleopatra*, *Antony and Cleopatra* by *Coriolanus*. It is evident that the artist was now completely roused. The impetus of his advance continued, and carried him without effort on from subject to subject. He could not put aside his stupendous task; neither would he accomplish any part of it imperfectly. In these years the utmost imaginative susceptibility is united with the utmost self-control. Every portion of his being is at length engaged in the magnificent effort. At first in the career of most artists a portion of their nature holds aloof from art, and is ready for application to other service. They have a poetical side, and a side which is prosaic. Gradually, as they advance towards maturity, faculty after faculty is brought into fruitful relation with the art-instinct, until at length the entire nature of the artist is fused in one, and his work becomes the expression of a complete personality. This period had now arrived for Shakespeare. In the great tragedies passion and thought, humour and pathos, severity and tenderness, knowledge and guess, are all accepted as workers together with the imagination.

Tragedy as conceived by Shakespeare is concerned with the ruin or the restoration of the soul, and of the life of men. In other words its subject is the struggle of good and evil in the world. This strikes down upon the roots of things. The comedies of Shakespeare had, in comparison, played upon the surface of life. The Histories, though very earnest, had not dealt with the deeper mysteries of being. *Henry V*, the ideal figure of the historical plays, has a real and firm grasp of the actual world; he has his religion, and he has his passion of love; but both are positive, practical, and limited. No more can his religion than his love ever embarrass Henry in his joyous mastery over men and things. His soldier-like piety and large, incurious trust in God suffice to resolve all questions with regard to that dark outlying region which surrounds the knowable and the practicable. With a devout optimism, Henry perceives there is "some soul of goodness in things evil," and he proceeds to confirm this principle by the very substantial and business-like instance that their bad neighbours, the French, had made his soldiers early stirrers. But such devout optimism was absolutely without avail for the spiritual needs of the man who had conceived Hamlet "To say to thee that I shall die" declares King Henry to Katharine, "is true; but for thy love,—by the Lord, no." Yet Shakespeare had discovered that to die for love may be the highest need of a life under certain extreme conditions. Juliet had died for love; Romeo had died for love; and in so doing they had fulfilled and accomplished their lives. Therefore this love of Henry is tested by Shakespeare, and declared to be a passion with limitation, serviceable for useful ends of marriage, and for the producing of children; but not that devotion of soul to soul which does not recognise the limitations of space or of time. "There is some soul of goodness in things evil," declares King Henry. And as comment upon such devout optimism, Shakespeare produces Goneril and Regan, Iago, and the Witches in *Macbeth*. Now, in the tragedies, Shakespeare has flung himself abroad upon the dim sea which moans around our little solid sphere of the known. Such easy and pious answers to the riddles of the world as constituted the working faith of a *Henry V* belong to a smaller and safer world of thought, feeling, and action; not to this.

There are certain problems which Shakespeare at once pronounces insoluble. He does not, like Milton, propose to give any account of the origin of evil. He does not, like Dante, pursue the soul of man through circles of unending torture, or spheres made radiant by the eternal presence of God. Satan in Shakespeare's poems does not come voyaging on gigantic vans across Chaos to find the earth. No great deliverer of mankind descends from the heavens. Here, upon the earth, evil *is*—such was Shakespeare's declaration in the most emphatic accent. Iago actually exists. There is also in the earth a sacred passion of deliverance, a pure redeeming ardour. Cordelia exists. This Shakespeare can tell for certain. But how Iago can be, and why Cordelia lies strangled across the breast of Lear—are these questions which you go on to ask? Something has been already said of the severity of Shakespeare. It is a portion of his severity to decline all answers to such questions as these. Is Ignorance painful? Well, then, it is painful. Little solutions of your large difficulties can readily be obtained from priest or *philosophe*. Shakespeare prefers to let you remain in the solemn presence of a mystery. He does not invite you into his little church or his little library brilliantly illuminated by philosophical or theological rushlights. You remain in the darkness. But you remain in the vital air. And the great night is overhead.

Critics of the last century were much exercised in mind about Shakespeare's violations of the rule of poetical justice. Dr Johnson, with his sturdy British morality, could not endure to read the last scenes of *King Lear*, and declared in favour of Nahum Tate's improvement on Shakespeare's play, according to which Edgar makes love to Cordelia, and she retires in the end "with victory and felicity." To die is so exceedingly uncomfortable; to live, and be a happy wife is so eminently satisfactory. Shakespeare's morality is somewhat more stern than that of the great moralist. Shakespeare introduces into the world no little ethical code. Such a little ethical code would flutter away in tatters across the tempest and the night of Lear's agony. But Shakespeare discovers the supreme fact,—that the moral world stands in sovereign independence of the world of the senses.* Cordelia lies upon the breast of Lear. "Upon such sacrifices the gods themselves throw incense." Cordelia, forgetting her father, might have returned to France, and have lived prosperously. But then *Cordelia,* the pure zeal of redeeming ardour, would indeed have ceased to be. Now she has fulfilled the end of her being. It is not so hard to die. Cordelia had accepted her lot with fortitude:

We are not the first
Who with best meaning have incurred the worst.

And for as the earth is made more beautiful by her life and by her death. That which satisfies our heart, that which brings us strength and consolation, is not that by happy concurrence of circumstances Cordelia should succeed in her enterprise, but merely that Cordelia existed. Lesser happiness can be dispensed with if we are granted the joy of the presence of beautiful, heroic souls. Cordelia has strengthened the bonds of humanity; she has enriched the tradition of human goodness. It is better for each of us to breathe because she has been a woman.

Thus although there was no possibility for Shakespeare to become a facile optimist, bearing jauntily a banner with the device *Whatever is, is best,* and singing to some tune secular or sacred the perfections of this the best of all possible worlds, he is equally far removed from despair. The absolute despair as represented by Shakespeare, that of Timon,—is despair of human virtue. And to such despair of human virtue Shakespeare never yielded himself. At the entrance to his long series of tragic writings stands the figure of Isabel, in Lucio's eyes "a thing ensky'd and sainted" in that Vienna where:

---

* Kreyssig describes Shakespeare's ethics as essentially identical with the ethics of Kant: "Von allen Tragödien Shakespeare's, ja von allen uns bekannten Tragödien alter und neuer Zeit scheint 'Lear' uns am vollständigsten die Bezeichnung, 'erhaben,' im Schiller'schen Sinne zu verdienen, insofern sie mit ganz besonderem Nachdruck die unbedingte souveräne Unabhängigkeit der sittlichen Welt von der der Sinne zur Anschauung bringt: die Tragödie des kategorischen Imperativ's von dem grössten germanischen Dichter geschaut und geschaffen, zwei Jahrhunderte ehe der grösste germanische Denker sein Gesetz wissenschaftlich begründete." *Shakespeare-Fragen,* p. 128.

> Corruption boils and bubbles
> Till it o'er-run the stew.

At the close stand Prospero and Hermione. The ills of life had sunk deep into Hamlet's soul:

> The oppressor's wrong, the proud man's contumely,
> The pangs of despised love, the law's delay,
> The insolence of office and the spurns
> That patient merit of the unworthy takes.

But presently by his side stood human virtue—Horatio, "a man that Fortune buffets and rewards"—these very ills which Hamlet enumerated—"had ta'en with equal thanks." Iago is a devouring gulf of evil "more fell than anguish, hunger, or the sea." But over against his malignity and cold impureness rises Desdemona, who cannot extend her imagination so far as to credit any breach of wifely faith or modesty in any woman. Goneril and Regan dismiss the old man into the tempest and the night; but Cordelia restores him with the warmth of her bosom.

This period during which Shakespeare was engaged upon his great tragedies was not, as it has been sometimes represented, a period of depression and of gloom in Shakespeare's spiritual progress. True, he was now sounding the depths of evil as he had never sounded them before. But his faith in goodness had never been so strong and sure. Hitherto it had not been thoroughly tested. In the over-strained loyalty of Valentine to his unworthy friend there is something fantastic and unreal. The graver friendship of Horatio for Hamlet is deeper and more genuine. There is gallantry in Portia's rescue of her husband's friend from death; but the devotion of Cordelia nourishes itself from springs of strength which lie farther down among the roots of things. Now, with every fresh discovery of crime Shakespeare made discovery of virtue which cannot suffer defeat. The knowledge of evil and of good grow together. While Shakespeare moved gaily upon the surface of life, it was the play of intellect that stirred within him the liveliest sense of pleasure. The bright speech and unsubduable mirth, not disjoined from common sense and goodness of heart of a

Rosalind or a Beatrice, filled him with a sense of quickened existence. Now that he had come to comprehend more of the sorrow and more of the evil of the earth—treachery, ingratitude, cruelty, lust—Shakespeare found perhaps less to delight him in mere brightness of intellect; he certainly gave his heart away with more fervour of loyalty to human goodness, to fortitude, purity of heart, self-surrender, self-mastery—to every noble expression of character. Such mellowing and enriching of Shakespeare's nature could not have proceeded during a period in which his moral being was in confusion, and heaven and earth seemed to lie chaotically around him. Were his delight in man and woman, his faith and joy in human goodness, stained with sullenness and ignoble resentment, could he have discovered Horatio and Kent, Cordelia and Desdemona? No. If the sense of wrong sank deep into his soul, if life became harder and more grave, yet he surmounted all sense of personal wrong, and while life grew more severe, it grew more beautiful.

I

The tragedy of *Othello* is the tragedy of a free and lordly creature taken in the toils, and writhing to death. In one of his sonnets, Shakespeare has spoken of

> Some fierce thing replete with too much rage
> Whose strength's abundance weakens his own heart.

Such a fierce thing, made weak by his very strength, is Othello. There is a barbaresque grandeur and simplicity about the movements of his soul. He sees things with a large and generous eye, not prying into the curious or the occult. He is a liberal accepter of life, and with a careless magnificence wears about him the ornament of strange experience; memories of

> Antres vast, and deserts idle,
> Rough quarries, rocks, and hills whose heads touch heaven,

memories of "disastrous chances, of moving accidents by flood and field." There is something of grand innocence in his loyalty to Venice, by which Mr Browning was not unaffected when he conceived his Moorish commander, Luria. Othello, a stranger, with tawny skin and fierce traditions in his blood, is fascinated by the grave senate, the nobly ordered life (possessing a certain rich colouring of its own), and the astute intelligence of the City of the Sea. At his last moment, through the blinding sandstorm of his own passion, this feeling of disinterested loyalty recurs to Othello, and brings him a moment's joy and pride. His history has been, indeed, a calamitous mistake; like the base Indian, he has thrown away "a pearl richer than all his tribe." But there is one fact with which the remembrance of him may go down to men, one fact which will rescue from complete deformity and absurd unreason the story of Othello:

> Set you down this;
> And say, besides, that in Aleppo once,
> Where a malignant and a turban'd Turk
> Beat a Venetian, and traduc'd the State,
> I took by the throat the circumcised dog,
> And smote him, thus.

With this loyalty to Venice, there is also an instinctive turning towards the barbaric glory which he has surrendered. He is the child of royal ancestry: "I fetch my life and being from men of royal siege." All the more joyous on this account it is to devote himself to the service of the State. And thus Othello has reached manhood, and passed on to middle life.

Then in the house of Brabantio this simple and magnificent nature found his fate. Desdemona, moving to and fro at her house-affairs, or listening with grave wonder, and eager, restrained sympathy to the story of his adventurous life, became to him, at first in an unconscious way, the type of beauty, gentleness, repose, and tender womanhood. And Desdemona, in her turn, brought up amidst the refinements and ceremonies of Venetian life, watching each day the same gondolas glide by, hearing her father's talk of some little new law of the Duke, found in the Moor strangeness and splendour of strong manhood, heroic simplicity, the charm of one who had suffered in solitude, and on whose history compassion might be lavished. Thus, while Brutus and Portia were indissolubly bound together by their likeness, Desdemona and Othello were mutually attracted by the wonder and grace of unlikeness. In the love of each there was a romantic element; and romance is not the highest form of the service which imagination renders to love. For romance disguises certain facts, or sees them, as it were, through a luminous mist; but the highest service which the imagination can render to the heart is the discovery of every fact, the hard and bare as well as the beautiful; and, to effect this, like a clear north wind it blows all mists away. There was a certain side of Othello's nature which it were well that Desdemona had seen, though she trembled.

But if Desdemona loves not with the most instructed heart, she yet loves purely and with tender devotion. And because her love was so entirely that of the heart, and of the imagination, Desdemona felt the tawny face, and the mature years, and half-barbaric origin of Othello, only as dim under-chords enriching the harmonies of her love. The whole current of her being, ordinarily so easy and tranquil, hurried forward with what to herself seemed "downright violence," to unite itself with the inmost being of the Moor:

> That I did love the Moor to live with him,
> My downright violence and storm of fortunes
> May trumpet to the world; my heart's subdued
> Even to the very quality of my lord;
> I saw Othello's visage in his mind,
> And to his honours and his valiant parts
> Did I my soul and fortunes consecrate.

Hazlitt has observed truly, "The extravagance of her resolutions, the pertinacity of her affections, may be said to arise out of the gentleness of her nature. They imply an unreserved reliance on the purity of her own intentions, and entire surrender of her fears to her love, a knitting of herself, heart and soul, to the fate of another."* And it is this being, who is to Othello "a wonder, and a beauty, and a terror,"

> A gentle tone
> Amid rude voices,—a beloved light,
> A solitude, a refuge, a delight,

it is this being whom he must hereafter cast away and trample under foot,—

* *Characters of Shakespeare's Plays*, by W. Hazlitt, p. 52, second edition.

O thou weed
Who art so lovely fair, and smell'st so sweet
That the sense aches at thee, would thou had'st
ne'er been born!

Portia was to Brutus the ideal of all he would fain become himself; the attraction was that of identical qualities: "O ye gods, render me worthy of this noble wife!" and Portia could come to Brutus and urge upon him her right of sharing in all that concerned him. Between Portia and Brutus, therefore, no errors of the heart were possible. But to Desdemona her husband was her lord, a being to be worshipped and served, and in his gentler mood to be played with, and graciously be contradicted and caressed. And Othello, for his part, has a care to stand between his gentle wife and the rough vexations, which beset himself. When roused at night by the brawl she appears in the streets, the Moor is doubly indignant with the offenders, because they have troubled her repose, and with affectionate force he turns her back from enquiring into what had caused him disturbance:

Look, if my gentle love be not raised up!
I'll make thee an example.
Des. What's the matter?
Oth. All's well now, sweeting; come away to bed.

The nature of Othello is free and open; he looks on men with a gaze too large and royal to suspect them of malignity and fraud; he is a man "not easily jealous":

My noble Moor
Is true of mind, and made of no such baseness
As jealous creatures are.

He has, however, a sense of his own inefficiency in dealing with the complex and subtle conditions of life in his adopted country. Where all is plain and broad, he relies upon his own judgment and energy. He is a master of simple, commanding action. When, upon the night of Desdemona's departure from her father's house, Brabantio and the officers with torches and weapons meet him, and a tumult seems inevitable, Othello subdues it with the untroubled, large validity of his will:

> Keep up your bright swords, for the dew will rust them.

But for curious inquiry into complex facts he has no faculty; he loses his bearings; "being wrought upon" he is "perplexed in the extreme." Then, too, his hot Mauritanian blood mounts quickly to the point of boiling. If he be infected, the poison hurries through his veins, and he rages in his agony.

Here upon the one side is material for a future catastrophe. And on the other, there is Desdemona's timidity. When she could stand by Othello's side, Desdemona was able to confront her father, and in presence of the Duke and magnificoes, declare that she would not return to the home she had abandoned. But during Othello's courtship Desdemona had shrunk from any speech upon this matter with Brabantio, and by innocent reserves and little dissemblings had kept him in ignorance of this great event in her history.* The Moor had moved her imagination by his strange nobility, his exotic grandeur. But how if afterwards her imagination be excited by some strange terror about her husband? What will her refined feminine accomplishments avail her then—her delicacy with her needle, the admirable music with which she "will sing the savageness out of a bear":

> I fear you, for you are fatal then,
> When your eyes roll so.

The handkerchief which she has lost becomes terrible to her, when Othello with oriental rapture into the marvellous describes its virtue:

> There's magic in the web of it:
> A sibyl that had number'd in the world
> The sun to course two hundred compasses,
> In her prophetic fury sew'd the work;
> The worms were hallow'd that did breed the silk,

---

* A circumstance which Iago afterwards turns to account against the peace of Othello's mind:

> She did deceive her father marrying you;
> And when she seem'd to shake and fear your looks,
> She loved them most.
> *Oth.* And so she did.

And it was dyed in mummy which the skilful
Conserved of maidens' hearts.

For Desdemona, with her smooth, intelligible girl's life in Venice, having at largest its little pathetic romance of her maid Barbara, with her song of "Willow," here flowed in romance too stupendous, too torrid, and alien to be other than dreadful. Shall we wonder that in her disturbance of mind she trembles to declare to her husband that this talisman could not be found. Underneath the momentary, superficial falsehood remains the constancy and fidelity of her heart; through alarm, and shock, and surprise, and awful alteration of the world, her heart never swerves from loyalty to her husband. If she had deceived Brabantio, as in his anger he declares, and if in this matter of the handkerchief she had faltered from the truth, Desdemona atones for these unveracities; not by acquisition of a confident candour,—such courageous dealing with difficulties was impossible for Desdemona,—but by one more falsehood, the sacred lie which is murmured by her lips as they grow for ever silent:

Emelia. O, who hath done this deed?
Des. Nobody; I myself; farewell;
Commend me to my kind lord; O, farewell.*

* In 1830, in period of full revolution in matters of dramatic art at Paris, the Othello translated and prefaced by Alfred de Vigny was acted at the Théâtre Français. The Duc de Broglie on this occasion published in the *Revue française* a remarkable article (reprinted by M. Guizot in his Shakespeare et son Temps, pp. 264-343) on the State of Dramatic Art in France. Of these last words of Desdemona, as delivered by Mlle. Mars, the Duc de Broglie writes: Nous devons le déclarer; l'effet de ce mot a été nul,—et franchement nous nous étions toujours douté qu'il en devait arriver ainsi [...]. Depuis le jour de son mariage Desdémona s'est considérée comme la propriété d'Othello, comme quelque chose dont Othello est le maitre d'user et d'abuser, comme une esclave qu'il peut battre ou tuer s'il lui en prend fantaisie; comment viendrait-elle à penser tout-à-coup qu' Othello coure aucun risque à propos d'elle, ni qu'il soit nécessaire de le mettre à l'abri d'une poursuite criminelle?" The criticism is more curious than just; but the recorded fact is interesting. See on the feeling towards Shakespeare in France at the time of this representation of Othello, "Histoire de l'Influence de Shakespeare sur le Théâtre Français (Septième Phase) par Albert Lacroix." (Bruxelles, 1856.)

If the same unknowable force which manifests itself through man, manifests itself likewise through the animal world, we might suppose that there were some special affinities between the soul of Othello, and the lion of his ancestral desert. Assuredly the same malignant power that lurks in the eye and that fills with venom the fang of the serpent would seem to have brought into existence Iago. "It is the strength of the base element that is so dreadful in the serpent; it is the very omnipotence of the earth [...]. It scarcely breathes with its one lung (the other shrivelled and abortive); it is passive to the sun and shade, and is cold or hot like a stone; yet 'it can outclimb the monkey, outswim the fish, outleap the zebra, outwrestle the athlete and crush the tiger.' It is a divine hieroglyph of the demoniac power of the earth,—of the entire earthly nature."* Such is the serpent Iago.

In the last scene of the play Othello calls on Cassio (for he cannot himself approach the horror) to interrogate Iago respecting the motives of his malignant crime:

> Will you, I pray, demand that demi-devil
> Why he hath thus ensnared my soul and body?

And Iago forecloses all such enquiry with the words,— they are the last words that he utters:

> Demand me nothing: what you know you know:
> From this time forth I never will speak word.

Shakespeare would have us believe that as there is a passion of goodness with no motive but goodness itself, so there is also a dreadful capacity in the soul for devotion to evil independently of motives, or out of all proportion to such motives, as may exist.† Iago is the absolute infidel; for he is devoid of all faith in

* Ruskin, "The Queen of the Air," pp. 83-84. The words quoted by Mr Ruskin are those of Mr Richard Owen.

† For a discussion of the motives of Iago, see Hebler "Aufsätze über Shakespeare" (Bern, 1865), pp. 42-60. The Duc de Broglie, in the article quoted already, endeavours to show that the character of Iago is incoherent. "Qu'est-ce qu' Iago? Est-ce le malin esprit ou du moins son représentant sur la terre? Othello a-t-il raison quand il le regarde aux pieds pour voir s'il ne les aurait pas fourchus? [...] Alors pourquoi donner à Iago des motivs humains et intéressés? Pourquoi nous montrer en lui

beauty and in virtue. Timon disbelieves, but he becomes desperate and abandons life. Iago finds it right and natural to live in a world, in which all men are knaves or fools, and all women are that which Desdemona is unable to name.

Together with everything beautiful, everything noble, there inevitably exists a gross element of the earth. It is upon this gross element alone that Iago battens, and he can discover it everywhere by denying and dismissing all that transforms, purifies and ennobles it. Othello with his heroic simplicity and royalty of soul

> Will as tenderly be led by the nose
> As asses are.

Cassio, who is full of chivalric enthusiasm for his great leader and the beautiful bride whom he has won, is to Iago "a knave very voluble; no further conscionable than in putting on the mere form of civil and humane feeling, for the better compassing of his salt and most hidden loose affection." Desdemona, exclaims Roderigo, is "full of most blessed condition." *Iago.* "Blessed fig's-end! the wine she drinks is made of grapes: if she had been blessed she would never have loved the Moor. Blessed pudding! Didst thou not see her paddle with the palm of his hand? Didst not mark that?" The Moor has inflamed her imagination with "bragging and telling her fantastical lies." Love "is merely a lust of the blood and a permission of the will."

une basse cupidité, le ressentiment d'une injure faite à son honneur; l'envie d'un poste plus élevé que le sien? [...] Ces passions de bas aloi détruisent tout le fantastique du rôle; le démon n'a ni humeur ni honneur; il n'a ni rancune, ni colére, ni convoitise; c'est un personnage désintéressé: il fait le mal parce que le mal est le mal, et qu'il est, lui, le malin. Iago est-il au contraire, comme il s'en fait gloire, le parfait égoiste, l'homme qui sait, au suprême degré s'aimer lui-méme, l'être qui sait subordonner hiérarchiquement ses désirs, selon leur degré d'importance, et disposer ensuite ses actions de manière à tendre invariablement à sa plus haute satisfaction, coûte que coûte à autrui, sans scrupule, sans remords, et aussi sans se laisser détourner par des velléités d'un ordre inférieur? Alors pourquoi poursuit-il en même temps trois ou quatre buts distincts, et d'une importance pour lui très inégale? [...] Pourquoi surtout prodigue-t-il, dans chaque occasion, cent fois plus de méchanceté que le besoin de la circonstance ne le comporte?" Reprinted in Guizot's "Shakespeare et son Temps," pp. 322-23.

Virtue is "a fig! 'tis in ourselves that we are thus or thus." "O, I have lost my reputation I" Cassio cries, "I have lost the immortal part of myself, and what remains is bestial. My reputation, Iago, my reputation." *Iago*. "As I am an honest man, I thought you had received some bodily wound." All this is the earthiness of the serpent; the dull eye which quickens only to fascinate and to strike; the muddy skin, discoloured with foul blotches; and the dust, which is the serpent's meat. This cold malignant power, passionless and intellectually sensual,—the soul itself having become more animal than the body can ever be,—is incarnated in the person of a man still young. Iago has reached the age of twenty-eight. And he would pass for a merry knave. While enticing Cassio to his ruin he entertains the company with clattering song:

> And let me the canakin clink, clink!
> And let me the canakin clink.

It is the grin of a death's head, the mirth of a ghoul.*

These are the chief forces, and the play of these forces constitutes the tragedy. Since Coleridge made the remark, all critics of Othello are constrained to repeat after him that the passion of the Moor is not altogether jealousy—it is rather the agony of being compelled to hate that which he supremely loved:

> Excellent wretch! Perdition catch my soul,
> But I do love thee, and when I love thee not,
> Chaos is come again.

Othello does not feel himself placed in rivalry with Cassio for the affection of his wife. Iago has contrived that the Moor shall overhear him conversing with Cassio about Bianca. Cassio,

---

* The passionless character of Iago, Coleridge says, "is all will in intellect;" and he notices well "the motive-hunting of a motiveless malignity," in Iago's soliloquy, Act i, Scene 3. Mr Hudson's study of the character of Iago is careful and discriminating. "Iago's creed," writes Mr Hudson, "is that the yielding to any inspirations from without argues an ignoble want of mental force [...]. Intellectuality is Iago's proper character; that is, intellect has in him cast off all allegiance to the moral reason, and become a law unto itself, so that the mere fact of his being able to do a thing is sufficient cause for doing it."

at thought of the extravagant pursuit of him by the Venetian courtesan, laughs aloud. It is then that Othello breaks out with the enraged cry, "How shall I murder him, Iago?" But Othello supposed that Cassio had been speaking of Desdemona, and that his laugh was a profane mockery of her fall. It was Cassio's supposed ignoble thought respecting Desdemona, even more than jealousy, which made him seem to Othello to merit mortal vengeance. Ordinarily Othello thinks little about Cassio. His agony is concentrated in the thought that the fairest thing on earth should be foul, that the fountain from which the current of his life had seemed to run so pure and free should be

A cistern for foul toads
To knot and gender in!

It is with an agonized sense of justice that he destroys the creature who is dearest to him in the world, knowing certainly that with hers his own true life must cease. Nay, it is not with the cessation of Desdemona's breath that the life of Othello ends; he is unable to survive the loss of faith in her perfect purity. All that had been glorious becomes remote and impossible for him if Desdemona be false. We hear the great childlike sob of Othello's soul:

O, now, for ever
Farewell the tranquil mind! farewell content!
Farewell the plumed troop, and the big wars
That make ambition virtue.

From the first suggestion of suspicion by his ensnarer, Othello is impatient for assurance, and finds suspense intolerable. Why? Not surely because he is eager to convict his wife of infidelity; but rather because he will not allow his passionate desire to believe her pure to abuse him, and retain him in a fool's paradise, while a great agony may possibly remain before him.

Of the tragic story what is the final issue? The central point of its spiritual import lies in the contrast between the two men, Iago and his victim. Iago, with keen intellectual faculties and manifold culture in Italian vice, lives and thrives after his fashion in a world from which all virtue and all beauty are absent.

Othello with his barbaric innocence and regal magnificence of soul must cease to live the moment he ceases to retain faith in the purity and goodness which were to him the highest and most real things upon earth. Or if he live, life must become to him a cruel agony. Shakespeare compels us to acknowledge that self-slaughter is a rapturous energy—that such prolonged agony is joy in comparison with the earthly life-in-death of such a soul as that of Iago. The noble nature is taken in the toils because it is noble. Iago suspects his wife of every baseness, but the suspicion has no other effect than to intensify his malignity. Iago could not be captured and constrained to heroic suffering and rage. The shame of every being who bears the name of woman is credible to Iago, and yet he can grate from his throat the jarring music:

> And let me the canakin clink, clink;
> And let me the canakin clink.

There is therefore, Shakespeare would have us understand, something more inimical to humanity than suffering—namely, an incapacity for noble pain. To die as Othello dies is indeed grievous. But to live as Iago lives, devouring the dust and stinging—this is more appalling.

Such is the spiritual motive that controls the tragedy. And the validity of this truth is demonstrable to every sound conscience. No supernatural authority needs to be summoned to bear witness to this reality of human life. No pallid flame of hell, no splendour of dawning heaven, needs show itself beyond the verge of earth to illumine this truth. It is a portion of the ascertained fact of human nature, and of this our mortal existence. We look upon "the tragic loading of the bed," and we see Iago in presence of the ruin he has wrought. We are not compelled to seek for any resolution of these apparent discords in any alleged life to come. That may also be; we shall accept it, if it be. But looking sternly and strictly at what is now actual and present to our sight, we yet rise above despair. Desdemona's adhesion to her husband and to love survived the ultimate trial. Othello dies "upon a kiss." He perceives his own calamitous error, and he recognizes Desdemona pure and loyal as she was. Goodness is justified of her child. It is evil which suffers defeat.

It is Iago whose whole existence has been most blind, purposeless, and miserable—a struggle against the virtuous powers of the world, by which at last he stands convicted and condemned.

II

There is a line in the play of *Macbeth*, uttered as the evening shadows begin to gather on the day of Banquo's murder, which we may repeat to ourselves as a motto of the entire tragedy, "Good things of day begin to droop and drowse." It is the tragedy of the twilight and the setting-in of thick darkness upon a human soul. We assist at the spectacle of a terrible sunset in folded clouds of blood. To the last, however, one thin hand's-breadth of melancholy light remains—the sadness of the day without its strength. Macbeth is the prey of a profound world-weariness. And while a huge *ennui* pursues crime, the criminal is not yet in utter blackness of night. When the play opens, the sun is already dropping below the verge. And as at sunset strange winds arise, and gather the clouds to westward with mysterious pause and stir, so the play of *Macbeth* opens with movement of mysterious, spiritual powers, which are auxiliary of that awful shadow which first creeps, and then strides across the moral horizon.

It need hardly be once more repeated that the Witches of Macbeth are not the broom-stick witches of vulgar tradition.* If they are grotesque, they are also sublime. The weird sisters of our dramatist may take their place beside the terrible old women of Michael Angelo, who spin the destinies of man. Shakespeare is no more afraid than Michael Angelo of being vulgar. It is the feeble, sentimental-ideal artist who is nervous about the dignity of his conceptions, and who, in aiming at the great, attains only the grandiose; he thins away all that is positive and material, in

* The theory of Messrs Clark and Wright (Clarendon Press edition of *Macbeth*) that the play is an alteration by Middleton of a tragedy of Shakespeare, is accepted by Mr Fleay, and carried farther into detail (Transactions of the New Shakespeare Society 1874). Mr Fleay is of opinion that the witches around the caldron, Act iv, Scene 1, are creations of Shakespeare; but he believes that they are entirely distinct from the three "weird sisters," the Nornae of Act i, Scene 3. He writes: "In

the hope of discovering some novelty of shadowy horror. But the great ideal artiste—Michael Angelo, Dante, Blake, Beethoven—see things far more dreadful than the vague horrors of the romanticist; they are perfectly fearless in their use of the material, the definite, the gross, the so-called vulgar. And thus Shakespeare fearlessly showed us his weird sisters, "the goddesses of destinie" brewing infernal charms in their wicked cauldron. We cannot quite dispense in this life with ritualism, and the ritualism of evil is foul and ugly; the hell-broth which the Witches are cooking bubbles up with no refined, spiritual poison; the quintessence of mischief is being brewed out of foul things, which can be enumerated; thick and slab the gruel must be made. Yet these weird sisters remain terrible and sublime. They tingle in every fibre with evil energy, as the tempest does with the electric current; their malignity is inexhaustible; they are wells of sin springing up into everlasting death; they have their raptures and ecstasies in crime; they snatch with delight

---

Holinshed we find that 'Macbeth and Banquo were met by iij women in straunge and ferly apparell resembling creatures of an elder world;' that they vanished; that at first by Macbeth and Banqno 'they were reputed but some vayne fantasticall illusion,' but afterwards the common opinion was that they were 'eyther the weird sisters—that is, *ye Goddesses of destinie*—or else some Nimphes or Feiries endewed with knowledge of prophesie by their Nicromanticall science' (Act ii, Scene 2). But in the part corresponding to IV, 1, Macbeth is warned to take heed of Macduff by 'certain wysardes;' but he does not kill him, because 'a certain witch whom he had in great trust' had given him the two other equivocal predictions. Now, it is to me incredible that Shakespeare, who in the parts of the play not rejected by the Cambridge editors never uses the word, or alludes to witches in any way, should have degraded 'ye Goddesses of destinie' to three old women, who are called by Paddock and Grimalkin, [...] sail in sieves, kill swine, serve Hecate, and deal in all the common charms, illusions, and incantations of vulgar witches. The three, who 'look not like the inhabitants o' th' earth, and yet are on't;' they who 'can look into the seeds of time and say which grain will grow;' they who 'seem corporal,' but 'melt into the air' like 'bubbles of the earth;' 'the weyward sisters,' who 'make themselves air,' and have 'more than mortal knowledge,' are not beings of this stamp." Mr Fleay's difficulty is that in III, iv, 133, and IV, i, 136, Macbeth calls the witches of IV, i, "the weird sisters," and he acknowledges that he cannot at present solve this difficulty. It is hardly perhaps a sound method of criticism to invent hypothesis which creates an insoluble difficulty.

at the relics of impiety and foul disease; they are the awful inspirers of murder, insanity, suicide.

The weird sisters, says Gervinus, "are simply the embodiment of inward temptation." They are surely much more than this. If we must regard the entire universe as a manifestation of an unknown somewhat which lies behind it, we are compelled to admit that there is an apocalypse of power auxiliary to vice, as really as there is a manifestation of virtuous energy. All venerable mythologies admit this fact. The Mephistopheles of Goethe remains as the testimony of our scientific nineteenth century upon the matter. The history of the race, and the social medium in which we live and breathe, have created forces of good and evil which are independent of the will of each individual man and woman. The sins of past centuries taint the atmosphere of to-day. We move through the world subject to accumulated forces of evil and of good outside ourselves. We are caught up at times upon a stream of virtuous force, a beneficent current which bears us onward towards an abiding-place of joy, of purity, and of sacrifice; or a counter-current drifts us towards darkness, and cold, and death. And therefore no great realist in art has hesitated to admit the existence of what theologians name divine grace, and of what theologians name Satanic temptation. There is, in truth, no such thing as "naked manhood." The attempt to divorce ourselves from the large impersonal life of the world, and to erect ourselves into independent wills, is the dream of the idealist. And between the evil within and the evil without subsists a terrible sympathy and reciprocity. There is in the atmosphere a zymotic poison of sin; and the constitution which is morally enfeebled supplies appropriate nutriment for the germs of disease; while the hardy moral nature repels the same germs. Macbeth is infected; Banquo passes free.* Let us, then, not inquire after the names of these fatal sisters. Nameless they are, and sexless. It is enough to know that such powers auxiliary to

---

* *Banquo.* Merciful powers
Restrain in me the cursed thoughts that nature
Gives way to in repose!

vice do exist outside ourselves, and that Shakespeare was scientifically accurate in his statement of the fact.

But it is also by no means difficult to believe that in the mere matter of superstition, in all that relates to presentiments, dreams, omens, ghost belief, and such like, Shakespeare would have failed to satisfy the requirements of enlightened persons of to-day, who receive their reports of the universe through the scientific article in the newest magazine:

> There are more things in heaven and earth, Horatio,
> Than are dreamt of in your philosophy.

"They say miracles are past;" Lafeu is speaking in *All's Well That Ends Well,* "and we have our philosophical persons, to make modern and familiar, things supernatural and causeless. Hence is it, that we make trifles of terrors; ensconcing ourselves into seeming knowledge, when we should submit ourselves to an unknown fear."* However we may account for it, the fact is unquestionable that some of the richest creative natures of the world have all their lives been believers, if not with their intellect, at least with their instinctive feelings and their imagination in much of the old-wives' lore of the nursery. Scott does not as a sceptic make use in his novels of ghostly and supernatural machinery merely for the sake of producing certain artistic effects. He retained at least a half-faith in the Gothic mythology of the north. Goethe for a time devoted himself to the pursuit of alchemy. In "The Spanish Gypsy" of George Eliot, from the necklace of Zarca dim mastering powers, blind yet strong, pass into his daughter's will; and in that poem the science of modern psychology accepts certain of the facts of old superstitions, accepts them and explains them. We slighter and smaller natures can deprive ourselves altogether of the sense for such phenomena; we can elevate ourselves into a rare atmosphere of intellectuality and incredulity. The wider and richer natures of creative artists have received too large an inheritance from the race, and have too fully absorbed all the influences of their environment for this to be possible in their case. While dim recollections and forefeelings haunt their blood they cannot

* Act ii, Scene 3.

enclose themselves in a little pinfold of demonstrable knowledge, and call it the universe.

"The true reason for the first appearance of the Witches," Coleridge has said, "is to strike the keynote of the character of the whole drama." They appear in a desert place, with thunder and lightning; it is the barren and blasted place where evil has obtained the mastery of things. Observe that the last words of the witches, in the opening scene of the play, are the first words which Macbeth himself utters,

> Fair is foul and foul is fair
> Hover through the fog and filthy air.*

Macbeth. "So foul and fair a day I have not seen." Shakespeare intimates by this that although Macbeth has not yet set eyes upon these hags, the connection is already established between his soul and them. Their spells have already wrought upon his blood. When the three sisters meet Macbeth and Banquo upon the heath, it is Banquo to whom they are first visible in the grey, northern air. To Banquo they are objective—they are outside himself, and he can observe and describe their strange aspect, their wild attire, and their mysterious gesture. Macbeth is rapt in silence, and then with eager longing demands, "Speak if you can: what are you?" When they have given him the three Hails, as Glamis, as Cawdor, and as King, the Hail of the past, of the present, of the future, Macbeth starts. "It is a full revelation of his criminal aptitudes," Mr Hudson has well said, "that so startles and surprises him into a rapture of meditation." And besides this, Macbeth is startled to find that there is a terrible correspondence established between the baser instincts of his own heart and certain awful external agencies of evil.

Shakespeare does not believe in any sudden transformation of a noble and loyal soul into that of a traitor and murderer. At the outset Macbeth possesses no real fidelity to things that are true, honest, just, pure, lovely. He is simply not yet in alliance with the powers of evil. He has aptitudes for goodness, and aptitudes for crime. Shakespeare felt profoundly that this

* Words uttered by all three witches, after each has singly spoken thrice.

careless attitude of suspense or indifference between virtue and vice cannot continue long. The kingdom of heaven suffers violence, and the violent take it by force. Those who lack energy of goodness, and drop into a languid neutrality between the antagonist spiritual forces of the world must serve the devil as slaves, if they will not decide to serve God as freemen.

But beside the vague yet mastering inspiration of crime received from the witches, there is the more definite inspiration received from his wife. Macbeth is excitably imaginative, and his imagination alternately stimulates, and enfeebles him. The facts in their clear-cut outline disappear in the dim atmosphere of surmise, desire, fear, hope, which the spirit of Macbeth effuses around the fact. But his wife sees things in the clearest and most definite outline. Her delicate frame is filled with high-strung nervous energy.* With her to perceive is forthwith to decide, to decide is to act. Having resolved upon her end a practical logic convinces her that the means are implied and determined. Macbeth resolves, and falters back from action; now he is restrained by his imagination, now by his fears, now by his lingering velleities towards a loyal and honourable existence. He is unable to keep in check or put under restraint any one of the various incoherent powers of his nature, which impede and embarrass each the action of the other. Lady Macbeth gains, for the time, sufficient strength by throwing herself passionately into a single purpose, and by resolutely repressing all that is inconsistent with that purpose. Into the service of evil she carries some of the intensity and energy of asceticism,—she cuts off from herself her better nature, she yields to no weak paltering with conscience. "I have given

* "According to my notion," Mrs Siddons wrote, "[Lady Macbeth's beauty] is of that character which I believe is generally allowed to be most captivating to the other sex—fair, feminine, nay, perhaps, even fragile." Dr Bucknill (before he was aware that Mrs Siddons held a similar opinion) wrote, "Lady Macbeth was a lady beautiful and delicate, whose one vivid passion proves that her organisation was instinct with nerve force, unoppressed by weight of flesh. Probably she was small; for it is the smaller sort of woman whose emotional fire is the most fierce, and she herself bears unconscious testimony to the fact that her hand was little."—*Mad Folk of Shakespeare*, p. 45. She is Maobeth's "dearest chuck."

suck," she exclaims, "and know how tender 'tis to love the babe that milks me;" she is unable to stab Duncan because he resembles her father in his sleep; she is appalled by the copious blood in which the old man lies, and the horror of the sight clings to her memory; the smell of the blood is hateful to her and almost insupportable; she had not been without apprehension that her feminine nature might fail to carry her through the terrible ordeal, through which she yet resolved that it should be compelled to pass. She must not waste an atom of her strength of will, which has to serve for two murderers,—for her husband as well as for herself. She puts into requisition with the aid of wine and of stimulant words the reserve of nervous force which lay unused. No witches have given her "Hail;" no airy dagger marshals her the way that she is going; nor is she afterwards haunted by the terrible vision of Banquo's gory head. As long as her will remains her own she can throw herself upon external facts and maintain herself in relation with the definite, actual surroundings; it is in her sleep, when the will is incapable of action, that she is persecuted by the past which perpetually renews itself, not in ghostly shapes, but by the imagined recurrence of real and terrible incidents.

The fears of Lady Macbeth upon the night of Duncan's murder are the definite ones, that the murderers may be detected, that some omission in the prearranged plan may occur, that she or her husband may be summoned to appear before the traces of their crime have been removed. More awful considerations would press in upon her and overwhelm her sanity, but that she forcibly repels them for the time:

> These deeds must not be thought
> After these ways; so, it will make us mad.

To her the sight of Duncan dead is as terrible as to Macbeth; but she takes the dagger from her husband; and with a forced jest, hideous in the self-violence which it implies, she steps forth into the dark corridor:

> If he do bleed
> I'll gild the faces of the grooms withal
> For it must seem their guilt.

"A play of fancy here is like a gleam of ghastly sunshine striking across a stormy landscape."* The knocking at the gate clashes upon her overstrained nerves and thrills her; but she has determination and energy to direct the actions of Macbeth, and rouse him from the mood of abject depression which succeeded his crime. A white flame of resolution glows through her delicate organisation, like light through an alabaster lamp:

> Infirm of purpose!
> Give me the daggers: the sleeping and the dead
> Are but as pictures: 'tis the eye of childhood
> That fears a painted devil.

If the hold which she possesses over her own faculties should relax for a moment all would be lost. For dreadful deeds anticipated and resolved upon, she has strength, but the surprise of a novel horror, on which she has not counted, deprives her suddenly of consciousness; when Macbeth announces his butchery of Duncan's grooms the lady swoons,—not in feigning but in fact,—and is borne away insensible.

Macbeth wastes himself in vague, imaginative remorse:

> Will not great Neptune's ocean wash this blood
> Clean from my hand? No, this my hand will rather
> The multitudinous seas incarnadine,
> Making the green one red.

Thus his imagination serves to dissipate the impression of his conscience. What is the worth of this vague, imaginative remorse? Macbeth retained enough of goodness to make him a haggard, miserable criminal; never enough to restrain him from a crime. His hand soon became subdued to what it worked in,—the blood in which it paddled and plashed. And yet the loose incoherent faculties ever becoming more and more disorganised and disintegrated somehow held together till the end. "My hands are of your colour," exclaims Lady Macbeth; "but I shame to wear a heart so white. A little water clears us of this deed." Yet it is she who has uttered no large words about "the multitudinous seas," who will rise in slumbery agitation,

---

* *Macbeth*, Clarendon Press Edition, p. 108.

and with her accustomed action eagerly essay to remove from her little hand its ineffaceable stain, and with her delicate sense sicken at the smell of blood upon it, which "all the perfumes of Arabia will not sweeten;" and last, will loosen the terrible constriction of her heart with a sigh that longs to be perpetual. It is the queen, and not her husband who is slain by conscience.

Yet the soul of Macbeth never quite disappears into the blackness of darkness. He is a cloud without water, carried about of winds; a tree whose fruit withers, but not even to the last quite plucked up by the roots. For the dull ferocity of Macbeth is joyless. All his life has gone irretrievably astray, and he is aware of this. His suspicion becomes uncontrollable; his reign is a reign of terror; and as he drops deeper and deeper into the solitude and the gloom, his sense of error and misfortune, futile and unproductive as that sense is, increases. He moves under a dreary cloud, and all things look gray and cold. He has lived long enough, yet he clings to life; that which should accompany old age "as honour, love, obedience, troops of friends," he may not look to have. Finally his sensibility has grown so dull that even the intelligence of his wife's death,—the death of her who had been bound to him by such close communion in crime,—hardly touches him, and seems little more than one additional incident in the weary, meaningless tale of human life:

> She should have died hereafter;
> There would have been a time for such a word.
> To-morrow, and to-morrow, and to-morrow,
> Creeps in this petty pace from day to day
> To the last syllable of recorded time;
> And all our yesterdays have lighted fools
> The way to dusty death. Out, out, brief candle!
> Life's but a walking shadow, a poor player
> That struts and frets his hour upon the stage,
> And then is heard no more; it is a tale
> Told by an idiot, full of sound and fury,
> Signifying nothing.

This world-weariness, which has not the energy of Timon's despair, is yet less remote from the joy and glory of true living than is the worm-like vivacity of Iago. Macbeth remembers that he once knew there was such a thing as human goodness. He stands a haggard shadow against the hand's breadth of pale sky which yields us sufficient light to see him. But Iago rises compact with fiend-like energy, seen brightly in the godless glare of hell. The end of Macbeth is savage, and almost brutal—a death without honour or loveliness. He fights now not like "Bellona's bridegroom lapp'd in proof," but with a wild and animal clinging to life:

> They have tied me to a stake; I cannot fly,
> But, bear-like, I must fight the course.

His followers desert him; he feels himself taken in a trap. The powers of evil in which he had trusted turn against him and betray him. His courage becomes a desperate rage. We are in pain until the horrible necessity is accomplished.

Shakespeare pursues Macbeth no farther. He does not follow him with yearning conjecture, as Mr Browning follows the murderer of his poem, "The Ring and the Book,"

> Into that sad obscure sequestered state,
> Where God unmakes but to re-make the soul
> He else made first in vain.

Our feet remain on solid Scottish earth. But a new and better era of history dawns. Macbeth and Siward's son lie dead; but the world goes on. The tragic deeds take up their place in the large life of a country. We suffer no dejection; "the time is free." Sane and strong, we expect the day when Malcolm will be crowned at Scone.

III

The tragedy of King Lear was estimated by Shelley, in his Defence of Poetry, as an equivalent in modern literature for the trilogy in the literature of Greece with which the Oedipus Tyrannus, or that with which the Agamemnon stands connected. *King Lear* is, indeed, the greatest single achievement in poetry of the Teutonic, or northern genius. By its largeness of conception, and the variety of its details, by its revelation of a harmony existing between the forces of nature and the passions of man, by its grotesqueness and its sublimity, it owns kinship with the great cathedrals of Gothic architecture. To conceive, to compass, to comprehend, at once in its stupendous unity and in its almost endless variety, a building like the cathedral of Rheims or that of Cologne is a feat which might seem to defy the most athletic imagination. But the impression which Shakespeare's tragedy produces, while equally large—almost monstrous—and equally intricate, lacks the material fixity and determinateness of that produced by these great works in stone. Everything in the tragedy is in motion, and the motion is that of a tempest. A grotesque head, which was peering out upon us from a point near at hand, suddenly changes its place and its expression, and now is seen driven or fading away into the distance with lips and eyes that, instead of grotesque, appear sad and pathetic. All that we see around us is tempestuously whirling and heaving, yet we are aware that a law presides over this vicissitude and apparent incoherence. We are confident that there is a logic of the tempest. While each thing appears to be torn from its proper place, and to have lost its natural supports and stays, instincts, passions, reason all wrenched and contorted, yet each thing in this seeming chaos takes up its place with infallible assurance and precision.

In *King Lear*, more than in any other of his plays, Shakespeare stands in presence of the mysteries of human life. A more impatient intellect would have proposed explanations of these. A less robust spirit would have permitted the dominant tone of the play to become an eager or pathetic wistfulness respecting the significance of these hard riddles in the destiny of man. Shakespeare checks such wistful curiosity, though it exists discernibly; he will present life as it is; if life proposes inexplicable riddles, Shakespeare's art must propose them also. But while Shakespeare will present life as it is, and suggest no inadequate explanations of its difficult problems, he will gaze at life not only from *within*, but, if possible, also from an extra-mundane, extra-human point of view, and gazing thence at life, will try to discern what aspect this fleeting and wonderful phenomenon presents to the eyes of gods. Hence a grand irony in the tragedy of Lear; hence all in it that is great is also small;

all that is tragically sublime is also grotesque. Hence it sees man walking in a vain shadow; groping in the mist; committing extravagant mistakes; wandering from light into darkness; stumbling back again from darkness into light; spending his strength in barren and impotent rages; man in his weakness, his unreason, his affliction, his anguish, his poverty and meanness, his everlasting greatness and majesty. Hence, too, the characters, while they remain individual men and women, are ideal, representative, typical; Goneril and Regan, the destructive force, the ravening egoism in humanity which is at war with all goodness; Kent, a clear, unmingled fidelity; Cordelia, unmingled tenderness and strength, a pure redeeming ardour. As we read the play, we are haunted by a presence of something beyond the story of a suffering old man; we become dimly aware that the play has some vast impersonal significance, like the Prometheus Bound of Æschylus, and like Goethe's Faust. We seem to gaze upon "huge, cloudy symbols of some high romance."

What was irony when human life was viewed from the outside, extra-mundane point of view, becomes, when life is viewed from within, Stoicism. For to Stoicism the mere phenomenon of human existence is a vast piece of unreason and grotesqueness, and from this unreason and grotesqueness Stoicism makes its escape by becoming indifferent to the phenomenon, and by devotion to the moral idea, the law of the soul, which is for ever one with itself, and with the highest reason. The ethics of the play of *King Lear* are Stoical ethics. Shakespeare's fidelity to the fact will allow him to deny no pain or calamity that befalls man. "There was never yet philosopher that could endure the toothache patiently."* He knows that it is impossible to

> Fetter strong madness in a silken thread,
> Charm ache with air, and agony with words.

He admits the suffering, the weakness of humanity; but he declares that in the inner law there is a constraining power stronger than a silken thread; in the fidelity of pure hearts, in

* *Much Ado about Nothing*, Act v, Scene 1.

the rapture of love and sacrifice, there is a charm which is neither air nor words, but indeed potent enough to subdue pain, and make calamity acceptable. Cordelia, who utters no word in excess of her actual feeling, can declare, as she is led to prison, her calm and decided acceptance of her lot:

> We are not the first
> Who, with best meaning, have incurred the worst;
> For thee, oppressed King, I am cast down;
> Myself could else out-frown false fortune's frown.*

But though ethical principles radiate through the play of *King Lear* its chief function is not, even indirectly, to teach or inculcate moral truth, but rather by the direct presentation of a vision of human life and of the enveloping forces of nature, to "free, arouse, dilate." We may be unable to set down in words any set of truths which we have been taught by the drama. But can we set down in words the precise moral significance of a fugue of Handel, or a symphony of Beethoven? We are kindled and aroused by them; our whole nature is quickened; it passes from the habitual, hard, encrusted, and cold condition into "the fluid and attaching state," the state in which we do not seek truth and beauty, but attract and are sought by them, the state in which "good thoughts stand before us like free children of God, and cry 'We are come.'"† The play or the piece of music is not a code of precepts, or a body of doctrine;‡ it is "a focus where a number of vital forces unite in their purest energy."

In the play of *King Lear* we come into contact with the imagination, the heart, the soul of Shakespeare, at a moment when they attained their most powerful and intense vitality.

---

* Compare also, as expressing the mood in which calamity must be confronted the words of Edgar,—

> Men must endure
> Their going hence, even as their coming hither;
> Ripeness is all.

† Goethe's Conversations with Eckermann, Feb. 24, 1824.

‡ Flathe, who ordinarily finds all preceding critics wrong, and himself profoundly right, discovers in *King Lear* Shakespeare's "warning letter against naturalism and pseudo-rationalism;" the play is translated into a didactic discourse on infidelity.

"He was here," Hazlitt wrote, "fairly caught in the web of his own imagination." And being thus aroused about deeper things, Shakespeare did not in this play feel that mere historical verisimilitude was of chief importance. He found the incidents recorded in history, and ballad, and drama; he accepted them as he found them. Our imagination must grant Shakespeare certain postulates, those which the story that had taken root in the hearts of the people already specified. The old *Chronicle History of King Lear* had assigned ingenious motives for the apparently improbable conduct ascribed to the King. He resolves that upon Cordelia's protesting that she loves him, he will say, "Then, daughter, grant me one request,—accept the husband I have chosen for you," and thus he will take her at a vantage. It would have been easy for Shakespeare to have secured this kind of verisimilitude; it would have been easy for him to have referred the conduct of Lear to ingeniously invented motives; he could, if he had chosen, by psychological fence have turned aside the weapons of those assailants who lay to his charge improbability and unnaturalness. But then the keynote of the play would have been struck in another mode. Shakespeare did not at all care to justify himself by special pleading and psychological fence. The sculptor of the Laocoon has not engraved below his group the lines of Virgil, which describe the progress of the serpent toward his victims; he was interested in the supreme moment of the father's agony, and in the piteous effort and unavailing appeal of the children. Shakespeare, in accordance with his dramatic method, drove forward across the intervening accidents toward the passion of Lear in all its stages, his wild revolt against humanity, his conflict with the powers of night and tempest, his restoration through the sacred balm of a daughter's love.

Nevertheless, though its chief purpose be to get the forces of the drama into position before their play upon one another begins, the first scene cannot be incoherent. In the opening sentence Shakespeare gives us clearly to understand that the partition of the kingdom between Albany and Cornwall is already accomplished. In the concluding sentences we are reminded of Lear's "inconstant starts," of "the unruly waywardness that infirm and choleric years bring with them." It is evidently intended that we should understand the demand made upon his daughters for a profession of their love to have been a sudden freak of self-indulged waywardness, in which there was something of jest, something of unreason, something of the infirmity which requires demonstrations of the heart.* Having made the demand, however, it must not be refused. Lear's will must be opposeless. It is the centre, and prime force of his little universe. To be thrown out of this passionate wilfulness, to be made a passive thing, to be stripped first of affection, then of power, then of home or shelter, last, of reason itself, and finally, to learn the preciousness of true love only at the moment when it must be for ever renounced,—such is the awful and purifying ordeal through which Lear is compelled to pass.

Shakespeare "takes ingratitude," Victor Hugo has said, "and he gives this monster two heads, Goneril [...] and Regan." The two terrible creatures are, however, distinguishable. Goneril is the calm wielder of a pitiless force, the resolute initiator of cruelty. Regan is a smaller, shriller, fiercer, more eager piece of malice. The tyranny of the elder sister is a cold, persistent pressure, as little affected by tenderness or scruple as the action of some crushing hammer; Regan's ferocity is more unmeasured,

---

* Coleridge writes, "The first four or five lines of the play let us know that the trial is but a trick; and that the grossness of the old King's rage is in part the natural result of a silly trick suddenly and most unexpectedly baffled and disappointed." Dr Bucknill maintains that the partition of the kingdom is "the first act of Lear's developing insanity." *Shakespeare Jahrbuch*, vol. ii, contains a short and interesting article by Ulrici on "Ludwig Devrient as King Lear." That great actor, if Ulrici might trust his own impression, would seem to have understood the first scene of the play in the sense in which Ulrici himself explains it, *viz.*, that Lear's demand for a declaration of his daughters' love was sudden and sportive, made partly to pass the time until the arrival of Burgundy and France. Having assigned their portions to Goneril and Regan there could not be a serious meaning in Lear's words to Cordelia,—

> What can you say to draw
> A third more opulent than your sisters?

The words were said with a smile, yet at the same time with a secret and clinging desire for the demonstration of love demanded. All the more is Lear surprised and offended by Cordelia's earnest and almost judicial reply. But Cordelia is at once suppressing and in this way manifesting her indignation against her sisters' heartless flattery.

and less abnormal or monstrous. Regan would avoid her father, and while she confronts him alone, quails a little as she hears the old man's curse pronounced against her sister:

> O the blest Gods! so will you wish on me
> When the rash mood is on.

But Goneril knows that a helpless old man is only a helpless old man, that words are merely words. When, after Lear's terrible malediction, he rides away with his train, Goneril, who would bring things to an issue, pursues her father, determined to see matters out to the end.* To complete the horror they produce in us, these monsters are amorous. Their love is even more hideous than their hate. The wars of

> Dragons of the prime
> That tare each other in their slime

formed a spectacle less prodigious than their mutual blandishments and caresses.

> *Regan.* I know your lady does not love her husband;
> I am sure of that: and at her late being here
> She gave strange oeillades and most speaking looks
> To noble Edmund.

To the last Goneril is true to her character. Regan is despatched out of life by her sister; Goneril thrusts her own life aside, and boldly enters the great darkness of the grave.

Of the secondary plot of this tragedy—the story of Gloucester and his sons—Schlegel has explained one chief significance: "Were Lear alone to suffer from his daughters, the impression would be limited to the powerful compassion felt by us for his private misfortune. But two such unheard-of examples taking place at the same time have the appearance of a great commotion in the moral world; the picture becomes gigantic, and fills us with such alarm as we should entertain at the idea that the heavenly bodies might one day fall from their appointed orbits."† The treachery of Edmund, and the torture to which

---

* It is Goneril who first suggests the plucking out of Gloucester's eyes. The points of contrast between the sisters are well brought out by Gervinus.

† *Lectures on Dramatic Art*, translated by J. Black, p. 412.

Gloucester is subjected, are out of the course of familiar experience; but they are commonplace and prosaic in comparison with the inhumanity of the sisters, and the agony of Lear. When we have climbed the steep ascent of Gloucester's mount of passion, we see still above us another *via dolorosa* leading to that

> Wall of eagle-baffling mountain,
> Black, wintry, dead, unmeasured,

to which Lear is chained. Thus the one story of horror serves as a means of approach to the other, and helps us to conceive its magnitude. The two, as Schlegel observes, produce the impression of a great commotion in the moral world. The thunder which breaks over our head does not suddenly cease to resound, but is reduplicated, multiplied, and magnified, and rolls away with long reverberation.

Shakespeare also desires to augment the moral mystery, the grand inexplicableness of the play. We can assign causes to explain the evil in Edmund's heart. His birth is shameful, and the brand burns into his heart and brain. He has been thrown abroad in the world, and is constrained by none of the bonds of nature, or memory, of habit or association.* A hard, sceptical intellect, uninspired and unfed by the instincts of the heart, can easily enough reason away the consciousness of obligations the most sacred. Edmund's thought is "active as a virulent acid, eating its rapid way through all the tissues of human sentiment."† His mind is destitute of dread of the Divine Nemesis. Like Iago, like Richard III, he finds the regulating force of the universe in the *ego*—in the individual will. But that terror of the unseen which Edmund scorned as so much superstition is "the initial recognition of a moral law restraining desire, and checks the hard bold scrutiny of imperfect thought into obligations which can never be proved to have any sanctity in the absence of feeling." We can, therefore, in some degree

---

* Gloucester (Act i, Scene 1) says of Edmund, "He hath been out nine years and away he shall again."

† This and the quotation next following will be remembered by readers of *Romola*; they occur in that memorable chapter entitled "Tito's Dilemma."

account for Edmund's bold egoism and inhumanity. What obligation should a child feel to the man who, for a moment's selfish pleasure, had degraded and stained his entire life? In like manner Gloucester's sufferings do not appear to us inexplicably mysterious:

> The gods are just, and of our pleasant vices
> Make instruments to plague us;
> The dark and vicious place where thee he got
> Cost him his eyes.

But having gone to the end of our tether, and explained all that is explicable we are met by enigmas which will not be explained. We were perhaps somewhat too ready to

> Take upon us the mystery of things
> As if we were God's spies.*

Now we are baffled, and bow the head in silence. Is it indeed the stars that govern our condition? Upon what theory shall we account for the sisterhood of a Goneril and a Cordelia? And why is it that Gloucester, whose suffering is the retribution for past misdeeds, should be restored to spiritual calm and light, and should pass away in a rapture of mingled gladness, and grief,

> His flaw'd heart,
> Alack! too weak the conflict to support!
> 'Twixt two extremes of passion, joy, and grief,
> Burst smilingly,—

while Lear, a man more sinned against than sinning, should be robbed of the comfort of Cordelia's love, should be stretched to the last moment upon "the rack of this tough world," and should expire in the climax of a paroxysm of unproductive anguish?

Shakespeare does not attempt to answer these questions. The impression which the facts themselves produce, their influence to "free, arouse, dilate," seems to Shakespeare more precious than any proposed explanation of the facts which cannot be verified. The heart is purified not by dogma, but by

---

* Words of Lear, Act v, Scene 3.

pity and terror. But there are other questions which the play suggests. If it be the stars that govern our conditions, if that be indeed a possibility which Gloucester in his first shock and confusion of mind declares,

> As flies to wanton boys are we to the gods;
> They kill us for their sport,

if, measured by material standards, the innocent and the guilty perish by a like fate,—what then? Shall we yield ourselves to the lust for pleasure? Shall we organise our lives upon the principles of a studious and pitiless egoism?

To these questions the answer of Shakespeare is clear and emphatic. Shall we stand upon Goneril's side, or upon that of Cordelia? Shall we join Edgar, or join the traitor? Shakespeare opposes the presence and the influence of evil not by any transcendental denial of evil, but by the presence of human virtue, fidelity, and self-sacrificial love. In no play is there a clearer, an intenser manifestation of loyal manhood, of strong and tender womanhood. The devotion of Kent to his master is a passionate, unsubduable devotion, which might choose for its watchword the saying of Goethe, "I love you; what is that to you?" Edgar's nobility of nature, is not disguised by the beggar's rags; he is the skilful resister of evil, the champion of right to the utterance. And if Goneril and Regan alone would leave the world unintelligible and desperate, there is

> One daughter
> Who redeems Nature from the general curse
> Which twain have brought her to.

We feel throughout the play that evil is abnormal; a curse which brings down destruction upon itself; that it is without any long career; that evil-doer is at variance with evil-doer. But good is normal; for it the career is long; and "all honest and good men are disposed to befriend honest and good men, as such."*

> *Cordelia.* O thou good Kent, how shall I live, and work,
> To match thy goodness! My life will be too short
> And every measure fail me.

* Butler, *Analogy*, Part 1, chap. iii.

Kent. To be acknowledged, madam, is o'erpaid.
All my reports go with the modest truth;
Nor more, nor clipped, but so.

Nevertheless, when everything has been said that can be said to make the world intelligible, when we have striven our utmost to realise all the possible good that exists in the world, a need of fortitude remains.

It is worthy of note that each of the principal personages of the play is brought into presence of those mysterious powers which dominate life, and preside over human destiny; and each according to his character is made to offer an interpretation of the great riddle. Of these interpretations, none is adequate to account for all the facts. Shakespeare (differing in this from the old play) placed the story in heathen times, partly, we may surmise, that he might be able to put the question boldly, "What are the gods?" Edmund, as we have seen, discovers no power or authority higher than the will of the individual, and a hard trenchant intellect. In the opening of the play he utters his ironical appeal:

I grow; I prosper—
Now gods stand up for bastards.*

It is not until he is mortally wounded, with his brother standing over him, that the recognition of a moral law forces itself painfully upon his consciousness, and he makes his bitter confession of faith:

The wheel is come full circle, I am here.

His self-indulgent father is, after the manner of the self-indulgent, prone to superstition; and Gloucester's superstition affords some countenance to Edmund's scepticism. "This is the excellent foppery of the world, that when we are sick in fortune—often the surfeit of our own behaviour—we make guilty of our disasters the sun, the moon, and the stars, as if we were villains by necessity; fools by heavenly compulsion; knaves, thieves,

* Compare Edmund's words (uttered with inward scorn) spoken of Edgar:

I told him the revenging gods
'Gainst parricides did all their thunders bend.

and treachers, by spherical predominance; drunkards, liars, and adulterers, by an enforced obedience of planetary influence; and all that we are evil in, by a divine thrusting-on."

Edgar, on the contrary, the champion of right, ever active in opposing evil and advancing the good cause, discovers that the gods are upon the side of right, are unceasingly at work in the vindication of truth, and the execution of justice. His faith lives through trial and disaster, a flame which will not be quenched. And he buoys up, by virtue of his own energy of soul, the spirit of his father, which, unprepared for calamity, is staggering blindly, stunned from its power to think, and ready to sink into darkness, and a welter of chaotic disbelief. Gloucester, in his first confusion of spirit, exclaims bitterly against the divine government:

> As flies to wanton boys are we to the gods,
> They kill us for their sport.

But before the end has come he "shakes patiently his great affliction off;" he will not quarrel with the "great opposeless wills" of the gods; nay, more than this, he can identify his own will with theirs, he can accept life contentedly at their hands, or death. The words of Edgar find a response in his own inmost heart:

> Thou happy father
> Think that the clearest gods, who make them honours
> Of men's impossibilities, have preserv'd thee.

And as Edgar, the justiciary, finds in the gods his fellow-workers in the execution of justice, so Cordelia, in whose heart love is a clear and perpetual illumination, can turn for assistance and co-operancy in her deeds of love to the strong and gentle rulers of the world:

> O you kind gods,
> Cure this great breach in his abused nature.

Kent possesses no vision, like that which gladdens Edgar, of a divine providence. His loyalty to right has something in it of a desperate instinct, which persists in spite of the appearances presented by the world. Shakespeare would have us know that there is not any devotion to truth, to justice, to charity more intense and real than that of the man who is faithful to them, out of the sheer spirit of loyalty, unstimulated and unsupported by any faith which can be called theological. Kent, who has seen the vicissitude of things, knows of no higher power presiding over the events of the world than fortune. Therefore, all the more, Kent clings to the passionate instinct of right-doing, and to the hardy temper, the fortitude which makes evil, when it happens to come, endurable. It is Kent, who utters his thought in the words:

> Nothing almost sees miracles
> But misery.

And the miracle he sees, in his distress, is the approaching succour from France, and the loyalty of Cordelia's spirit. It is Kent again, who, characteristically making the best of an unlucky chance, exclaims, as he settles himself to sleep in the stocks,

> Fortune, good night; smile once more, turn thy wheel.

And again:

> It is the stars,
> The stars above us, govern our conditions.

And again (of Lear):

> If Fortune brag of two she lov'd and hated,
> One of them we behold.

Accordingly there is at once an exquisite tenderness in Kent's nature, and also a certain roughness and hardness, needful to protect, from the shocks of life, the tenderness of one who finds no refuge in communion with the higher powers, or in a creed of religious optimism.

But Lear himself—the central figure of the tragedy—what of him? What of suffering humanity that wanders from the darkness into light, and from the light into the darkness? Lear is grandly passive—played upon by all the manifold forces of nature and of society. And though he is in part delivered from his imperious self-will, and learns at last what true love is, and that it exists in the world—Lear passes away from our sight, not in any mood of resignation, or faith, or illuminated peace, but in a piteous agony of yearning for that love which he had found only to lose for ever. Does Shakespeare mean to contrast the pleasure in a demonstration of spurious affection in the first scene, with the agonised cry for real love in the last scene, and does he wish us to understand that the true gain from the bitter discipline of Lear's old age, was precisely this—his acquiring a supreme need of what is best, though a need which finds, as far as we can learn, no satisfaction?

We guess at the spiritual significance of the great tragic facts of the world, but after our guessing their mysteriousness remains.

Our estimate of this drama as a whole, Mr Hudson has said, depends very much on the view we take of the Fool; and Mr Hudson has himself understood Lear's "poor boy" with such delicate sympathy that to arrive at precisely the right point of view we need not go beyond his words. "I know not how I can better describe the Fool than as the soul of pathos in a sort of comic masquerade; one in whom fun and frolic are sublimed and idealized into tragic beauty [...]. His 'labouring to out jest Lear's heart-struck injuries' tells us that his wits are set a-dancing by grief; that his jests bubble up from the depths of a heart struggling with pity and sorrow, as foam enwreaths the face of deeply-troubled waters [...]. There is all along a shrinking, velvet-footed delicacy of step in the Fool's antics, as if awed by the holiness of the ground; and he seems bringing diversion to the thoughts, that he may the better steal a sense of woe into the heart. And I am not clear whether the inspired antics that sparkle from the surface of his mind are in more impressive contrast with the dark tragic scenes into which they are thrown, like rockets into a midnight tempest, or with the undercurrent of deep tragic thoughtfulness out of which they falteringly issue and play."*

Of the tragedy of King Lear a critic wishes to say as little as may be; for in the case of this play, words are more than ordinarily inadequate to express or describe its true impression. A tempest or a dawn will not be analysed in words; we must feel

---

* *Shakespeare's Life, Art and Characters*, vol. ii, pp. 351-52. What follows, too long to quote, is also excellent.

the shattering fury of the gale, we must watch the calm light broadening.* And the sensation experienced by the reader of *King Lear* resembles that produced by some grand natural phenomenon. The effect cannot be received at second hand; it cannot be described; it can hardly be suggested.†

* In Victor Hugo's volume of dithyrambic prophesying entitled *William Shakespeare*, a passage upon *King Lear* (ed. 1869, pp. 205-09) is particularly note-worthy. His point of view—that the tragedy is "Cordelia," not "King Lear," that the old King is only an occasion for his daughter—is absolutely wrong; but the criticism, notwithstanding, catches largeness and passion from the play. "Et quelle figure que le père! quelle cariatide! C'est l'homme courbé. Il ne fait que changer de fardeaux, toujours plus lourds. Plus le vieillard faiblit, plus le poids augmente. Il vit sous la surcharge. Il porte d'abord l'empire, puis l'ingratitude, puis l'isolement, puis le désespoir, puis la faim et la soif, puis la folie, puis toute la nature. Les nuées viennent sur sa tête, les forêts l'accablent d'ombre, l'ouragan s'abat sur sa nuque, l'orage plombe son manteau, la pluie pèse sur ses épaules, il marche plié et hagard, comme s'il avait les deux genoux de la nuit sur son dos. Eperdu et immense, il jette aux bourrasques et aux grêles ce cri épique: Pourquoi me haïssez-vous, tempêtes? pourquoi me persécutez-vous? *vous n'êtes pas mes filles.* Et alors, c'est fini; la lueur s'éteint, la raison se décourage, et s'en va, Lear est en enfance. Ah! il est enfant, ce vieillard. Eh bien! il lui faut une mère. Sa fille parait. Son unique fille, Cordelia. Car les deux autres, Regane et Goneril ne sont plus ses filles que de la quantité nécessaire pour avoir droit au nom de parricides." For the description of "l'adorable allaitement," "the maternity of the daughter over the father," see what follows, p. 208.

† In addition to the medical studies of Lear's case by Doctors Bucknill and Kellogg, we may mention the "König Lear" of Dr Carl Stark, (Stuttgart, 1871) favourably noticed in *Shakespeare Jahrbuch*, vol. vi, and again by Meissner in his study of the play, *Shakespeare Jahrbuch*, vol. vii, pp. 110-15.

6

The Roman Plays

I

The two books which contributed the largest material towards the building-up of Shakespeare's art-structure were the *Chronicles of Holinshed,* a quarry worked by the poet previous to 1600; and *North's translation of Plutarch's Lives,* a quarry worked after 1600. To this latter source we owe Julius Caesar, Coriolanus, Antony and Cleopatra, and, in part, Timon of Athens. Shakespeare treated the material which lay before him in Holinshed and in Plutarch with reverent care. It was not a happy falsifying of the facts of history to which he, as dramatist, aspired, but an imaginative rendering of the very facts themselves. Plutarch he followed even more studiously and closely than he followed Holinshed. Yet it is to be noted that, while Shakespeare is profoundly faithful to Roman life and character, it is an ideal truth, truth spiritual rather than truth material, which he seeks to discover. His method, as critics have pointed out, is widely different from that of his contemporary, Ben Jonson. Mr Knight, treating this subject, has said, "Jonson has left us two Roman plays produced essentially upon a different principle. In his Sejanus there is scarcely a speech or an incident that is not derived from the ancient authorities; and Jonson's own edition of the play is crowded with references as minute as would have been required from any modern annalist [...]. His characters [...] are made to speak according to the very words of Tacitus and Suetonius; but they are not living men."* Shakespeare was aware that his personages

* Charles Knight, *Studies of Shakespeare,* 1851, p. 405.

must be men before they were Romans; he felt that the truth of poetry must be vital and self-evidencing; that if it has got hold of the fact, no reference to authority will make the validity of the fact more valid. He knew that the buttressing up of art with erudition will not give stability to that which must stand by no aid of material props and stays, but, if at all, by virtue of the one living soul of which it is the body.

The German Romanticist critic Franz Horn has said that the hero of Shakespeare's King John "stands not in the list of personages, and could not stand with them [...]. The hero is England." Mr Knight adds, that the hero of Shakespeare's great classical trilogy is Rome. Important, however, as the political significance doubtless is there is something more important. Whether at any time Shakespeare was concerned as deeply about corporate life,—ecclesiastical, political, or even national, as he was about the life and destiny of the individual man, may well be questioned. But at this time the play of social forces certainly did not engage his imagination with exclusive or supreme interest. The struggle of patrician and plebeian is not the subject of *Coriolanus*, and the tragedy resolves itself by no solution of that political problem. Primarily the tragedy is that of an individual soul. It is important to note the dates of these plays. *Julius Caesar*, which Malone assigned to the year 1607, is now with good reason carried back as early as 1601, and thus it lies side by side in point of time with *Hamlet*.* After an interval of seven years or upwards, the second of the Roman Plays, *Antony and Cleopatra*, was written.† The events of Roman

* Mr Halliwell pointed out the following lines in Weever's "Mirror of Martyrs," 1601,—

> The many-headed multitude were drawn
> By Brutus' speech, that Caesar was ambitious;
> When eloquent Mark Antony had shown
> His virtues, who but Brutus then was vicious?

The theory of Mr Fleay (New Shakespeare Society's Transactions, 1874) that our present Julius Caesar is a play of Shakespeare's altered by Ben Jonson about 1607, is unsupported by any sufficient evidence, internal or external. Delius dates Julius Caesar "before December 1604."

† There is an entry in the Stationers' Registers, by Edward Blount, May 20, 1608, of "a booke called Antony and Cleopatra." This is generally supposed

history connect *Antony and Cleopatra* immediately with *Julius Caesar*; yet Shakespeare allowed a number of years to pass, during which he was actively engaged as author, before he seems to have thought of his second Roman play. What is the significance of this fact? Does it not mean that the historical connection was now a connection too external and too material to carry Shakespeare on from subject to subject, as it had sufficed to do while he was engaged upon his series of English historical plays? The profoundest concerns of the individual soul were now pressing upon the imagination of the poet. Dramas now written upon subjects taken from history became not chronicles but tragedies. The moral interest was supreme. The spiritual material dealt with by Shakespeare's imagination in the play of *Julius Caesar* lay wide apart from that which forms the centre of the *Antony and Cleopatra*. Therefore the poet was not carried directly forward from one to the other.

But having in *Macbeth* (about 1606), studied the ruin of a nature which gave fair promise in men's eyes of greatness and nobility, Shakespeare, it may be, proceeded directly to a similar study in the case of Antony. In the nature of Antony as in the nature of Macbeth, there is a moral fault or flaw which circumstances discover, and which in the end works his destruction. In each play the pathos is of the same kind,—it lies in the gradual severing of a man, through the lust of power, or through the lust of pleasure, from his better self. By the side of Antony as by Macbeth's side there stood a terrible force, in the form of a woman, whose function it was to realise and ripen the

---

to have been Shakespeare's play (so Malone, Chalmers, Drake, Collier, Delius, Gervinus, Hudson, Fleay and others). Knight and Verplanck assign a later date. Mr Halliwell on comparing the early editions of North's Plutarch—1579, 1595, 1603, 1612—noticed many small differences between them, "and in one case, in *Coriolanus*, hit on a word 'vnfortunate,' altered by the 1612 edition from the former one's 'vnfortunately,' which 'vnfortunate' was the word used by Shakespeare in his tragedy of *Coriolanus*. This was therefore *primâ facie* evidence that Shakespeare used the 1612 edition of North for his *Coriolanus*, if not for his other Roman plays." (Transactions of the New Shakespeare Society.) Mr Paton claims for a copy of North's Plutarch now in the Greenock library the honour of having been Shakespeare's own copy. In it appear the initials W.S.; it is a copy of the 1612 edition.

unorganised and undeveloped evil of his soul. Antony's sin was an inordinate passion for enjoyment at the expense of Roman virtue and manly energy; a prodigality of heart, a superb egoism of pleasure. After a brief interval Shakespeare went on to apply his imagination to the investigating of another form of egoism—not the egoism of self-diffusion but of self-concentration. As Antony betrays himself and his cause through his sin of indulgence and laxity, so Coriolanus does violence to his own soul, and to his country through his sin of haughtiness, rigidity, and inordinate pride. Thus an ethical tendency connects these two plays which are also connected in point of time. While *Antony and Cleopatra*, although historically a continuation of *Julius Caesar*, stands separated from it, both in the chronological order of Shakespeare's plays, and in the logical order assigned by successive developments of the conscience, the intellect and the imagination of the dramatist.

The theme of the English historical plays is the success and the failure of men to achieve noble practical ends. Shakespeare observed that there are two classes of men in the world—those who use the right means for effecting their ends, who, if they want fruit, plant fruit-trees; and, secondly, those who will not accept the fact, who try to get fruit by various ingenious methods, only not by planting fruit-trees. Success in the visible material world, the world of noble positive action, is the measure of greatness in the English historical plays; and the ideal, heroic character of those plays is that of the king who so gloriously succeeded,—Henry V. But in the tragedies, the men who fail are not necessarily less worthy of admiration than the men who succeed. Octavius, who deals skilfully with life, and is misled by no enthusiasms, whose cool heart does not disturb his efficient hand, who sees the fact with clear-cut edges, and achieves the necessary deed with logical precision, which is pitiless but not cruel,—Octavius is successful. Yet we should rather fail with Brutus. Prosperity or adversity in the material world is here a secondary affair. By this time Shakespeare himself, by use of means which he would not reject, however distasteful they were, had succeeded: he had practically mastered life from the material point of view. But the breaking down or the building up of character seemed to him, now more than ever before, of supreme importance.

In *Julius Caesar*, Shakespeare makes a complete imaginative study of the case of a man predestined to failure, who nevertheless retains to the end the moral integrity which he prized as his highest possession and who with each new error advances a fresh claim upon our admiration and our love. To maintain the will in a fruitful relation with facts, that was what Romeo could not do, because he brooded over things as they reflected and repeated themselves in his own emotions; what Hamlet could not do, because he would not or could not come into direct contact with events, but studied them as they endlessly repeated and reflected themselves in his own thinking. Henry V had been a ruler of men, because, possessing a certain plain genius for getting into direct relation with concrete fact, and possessing also entire moral soundness, his will, his conscience, his intellect, and his enthusiasms had all been at one, and had all tended to action. Shakespeare's admiration of the great men of action is immense, because he himself was primarily not a man of action. He is stern to all idealists, because he was aware that he might too easily yield himself to the tendencies of an idealist. When Shakespeare feels himself shooting up too rapidly he "stops" himself, as gardeners do a plant, that he may throw out shoots below, and increase in strength and massiveness. If his feelings begin to idealise, he stops them, in order that by coming into more fruitful relation with fact he may add force and amplitude to his feelings. If his ideas tend to become abstract and notional, he plunges them into concrete matter in order that they may enrich and vitalise themselves. Against his idealising tendency Shakespeare constantly plays off his humour, resolved that he will not let himself escape from the real world, and from the whole of it. But with his sternness to idealists there is mingled a passionate tenderness. He shows us remorselessly their failure, but while they fail we love them.

Shakespeare "stops" himself, because he has entire confidence in the vigour of both his intellect and of his heart, and also in the good powers of this present world. He does not suppose that his thoughts will be less strong and fruitful because he plunges his ideas back into concrete fact. He does not suppose that he will cease to love because he chooses to see things as they are, and each thing on every side, rather than refine things away into the abstractions of the heart, which are desired by the purist or the sentimentalist. He does not fear that his will may grasp things with less energy or less tenacity, because he knows his purpose, and can refrain. And accordingly, while we may note many particulars which distinguish Shakespeare's later writings from those of his earlier years, the great distinction of all is this, that his power of thought, while losing none of its litheness and celerity, became, as time went on, more massive and sternly capable of endurance, so that he dared to confront the most awful problems of life, and could at will either stoically detain his mind from contemplation of the unknown, or could brood upon it with long and wistful intensity; and at the same time his feelings, increasing in ardour and swiftness, grew in massiveness and complexity, until from such lyric melody of passion as reaches us from *Romeo and Juliet* we make transition to the orchestral symphony of emotion which envelops us when we approach *King Lear*.

Brutus is the political Girondin. He is placed in contrast with his brother-in-law Cassius, the political Jacobin. Brutus is an idealist; he lives among books; he nourishes himself with philosophies; he is secluded from the impression of facts. Moral ideas and principles are more to him than concrete realities; he is studious of self-perfection, jealous of the purity of his own character, unwilling that so clear a character should receive even the apparent stain of misconception or misrepresentation. He is, therefore, as such men are, too much given to explanation of his conduct. Had he lived he would have written an Apology for his life, educing evidence, with a calm superiority, to prove that each act of his life proceeded from an honourable motive. Cassius, on the contrary, is by no means studious of moral perfection. He is frankly envious, and hates Caesar. Yet he is not ignoble. Brutus loves him, and the love of Brutus is a patent which establishes a man's nobility:

> The last of all the Romans, fare thee well!
> It is impossible that ever Rome
> Should breed thy fellow.*

And Cassius has one who will die for him. Titinius crowns the dead brow of the conspirator:

> Brutus come apace,
> And see how I regarded Caius Cassius.
> By your leave, gods—this is a Roman's part:
> Come Cassius' sword, and find Titinius' heart.

Cassius has a swift and clear perception of the fact. He is not, like Brutus, a theorist, but "a great observer," who "looks quite through the deeds of men." Brutus lives in the abstraction, in the idea; Cassius lives in the concrete, in the fact.

The conspiracy has been conceived and hatched by Cassius. The one thing wanting to the conspirators, as he perceives, is moral elevation, and that prestige which would be lent to the enterprise by a disinterested and lofty soul like that of Brutus. The time is the feast of Lupercal, and Antony is to run in the games. Caesar passes by, and as he passes a soothsayer calls in shrill tones from the press of people, "Beware the Ides of March." Caesar summons him forward, gazes in his face, and dismisses him with authoritative gesture, "He is a dreamer; let us leave him: pass." It is evidently intended that Caesar shall have a foible for supposing that he can read off character from the faces of men:

> Yond Cassius has a lean and hungry look.

Caesar need not condescend to the ordinary ways of obtaining acquaintance with facts. He asks no question of the soothsayer. He takes the royal road to knowledge,—intuition. This self-indulgence of his own foibles is, as it were, symbolized by his physical infirmity, which he admits in lordly fashion—"Come on my right hand, for this ear is deaf." Caesar is entitled to own

* These lines are taken almost word for word from *North's Plutarch*. Besides having read *Plutarch* it seems probable that Shakespeare was acquainted with the translation of *Appian*, 1578, from which he probably obtained the hints for his great speeches of Brutus and of Antony.

such a foible as deafness; it may pass well with Caesar. If men would have him hear them, let them come to his right ear. Meanwhile, things may be whispered which it were well for him if he strained an ear—right or left—to catch. In Shakespeare's rendering of the character of Caesar, which has considerably bewildered his critics, one thought of the poet would seem to be this,—that unless a man continually keeps himself in relation with facts, and with his present person and character, he may become to himself legendary and mythical. The real man Caesar disappears for himself under the greatness of the Caesar myth. He forgets himself as he actually is, and knows only the vast legendary power named Caesar. He is a *numen* to himself, speaking of Caesar in the third person, as if of some power above and behind his consciousness. And at this very moment—so ironical is the time-spirit—Cassius is cruelly insisting to Brutus upon all those infirmities which prove this god no more than a pitiful mortal.

Julius Caesar appears in only three scenes of the play. In the first scene of the third act he dies. Where he does appear the poet seems anxious to insist upon the weakness rather than the strength of Caesar. He swoons when the crown is offered to him, and upon his recovery enacts a piece of stagey heroism; he suffers from the falling sickness; he is deaf; his body does not retain its early vigour. He is subject to the vain hopes and vain alarms of superstition. His manner of speech is pompous and arrogant; he accepts flattery as a right; he vacillates, while professing unalterable constancy; he has lost in part his gift of perceiving facts, and of dealing efficiently with men, and with events. Why is this? And why is the play, notwithstanding, "Julius Caesar?" Why did Shakespeare decide to represent in such a light the chief man of the Roman world? Passages in other plays prove that Shakespeare had not really misconceived "the mightiest Julius," "broad-fronted Caesar," the conqueror over whom "Death makes no conquest."* "The poet," writes Gervinus, "if he intended to make the attempt of the republicans his main theme, could not have ventured to create too great an

* *Hamlet,* Act i, Scene 1; *Antony and Cleopatra,* Act i, Scene 5. *K. Richard III,* Act iii, Scene 1.

interest in Caesar; it was necessary to keep him in the background, and *to present that view of him which gave* a *reason for the conspiracy.* According even to Plutarch, [...] Caesar's character altered much for the worse shortly before his death, and Shakespeare has represented him according to this suggestion."* Mr Hudson offers a somewhat similar explanation. "I have sometimes thought that the policy of the drama may have been to represent Caesar not as he was indeed, but as he must have appeared to the conspirators; to make us see him as they saw him, in order that they, too, might have fair and equal judgment at our hands. For Caesar was literally too great to be seen by them, save as children often see bugbears by moonlight, when their inexperienced eyes are mocked with air." And Mr Hudson believes that he can detect a "refined and subtile irony;" diffusing itself through the texture of the play; that Brutus, a shallow idealist, should outshine the greatest practical genius the world ever saw, can have no other than an ironical significance.

Neither Gervinus nor Mr Hudson has solved the difficulty. Julius Caesar is indeed protagonist of the tragedy: but it is not the Caesar whose bodily presence is weak, whose mind is declining in strength and sure-footed energy, the Caesar who stands exposed to all the accidents of fortune. This bodily presence of Caesar is but of secondary importance, and may be supplied when it actually passes away, by Octavius as its substitute. It is the spirit of Caesar which is the dominant power of the tragedy; against this—the spirit of Caesar—Brutus fought; but Brutus, who for ever errs in practical politics, succeeded only in striking down Caesar's body; he who had been weak now rises as pure spirit, strong and terrible, and avenges himself upon the conspirators. The contrast between the weakness of Caesar's bodily presence in the first half of the play, and the might of his spiritual presence in the latter half of the play, is emphasized and perhaps over-emphasized by Shakespeare. It was the error of Brutus that he failed to perceive wherein lay the true Caesarean power, and acted with short-

* Gervinus, *Shakespeare Commentaries*, 1863, vol. ii, p. 350.

sighted eagerness and violence. Mark Antony, over the dead body of his lord, announces what is to follow:

> Over thy wounds now do I prophesy,—
> . . . . . .
> A curse shall light upon the limbs of men;
> Domestic fury and fierce civil strife
> Shall cumber all the parts of Italy;
> . . . . . .
> And Caesar's spirit, ranging for revenge,
> With Ate by his side come hot from hell,
> Shall in these confines with a monarch's voice
> Cry "Havoc," and let slip the dogs of war.

The ghost of Caesar (designated by Plutarch only the "evil spirit" of Brutus), which appears on the night before the battle of Philippi, serves as a kind of visible symbol of the vast posthumous power of the dictator. Cassius dies with the words:

> Caesar thou art revenged
> Even with the sword that killed thee.

Brutus, when he looks upon the dead face of his brother, exclaims:

> O Julius Caesar thou art mighty yet!
> Thy spirit walks abroad, and turns our swords
> In our own proper entrails.

Finally, the little effort of the aristocrat republicans sinks to the ground foiled and crushed by the force which they had hoped to abolish with one violent blow. Brutus dies:

> Caesar, now be still:
> I kill'd not thee with half so good a will.

Brutus dies; and Octavius lives to reap the fruit whose seed had been sown by his great predecessor. With strict propriety, therefore, the play bears the name of Julius Caesar.*

---

* I am in great part indebted for this explanation of the difficulty to the article "Die Dramatische Einheit im Julius Cäsar," by Dr Albert Lindner, in the *Jahrbuch der Deutschen Shakespeare-Gesellschaft*, vol. ii, pp. 90-95. Dr Lindner fails however to bring out the relation of Shakespeare's conception of Caesar in this play to the character and act of Brutus.

Brutus has seen Antony going to the course where he is to run with others. The feast of Lupercal in honour of the god Pan is being celebrated, and Antony is present as chief of one of the companies of priests. The Stoic Brutus looks upon all this as an offence. He despises Antony, because Antony is "gamesome," and he loves the dignified gravity of his own character:

Cas. Will you go see the order of the course?
Bru. Not I.
Cas. I pray you, do.
Bru. I am not gamesome; I do lack some part
Of that quick spirit that is in Antony.
Let me not hinder, Cassius, your desires;
I'll leave you.

Antony is a man of genius without moral fibre; a nature of a rich, sensitive, pleasure-loving kind; the prey of good impulses and of bad; looking on life as a game, in which he has a distinguished part to play, and playing that part with magnificent grace and skill. He is capable of personal devotion (though not of devotion to an idea), and has indeed a gift for subordination,—subordination to a Julius Caesar, to a Cleopatra. And as he has enthusiasm about great personalities, so he has a contempt for inefficiency and ineptitude. Lepidus is to him "a slight, unmeritable man meet to be sent on errands," one that is to be talked of not as a person, but as a property. Antony possesses no constancy of self-esteem; he can drop quickly out of favour with himself; and being without reverence for his own type of character, and being endowed with a fine versatility of perception and feeling, he can admire qualities the most remote from his own. It is Antony who utters the *éloge* over the body of Brutus at Philippi. Antony is not without an aesthetic sense and imagination, though of a somewhat unspiritual kind: he does not judge men by a severe moral code, but he feels in an aesthetic way the grace, the splendour, the piteous interest of the actors in the exciting drama of life, or their impertinence, ineptitude and comicality; and he feels that the play is poorer by the loss of so noble a figure as that of a Brutus. But Brutus, over whom his ideals dominate, and who is blind to facts which are not in harmony with his theory of the universe, is quite unable to perceive the power for good or for evil that is lodged in Antony, and there is in the great figure of Antony nothing which can engage or interest his imagination; for Brutus' view of life is not imaginative, or pictorial, or dramatic; but wholly ethical. The fact that Antony abandons himself to pleasure, is "gamesome," reduces him in the eyes of Brutus to a very ordinary person,—one who is silly or stupid enough not to recognise the first principle of human conduct, the need of self-mastery; one against whom the laws of the world must fight, and who is therefore of no importance. And Brutus was right with respect to the ultimate issues for Antony. Sooner or later Antony must fall to ruin. But before the moral defect in Antony's nature destroyed his fortune much was to happen. Before Actium might come Philippi.

The procession passes on; Caesar and Antony are out of sight; Brutus and Cassius are left alone. Cassius complains of want of warmth and gentleness in the bearing of Brutus towards him of late. The manner of self-restraint habitual to Brutus is noticeable, his grave courtesy, and desire for a sincere explanation and vindication of himself. Cassius now endeavours to gain over Brutus to the conspiracy, avoiding any suggestion of an interested motive, but holding up as it were a mirror in which Brutus may see himself reflected, and thence infer what lofty achievement is expected by Rome from one so noble. As his own credentials Cassius puts forward his freedom from those vices which Brutus most contemns, as if there were no dangers from the man whose life is not lax, ostentatious and self-indulgent:

> And be not jealous on me, gentle Brutus.
> Were I a common laugher, or did use
> To stale with ordinary oaths my love
> To every new protester; if you know
> That I do fawn on men and hug them hard
> And after scandal them, or if you know
> That I profess myself in banqueting
> To all the rout, then hold me dangerous.

It is noteworthy that while Cassius thus plays with Brutus and secures him, almost using him as his tool, he is fully conscious of the superiority of Brutus. The very weaknesses of Brutus come from the nobility of his nature. He cannot credit or conceive the base facts of life. He has no instrument by which to gauge the littleness of little souls.

The last scene of the first act brings us to the tempestuous night of prodigies which preceded the death of Julius Caesar. Casca appears with the superficial garb of cynicism dropt. Does Shakespeare in this play mean to signify to us unobtrusively that the philosophical creed which a man professes grows out of his character and circumstances as far as it is really a portion of his own being; and that as far as it is received by the intellect in the calm of life from teachers and schools, such a philosophical creed does not adhere very closely to the soul of a man, and may, upon the pressure of events or of passions, be cast aside? The Epicurean Cassius is shaken out of his philosophical scepticism by the portents which appeared upon the march to Philippi:

> You know that I held Epicurus strong,
> And his opinion; now I change my mind,
> And partly credit things that do presage.

The Stoic Brutus, who by the rules of his philosophy blamed Cato for a self-inflicted death, runs upon his own sword and dies. The dramatic self-consistency of the characters created by certain writers is to be noticed; we must notice in the case of Shakespeare, as a piece of higher art, the dramatic inconsistency of his characters. In the preceding scene, describing in his cynical mood the ceremony at which an offer of the crown was made to Caesar, Casca utters himself in prose; here Shakespeare puts verse into his mouth. "Did Cicero say anything?" Cassius inquired in the preceding conversation, and Casca answered with curt scorn, "Ay, he spoke Greek." But now so moved out of himself is Casca by the portents of the night, that he enlarges himself and grows effusive to this very Cicero, the recollection of whom he had dismissed with such impatient contempt.

Cicero passes along the streets perceiving no more than a storm from which it is prudent that an old man should be housed; his spirit is insulated by a thin, non-conducting web of scepticism and intellectuality from the electric atmosphere of the time. This electric atmosphere plays through every nerve of Cassius. His energy of brain and limb is stimulated and intensified, until it needs to relieve itself in movement. It is to him a night of high-strung delight. Besides, Cassius has much work to do, and the tempest suits his purposes:

> For my part, I have walk'd about the streets,
> Submitting me unto the perilous night;
> And thus, unbraced, Casca, as you see,
> Have bar'd my bosom to the thunder-stone;
> And when the cross blue lightning seem'd to open
> The breast of heaven, I did present myself
> Even in the aim and very flash of it.

Brutus is in his orchard alone. He has stolen away from Portia; he is seeking to master himself in solitude, and bring under the subjection of a clear idea and a definite resolve the tumultuary powers of his nature, which have been roused and thrown into disorder by the suggestions of Cassius. In the soliloquy of Brutus, after he has been left alone, will be found an excellent example of the peculiar brooding or dwelling style which Shakespeare appropriated at this period to the soliloquies of men. The soliloquies of his women are conceived in a different manner. Of this speech Coleridge has said, "I do not at present see into Shakespeare's motive, his *rationale,* or in what point of view he meant Brutus' character to appear." Shakespeare's motive is not far to seek. He wishes to show upon what grounds the political idealist acts. Brutus resolves that Caesar shall die by his hand as the conclusion of a series of hypotheses; there is, as it were, a sorties of abstract principles about ambition, and power, and reason, and affection; finally, a profound suspicion of Caesar is engendered, and his death is decreed. It is idealists who create a political terror; they are free from all desire for blood-shedding; but to them the lives of men and women are accidents; the lives of ideas are the true realities; and, armed with an abstract principle and a suspicion, they perform deeds which are at once beautiful and hideous:

> 'Tis a common proof
> That lowliness is young Ambition's ladder,
> Whereto the climber-upward turns his face;

But when he once attains the utmost round,
He then unto the ladder turns his back,
Looks in the clouds, scorning the base degrees
By which he did ascend; so Caesar may;
Then, lest he may, prevent!

The written instigations which Cassius has caused to be thrown in at Brutus' window add the final confirmation to his resolve; and at this moment the conspirators enter. While Brutus and Cassius converse apart, and the others are turned in the direction of the east, the first grey lines of morning begin doubtfully to fret the clouds. Nature, with her ministries of twilight and day-dawn, suffers no interruption of her calm, beneficent operancy, and, after tempest, another morning is broadening for all Rome. Casca points his sword toward the Capitol, and at the same moment the sun arises. "Is there not," asks Mr Craik, "some allusion, which the look and tone of the speaker might express more clearly than his words, to the great act about to be performed in the Capitol, and the change as of a new day that was expected to follow it?" Observe how strongly Shakespeare marks the passage of time up to the moment of Caesar's death; night, dawn, eight o'clock, nine o'clock, that our suspense may be heightened, and our interest kept upon the strain.

It is characteristic of Brutus that he will allow no oath to be taken by the conspirators. He who has been all his life cultivating reliance on the will apart from external props, cannot now fall back for support upon the objective bond of a vow or pledge. Their enterprise looks more clear and beautiful in the light of its own courage and justice than when associated with a vulgar formula of words:

Do not stain
The even virtue of our enterprise,
Nor the insuppressive mettle of our spirits,
To think that or our cause, or our performance
Did need an oath.

Cassius now proposes to bring Cicero into the plot; Casca, Cinna, and Metellus Cimber warmly concur. Brutus objects (and it is to be noticed that Shakespeare did not obtain from Plutarch this fine trait):

> O, name him not; let us not break with him;
> *For he will never follow anything*
> *That other men begin.*

And by mere force of his moral authority, Brutus carries his point. So again with the next matter under discussion. Cassius estimating the importance of Antony justly urges that Antony should perish with Caesar. But Brutus again objects. The political Girondin is not warring against men but against ideas:

> Let us be sacrificers, but not butchers, Caius.
> We all stand up against the spirit of Caesar;
> And in the spirit of men there is no blood.

Besides, apart from Caesar, Antony can do nothing. Is he not given "to sports, to wildness, and much company," and therefore an insignificant person? A shortsighted idealism! Yet it was better that Brutus should die with foiled purpose at Philippi than that he should sully the brightness of his virtue by the stain of what seemed to him needless bloodshedding. Like the Girondin that he is, Brutus trusts to moral forces and ideas, which operate in the real world in a large incalculable way, unlike that allowed for in any of our idealistic schemes of the world. While committing an act of violence against constituted authority, Brutus fails to perceive the necessary consequences of that act. Cassius, who with Caesar would have stabbed Antony, might have served his cause better than did Brutus. The gift with which Brutus enriched the world was the gift of himself, a soul of incorruptible virtue.

As the conspirators depart, Brutus, who is not fashioned for conspiracy, bids them look fresh and merrily,

> And bear it as our Roman actors do
> With untir'd spirits and formal constancy.

How ill Brutus can conceal his inward trouble appears from what immediately follows. Portia enters. The strange behaviour and distraught aspect of Brutus have roused her tenderest wifely anxieties. No relation of man and woman in the plays of

Shakespeare is altogether so noble as that of Portia and Brutus. The love of Brutus could not be given except with admiration equal to his love. He could not separate a public life of action from his life of the home, or sink down upon mild domestic comfort, some "gracious silence" like the Virgilia of Coriolanus. His love must be strenuous like every other part of his character, and must constantly infuse vigour and ardour into his life. Portia, while perfectly a woman, must be to him more than a woman; she must be an ideal of august and adorable heroism. Portia, Cato's daughter, Brutus' wife, is a Stoic like her husband. To test her constancy she had inflicted upon herself a wound in the thigh,—the will dealing hardly with the body, the idea daring to transform itself with eagerness and keen convention into the act. We read of no embrace, no touch of hands or lips, between Brutus and Portia; but we know that their souls have met, that they are inseparably one, and absolutely equal. Juliet, heroic nature though hers be, is but a passionate girl by the side of this perfect woman. And the nobility of Portia makes the love of Brutus for her almost a religion:

O ye gods,
Render me worthy of this noble wife!

He had thought not to burden her with the secret of the conspiracy; the sense of something concealed has made his manner toward her constrained. Now as an equal she demands her right, she pleads for her happiness of sharing all that concerns her husband. She will not be put off with kind evasions; she presses forward to know the formidable truth; and pleads upon her knees before the husband whom she venerates even as he venerates her:

Upon my knees
I charm you, by my once commended beauty,
By all your vows of love, and that great vow
Which did incorporate and make us one,
That you unfold to me, your self, your half,
Why you are heavy.

And Brutus grants her the share in his enterprise to which she is entitled.

With this scene may be compared and contrasted the scene in the first part of King Henry IV (Act ii, Scene 3), in which Lady Percy, alarmed by the evidences of excitement which her husband cannot conceal, but of which he will not render an account, persecutes him with loving importunity to disclose his secret. Lady Percy loves Hotspur as a loyal wife; but she has no serious confidence in her own influence with her gallant madcap Harry; and while playfully insisting on her demands she expects a refusal:

> Come, come you paraquito, answer me
> Directly unto this question that I ask;
> In faith I'll break thy little finger, Harry,
> An if thou wilt not tell me all things true.

Hotspur, through his seeming recklessness, has in reality a genuine manly tenderness for his wife; he is troubled by her importunities, and anxious to escape from them; but he is not going to be so weak as to betray his secret to a woman:

> Whither I must, I must; and, to conclude,
> This evening must I leave you, gentle Kate.
> I know you wise, but yet no farther wise
> Than Harry Percy's wife; constant you are,
> But yet a woman; and for secrecy
> No lady closer; for I will believe
> Thou wilt not utter what thou dost not know;
> And so far will I trust thee, gentle Kate.
> *Lady.* How! so far?
> *Hot.* Not an inch further.

And then comes the explanation of his apparent roughness:

> But hark you, Kate:
> Whither I go, thither shall you go too;
> To-day will I set forth, to-morrow you.
> Will this content you, Kate?
> *Lady.* It must of force.

The relation of husband and wife as conceived in the historical plays differs throughout from that relation as conceived in the tragedies.

In the fourth scene we again meet Portia. Brutus has gone forth to bring Caesar to the Capitol. Portia is standing without the door of her house, straining her ear to catch any sound the wind may bear from that direction. "Think you," asked Portia in the preceding scene, "I am no stronger than my sex?" Now she discovers her womanhood:

> O constancy, be strong upon my side,
> Set a huge mountain 'tween my heart and tongue!
> I have a man's mind, but a woman's might.

She is one strung nerve of suspense and anxiety. She is uncontrollably eager (for this stoical woman is of an organization as far as possible removed from the phlegmatic); yet when the soothsayer speaks, adding to her anxiety as to the event, the apprehension that the plot has been discovered, she for the time controls herself, and appears calm. When he is gone, she can endure no longer:

> I must go in. Ay me, how weak a thing
> The heart of woman is!

Such a woman as Portia pays a terrible tax for her self-mastery. The cheap payment of effusive tears and hysterical cries she cannot render as her tribute to the tyrannous powers. When tears escape her, each one is distilled from an intense agony. And because she yields less than others, she may snap the more suddenly. "It is the strongest hearts," said Landor, "that are the soonest broken." Had Portia been less her husband's equal, less absolutely one with him in his aims and endeavours, she might have lived. Her death, like her life, excludes all common grief and joy; the pain is a pain which makes us stronger; the joy is stricter than duty, and of higher power to constrain to all that is excellent. Shakespeare, with fine judgment, has allowed us to see Portia seldom in the play; otherwise an interest alien from that which he intended might have grown predominant.*

---

* Mr Hudson (*Shakespeare: His Life, Art and Characters*, vol. ii, p. 239) notices a touching incident from Plutarch, respecting Portia, which Shakespeare did not use. At the parting of Portia from Brutus in the sea-side city of Elea, she tried to dissemble her sorrow. "But a certain

Upon the death of Caesar, Cassius parts the crowd, and delivers an oration. This speech of Cassius Shakespeare has not recorded for us. We may be certain that it was fiery, triumphant, and effective; we may be certain that he did not, like Brutus, make studious effort to exclude all appeal to passion. It is characteristic of the idealist that he should treat the Roman crowd—that sensitive, variable, irrational mass—as if it must not be indulged in any manner of persuasion except a calm appeal to reason, and the presentation of an ideal of Justice. He begins with a vindication of his own conduct, an apology for Brutus. His manner is deliberate and constrained until he passes from self-defence to a direct appeal to his countrymen's patriotism and love of freedom; and it is noticeable that at this point his speech, which began as prose, if not actually verse, hovers on the brink of verse. But Brutus, who is utterly unable to calculate the composition of concrete forces, commits a yet graver error. When Antony, after the assassination, comes into the presence of the leaders of the conspiracy, Brutus addresses him also with a speech of explanation, an *apologia*. Cassius, who at their private conclave had urged Mark Antony's death, now comes forward with a brief and effective appeal to Antony's interests:

> Your voice shall be as strong as any man's
> In the disposing of new dignities.

Antony begs to be allowed to speak at Caesar's funeral. In the joy of having achieved an eminent deed which though it look savage, was indeed merciful, and for which he can render ample "reasons,"—Brutus is well pleased to act generously to a partizan of Caesar, and gives consent. Cassius is still urgent to have the future relation of Antony to the conspirators determined and made clear:

---

painting bewrayed her in the end. The device was taken out of the Greek stories, how Andromache accompanied her husband Hector when he went out of Troy to the wars, and how Hector delivered her his little son, and how her eyes were never off him. Portia, seeing this picture, and likening herself to be in the same case, fell a-weeping; and coming thither oftentimes in a day to see it, she wept still."

Will you be pricked in number of our friends;
Or shall we on, and not depend on you?

Upon hearing Brutus give consent to Antony's request, Cassius interposes:

Brutus, a word with you.
You know not what you do; do not consent
That Antony speak in his funeral.

But Brutus replies that he will himself go first into the pulpit, "And show the reason of our Caesar's death." Show the reason! After which, doubtless, appeal to the passions of a Roman crowd must be ineffectual. But in reality the speech of Brutus is unable to rouse any enthusiasm among his hearers for Liberty or an ideal of Justice. The people require a Caesar, and if their former lord be dead, then they will have Brutus himself for their new lord:

1. *Cit.* Bring him in triumph home unto his house.
2. *Cit.* Give him a statue with his ancestors.
3. *Cit.* Let him be Caesar.

This is not the mood in which the citizens can offer resistance to the appeals of Antony. The political idealist adds another to his series of fatal miscalculations.*

---

* Mr Hudson notices that "Plutarch has a short passage which served as a hint, not indeed of the matter, but for the style of that speech [of Brutus]. 'They do note,' says he, 'that in some of his epistles he counterfeited that brief compendious manner of the Lacedaemonians. As, when the war was begun, he wrote to the Pergamenians in this sort; 'I understand you have given Dolabella money: if you have done it willingly, you confess you have offended me; if against your wills, show it by giving me willingly.' This was Brutus' manners of letters, which were honoured for their briefness.'" *Shakespeare: His Life, Art and Characters*, vol. ii, pp. 234-35. This peculiarity of style is not confined to Brutus' address to the people. It appears, for example, in his final and deliberate reply to Cassius, Act i, Scene 2:

That you do love me I am nothing jealous;
What you would work me to I have some aim;
. . . .
. . . . . What you have said
I will consider; what you have to say
I will with patience hear.

The second scene of the fourth act was already celebrated in Shakespeare's own day. Leonard Digges records its popularity. It was imitated by Beaumont and Fletcher in *The Maid's Tragedy*, and afterwards by Dryden in *All for Love*. "I know no part of Shakespeare," Coleridge wrote, "that more impresses on me the belief of his genius being superhuman, than this scene between Brutus and Cassius." Brutus has alienated his friend by uncompromising adherence to his own ideal standard of purity: he has condemned Lucius Pella for taking bribes, although Cassius had written in his behalf. Brutus loves virtue and despises gold; but in the logic of facts there is an irony cruel or pathetic. Brutus maintains a lofty position of immaculate honour above Cassius; but ideals, and a heroic contempt for gold, will not fill the military coffer, or pay the legions, and the poetry of noble sentiment suddenly drops down to the prosaic complaint that Cassius had denied the demands made by Brutus for certain sums of money.* Nor is Brutus, though he worships an ideal of Justice, quite just in matters of concrete practical detail:

Cas. I denied you not.
Bru. You did.
Cas. I did not; he was but a fool
That brought my answer back. Brutus hath riv'd my heart;
A friend should bear his friend's infirmities,
But Brutus makes mine greater than they are.

Each is naturally and inevitably aggrieved with the other; one from the practical, the other from the ideal standpoint. Shakespeare, in his infinite pity for human error and frailty, makes us love Brutus and Cassius the better through the little wrongs which bring the great wealth of their love and true fraternity to light. Brutus calls for a bowl of wine in which to pledge their reconciliation. Then when their hearts are tenderest comes the confession of the sorrow which Brutus could not utter as long as a shadow lay between his soul and his friend's:

Cas. I did not think you could have been so angry.
Bru. O Cassius, I am sick of many griefs.

* Kreyssig, *Vorlesungen über Shakespeare* (ed. 1874), vol. i, p. 424.

Cas. Of your philosophy you make no use,
If you give place to accidental evils.
Bru. No man bears sorrow better. Portia is dead.

But Brutus is sustained by the spirit of Portia. To live in her spirit of Stoicism becomes now the highest act of religion to her memory.

Speak no more of her. Give me a bowl of wine;—
In this I bury all unkindness, Cassius.

The armed men talking so gravely, before the great day which is to decide the fate of the world of the "insupportable and touching loss" make us know what this woman was. Profound emotion, Shakespeare was aware, can express itself quietly and with reserve. The noisy demonstration of grief over the supposed dead Juliet is the extravagant abandonment to sorrow, partly real and partly formal, of hearts which were little sensitive, and which had little concerned themselves about the joy or misery of Juliet living. Laertes' rant in the grave of Ophelia is reproved by the more violent hyperbole of Hamlet. Brutus will henceforth be silent, and possess his soul:

Cas. Portia, thou art gone.
Bru. No more I pray you.

The remainder of the life of Brutus is a sad, sustained devotion to his cause.

And now once more he helps to ruin that cause. Cassius with good reason urges that the army should not advance upon Philippi; Brutus is in favour of advancing. Cassius, as always, is in the right; Brutus, as always, carries his point. Night has crept upon their talk, and with a profound reconciliation, with a sense of full and measureless fraternity they part. The Roman leader, now that the great battle has drawn near, does not occupy himself like Henry V before the morning of Agincourt in moving from sentinel to sentinel with words of cheer. He is in his tent, and the boy Lucius touches his instrument, drowsily fingering the strings.* Brutus, with his beautiful freedom from

---

* Brutus loves music; but of Cassius, Caesar notes "he hears no music." Compare *Merchant of Venice*, Act v, Scene 1:

the petty self-interests of daily life, is gentle and considerate towards everyone. The servants have lain down. Lucius drops away into the irresistible sleep of boyhood. Brutus, who at the call of duty and honour could plunge his dagger into Caesar, cannot wake a sleeping boy. Shakespeare had somehow learnt

> The devotion to something afar
> From the sphere of our sorrow.

Brutus gently disengages the instrument from the hand of Lucius, and continues his book where he had left it off last night. There is nothing more tender in the plays of Shakespeare than this scene. The tenderness of a man who is stern is the only tenderness which is wholly delicate and refined.

In the battle at Philippi it is Brutus who, by his inconsiderate rashness and miscalculation of facts, ensures defeat. This is his last error. He is willing that Strato should hold the sword while he falls upon it:

> Thou art a fellow of a good respect,
> Thy life hath had some smatch of honour in it;
> Hold then my sword.

Brutus must die by no ignoble hand. To the last moment he reveres himself. And the concluding words of the play convey to us an assurance, which we require, that his body shall suffer no wrong.

The life of Brutus, as the lives of such men must be, was a good life, in spite of its disastrous fortunes. He had found no man who was not true to him. And he had known Portia. The idealist was predestined to failure in the positive world. But for him the true failure would have been disloyalty to his ideals. Of such failure he suffered none. Octavius and Mark Antony remained victors at Philippi. Yet the purest wreath of victory rests on the forehead of the defeated conspirator.

> The man that hath no music in himself,
> Nor is not moved with concord of sweet sounds,
> Is fit for treasons, stratagems, and

U

II

The transition from the *Julius Caesar* of Shakespeare to his *Antony and Cleopatra* produces in us the change of pulse and temper experienced in passing from a gallery of antique sculpture to a room splendid with the colours of Titian and Paul Veronese. In the characters of the *Julius Caesar* there is a severity of outline; they impose themselves with strict authority upon the imagination; subordinated to the great spirit of Caesar, the conspirators appear as figures of life-size, but they impress us as no larger than life. The demand which they make is exact; such and such tribute must be rendered by the soul to each. The characters of the *Antony and Cleopatra* insinuate themselves through the senses, trouble the blood, ensnare the imagination, invade our whole being like colour or like music. The figures dilate to proportions greater than human, and are seen through a golden haze of sensuous splendour. *Julius Caesar* and *Antony and Cleopatra* are related as works of art rather by points of contrast than by points of resemblance. In the one an ideal of duty is dominant; the other is a divinisation of pleasure, followed by the remorseless Nemesis of eternal law. Brutus, the Stoic, constant, loyal to his ideas, studious of moral perfection, bent upon gaining self-mastery, unsullied and untarnished to the end, stands over against Antony, swayed hither and thither by appetites, interests, imagination, careless of his own moral being, incapable of self-control, soiled with the stains of passion and decay. And of Cleopatra what shall be said? Is she a creature of the same breed as Cato's daughter, Portia? Does the one word woman include natures so diverse? Or is Cleopatra—Antony's "serpent of old Nile"—no mortal woman, but Lilith who ensnared Adam before the making of Eve? Shakespeare has made the one as truly woman as the other; Portia, the ideal of moral loveliness, heroic and feminine; Cleopatra, the ideal of sensual attractiveness, feminine also:

> A bliss in proof, and proved, a very woe;
> Before, a joy proposed; behind, a dream.*

We do not once see the lips of Brutus laid on Portia's lips as seal

* Shakespeare's *Sonnets*, cxxix.

of perfect union, but we know that their beings and their lives had embraced in flawless confidence, and perfect, mutual service. Antony embracing Cleopatra exclaims,

> The nobleness of life
> Is to do thus; when such a mutual pair
> And such a twain can do't, in which I bind,
> On pain of punishment, the world to weet
> We stand up peerless.

Yet this "mutual pair," made each to fill the body and soul of the other with voluptuous delight, are made also each for the other's torment. Antony is haunted by suspicion that Cleopatra will betray him; he believes it possible that she could degrade herself to familiarity with Caesar's menials. And Cleopatra is aware that she must weave her snares with endless variety, or Antony will escape.

The spirit of the play, though superficially it appear voluptuous, is essentially severe. That is to say, Shakespeare is faithful to the fact. The fascination exercised by Cleopatra over Antony, and hardly less by Antony over Cleopatra, is not so much that of the senses as of the sensuous imagination. A third of the world is theirs. They have left youth behind with its slight, melodious raptures and despairs. Theirs is the deeper intoxication of middle age, when death has become a reality, when the world is limited and positive, when life is urged to yield up quickly its utmost treasures of delight. What may they not achieve of joy who have power, and beauty, and pomp, and pleasure all their own? How shall they fill every minute of their time with the quintessence of enjoyment and of glory?

> Let Rome in Tiber melt! and the wide arch
> Of the rang'd empire fall? here is my space.

Only *one* thing they had not allowed for,—that over and above power, and beauty, and pleasure, and pomp, there is a certain inevitable fact, a law which cannot be evaded. Pleasure sits enthroned as queen; there is a revel, and the lords of the earth, crowned with roses, dance before her to the sound of lascivious flutes. But presently the scene changes; the hall of revel is transformed to an arena; the dancers are armed gladiators; and as they advance to combat they pay the last homage to their Queen with the words, *Morituri te salutant.*

The pathos of Antony and Cleopatra resembles the pathos of Macbeth. But Shakespeare like Dante allows the soul of the perjurer and murderer to drop into a lower, blacker, and more lonely circle of Hell than the soul of the man who has sinned through voluptuous self-indulgence. Yet none the less Antony is daily dropping away farther from all that is sound, strong, and enduring. His judgment wanes with his fortune. He challenges to a combat with swords his clear-sighted and unimpassioned rival into whose hands the empire of the world is about to fall. He abandons himself to a senseless exasperation:

> I will be treble-sinew'd, hearted, breathed,
> And fight maliciously; for when mine hours
> Were nice and lucky, men did ransom lives
> Of me with jests; but now I'll set my teeth,
> And send to darkness all that stop me.

He sees his fate closing in upon him; he will sell his life dearly; and meantime, like a man condemned to execution upon the morrow, he will have one more night of pleasure:

> Come,
> Let's have one other gaudy night: call to me
> All my sad captains; fill our bowls once more;
> Let's mock the midnight bell
> *Cleo.* It is my birthday.

But Antony's struggle after boisterous mirth proves a piteous mockery. The banquet is a valediction; the great leader's followers are transformed to women; Enobarbus turns away "onion-eyed." Antony makes one rude effort to lift himself up above the damps and depression which have fallen on his spirit, one effort fling aside the consciousness of the failure of his life, which yet clings to him:

> Ho, ho, ho!
> Now the witch take me, if I meant it thus!
> Grace grow where those drops fall! My hearty friends,
> You take me in too dolorous a sense;
> For I spake to you for your comfort; did desire you

To burn this night with torches: know, my hearts,
I hope well of to-morrow; and will lead you
Where rather I'll expect victorious life
Than death and honour. Let's to supper, come,
And drown consideration.

Hercules, the generous wielder of strength, whom Antony loved, is departing from him; music heard at midnight by the sentinels warn them of the withdrawal of the favour of the divinity. Experience, manhood, honour, more and more violate themselves in Antony. Cleopatra's ship turns the rudder and flies from the sea-fight. Antony, regardless of fortune and of shame,

Claps on the sea-wing and like a doting mallard,
Leaving the fight in height, flies after her.

He is indeed the ruin of Cleopatra's magic; yet he is a lordly and eminent ruin, and before all sinks in blackness and ashes, there is a last leaping-up of the flame of his fortune by which we see the figure of Antony, still majestic, pathetically illuminated by a glory that passes away. He is made glad with one hour's victory. Though deserted by Enobarbus, Scarus has been faithful and is at his side, red from honourable wounds:

Give me thy hand;
Enter Cleopatra, attended.
To this great fairy I'll commend thy acts,
Make her thanks bless thee [*To Cleo.*], O thou day o' the world,
Chain mine armed neck; leap thou, attire and all,
Through proof of harness to my heart, and there
Ride on the pants triumphing!
Cleo. Lord of lords!
O infinite virtue, comest thou smiling from
The world's great snare uncaught?
Ant. My nightingale,
We have beat them to their beds. What girl? though gray
Do something mingle with our younger brown,
Yet ha' we a brain that nourishes our nerves,
And can get goal for goal of youth.

Measure things only by the sensuous imagination, and everything in the world of oriental voluptuousness, in which Antony lies bewitched, is great. The passion and the pleasure of the Egyptian queen, and of her paramour, toil after the infinite. The Herculean strength of Antony, the grandeur and prodigal power of his nature, inflate and buoy up the imagination of Cleopatra:

> The demi-Atlas of this earth, the arm
> And burgonet of men.

While he is absent, Cleopatra would, if it were possible, annihilate time:

> *Charmian.* Why, madam?
> *Cleo.* That I might sleep out this great gap of time.
> My Antony is away.

When Antony dies the only eminent thing in the earth is gone, and an universal flatness, an equality of insignificances remains:

> Young boys and girls
> Are level now with men; the odds is gone,
> And there is nothing left remarkable
> Beneath the visiting moon.

We do not mistake this feeling of Cleopatra towards Antony for love; but he has been for her (who had known Caesar and Pompey), the supreme sensation. She is neither faithful to him nor faithless; in her complex nature, beneath each fold or layer of sincerity, lies one of insincerity, and we cannot tell which is the last and innermost. Her imagination is stimulated, and nourished by Antony's presence. And he in his turn finds in the beauty and witchcraft of the Egyptian, something no less incommensurable and incomprehensible. Yet no one felt more profoundly than Shakespeare,—as his *Sonnets* abundantly testify,—that the glory of strength and of beauty is subject to limit and to time. What he would seem to say to us in this play, not in the manner of a doctrinaire or a moralist, but wholly as an artist, is that this sensuous infinite is but a dream, a deceit, a snare. The miserable change comes upon Antony. The remorseless practice of Cleopatra upon his heart has done him to death. And among things which the barren world offers to the Queen she now finds death, a painless death, the least hateful. Shakespeare, in his high impartiality to fact, denies none of the glory of the lust of the eye and the pride of life. He compels us to acknowledge these to the utmost. But he adds that there is another demonstrable fact of the world, which tests the visible pomp of the earth, and the splendour of sensuous passion, and finds them wanting. The glory of the royal festival is not dulled by Shakespeare or diminished; but also he shows us in letters of flame the handwriting upon the wall.

This Shakespeare effects, however, not merely or chiefly by means of a catastrophe. He does not deal in precepts or moral reflections, or practical applications. He is an artist, but an artist who grasps truth largely. The ethical truth lives and breathes in every part of his work as artist, no less than the truth to things sensible and presentable to the imagination. At every moment in this play we assist at a catastrophe—the decline of a lordly nature. At every moment we are necessarily aware of the gross, the mean, the disorderly womanhood in Cleopatra, no less than of the witchery and wonder which excite, and charm, and subdue. We see her a dissembler, a termagant, a coward; and yet "vilest things become her." The presence of a spirit of *life* in Cleopatra, quick, shifting, multitudinous, incalculable, fascinates the eye, and would, if it could, lull the moral sense to sleep, as the sea does with its endless snake-like motions in the sun and shade. She is a wonder of the world, which we would travel far to look upon. Enobarbus, while contemptuously ironical, and looking through her manifest practice upon Mark Antony with perfect clearness of vision, admits also that she repays the cost of inspection:

Ant. She is cunning past man's thought.

Eno. Alack, sir, no; her passions are made of nothing but the finest part of pure love; we cannot call her winds and waters, sighs and tears; they are greater storms and tempests than almanacs can report; this cannot be cunning in her—if it be, she makes a shower of rain as well as Jove.

Ant. Would I had never seen her!

Eno. O, sir, you had then left unseen a wonderful piece of work, which not to have been blest withal would have discredited your travel.

"Great crimes, springing from high passions, grafted on high qualities, are the legitimate source of tragic poetry. But to make the extreme of littleness produce an effect like grandeur—to make the excess of frailty produce an effect like power—to heap up together all that is most unsubstantial, frivolous, vain, contemptible, and variable, till the worthlessness be lost in the magnitude, and a sense of the sublime spring from the very elements of littleness—to do this, belonged only to Shakespeare, that worker of miracles. Cleopatra is a brilliant antithesis, a compound of contradictions, of all that we most hate, with what we most admire."*

If we would know how an artist devoted to high moral ideals would treat such a character as that of the fleshly enchantress we have but to turn to the Samson Agonistes. Milton exposes Dalila only to drive her explosively from the stage. Shakespeare would have studied her with equal delight and detestation. Yet the severity of Shakespeare, in his own dramatic fashion, is as absolute as that of Milton. Antony is dead. The supreme sensation of Cleopatra's life is ended, and she seems in the first passionate burst of chagrin to have no longer interest in anything but death. By-and-by she is in the presence of Caesar, and hands over to him a document, the "brief of money, plate, and jewels" of which she is possessed. She calls on her treasurer Seleucus to vouch for its accuracy:

Speak the truth, Seleucus.

Sel. Madam,
I had rather seal my lips than to my peril
Speak that which is not.

Cleo. What have I kept back?

Sel. Enough to purchase what you have made known.

---

* Mrs Jameson, *Characteristics of Women*, vol. ii, p. 122, ed. 1858. The study of Cleopatra's character is among the best of this writer's criticisms of Shakespeare.

Caes. Nay, blush not, Cleopatra; I approve
Your wisdom in the deed.

In her despair, while declaring that she will die "in the high Roman fashion," Cleopatra yet clings to her plate and jewels. And the cold approval of Caesar, who never gains the power which passion supplies, nor loses the power which passion withdraws and dissipates, the approval of Caesar is confirmed by the judgment of the spectator. It is right and natural that Cleopatra should love her jewels, and practise a fraud upon her conqueror.

Nor is her death quite in that "high Roman fashion" which she had announced. She dreads physical pain, and is fearful of the ravage which death might commit upon her beauty;* under her physician's direction she has "pursued conclusions infinite of easy ways to die." And now to die painlessly is better than to grace the triumph of Octavius. In her death there is something dazzling and splendid, something sensuous, something theatrical, something magnificently coquettish, and nothing stern. Yet Shakespeare does not play the rude moralist; he needs no chorus of Israelite captives to utter invective against this Dalila. Let her possess all her grandeur, and her charm. Shakespeare can show us more excellent things which will make us proof against the fascination of these:

Cleo. Give me my robe, put on my crown; I have
Immortal longings in me: now no more
The juice of Egypt's grape shall moist this lip;
Yare, yare, good Iras; quick. Methinks I hear
Antony call; I see him rouse himself
To praise my noble act; I hear him mock
The luck of Caesar, which the gods give men
To excuse their after-wrath: husband, I come:
Now to that name my courage prove my title!

---

* Shall they hoist me up,
And show me to the shouting varletry
Of censuring Rome? Rather a ditch in Egypt
Be gentle grave unto me! rather on Nilus' mud
Lay me stark naked, and let the water-flies
Blow me into abhorring.

I am fire and air; my other elements
I give to baser life. So; have you done?
Come then, and take the last warmth of my lips.
Farewell, kind Charmian; Iras, long farewell.
[*Kisses them. Iras falls and dies.*]
Have I the aspic in my lips? Dost fall?
If thou and nature can so gently part
The stroke of death is as a lover's pinch,
Which hurts and is desired. Dost thou lie still?
If thus thou vanishest, thou tell'st the world
It is not worth leave-taking.

Char. Dissolve, thick cloud, and rain, that I may say
The gods themselves do weep!

Cleo. This proves me base:
If she first meet the curled Antony,
He'll make demand of her, and spend that kiss
Which is my heaven to have. Come, thou mortal wretch:
[*To an asp, which the applies to her breast.*]
With thy sharp teeth this knot intrinsicate
Of life at once untie: poor venomous fool,
Be angry and despatch. O couldst thou speak,
That I might hear thee call great Caesar ass
Unpolicied!

Char. O eastern star!

Cleo. Peace, peace!
Dost thou not see my baby at my breast
That sucks the nurse asleep?

Char. O break! O break!

Cleo. As sweet as balm, as soft as air as gentle,—
O Antony!—Nay, I will take thee too:
[*Applying another asp to her arm.*
What should I stay— [*Dies.*

Char. In this vile world? So, fare thee well.
Now boast thee, death, in thy possession lies
A lass unparalleled. Downy windows, close,
And golden Phoebus never be beheld
Of eyes again so royal.

III

The subject of *Coriolanus* is the ruin of a noble life through the sin of pride. If duty be the dominant ideal with Brutus, and pleasure of a magnificent kind be the ideal of Antony and Cleopatra, that which gives tone and colour to Coriolanus is an ideal of self-centred power. The greatness of Brutus is altogether that of the moral conscience; his external figure does not dilate upon the world through a golden haze like that of Antony, nor bulk massively and tower like that of Coriolanus. Brutus venerates his ideals, and venerates himself; but this veneration of self is in a certain sense disinterested. A haughty and passionate personal feeling, a superb egoism are with Coriolanus the sources of weakness and of strength. Brutus is tender and considerate to all—to his household servants, to the boy Lucius, to the poor peasantry from whom he will not wring their petty hard-earned gains. The Theseus of *A Midsummer Night's Dream*, the great lord and conqueror, now in his mood of leisure and enjoyment, is graciously indulgent to the rough-handed and thick-witted mechanicals of Athens. In Henry V Shakespeare had drawn the figure of a man right royal, who yet keeps his sympathies in living contact with the humblest of his subjects, and who by his real rising above self, his noble disinterestedness is saved from arrogance and haughty self-will. On the ground of common manhood he can meet John Bates and Michael Williams; and the great king, strong because he possesses in himself so large a fund of this plain, sound manhood, finds comfort and support in his sense of equality with his subjects and fellow soldiers. "For though I speak it to you," says Henry while playing the private soldier on the night before the battle, "I think the king is but a man as I am; the violet smells to him as it doth to me; the element shows to him as it doth to me; all his senses have but human conditions; his ceremonies laid by, in his nakedness he appears but a man; and though his affections are higher mounted than ours, yet when they stoop they stoop with the like wing." Only the greatness of a high responsibility distinguishes the king, and gives him weightier cares and nobler toil. Such is the spirit, neither aristocratic nor, in the modern doctrinaire sense, democratic, of Shakespeare's *Henry V*.

"The whole dramatic moral of Coriolanus," Hazlitt wrote, "is that those who have little shall have less, and that those who have much shall take all that others have left. The people are poor, therefore they ought to be starved. They are slaves, therefore they ought to be beaten. They work hard, therefore they ought to be treated like beasts of burden. They are ignorant, therefore they ought not to be allowed to feel that they want food, or clothing, or rest, that they are enslaved, oppressed, and miserable."* This is simply impossible; this is extravagantly untrue, a piece of the passionate injustice which breaks forth every now and again in Hazlitt's writings. The dramatic moral of *Coriolanus* lies far nearer to the very opposite of Hazlitt's statement. Had the hero of the play possessed some of the human sympathies of Henry V, the tragic issue would have become impossible.

"Shakespeare," a great modern poet has said, "is incarnated, uncompromising feudalism in literature."† Shakespeare is surely something more human and permanent than feudalism: but it is true that he is not in a modern sense democratic. That he recognized the manly worth and vigour of the common English character is evident. It cannot be denied, however, that when the people are seen in masses in Shakespeare's plays, they are nearly always shown as factious, fickle, and irrational. To explain this fact we need not suppose that Shakespeare wrote to flatter the prejudice of the *jeunesse dorée* of the Elizabethan theatre.‡ How could Shakespeare represent the people otherwise? In the Tudor period the people had not yet emerged. The people, like Milton's half-created animals, is still pawing to get free its hinder parts from the mire. The mediaeval attempts to resist oppression, the risings of peasants or of citizens, inaugurated commonly by the murder of a Lord or of a Bishop, were for the most part desperate attempts, rash and dangerous, sustained by no sense of adequate moral or material power. It is only after such an immense achievement as that of 1789, such a proof of

---

* *Characters of Shakespeare's Plays*, p. 74 (ed. 1818).

† Walt Whitman, *Democratic Vistas*, p. 81.

‡ See Rümelin, *Shakespeare-Studien*, p. 222.

power as the French Revolution afforded, that moral dignity, the spirit of self-control and self-denial, the heroic devotion of masses of men to ideas and not merely interests, could begin to manifest themselves. Shakespeare studied and represented in his art the world which lay before him. If he prophesied the future, it was not in the ordinary manner of prophets, but only by completely embodying the present, in which the future was contained.

It has been asked, if Shakespeare had been born a generation later what side would he have taken in that great conflict, in which Milton struggled so nobly on the side of liberty. A critic of admirable insight, already referred to—H.A. Werner—discovers in the author of *Hamlet* and of *Lear* a thinker in the foremost ranks of modern and patriotic spirits, a forerunner of the struggle in which England was to engage first among the nations of Europe. The drama of *Hamlet* is "a Prometheus-sigh for freedom and deliverance, for honour and influence, for security and peace." It portrays the collision between an effete society buttressing itself up against the past, and "an idea, ever young, to which all the future belongs." But Shakespeare's statement of the fact concerning the revolutionary epochs of the world is uttered, the critic adds, not as a piece of political instruction, but as a question to fate; it is, as it were, "the first half of a Book of Job," a solemn balancing of good and evil in the world, wherein neither appears preponderant; and the longer the poet thought, the more definitely the political phenomenon, and its influence upon the life and character of individual man assumed the shape of an insoluble riddle.* It is impossible to accept this interpretation of Shakespeare's political tendencies otherwise than as an ingenious reading-in of modern ideas between the lines of Shakespeare's art.

But neither can we admit with the champion of so-called "realist" criticism, Rümelin, that Shakespeare perceived the existence already in Elizabeth's time of the Royalist and Roundhead parties, and that being personally associated with

* Ueber das Dunkel in der Hamlet-Tragödie. Von H.A. Werner, *Jahrbuch der Deutschen Shakespeare-Gesellschaft*, vol. v, pp. 37-81.

the young Elizabethan nobility, and as actor, playwright, and stage-manager, opposed to the Puritan *bourgeoisie*, "Shakespeare was an extreme Royalist, and an adherent of the purest water to the Court party and the nobles."* No; had Shakespeare lived when Milton lived, he would probably have passed through his life and gone to the grave in silence. He would certainly never have consumed himself in writing passionate pamphlets of huge dimensions as Milton did on behalf either of this party or of that. We cannot suppose that he would have been satisfied with the cavalier ideal of manhood, with its gallantry of showy devotion to church and king—to the church of Laud and the royalty of Charles. We cannot imagine Shakespeare among the Court singers who grated "lean and flashy songs" on scrannle pipes. But neither could he have accepted as complete the Puritan ideal. Sir Toby Belch is not an embodiment of the highest wisdom; but Malvolio has no answer when the irrepressible knight addresses him: "Dost thou think because thou art virtuous there shall be no more cakes and ale?" Ginger is hot in the mouth, Feste the clown justly declares; and *that* fact must enter into every adequate idea of human life. Had Shakespeare lived when Milton lived, he would have seen and mourned over the breach in humanity, the violence done to human happiness and human culture by two opposite ideals which tore the truth in sunder. It would have been impossible for him to attain his own complete development either as an artist or as a man. He would have looked on, and uttered now and again the cry of pain and indignation, "A plague on both your houses!"

What were Shakespeare's political views? It is matter of congratulation that Shakespeare approached history not through political theories, or philosophies, but through a wide and deep sympathy with human action, and human suffering. That a poet of the nineteenth century should disregard political theories, and philosophies of history, would prove that he was lacking in that very sympathy with humanity which made Shakespeare what he was. But the seventeenth century was one in which, in the world of politics, nation struggled with nation,

* Rümelin, *Shakespeare-Studien*, p. 217.

and man with man, rather than idea with idea. Shakespeare has no political doctrine to apply to the civil contest of the houses of Lancaster and York, by which to resolve the claims of the contending parties. If we discover any principle in which he had faith, it is that of the right of the kingliest nature to be king. The divine right of Richard II, gallantly urged by the Bishop of Carlisle, is hardly as sacred in Shakespeare's eyes as the divine right of the son of the usurping Bolingbroke. It is Henry VI whose over-irritable conscience suggests to him doubts respecting the title of his house. Happily we are not afflicted by Shakespeare with doctrinaire utterances, with sentiments liberal or reactionary uttered by the heroes of monarchy or of republicanism. A time will perhaps come, more favourable to true art than the present, when ideas are less outstanding factors in history than they have been in this century; when thought will be obscurely present in instinctive action, and in human emotion, and will vitalize and inspire these joyously rather than tyrannically dominate them. And then men's sympathy with the Elizabethan drama will be more prompt and sure than in our day it can be.

Party-spirits are baffled by the great human poet. They can with entire ease and self-satisfaction read their several creeds, political and religious, into the poetry of Shakespeare; but *find* them there they cannot. Only if we look for what is truly human and of permanent interest to man we shall not be disappointed. "Many reproaches have been uttered against Shakespeare. But the hypocrite whom his poetry does not unmask and cover with confusion, the tyrant who does not suffer in himself the pangs of conscience, and earn the general hatred, the coward who is not made a laughing-stock, the dressed-up imposition, who, discovered in his nakedness, does not experience the poet's annihilating scorn, is in vain to be sought for among the historical figures of these dramas."*

* F. Kreyssig, *Shakespeare-Fragen*, pp. 97-98. The discussion of this subject by Kreyssig is excellent. "Shakespeare hätte sich bei seinen Zuschauern so wenig Dank verdient als bei den Behörden, wenn er etwa in der Schilderung des König Johann für die Barone und die Communen gegen den König Partei genommen hätte, statt für England gegen Frankreich und gegen den Papst. Ja, er hätte ganz aus der ihn umgebenden geistigen

That the people should appear at all in the histories of Shakespeare is worthy of note. In French tragedy the people plays no part; and naturally, for "French history does not speak of the people before the nineteenth century."* Shakespeare's representation of the people is by no means harsh or ungenial. He does not discover in them heroic virtues; he does not think that a crowd of citizens is invariably very wise, patient, or temperate; and he has a certain aversion, quite under control however, to the sweaty caps, and grimy hands, and stinking breath of garlic-eaters, and men of occupation.† Nevertheless, Shakespeare recognises that the heart of the people is sound; their feelings are generally right, but their view of facts is perverted by interests, by passions, by stupidity. In the play of *Coriolanus* the citizens are not insensible to the virtues of the great Consul; they appreciate the humorous kindliness of the patrician Menenius. But they are as wax in the hands of their demagogues. Is Shakespeare's representation so wholly unjust to the seventeenth century, or even to the nineteenth? He had no political doctrinaire philosophy, no humanitarian idealism, to put between himself and the facts concerning the character of the people. His age did not supply him with humanitarian idealism; but man delighted Shakespeare and woman also. Thersites was not beyond the range of his sympathy. And to

---

Atmosphäre heraustreten müssen, um nach politischer Gesinnungstüchtigkeit und Geschichtsphilosophie im Sinne seiner heutigen Kritiker und Nachahmer zu trachten. Man wird seine Historien vergeblich nach liberalen Sentenzen durchsuchen. Wenn er dann aber, von seinem Standpuncte, dabei im Rechte war: sind es seine Gegner von dem ihrigen nicht ebenso sehr, indem sie sich lieber an den Gedanken- und Gesinnungshelden unserer modernen historischen Dramen erbauen als an den Schlagezu's und Haltefest's, den unbarmherzigen Tyrannen, den hochfahrenden Rittern, den intriguanten Priestern und leidenschaftlichen Weibern der Shakespeare'schen Historien?" *Shakespeare-Fragen*, p. 92. I am indebted to other passages in the same lecture for some suggestions.

* A. Mézières, *Shakespeare, ses Œuvres et ses Critiques*, p. 154. M. Mézières studies the historical dramas of Shakespeare in a highly interesting manner, throwing the characters into groups,—the women, the children, the people, the lords, the prelates, the kings.

† Kreyssig, *Shakespeare-Fragen*, p. 95.

Shakespeare the people did not appear as Thersites; at worst it appeared as Caliban.

Further if Shakespeare exposes the vices of a mob, he shrinks as little from exposing the vices of a court. The wisdom of the populace is not inferior to the wisdom of a Polonius. The manners of handicraftsmen are as truly gentle as the manners of Osric. Of ceremony Shakespeare was no lover, but he was deeply in love with all that is sound, substantial, honest. Prince Henry flies from the inanimate, bloodless, and insincere world of his father's court to the society of drawers and carriers in Eastcheap. In the play of *Coriolanus*, the intolerant haughtiness and injustice of the patrician is brutal and stupid, not less, but rather more, than the plebeian inconstancy and turbulence.

In Shakespeare's late play, *The Tempest*, written when he was about to retire for good to his Stratford home, he indulges in a sly laugh at the principles of communism. He who had earned the New Place, and become a landed gentleman by years of irksome toil, did not see that he was bound to share his tenements and lands with his less industrious neighbours. On the contrary he meant to hold them himself by every legal title, and at his decease to hand them down to his daughter and her sons, and sons' sons. Into the mouth of the honest old counsellor, Gonzalo, the dramatist puts the pleasant theory of communism and of human perfectibility, and Gonzalo is amusingly landed in the inconsequence of resolving to be himself sovereign of his kingless commonwealth.* In Shakespeare's earliest play, or one of the earliest, *Henry VI*, and in a passage certainly not written by Marlowe, nor in the manner of Greene, Jack Cade announces his intended reformation of the state of England. "Be brave, then; for your captain is brave, and vows reformation. There shall be in England seven halfpenny loaves sold for a penny; the three-hooped pot shall have ten hoops; and I will make it felony to drink small beer; all the realm shall be in common, and in

* Shakespeare borrows his imaginary commonwealth from Montaigne. On Shakespeare's obligations to Montaigne, see M. Philarète Chasles, *Études sur Shakespeare*, pp. 162-87.

Cheapside shall my palfrey go to grass: and when I am king, as king I will be—." And the people shout, "God save your Majesty!" George Bevis and John Holland discuss affairs of State:

Bevis. I tell thee, Jack Cade the clothier means to dress the commonwealth, and turn it, and get a new nap upon it.
Holl. So he had need, for 'tis threadbare. Well, I say it was never merry world in England since gentlemen came up.
Bevis. O miserable age! virtue is not regarded in handicraftsmen.
Holl. The nobility think scorn to go in leather aprons.
Bevis. Nay, more, the King's council are no good workmen.
Holl. True; and yet it is said labour in thy vocation: which is as much as to say, let the magistrates be labouring men; and therefore should we be magistrates.
Bevis. Thou hast hit it; for there's no better sign of a brave mind than a hard hand.

"An audience," writes Mr Walter Bagehot, "which *bona fide* entered into the merit of this scene, would never believe in everybody's suffrage. They would know that there is such a thing as nonsense, and when a man has once attained to that deep conception, you may be sure of him ever after [...]. The author of *Coriolanus* never believed in a mob, and did something towards preventing anybody else from doing so. But this political idea was not exactly the strongest in Shakespeare's mind [...]. He had two others stronger, or as strong. First, the feeling of loyalty to the ancient polity of this country, not because it was good, but because it existed [...]. The second peculiar tenet which we ascribe to his political creed is a disbelief in the middle classes. We fear he had no opinion of traders [...]. You will generally find that when a 'citizen' is mentioned, he does or says something absurd.* Shakespeare had a clear perception that it is possible to bribe a class as well as an individual [...]. He everywhere speaks in praise of a tempered, and ordered, and qualified polity, in which the pecuniary classes have a certain influence, but no more; and shows in every page a keen

* Not always. See, for example, *King Richard III*, Act ii, Sc. 3, where a "divine instinct" informing men's minds of coming danger moves in the breasts of the citizens.

sensibility to the large views and high-souled energies, the gentle refinements and disinterested desires in which those classes are likely to be especially deficient. He is particularly the poet of personal nobility, though throughout his writings there is a sense of freedom; just as Milton is the poet of freedom, though with an underlying reference to personal nobility; indeed, we might well expect our two poets to combine the appreciation of a rude and generous liberty with that of a delicate and refined nobleness, since it is the union of these two elements that characterises our society and their experience."*

Although the play of *Coriolanus* almost inevitably suggests a digression into the consideration of the politics of Shakespeare, it must once again be asserted that the central and vivifying element in the play is not a political problem, but an individual character and life. The tragic struggle of the play is not that of patricians with plebeians, but of Coriolanus with his own self. It is not the Roman people who bring about his destruction; it is the patrician haughtiness and passionate self-will of Coriolanus himself. Were the contest of political parties the chief interest of Shakespeare's drama, the figures of the Tribunes must have been drawn upon a larger scale. They would have been endowed with something more than "foxship." As representatives of a great principle, or of the power constantly tending in one direction, they might have appeared worthy rivals of the leaders of the patrician party; and the fall of Coriolanus would be signalised by some conquest and advance of the tide of popular power.† Shakespeare's drama is the drama of individuality, including under this name all those bonds of duty and of affection which attach man to his fellow-man, but not impersonal principles and ideas.‡ The passion of

* Walter Bagehot, *Estimates of some Englishmen and Scotchmen*, pp. 257-60. See on the subject generally of the literature of aristocratic and of democratic epochs the writer's article, "The Poetry of Democracy—Walt Whitman," *Westminster Review*, July 1871.

† I owe this observation to Professor H.Th. Rötscher, *Shakespeare in seinen höchsten Charactergebilden, &c.* Dresden, 1864, p. 20.

‡ "His [Shakespeare's] drama is the drama of *individuality* [...]. Shakespeare shows neither the consciousness of a law, nor of humanity the future is mute in his dramas, and enthusiasm for great principles unknown. His

patriotism, high-toned and enthusiastic, stands with Shakespeare instead of general political principles and ideas, and the life of the individual is widened and elevated by the national life, to which the individual surrenders himself with gladness and with pride.

The pride of Coriolanus is however not that which comes from self-surrender to and union with some power, or person, or principle higher than oneself. It is two-fold, a passionate self-esteem which is essentially egoistic; and secondly a passionate prejudice of class. His nature is the reverse of cold or selfish; his sympathies are deep, warm and generous; but a line, hard and fast, has been drawn for him by the aristocratic tradition, and it is only within that line that he permits his sympathies to play. To the surprise of the Tribunes, he can accept well-pleased a subordinate command under Cominius. He yields with kindly condescension to accept the devotion and fidelity of Menenius, and cherishes towards the old man a filial regard—the feeling of a son, who has the consciousness that he is greater than his father. He must dismiss Menenius disappointed from the Volscian camp; but he contrives an innocent fraud by means of which the old senator will fancy that he has affected more for the peace of Rome than another could. For Virgilia, the gentle woman in whom his heart finds rest, Coriolanus has a manly tenderness, and constant freshness of adhesion:

O, a kiss
Long as my exile, sweet as my revenge!
Now by the jealous queen of heaven, that kiss
I carried from thee, dear; and my true lip
Hath virgin'd it e'er since.

In his boy he has a father's joy, and yields to an ambitious hope, and a yearning forward to his son's possible future of heroic action, in which there is something of touching, paternal weakness:

---

genius comprehends and sums up the past and the present; it does not initiate the future. He interpreted an epoch; he announced none." Joseph Mazzini, *Life and Writings*, vol. ii, pp. 133-34. See Rümelin, *Shakespeare-Studien*, pp. 169-70.

> The god of soldiers,
> With the consent of supreme Jove, inform
> Thy thoughts with nobleness; that thou may'st prove
> To shame unvulnerable, and stick i' the wars
> Like a great sea-mark, standing every flaw,
> And saving those that eye thee!

His wife's friend Valeria is the "moon of Rome":

> Chaste as the icicle
> That's curdied by the frost from purest snow
> And hangs on Dian's temple.*

In his mother Volumnia, the awful Roman matron, he rejoices with a noble enthusiasm and pride; and while she is present always feels himself by comparison with this great mother, inferior and unimportant.

But Cominius, Menenius, and Virgilia, Valeria and Volumnia, and his boy belong to the privileged class, they are patrician. Beyond this patrician class neither his sympathies nor his imagination find it possible to range. The plebeians are "a common cry of curs" whose breath Coriolanus hates. He cannot like Bolingbroke flatter their weakness while he despises them inwardly. He is not even indifferent towards them; he rather rejoices in their malice and displeasure; if the nobility would let him use his sword he would make a quarry "with thousands of these quarter'd slaves," as high as he could pick his lance. Sicinius the Tribune is "the Triton of the minnows." When Coriolanus departs from Rome, as though all the virtue of the city were resident in himself, he reverses the apparent fact and pronounces a sentence of banishment against those whom he leaves behind: "*I banish you.*" Brutus is warranted by the fact when he says:

---

* Observe the extraordinary vital beauty, and illuminating quality of Shakespeare's metaphors and similes. A common-place poet would have written "as chaste as snow;" but Shakespeare's imagination discovers degrees of chastity in ice and snow, and chooses the chastest of all frozen things. On this subject see an excellent study by Rev. H.N. Hudson, *Shakespeare: His Life, Art and Characters,* vol. i, pp. 217-37.

You speak o' the people
As if you were a god to punish, not
A man of their infirmity.

And yet the weakness, the inconstancy, and the incapacity of apprehending facts which are the vices of the people, reflect and repeat themselves in the great patrician; his aristocratic vices counterbalance their plebeian. He is rigid and obstinate; but under the influence of an angry egoism he can renounce his principles, his party and his native city. He will not bear away to his private use the paltry booty of the Volces; but to obtain the consulship he is urged by his proud mother and his patrician friends to stand bareheaded before the mob, to expose his wounds, to sue for their votes, to give his heart the lie, to bend the knee like a beggar asking an alms. The judgment and blood of Coriolanus are ill commingled; he desires the end, but can only half submit to the means which are necessary to attain that end; he has not sufficient self-control to enable him to dispose of those chances of which he is lord. And so he mars his fortune. The pride, of Coriolanus, as Mr Hudson has observed, is "rendered altogether inflammable and uncontrollable by passion; insomuch that if a spark of provocation is struck into the latter, the former instantly flames up beyond measure, and sweeps away all the regards of prudence, of decorum, and even of common sense."* Now such passion as this Shakespeare knew to be weakness and not strength; and by this uncontrollable violence of temper Coriolanus draws down upon himself his banishment from Rome, and his subsequent fate.

At the moment when he passes forth through the gates of the city, and only then, his passion instead of breaking violently forth, subdues his nature in a more evil fashion and becomes dark and deadly. He feels that he has been deserted by "the dastard nobles," and given over as a prey to the mob. He who had been so warm, so generous, so loyal towards his class now feels himself betrayed; and the deadly need of revenge, together with the sense that he is in solitude and must depend upon his own strength and prudence, makes him calm. He endeavours

* *Shakespeare: His Life, Art and Characters*, vol. ii, p. 473.

to pacify his mother, and to check the old man's tears; he utters no violent speech. Only one obscure and formidable word escapes his lips:

I go alone
Like to a lonely dragon that his fen
Makes fear'd and talked of more than seen.

And in this spirit he strides forward towards Corioli.

No passage in the play is quick with such bright, spontaneous, almost lyrical feeling as the address of his defeated rival to Coriolanus, when he finds the great leader an unbidden guest within his house at Antium. Enthusiasm about great personalities finds nobler expression perhaps in the writings of Shakespeare than in those of any other poet of any country. The reader will recall that wonderful outbreak of admiration and homage from the aged Nestor when he gazes for the first time upon Hector's unhelmeted head:

I have, thou gallant Trojan, seen thee oft,
Labouring for destiny, make cruel way
Through ranks of Greekish youth, and I have seen thee
As hot as Perseus spur thy Phrygian steed,
Despising many forfeits and subduements,
When thou hast hung thy advanced sword i' the air,
Not letting it decline on the declined,
That I have said to some my standers by,
'Lo Jupiter is yonder, dealing life!'
And I have seen thee pause and take thy breath,
When that a ring of Greeks have hemm'd thee in,
Like an Olympian wrestling.

And the old man continues in the like strain until almost breath must fail him. The instantaneous and involuntary homage paid by Aufidius to Coriolanus is the same in kind—the overwhelming joy of standing face to face with veritable human greatness and nobility. But Coriolanus has found in Antium no second home. Honoured and deferred to, tended on, and treated as almost sacred, he is still the "lonely dragon that his fen makes fear'd." Cut off from his kindred and his friends, wronged by his own passionate sense of personality, his violent egoism, he resolves to stand:

> As if a man were author of himself,
> And knew no other kin.

But the loves and loyalties to which he has done violence, react against him. The struggle, prodigious and pathetic, begins, between all that is massive, stern, inflexible and all that is tender and winning in his nature; and the strength is subdued by the weakness. It is as if an oak were rent and uprooted not by the stroke of lightning, but by some miracle of gentle yet irresistible music. And while Coriolanus yields under the influence of an instinct not to be controlled, he possesses the distinct consciousness that such yielding is mortal to himself. He has come to hate and to conquer, but he must needs perish and love:

> My wife comes foremost; then the honour'd mould
> Wherein this trunk was framed, and in her hand
> The grandchild to her blood. But, out, affection!
> All bond and privilege of nature, break
> Let it be virtuous to be obstinate!
> What is that curt'sy worth? Or those doves' eyes,
> Which can make gods forsworn? I melt, and am not
> Of stronger earth than others. My mother bows;
> As if Olympus to a molehill should
> In supplication nod; and my young boy
> Hath an aspect of intercession, which
> Great nature cries 'Deny not.'

The convulsive efforts to maintain his hardness and rigidity are in vain; Coriolanus yields; his obstinacy and pride are broken; he is compelled to learn that a man cannot stand as if he were author of himself. And so the fortunes of Coriolanus fall, but the man rises with that fall.

Delivered from patrician pride, and his long habit of egoism, Coriolanus cannot be. The purely human influences have reached him through the only approaches by which he was accessible—through his own family. To the plebeian class he must still remain the intolerant patrician. Nevertheless, he has undergone a profound experience; he has acknowledged purely human influences in the only way in which it was possible for him to do so. No single experience, Shakespeare was aware, can deliver the soul from the long habit of passionate egoism. And, accordingly, at the last it is this which betrays him into the hands of the conspirators. His conduct before Rome is about to be judicially enquired into at Antium. But the word "boy," ejaculated against him by Aufidius, "touches Coriolanus into an ecstasy of passionate rage":

> Boy! O slave!
> Pardon me, lords, 'tis the first time that ever
> I was forced to scold. . . .
> Boy! false hound!
> If you have writ your annals true, 'tis there
> That, like an eagle in a dove-cote, I
> Flutter'd your Volscians in Corioli;
> Alone, I did it. Boy!

And in a moment the swords of the conspirators have pierced him. A Volscian lord, reverent for fallen greatness, protects the body:

> Tread not upon him. Masters all, be quiet;
> Put up your swords.

So suddenly has he passed from towering passion to the helplessness of death; the victim of his own violent egoism, and uncontrollable self-will. We remain with the sense that a great gap in the world has been made; that a sea-mark "standing every flaw" has for all time disappeared. We see the lives of smaller men still going on; we repress all violence of lamentation, and bear about with us a memory in which pride and pity are blended.

7

The Humour of Shakespeare

A study of Shakespeare which fails to take account of Shakespeare's humour must remain essentially incomplete. The character and spiritual history of a man who is endowed with a capacity for humorous appreciation of the world must differ throughout and in every particular from that of the man whose moral nature has never rippled over with genial laughter. At whatever final issue Shakespeare arrived after long spiritual travail as to the attainment of his life, that precise issue rather than another was arrived at in part by virtue of the fact of Shakespeare's humour. In the composition of forces which determined the orbit traversed by the mind of the poet this must be allowed for as a force among others, in importance not the least, and efficient at all times, even when little apparent. A man whose visage "holds one stern intent" from day to day, and whose joy becomes at times almost a supernatural rapture, may descend through circles of hell to the narrowest and the lowest; he may mount from sphere to sphere of Paradise until he stands within the light of the divine majesty; but he will hardly succeed in presenting us with an adequate image of life as it is on this earth of ours in its oceanic amplitude and variety. A few men of genius there have been, who, with vision penetrative as lightning, have gazed as it were through life, at some eternal significance of which life is the symbol. Intent upon its sacred meaning they have had no eye to note the forms of the grotesque hieroglyph of human existence. Such men are not framed for laughter. To this little group the creator of Falstaff, of Bottom, and of Touchstone does not belong.

Shakespeare, who saw life more widely and wisely than any other of the seers, could laugh. That is a comfortable fact to bear in mind; a fact which serves to rescue us from the domination of intense and narrow natures, who claim authority by virtue of their grasp of one half of the realities of our existence and their denial of the rest. Shakespeare could laugh. But we must go on to ask "What did he laugh at? and what was the manner of his laughter?" There are as many modes of laughter as there are facets of the common soul of humanity to reflect the humorous appearances of the world. Hogarth in one of his pieces of coarse, yet subtile engraving, has presented a group of occupants of the pit of a theatre sketched during the performance of some broad comedy or farce. What proceeds upon the stage is invisible and undiscoverable save as we catch its reflection on the faces of the spectators, in the same way that we infer a sunset from the evening flame upon windows that front the west. Each laughing face in Hogarth's print exhibits a different mode or a different stage of the risible paroxysm. There is the habitual enjoyer of the broad comic abandoned to his mirth which is open and unashamed, mirth which he is evidently a match for, and able to sustain. By his side is a companion female portrait, a woman with head thrown back to ease the violence of the guffaw; all her loose redundant flesh is tickled into an orgasm of merriment; she is fairly overcome. On the other side sits the spectator who has passed the climax of his laughter; he wipes the tears from his eyes, and is on the way to regain an insecure and temporary composure. Below appears a girl of eighteen or twenty, whose vacancy of intellect is captured and occupied by the innocuous folly still in progress; she gazes on expectantly, assured that a new blossom of the wonder of absurdity is about to display itself. Her father, a man who does not often surrender himself to an indecent convulsion, leans his face upon his hand, and with the other steadies himself by grasping one of the iron spikes that enclose the orchestra. In the right corner sits the humourist, whose eyes, around which the wrinkles gather, are half-closed, while he already goes over the jest a second time in his imagination. At the opposite side an elderly woman is seen, past the period when animal violences are possible, laughing because she knows there is something to laugh at, though she is too dull-witted to know precisely what. One spectator, as we guess from his introverted air, is laughing to think what somebody else would think of this. Finally, the thin-lipped, perk-nosed person of refinement looks aside, and by his critical indifference condemns the broad, injudicious mirth of the company.

All these laughers of Hogarth are very commonplace, and some are very vulgar persons; one trivial, ludicrous spectacle is the occasion of their mirth. When from such laughter as this we turn to the laughter of men of genius, who gaze at the total play of the world's life, and when we listen to this, as with the ages it goes on gathering and swelling, our sense of hearing is enveloped and almost annihilated by the chorus of mock and jest, of antic and buffoonery, of tender mirth and indignant satire, of monstrous burlesque and sly absurdity, of desperate misanthropic derision, and genial, affectionate caressing of human imperfection and human folly. We hear from behind the mask the enormous laughter of Aristophanes, ascending peal above peal, until it passes into jubilant ecstasy or from the uproar springs some exquisite lyric strain. We hear laughter of passionate indignation from Juvenal, the indignation of "the ancient and free soul of the dead republics."* And there is Rabelais, with his huge buffoonery, and the earnest eyes intent on freedom which look out at us in the midst of the zany's tumblings and indecencies. And Cervantes, with his refined Castilian air, and deep melancholy mirth at odds with the enthusiasm which is dearest to his soul. And Molière, with his laughter of unerring good sense, undeluded by fashion, or vanity, or folly, or hypocrisy, and brightly mocking these into modesty. And Milton, with his fierce objurgatory laughter, Elijah-like insult against the enemies of freedom and of England. And Voltaire, with his quick intellectual scorn, and eager malice of the brain. And there is the urbane and amiable play of Addison's invention, not capable of large achievement, but stirring the corners of the mouth with a humane smile,—gracious gaiety for

* "Juvénal, c'est la vieille âme libre des républiquès mortes; il a en lui une Rome dans l'airain de laquelle sont fondues Athènes et Sparte." Victor Hugo, *William Shakespeare*, p. 45 (ed. 1869).

the breakfast tables of England. And Fielding's careless mastery of the whole, broad, common field of mirth. And Sterne's exquisite curiosity of oddness, his subtile extravagances and humours prepense. And there is the tragic laughter of Swift, which announces the extinction of reason, and loss beyond recovery of human faith, and charity, and hope. How in this chorus of laughters, joyous and terrible, is the laughter of Shakespeare distinguishable?

In the first place the humour of Shakespeare like his total genius is many-sided. He does not pledge himself as dramatist to any one view of human life. If we open a novel by Charles Dickens, we feel assured beforehand that we are condemned to an exuberance of philanthropy; we know how the writer will insist that we must all be good friends, all be men and brothers intoxicated with the delight of one another's presence; we expect him to hold out the right hand of fellowship to man, woman, and child; we are prepared for the bacchannalia of benevolence. The lesson we have to learn from this teacher is that, with the exception of a few inevitable and incredible monsters of cruelty, every man naturally engendered of the offspring of Adam is of his own nature inclined to every amiable virtue. Shakespeare abounds in kindly mirth; he receives an exquisite pleasure from the alert wit and bright good sense of a Rosalind; he can dandle a fool as tenderly as any nurse qualified to take a baby from the birth can deal with her charge. But Shakespeare is not pledged to deep-dyed, ultra-amiability. With Jacques he can rail at the world, while remaining curiously aloof from all deep concern about its interests, this way or that. With Timon he can turn upon the world with a rage no less than that of Swift, and discover in man and woman a creature as abominable as the Yahoo. In other words, the humour of Shakespeare, like his total genius, is dramatic.

Then again, although Shakespeare laughs incomparably, mere laughter wearies him. The only play of Shakespeare's, out of nearly forty, which is farcical, *The Comedy of Errors*, was written in the poet's earliest period of authorship, and was formed upon the suggestion of a preceding piece. It has been observed with truth by Gervinus that the farcical incidents of this play have been connected by Shakespeare with a tragic background, which is probably his own invention. With beauty, or with pathos, or with thought, Shakespeare can mingle his mirth, and then he is happy, and knows how to deal with play of wit or humorous characterization; but an entirely comic subject somewhat disconcerts the poet. On this ground, if no other were forthcoming, it might be suspected that the *Taming of the Shrew* was not altogether the work of Shakespeare's hand. The secondary intrigues and minor incidents were of little interest to the poet. But in the buoyant force of Petruchio's character, in his subduing tempest of high spirits, and in the person of the foiled revoltress against the law of sex, who carries into her wifely loyalty the same energy which she had shown in her virgin *sauvagerie,* there were elements of human character in which the imagination of the poet took delight.*

Unless it be its own excess, however, Shakespeare's laughter seems to fear nothing. It does not, when it has once arrived at its full development, fear enthusiasm, or passion, or tragic intensity; nor do these fear it. The traditions of the English drama had favoured the juxtaposition of the serious and comic; but it was reserved for Shakespeare to make each a part of the other; to interpenetrate tragedy with comedy, and comedy with tragic earnestness. In Marlowe's *Doctor Faustus,* as we now possess it, the scenes of extravagant burlesque are merely a *divertissement* after the terror and awful solemnity of the tragic

* "Farmer nearly a hundred years ago said that Shakespeare wrote only the Petruchio scenes in the *Taming of the Shrew*. Mr Collier hesitatingly adopted this view. Mr Grant White developt it, and I (and Mr Fleay afterwards) turned it into figures, making the following parts Shakespeare's though in many places they are workt up by him from the old *Taming of a Shrew*: Induction; Act II, sc. i, 1. 168-326 (? touching 115-67); III, ii, 1, 125, 151-240; IV, i (and ii, Dyce); IV, iii, v (iv, vi Dyce); V, ii, 1-180; in short the parts of Katherine and Petruchio, and almost all Grumio, with the characters on the stage with them, and possible occasional touches elsewhere. (New Sh. Soc. Trans. 1874, 103-10). The rest is by the alterer and adapter of the old *A Shrew* probably Marlowe, as there are deliberate copies or plagiarisms of him in ten passages (G. White)." F.J. Furnivall, Preface to Gervinus' *Shakespeare Commentaries,* 1874. I cannot accept the opinion that Marlowe was the adapter of the *Taming of a Shrew.*

scenes. One cannot but desire to believe that such passages of rude burlesque were the invention of some clumsy playwright, and not the laborious degradation of his own art by Marlowe, who possessed no gift of humour. In *Doctor Faustus* the juxtaposition of the elevated and the burlesque scenes produces an effect as incongruous as if a group of Dutch boors carousing in a tavern of Teniers were transferred into some great sacred or classical composition by Lionardo da Vinci or Raffaele. The serious and the comic portions of the play move upon different planes of feeling, and the one cannot assist or co-operate with the other. In Shakespeare's earliest tragedy his method is already in existence. He is not afraid that the passion and the anguish of the lives of Romeo and Juliet will suffer abatement because Mercutio coruscates and scintillates, or because the Nurse puffs and perspires, tells long-winded stories and tipples her *aqua vitae*. In *The Two Gentlemen of Verona*, while Julia standing by disguised hears her faithless lover devoting himself to Silvia, the Host falls sound asleep. This is quite as it should be. The world is not all made for passionate young gentlemen and ladies. The stout body of mine Host has its rights and dues also: "By my halidom I was fast asleep." Shakespeare's humour here is a portion of his fidelity to the fact, his content in seeing things as they are, his justice, his impartiality. The clown laughs at the lover, and not without a fair show of clown-like common sense. Shakespeare is disposed to let no side of a fact escape him. If it have a trivial, ludicrous aspect, by all means let us have that put upon record. The valet-de-chambre range of emotion is as undeniable a piece of reality as is the heroic; and the world somehow is wide enough for both valet and hero. It is desirable to ascertain what lights the one may throw upon the other.

This apparent holding himself aloof from, and above his own creations, his perfect impartiality towards each person, and sometimes towards the entire action of his drama, is what Schlegel has spoken of as Shakespeare's irony. This irony Schlegel has said is "the grave of enthusiasm. We arrive at it only after we have had the misfortune to see human nature through and through; and when no choice remains but to adopt the melancholy truth that 'no virtue or greatness is altogether pure or genuine,' or the dangerous error that 'the highest perfection is attainable.'" "Here," the critic continues, "we therefore may perceive in the poet himself, notwithstanding his power to excite the most fervent emotions, a certain cool indifference, but still the indifference of a superior mind, which has run through the whole sphere of human existence and survived feeling."*

In this criticism by Schlegel there is an appearance of truth, but no more than an appearance. Shakespeare's impartiality towards the persons and motives of his plays is not real aloofness. It rather proceeds from his profound interest in his subject, his determination to do justice to every side of it. "In troth," exclaims Prince Henry, "I do now remember the poor creature small beer, but, indeed, these humble considerations make me out of love with my greatness." Does Shakespeare feel less enthusiasm for the glorious manhood of Henry because Henry remembers the poor creature small beer? No; Shakespeare is prepared to admit that Henry is every whit human, and therefore it is that the splendour of his manhood strengthens us, and fills us as it were with a personal pride and joy:

> I saw young Harry with his beaver on,
> His cuisses on his thighs, gallantly arm'd,
> Rise from the ground like feather'd Mercury,
> And vaulted with such ease into his seat,
> As if an angel dropp'd down from the clouds,
> To turn and wind a fiery Pegasus
> And witch the world with noble horsemanship.

It is because Shakespeare so entirely acknowledges the heroic in Henry that he has no timidity in risking his reputation as hero, by confession of the common incidents of humanity, heroic as well as non-heroic. That a most Christian king should each morning receive his peruke inserted upon a cane through an aperture of his bed-curtains is entirely correct; for the valet cannot retain faith in a perukeless grand monarch. But Shakespeare dares to inspect his hero as "unaccommodated man." "Unaccommodated man is no more but such a poor,

* *Lecture on Dramatic Art and Literature*, by A.W. Schlegel (ed. 1846), p. 369.

bare, forked animal as thou art," exclaims Lear to the shivering Edgar; and yet he is at the same time "How noble in reason! how infinite in faculty! in form and moving how express and admirable! in action how like an angel! in apprehension how like a god! the beauty of the world! the paragon of animals!"

Shakespeare recognized both our human imperfection and our human greatness; he denied the one as little as the other; hence his enthusiasm is not suppressed by, but at one with his tenderness, his pity, his pathos. Desdemona falters from the truth before the terrible eye of her husband; but she utters her dying and redeeming falsehood. Imogen's quick resentment wrongs for a moment the honour of Posthumus; but Imogen's arms around Posthumus' neck do more than make amends. A woman is dearer to Shakespeare than an angel; a man is better than a god. At the Diet of Worms in 1521, his imperial Majesty, who did not know high German, required Martin Luther to repeat his long defence in the Latin tongue. The sweat flowed on Luther's forehead; his lungs were exhausted, his throat was parched. The Duke of Brunswick, who sat by his side, despatched a servant for three flagons of the best Eimbeck beer. "I shall never forget that noble action," writes Heine, with a genuine burst of delight in the homely heroism of our dear master Martin Luther, "which does so much honour to the house of Brunswick."* The Host falls fast asleep while Julia's heart is only just sound and strong enough to keep from breaking. Does the propinquity of the snoring host make the anguish of Julia less real? Must we suppose that love was an illusion which Shakespeare had transcended because Friar Laurence moralizes on the violent ends of violent delights? In *Antony and Cleopatra* a clown bears the basket in which is hidden "the pretty worm of Nilus that kills and pains not." Is Shakespeare indifferent to the gravity of dying because a grotesque rustic becomes the messenger of death to the great Egyptian queen? Is dying not altogether a reality? Assuredly, though a clown has brought the basket, the worm "will do his kind" upon Iras, and Chairman, and Cleopatra. Death is real. Anguish and love are real, though

---

* Heinz, *Sämmtliche Werke*, vol. v, Ueber Deutschland, p. 76.

Peter call for some "merry dump" to comfort him, and though mine Host yield to the luxurious obsession of a snooze.

Tragedy with Shakespeare becomes more tragic because it lies surrounded by the common realities of life. Heroics which are so elevated as to disdain all that is actual and ordinary, like those of the Restoration drama and that of a subsequent period, tend rapidly to become pseudo-heroics, and affect us, in the end, as actually comic,—a ridiculous, undersigned parody of genuine nobility of feeling and conduct. Hector becomes Drawcansir. The statuesque group of which Whiskerandos is the centre,—uncles and nieces,—stand in menacing attitude at a deadlock, each with a dagger at the breast. Shakespeare, a German poet has said, inoculates his tragedy with a comic virus, and thus it is preserved from the great disease of absurdity.* Abstract from *Romeo and Juliet* the scenes in which the serving-men bite thumbs, the scenes in which Mercutio jests, those in which the nurse lets loose her wanton tongue, those in which old Capulet fusses and frets, and leave only the passages of joy and of sorrow between the lovers,—how insubstantial the joy and the sorrow appear! In order that the angels in the dream of Jacob might descend to this abiding-place of ours, and might ascend again, there was needed "a ladder set up on the earth, the top of which reached to heaven." The ardours and virtues,

---

* Das Komische ist der natürliche Feind des Gravitätischen, es ver-hält sich zum Tragischen wie die sogenannte geforderte Farbe zu der andern (Göthe); wenn man nicht Roth mit Grün abwechseln lässt, so wird zuletzt das Roth selber Grün. So wird das Tragische komisch, das Komische langweilig. In der Beimischung von Humor liegt eine Art Inoculation der komischen Kuhpocken, damit nicht die Menschen-pocken, *d.i.*, der Umschlag in's Lächerliche eintrete. Dann vollendet sich durch die Hinzuthat des Komischen zum Tragischen erst die Welt-ganzheit, die Ganzheit des Lebens. So haben Shakespeare's Figuren ihr charakteristisches Pathos nicht immer wie ein Kleid am Leibe, sie haben noch andere leichtere Charakterzüge, die in mittleren Zuständen jene so lange ersetzen, bis sie wieder eintreten, und besonders in diesem Wechsel liegt eine wunderbare Wirklichkeit ihres Lebens und des ganzen Stückes. Die vertraulichste Sprache gewöhnlicher Zustände und der kühnste Schwung des Pathos in den ausserordentlichsten Situationen; dazwischen eine Unendlichkeit von Mitteltinten." Otto Ludwig, *Shakespeare-Studien*, pp. 7-8.

and spiritual presences of the human soul are most energetically operant when they find footing on this ladder, which has its base upon the common ground.

Can we discover any single expression which will resume the various humorous appearances of life as they presented themselves to Shakespeare? It would be hazardous to adopt any such expression and make of it a theory of Shakespearian humour, with which facts must be compelled to square. Yet, by contrasting the tragic with the comic developments of human character in the drama of Shakespeare, it is possible to discover at least one main feature of the comic as it was conceived by the poet.* Every embodiment of thought, of passion, or of will, which passes considerably beyond the normal standard, is tragic, or contains within it potential elements of tragedy. All embodiments of thought, passion, and volition which fall considerably below the normal standard are comic, or contain possible comic elements. Romeo is a tragic personage, because in him the passion of love has grown supremely great, and under its influence his external, material life, the life of limitation, is wrecked and ruined. Hamlet is a tragic personage, because in him thought has developed itself in a way and degree which is without suitability or proportion to this finite life. Richard III is tragic, because his will is unsatisfied by ever-renewed victory, and still needs to wreak itself absolutely upon the world. But Slender is comic, whose love of sweet Anne Page is so faint a velleity that he is compelled to borrow all the suggestions of his passion from his uncle:

Shallow. Mistress Anne, my cousin loves you.

Slender. Ay, that I do; as well as I love any woman in Gloucestershire.

Shal. He will maintain you like a gentlewoman.

Slen. Ay, that I will, come cut and long-tail, under the degree of a squire.

Shal. He will make you a hundred and fifty pounds jointure.

Anne. Good Master Shallow, let him woo for himself.

* See Gervinus on the different branches of the drama: *Shakespeare Commentaries* (ed. 1863), vol. ii, pp. 597-612.

Slender too evidently is not a Romeo; and when he is put in the embarrassing position of being allowed to woo for himself, the dialogue proceeds:

Anne. Now, Master Slender—

Slen. Now, good Mistress Anne—

Anne. What is your will?

Slen. [*Brightening up under the inspiration of a happy thought.*] My will! 'ods heartlings, that's a pretty jest indeed! I ne'er made my will yet, I thank heaven; I am not such a sickly creature, I give heaven praise.

Anne. I mean, Master Slender, what would you with me?

Slen. Truly, for mine own part, I would little or nothing with you; your father and my uncle have made motions; if it be my luck, so; if not, happy man be his dole! They can tell you how things go better than I can; you may ask your father.

Slender's meek resignation to a successful issue of his wooing, "If it be my luck, so," brought doubtless an arch smile, quickly smoothed away, to the lips, and an amused twinkle to the eyes of sweet Anne Page. The painful obligation of making love, which he makes with all his heart, and with his largest oaths, ("'ods heartlings!") is submitted to by Slender with the same good grace with which Falstaff's ragged conscripts accept the necessity of fighting. Slender, under the conduct of love, advances to conquest with a like gallantry to that exhibited by Mouldy, Shadow, and Feeble, when marshalled for war under the banner of patriotism and honour. Sir Andrew Aguecheek is a comic personage, whose being as it trembles upon the border of non-existence, is kept from quite vanishing away by the faint reflections it catches of Sir Toby's boisterous vitality. Through his soft veil of silliness and imbecility (Providence tempering the wind to the shorn lamb) glimmers for a moment the faint suspicion that he is an ass; but any want of brilliancy on Sir Andrew's part is to be set down to accidental, and not inherent causes: "Methinks sometimes I have no more wit than a Christian or an ordinary man has; but I am a great eater of beef; and I belief that does harm to my wit." And Dogberry is comic with his laborious inefficiency, delivering to the Watch most painful instructions how to do nothing:

Dog. You shall comprehend all vagrom men; you are to bid any man stand in the Prince's name.

Second Watch. How if a' will not stand?

Dog. Why, then, take no note of him, but let him go, and presently call the rest of the watch, and thank God you are rid of a knave.

Alike in the tragic and in the comic there is an incongruity to be found. The tragic incongruity arises from the disproportion between the world and the soul of man; life is too small to satisfy the soul; the desires of man are infinite, and all possible attainment exists under strictest limitation. The comic incongruity is the reverse of this. It arises from the disproportion between certain souls of men, and even this very ordinary world of ours. When a man's wits are so unjointed and so ill-trained that, if put into motion, they forthwith get at cross purposes with themselves, while the happy imbecile remains supremely unconscious of his incapacity, we are in presence of an example of the comic incongruity. Hamlet brooding wistfully upon the unknown, until the mind's eye is baffled by the darkness—that is an example of grand incongruity, essentially tragic. Romeo would love infinitely, and be loved; and there lies his body motionless and senseless in the tomb of the Capulets. Cordelia spends all her wealth of piety to redeem her father from inhumanity and solitude; and Lear hangs over her body comfortless and desperate. We can endure these sights because we know that there is no absolute failure for the love and devotion which necessarily scorn all such consequences as these, and which do not owe allegiance to accident, or time, or place. Nevertheless there remains a terrible tragic incongruity. Hamlet's baffled movement, his beating to and fro in a vast and obscure world which he cannot comprehend, has in it something pathetic and something sublime. Polonius, with his mastery of court manners, and secrets, and policy, with his assumed omniscience and real ineptitude, excites a smile which carries with it something of contempt. His knowledge of the world falls so ludicrously short of what true knowledge is. If personal nullity be dressed up in formal dignity, and the pretension of office, it becomes more conspicuous. If, where incapacity be all but absolute, there yet are discovered degrees of incapacity greater and less, we dilate in presence of the infinitely little, and expect inexhaustibly varied and ever diminishing *quantums* of sense on this side of idiocy.* Dogberry, the city officer, is not a very competent person, but he is in a position to apologise for the feebler intellect of Verges, whom he patronises, as a condescending superior person should. "Goodman Verges, sir, speaks a little off the matter; an old man, sir, and his wits are not so blunt as, God help, I would desire they were; but in faith, honest as the skin between his brows."

Persons who are curious about possessing the most delicate sentiments might maintain that incapacity of heart, or will, or understanding is the appropriate object of sympathy and pity rather than of mirth. There is indeed an incapacity which is pathetic—that which being conscious of itself, yearns for a higher comprehension of things, for a more understanding heart, as a dog dumbly yearns for more full intelligence of his master's wishes and thoughts. But the kindly laugh of Shakespeare at self-complacent folly and ineptitude is a much more sincere and wholesome manifestation of feeling than the refinements of sympathy dear to the heart of the pathos-monger. It is deeply lamentable, no doubt, that some of our neighbours are not qualified to stand as models for an Apollo Belvedere, or a Venus of Melos. Still to weep because middle-aged gentlemen display at times an ungraceful rotundity of person, or because every nose is not straight, would hardly improve the condition of the world. These facts are recognized and allowed for most wholesomely by an honest laugh like that of Cruikshank or of Leech. It is well to smile at these grotesque departures from the ideal, and reserve our tears for higher uses. The genial laughter of Shakespeare at human absurdity is free from even that amiable cynicism, which gives to the humour of Jane Austen a certain piquant flavour; it is like the play of summer lightning, which hurts no living creature, but surprises, illuminates and charms.

* See Hazlitt on Shallow and Silence. *English Comic Writers*, Lecture ii, pp. 41-42 (ed. 1869).

To keep us constantly sensible of the grotesque which surrounds us is indeed to render us a service of no slight importance; for we are too ready to accept imperfection, and rapidly to forget it when once accepted. With most of us so habituated has the eye become to the visible grotesque in human face and form, costume and gesture, that we are unable at first to recognize the profound fidelity of such matter-of-fact pictures as those of Hogarth, or the ideal truth which exists as living centre of the inexhaustible, fantastic inventions of Cruikshank. We need to have our sense of seeing renewed and rendered fresh and childlike before we can perceive in every street through which we walk the types of our Cruikshank and our Hogarth. And around the life of each of us there is forever gathering an accretion of the grotesque in habit and character to which we quickly become insensible. To deliver the ideal man from this requires constant freshness of perception, and vigilance of will. Shakespeare does not seem to feel that Dogberry and Verges are creatures of another breed from himself. He stands, it is true, at the opposite pole of humanity; nevertheless, a potential Dogberry element existed even in Shakespeare. "Common people," as Mr Bagehot has happily said, "could be cut out of Shakespeare;" just as the robust and prosaic statesman of Westmoreland could have been cut out of the great spiritual thinker and poet of the Lake district. Therefore, apart from the interest of sympathy, we have a personal interest in understanding the common features of the most ordinary lives. Our own life is akin to them, and may readily lapse into a resemblance curiously exact. But as long as we can smile at them we are safe; our sense of humour is servant of our passion for perfection; we have, no need to grow impatient or indignant with these grotesque portions of humanity; that would unnecessarily disturb the balance of our lives, and the purity of our perceptions; we only need to understand them, and to smile.

The humour of Shakespeare, however, is much more than a laughter-producing power. It is a presence and pervading influence throughout his most earnest creations. This it is which preserves Shakespeare from all eager and shrill intensity; this it is which makes his emotions voluminous and massive. And of this humour there are two principal stages or degrees. First,—given a person or an event, a passion or a thought, Shakespeare examines it on every side, compares it with all other objects with which it may naturally be connected, or may happen to be associated; puts it in its environment, sees the fine and the coarse, the poetic and the prosaic, and thus acquires a rich and pregnant feeling for it. So abundant and varied is the body of fact which he is possessed of that one portion, as it were, balances the other, and he is saved from all the violence and extravagance that originate in the partial views of the idealist. Ophelia's death is pathetic; but the pathos of Shakespeare is not the pretty pathos of Beaumont and Fletcher, a soft, a sweet and tender sorrow, a gentle investiture of melancholy. Shakespeare sees the fact from the Queen's point of view, and from Hamlet's; from the priest's and from the grave-digger's points of view. That is to say, he sees the fact in the round; and the pathos of Ophelia's death is in the drama as real as it would be, if the occurrence became actual. This is the manner in which the humour of Shakespeare works in the first stage or degree.

But secondly, when all realities of this world and of time have been represented as far as they can be in their totality, Shakespeare measures these by absolute standards. He lays the measuring-reed of the infinite by the side of what is finite, and he perceives how little, how imperfect, the finite is. And he smiles at human greatness, while yet he pays loyal homage to what is great; he smiles at human love, and human joy, while yet they are deeply real to him (more real to him than they could possibly be to an eager intense Shelley); it is Prospero's smile upon seeing the new happiness of the youthful lovers:

> So glad of this as they I cannot be,
> Who are surprised with all; but my rejoicing
> In nothing can be more.

And he smiles at human sorrow, while he enters into the deep anguish of the soul; he knows that for it too there is an end and a quietus. The greatest poetic seers are not angry, or eager, or hortatory, or objurgatory, or shrill. Homer and Shakespeare are "too great for contest; [...] men to whose unoffended, uncondemning sight, the whole of human nature reveals itself in a pathetic weakness, with which they will not strive, or in mournful and transitory strength, which they dare not praise."* Shakespeare sees with purged eyes; and he loves and pities men. But while this view of things from an extra-mundane point of vision is to be taken account of in any study of Shakespeare's mind and art, it must be insisted upon that the facts are at the same time thoroughly apprehended, studied, and felt from the various points which are strictly finite and mundane.

But it is not alone Shakespeare's humour, and the laughter of Shakespeare which are significant. There is something also to be discovered from the *history of* his laughter. Every man must be aware that in his own case his laughter has had a history, and that if the history were faithfully made out a good deal would necessarily be ascertained respecting the development of his whole moral nature. Now we have documents which contain the history of Shakespeare's laughter during a period of upwards of twenty years. Surely from these something about the growth of his intellect and character must be ascertainable.

In Shakespeare's life as artist we may distinguish four periods. First of these is the tentative period, the years of experiments. The dramatist has not as yet got a sure and firm grasp upon life. He is somewhat deficient in the material of deep thought and of deep emotion. Both of these originate through a vital connection between the soul and the graver realities of life, and such a connection is as yet only establishing itself for Shakespeare. A man who is not as yet under the controlling influence of any of the graver realities of human life, and who at the same time possesses extraordinary mental gifts, will take pleasure in the mere play of his wits apart from the special occasion or object which sets his wits to work. If he have high spirits, he will enjoy fun pure and simple, comical surprises and grotesque incidents. If he have a turn for satire, the objects of his gay, satirical attack will be superficial oddities, follies, and affectations of the world. It is during this period of clever

* *Afternoon Lectures*, 1869. "The Mystery of Life and Its Arts," by John Ruskin, p. 109.

"youngmanishness" (Mr Furnivall's descriptive word) that Shakespeare's laughter first becomes audible to us. *The Two Gentlemen of Verona, Love's Labour's Lost,* and *The Comedy of Errors* sufficiently represent this stage in the history of the growth of Shakespeare's mind. In *Love's Labour's Lost,* as was attempted to be shown in a former chapter, there is a serious underlying intention. It concerns itself, as the work of a young man naturally may, with the subject of self-culture, and it gaily maintains the thesis that in our schemes of self-improvement the first requisite is this—that we take account of all the facts of human nature, including its appetites, instincts, and passions, and that any attempt to idealize these away will surely end in failure and egregious folly. Such is the underlying serious intention of the play. But by the way the poet takes an opportunity to have his laugh and skit at the fashionable affectations of the time.

Nearly at this same period Spenser in 'The Tears of the Muses' was lamenting the condition of the English comic drama; the stage had been made the means of cruel personal and party satire; "seasoned wit," and "goodly pleasure" had disappeared from comedy; in place of these, "scoffing scurrility," and "scornful folly" had possessed the stage,

> Rolling in rhymes of shameless ribaldry,
> Without regard of due decorum kept.

Whether Spenser's words in this passage, "Our pleasant Willy, ah! is dead of late," refer to some temporary silence of Shakespeare, or have no such reference, it is at least worthy of note that Shakespeare abstained altogether from this abusing of the stage to unworthy purposes, and found the objects of his mirth in fashions and follies of the time, not in the misfortunes or weaknesses of individuals.* Shakespeare was probably not without enemies. He was successful, and that secured for him the hatred of men who failed. Greene, upon his death-bed, assailed him with bitter and insolent words, and wrote as if his

* The identity of Holofernes with Florio of dictionary-making celebrity must be supported by better evidence before we regard it as other than an ingenious conjecture.

feeling would naturally be shared by Peele, by Lodge or Nash, and by Marlowe. Yet we do not anywhere find the name of Shakespeare, as we find the names of Jonson and Dekker, and other contemporary dramatists, occupying a place in the record of the quarrels of authors. The light and airy satire of *Love's Labour's Lost,* with its grave, underlying intention, is thus characteristic of the youthful Shakespeare, both in a positive way, and also negatively, because it contains no particle of the scurrility and ribaldry of which Spenser made complaint. The pleasure which Shakespeare derives from the quick encounter of wits, from the bandying of a jest to and fro in the air until at last it falls, in elaborate play upon words,—this was in part a pleasure of the period, and in part it is significant of the fact that Shakespeare, in his years of clever "youngmanishness," enjoyed the mere exercise of a nimble brain. "Now by the salt wave of the Mediterranean, a sweet touch; a quick venew of wit; snip snap, quick and home; it rejoiceth my intellect."

In this tentative period the comic and the serious, tender or sentimental elements of the drama exist side by side, and serve as a kind of criticism each upon the other; the lover serves to convict the clown of insensibility to the higher facts of life, and the clown convicts the lover of the blindness or extravagance of passion. But though the comic and the tender or serious elements exist side by side, and reflect certain lights one upon the other, they do not as yet interpenetrate. One set of personages is reserved for the grave or tender business of the drama; and a different set of personages is told off for the comic business. In *The Two Gentlemen of Verona* the comedy is entrusted to a pair of clowns. Speed and Launce: Speed is the professed wit; after serving his turn he finally disappears from the fully developed drama of Shakespeare. Launce, on the other hand, is a humourist, who, not without a sufficiency of clownish sense, blunders into mirthful matter of a more vital, more pregnant kind, than the nimble tongue of Speed can command. Launce, attended by his dog Crab, heads the procession of Shakespeare's humorous characters; there march behind him a long train, including manifold varieties of the mirth-provoking tribe,—from the naive, comic Touchstone, with his mingled instinct of sense and nonsense, to Hotspur and Mercutio, in whom overflowing energy or an exquisite zest in living produces a humorous extravagance, and again from these to Falstaff, in whom humour has acquired clear consciousness of itself and become free; and yet again from Falstaff to the pathetic, tragically earnest figure of the Fool in *Lear*.*

In *A Midsummer Night's Dream* Shakespeare's humour has enriched itself by coalescing with the fancy. The comic is here no longer purely comic; it is a mingled web, shot through with the beautiful. Bottom and Titania meet; and this meeting of Bottom and Titania may be taken, by any lover of symbolism that pleases, as an undesigned symbol of the fact that the poet's faculties, which at first had stood apart, and were accustomed to go to work each faculty by itself, were now approaching one another. At a subsequent period, when the shocks of life had roused to highest energy every nerve, every fibre of the genius of Shakespeare, the actions of all faculties were fused together in one. Bottom is incomparably a finer efflorescence of the absurd than any preceding character of Shakespeare's invention. How lean and impoverished his fellows, the Athenian craftsmen, confess themselves in presence of the many-sided genius of Nick Bottom! Rarely is a great artist appreciated in the degree that Bottom is—"He hath simply the best wit of any handicraft man in Athens; yea, and the best person too; and he is a very paramour for a sweet voice." With what a magnificent multiplicity of gifts he is endowed! How vast has the bounty of nature been to him! The self-doubtful Snug hesitates to undertake the moderate duties assigned to the lion. Bottom, though his chief humour is for a tyrant, knows not how to suppress his almost equal gift for playing a lady. How, without a pang, can he deprive the world, through devotion to "the Ercles vein," of the monstrous little voice in which he can utter "Thisne, Thisne—Ah Pyramus, my lover dear! thy Thisby dear and lady dear!" And as to the part assigned to the too bashful Snug,—that Bottom can undertake in either of two styles, or in

* See the hierarchy of comic characters as made out by Dr Eduard Vehse in *Shakespeare als Protestant, Politiker, Psycholog und Dichter*, vol. ii, pp. 5-6.

both, so that the Duke must say, "Let him roar again, let him roar again," or the ladies may be soothed by the "aggravated voice" in which he will "roar you as gently as any sucking dove." But from these dreams of universal ambition he is recalled by Quince to his most appropriate impersonation: "You can play no part but Pyramus, for Pyramus is a sweet-faced man; a proper man as one shall see in a summer's day; a most lovely, gentleman-like man; therefore you must needs play Pyramus."

During the second period of the development of Shakespeare's genius, he was gaining a sure grasp of the positive facts of life. This is the period of the histories. At first, impressed perhaps by a sense of the dignity of the historical drama, Shakespeare held his humour aloof. In *Richard II* there is no humorous scene. Had Shakespeare written the play a few years later, we may be certain that the gardener and servants (Act iii, Sc. 4) would not have uttered stately speeches in verse, but would have spoken homely prose, and that humour would have mingled with the pathos of this scene. The same remark maybe made with reference to the subsequent scene, in which his groom visits the dethroned king in the Tower. But as yet the pathetic, although with Shakespeare approximating to the humorous, looked at it somewhat askance and suspiciously. In *Richard III* there is a certain grim humour, humour of the diabolic kind, which is part of the daemonic personality of Richard, and has for its central element a fierce contempt of humanity. Richard kneels before Anne, and she offers at his breast with the sword; but the sword falls; Anne is overpowered by the malign strength of Richard's volition, and presently his ring is on her finger. The sense of power, which stands with Richard in the place of joy and beauty and virtue, is flattered by his achievement; his triumph over Anne is an insult to womanhood. That Richard should be supreme, the order of things must be inverted, the moral facts of the world must be reversed, and a new empire of the diabolic and the grotesque must be accepted as the normal condition of things. It is as if we stood beneath some monument before which men were bowing, and when we looked up we beheld the mocking figure of the Fiend upon the pedestal.

Except grim irony of this description, *Richard III,* like *Richard II,* contains no comic element. In the Jack Cade scenes of *Henry VI,* the satire effective, if at times rude, which Shakespeare directs against the weaker side of popular political movements, appears in its frankest and least subtile form. But it is in the play of *King John* that the humorous element first breaks forth energetically and in reckless defiance of the dignity of history. Something genuine, hearty, spontaneous, was especially needed in this play. A spurious appearance of majesty, with inward rottenness, the selfish policy of kings, the craft of priests, the barter of hearts and of lives, all these are exposed and explained by the one honest thing in the play,—the character of Faulconbridge, the bounding courage in his veins, his loyalty to the memory of the father who had given him a dishonourable birth, his dauntless, patriotic enthusiasm in presence of his country's disaster, and not inconsistent with this, his humorous assumption of a baseness and selfishness of which he was incapable.*

The two parts of *King Henry IV* exhibit a further advance of the comic element in connection with the historical drama. Already the humour of Shakespeare has marvellously deepened and enriched itself since the period of *Love's Labour's Lost* and *The Comedy of Errors.* Sir John Falstaff is a conception hardly less complex, hardly less wonderful than that of Hamlet. He is forever creating a fresh series of impressions, which seems at first inconsistent with the preceding series, and which yet after awhile somehow conciliates itself in an obscure and vital way with all that had gone before. "He is a man at once young and old, enterprising and fat, a dupe and a wit, harmless and wicked, weak in principle and resolute by constitution, cowardly in appearance and brave in reality, a knave without malice, a liar without deceit, and a knight, a gentleman, and a soldier, without either dignity, decency, or honour. This is a character which, though it may be decompounded, could not, I believe, have

* Notice how the Bastard's utterance in sonnet-form, Act ii, Sc. 2, beginning

"Drawn in the flattering table of her eye,"

serves to expose the true character of the Dauphin's elaborately complimentary wooing of Blanch and her dowry.

been formed, nor the ingredients of it duly mingled, upon any receipt whatever; it required the hand of Shakespeare himself to give to every particular part a relish of the whole, and of the whole to every particular part;—alike the same incongruous, identical Falstaff, whether to the grave Chief Justice he vainly talks of his youth and offers to caper for a thousand, or cries to Mrs Doll, 'I am old! I am old!' although she is seated on his lap, and he is courting her for busses."*

Sir John, although, as he truly declares, "not only witty in himself, but the cause that wit is in other men," is by no means a purely comic character. Were he no more than this, the stern words of Henry to his old companion would be unendurable. The central principle of Falstaff's method of living is that the facts and laws of the world may be evaded or set at defiance, if only the resources of inexhaustible wit be called upon to supply by brilliant ingenuity whatever deficiencies may be found in character and conduct.† Therefore Shakespeare condemned Falstaff inexorably. Falstaff, the invulnerable, endeavours, as was said in a preceding chapter, to coruscate away the realities of life. But the fact presses in upon Falstaff at the last relentlessly. Shakespeare's earnestness here is at one with his mirth; there is a certain sternness underlying his laughter. Mere detection of his stupendous unveracities leaves Sir John just where he was before; the success of his lie is of less importance to him than

* "An Essay on the Dramatic Character of Sir John Falstaff," by Maurice Morgann, Esq., pp. 150-51 (ed. 1825). No piece of 18th century criticism of Shakespeare is more intelligently and warmly appreciative than is this delightful essay.

† "Falstaff's innerste Natur geht vielmehr auf die Auflösung alles Ernstes des Lebens, aller Leidenschaft, aller Affecte, welche den Menschen unter ihre Herrschaft bringen, ihn beschränken, und ihm die volle Freiheit des Gemüths rauben. Der Ernst des Lebens fordert eine Vertiefung in den Inhalt des Lebens; der Ernst concentrirt den Menschen auf einen bestimmten und daher nothwendig beschränkten Inhalt und Zweck, der sein Wohl und Wehe ausmacht [...]. Falstaff ist daher dor natürliche Feind aller idealen Interessen und Leidenschaften, denn sie rauben zugleich dem Gemüth die Behaglichkeit und beeinträchtigen natürlich eben, weil sie den Menschen concentriren, die unbeschränkte Freiheit der Seele."—Dr H. Th. Rötscher, "Shakespeare in seinen höchsten Charaktergebilden," p. 70.

is the glory of its invention. "There is no such thing as totally demolishing Falstaff; he has so much of the invulnerable in his frame that no ridicule can destroy him; he is safe even in defeat, and seems to rise, like another Antaeus, with recruited vigour from every fall."* It is not ridicule, but some stern invasion of fact—not to be escaped from—which can subdue Falstaff. Perhaps Nym and Pistol got at the truth of the matter when they discoursed of Sir John's unexpected collapse:

> *Nym.* The king hath run bad humours on the knight; that's the even of it.
>
> *Pistol.* Nym, thou hast spoke the right;
> His heart is fracted and corroborate.

In the relation by Mrs Quickly of the death of Falstaff pathos and humour have run together and become one. "A' made a finer end and went away an' it had been any christom child; a' parted even just between twelve and one, even at the turning o' the tide: for after I saw him fumble with the sheets, and play with flowers and smile upon his fingers' ends, I knew there was but one way; for his nose was as sharp as a pen, and a' babbled of green fields."† Here the smile and the tear rise at the same instant. Nevertheless, the union of pathos with humour as yet extends only to an incident; no entire pathetic-humorous character has been created like that of Lear's Fool.

Pathetically, however, the fat knight disappears, and disappears for ever. The Falstaff of *The Merry Wives of Windsor* is another person than the Sir John who is "in Arthur's bosom, if ever man went to Arthur's bosom." The epilogue to the second part of *Henry IV* (whether it was written by Shakespeare or not remains doubtful) had promised that "our humble author will continue the story with Sir John in it." But our humble author decided (with a finer judgment than Cervantes in the case of his hero) that the public was not to be indulged in laughter for laughter's sake at the expense of his play. The tone

* Maurice Morgann, "Essay on the Character of Sir John Falstaff," p. 180.

† Dr Newman incidentally (by way of illustration) discusses the claim of Theobald's emendation to stand is the text. *Grammar of Assent*, pp. 264-70.

of the entire play of *Henry V* would have been altered if Falstaff had been allowed to appear in it. During the monarchy of a Henry IV no glorious enthusiasm animated England. It was distracted by civil contention. Mouldy, Shallow, and Feeble were among the champions of the royal cause. Patriotism and the national pride of England could not under the careful policy of a Bolingbroke burst forth as one ascending and universal flame. At such a time our imagination can loiter among the humours and frolics of a tavern. When the nation was divided into various parties, when no interest was absorbing and supreme, Sir John might well appear upon his throne at Eastcheap, monarch by virtue of his wit, and form with his company of followers a state within the state. But with the coronation of Henry V opens a new period, when a higher interest animates history, when the national life was unified, and the glorious struggle with France began. At such a time private and secondary interests must cease; the magnificent swing, the impulse and advance of the life of England occupy our whole imagination. It goes hard with us to part from Falstaff, but, like the king, part from him we must; we cannot be encumbered with that tun of flesh; Agincourt is not the battle-field for splendid mendacity. Falstaff, whose principle of life is an attempt to coruscate away the facts of life, and who was so potent during the Prince's minority, would now necessarily appear trivial. There is no place for Falstaff any longer on earth; he must needs find refuge "in Arthur's bosom."*

At the close of this second period in the development of Shakespeare's mind and art the brightest and loveliest comedies were written. In these years were created Rosalind and Viola, Jacques and Malvolio, Beatrice and Benedict. The essential characteristic of the close of the second period is this: Shakespeare had quite left behind him his spirit of clever "youngmanishness;" he had come into possession of himself and of his own powers, and he had entered into vital union

* This is well brought out by Rotscher, "Shakespeare in seinen höchsten Charaktergebilden," p. 77.

with the real life of the world; but as yet (concerned, as he was, a good deal about material success) he had not started upon any profound enquiry concerning the deeper and more terrible problems of existence. He had not begun to prosecute his prolonged investigation of evil. It was precisely the period at which Shakespeare's mirth was freest for disport. He had put aside the massive material supplied by history. He had not as yet fallen profoundly under the influence of those obscure and passionate interests of life which lie about the roots of tragedy. If ever there was a time when Shakespeare's laughter would be clear, and musical, and free, it was this time. Comedy, which had been involved with the grave matter of history, now disengages itself, and appears as something widely different from the tentative comedy of Shakespeare's earliest period. If we compare Touchstone with Speed, Rosalind with Rosaline, the scenes of mistaken identity in *Twelfth Night* with those of *The Comedy of Errors*, we shall have a measure of the distance traversed.

From among the plays so bright, so tender, so gracious of these years, one play—*The Merry Wives of Windsor*—stands apart with an unique character. It is essentially prosaic, and is indeed the only play of Shakespeare written almost wholly in prose. There is no reason why we should refuse to accept the tradition put upon record by Dennis and by Rowe that *The Merry Wives* was written by Shakespeare upon compulsion, by order of Elizabeth, who in her lust for gross mirth, required the poet to expose his Falstaff to ridicule, by exhibiting him, the most delightful of egoists, in love. Shakespeare yielded to the necessity. His *Merchant of Venice* might pass well enough with the miscellaneous gathering of upper, middle, and lower classes which crowded to a public theatre. Now he had to cater specially for gentlefolk and for a queen. And knowing how to please every class of spectators, he knew how to hit off the taste of "the barbarian." *The Merry Wives of Windsor* is a play written expressly for the barbarian aristocrats with their hatred of ideas, their insensibility to beauty, their hard efficient manners, and their demand for impropriety. The good folk of London liked to see a prince or a duke, and they liked to see him made gracious and generous. These royal and noble persons at Windsor wished to see the interior life of country gentlemen of the middle-class, and to see the women of the middle-class with their excellent bourgeois morals, and rough, jocose ways. The comedy of hearing a French physician and a Welsh parson speak broken English was appreciated by these spectators who uttered their mother-tongue with exemplary accent. Shakespeare did not make a grievance of his task. He threw himself into it with spirit, and despatched his work quickly,—in fourteen days, if we accept the tradition. But Falstaff he was not prepared to recall from heaven or from hell. He dressed up a fat rogue, brought forward for the occasion from the back premises of the poet's imagination, in Falstaff's clothes; he allowed persons and places and times to jumble themselves up as they pleased; he made it impossible for the most laborious nineteenth century critic to patch on *The Merry Wives* to *Henry IV.* But the Queen and her Court laughed as the buck-basket was emptied into the ditch, no more suspecting that its gross lading was not the incomparable jester of Eastcheap, than Ford suspected the woman with a great beard to be other than the veritable Dame Pratt.*

* With respect to the difficulty of identifying the characters of Mrs Quickly, Pistol, Bardolph and Sir John with the persons bearing the same names in the historical plays, see Mr Halliwell's introduction to *The First Sketch of the Merry Wives of Windsor* (Shakespeare Society, 1842). My impression of this play is confirmed by that of competent critics. Mr Hudson writes "That the free impulse of Shakespeare's genius, without suggestion or inducement from any other source, could have led him to put Falstaff through such a series of uncharacteristic delusions and collapses, is to me well nigh incredible." *Shakespeare, His Life and Characters,* vol. i, p. 298. See also Hazlitt's criticism of the play. Hartley Coleridge writes: "That Queen Bess should have desired to see Falstaff making love proves her to have been, as she was, a gross-minded old baggage. Shakespeare has evaded the difficulty with great skill. He knew that Falstaff could not be in love; and has mixed but a little, a very little *pruritus* with his fortune-hunting courtship. But the Falstaff of *The Merry Wives,* is not the Falstaff of *Henry the Fourth.* It is a big-bellied impostor, assuming his name and style, or at best it is Falstaff in dotage. The Mrs Quickly of Windsor is not mine Hostess of the Boar's Head; but she is a very pleasant, busy, good-natured, unprincipled old woman, whom it is impossible to be angry with. Shallow should not have left his seat in Gloucestershire and his magisteral duties. Ford's jealousy is of too serious a complexion for the rest of the play. The merry wives are a delightful

The third period of Shakespeare's development is that which contains the great tragedies. Shakespeare's laughter now is more than pathetic,—though pathetic it is as it had never been before,—it is also tragic and terrible. The gaze of the poet during this period was concentrated upon the evil in man's heart, the deepest mystery of being, and upon the good which is at odds in the world with this evil. He studies human life now with reference to its most solemn issues. Of unalloyed mirth, of bright and tender fancy we can now look for none. In Shakespeare's earliest tragedy, Mercutio disappears before half the play is over; and the gloom instantly deepens upon the withdrawal of his gleaming vivacity. The Mercutio in Shakespeare's brain also disappears when the tragedy of life becomes with him very grave and real. In *Hamlet*, the humorous figures of the court are all a little contemptible, and odious. Polonius, Osric, Rosencrantz and Guildenstern serve as irritants to stimulate Hamlet's dissatisfaction with living and impatience of the world. The grave-diggers have a grim grotesqueness, and might almost appear as figures in the *Danses macabres* of the middle ages; each a humorous jester in the court of Death; hail-fellow-well-met with chap-fallen skulls; a go-between for my lady Worm and him she desires; a connoisseur in corpses; a chronicler of dead men's bones.

The scene of the knocking in *Macbeth* has similarly a grave significance.* To the criticism of De Quincey, nothing from the aesthetic point of view, remains to be added. "The retiring of

---

pair. Methinks I see them, with their comely, middle-aged visages, their dainty white ruffs and toys, their half-witch-like conic hats, their full farthingales, their neat though not overslim waists, their housewifely keys, their girdles, their sly laughing looks, their apple-red cheeks, their brows the lines whereon look more like the work of mirth than years. And sweet Anne Page—she is a pretty little creature whom one would like to take on one's knee." *Essays and Marginalia*, vol. ii, pp. 133-34. It is noteworthy that Maurice Morgann in his Essay on Falstaff avoids the Merry Wives.

* Coleridge rejected the porter's soliloquy with the exception of two lines, *viz.*—"I'll devil-porter it no further, I had thought to let in some of all professions, that go the primrose way to the everlasting bonfire." On the other side, see (Trans. New Shak. Soc., 1874) Mr Hales "On the Porter in

the human heart, and the entrance of the fiendish heart was to be expressed and made sensible. Another world has stept in: and the murderers are taken out of the region of human things, human purposes, human desires. They are transfigured. Lady Macbeth is "unsexed;" Macbeth has forgot that he was born of woman; both are conformed to the image of devils; and the world of devils is suddenly revealed. But how shall this be conveyed and made palpable? In order that a new world may step in, this world must for a time disappear. The murderers and the murder must be insulated—cut off by an immeasurable gulf from the ordinary tide and succession of human affairs; we must be made sensible that the world of ordinary life is suddenly arrested,—laid asleep,—tranced,—racked into a dread armistice; time must be annihilated, relations to things without abolished; and all must pass self-withdrawn into a deep syncope and suspension of earthly passion. Hence it is, that when the deed is done, when the work of darkness is perfect, then the world of darkness passes away like a pageantry in the clouds; the knocking at the gate is heard; and it makes known audibly that the reaction has commenced; the human has made its reflux upon the fiendish; the pulses of life are beginning to beat again; and the re-establishment of the goings on of the world in which we live, first makes us profoundly sensible of the awful parenthesis that had suspended them."*

Macbeth." Mr Hales endeavours to establish the genuineness of the speech on the grounds:

(i) That a Porter's speech is an integral part of the play.

(ii) That it is necessary as a relief to the surrounding horror.

(iii) That it is necessary according to the law of contrast elsewhere obeyed.

(iv) That the speech we have is dramatically relevant.

(v) That its style and language are Shakespearian.

* De Quincey's Works, (1st ed.) vol. xiv, p. 197. Bodenstedt (quoted by Furness; *Variorum Shakespeare*: *Macbeth*, p. 110) writes of the Porter, "After all, his uncouth comicality has a tragic background: he never dreams, while imagining himself a porter of hell, how near he comes to the truth. What are all these petty sinners who go the primrose way to the everlasting bonfire, compared with those great criminals whose gates he guards?"

In *Lear*, where all else of Shakespeare's art attains a deeper and more intense life than in any other of his poems, the interpenetration of the humorous, the pathetic, and the tragic, has become complete. When Lear, assisted by the most learned justicer, poor Tom, and his yoke-fellow in equity, the Fool, arraigns a joint-stool as Goneril, we do not smile, we hardly as yet can pity; we gaze on with suspended intellect as if the entire spectacle were some mysterious, grotesque hieroglyph, the secret of which we were about to discover. In the smallest atom of the speeches of Lear, of Edgar, of the Fool, and equally in the entire drama, tragic earnestness is seen arrayed in fantastic motley. It is as if the writer were looking down at human life from a point of view without and above life, from which the whole appears as some monstrous farce-tragedy, in which all that is terrible is ludicrous, and all that is ludicrous, terrible.

If, during this tragic period, Shakespeare retain any tendency to observe the comedy of incident in life, the incident will be of another sort from that which moves our laughter in *The Comedy of Errors*. It will rather be a fragment of titanic burlesque, overhung by some impending horror, and inspired by a deep "idea of world-destruction."* Such a stupendous piece of burlesque, inspired by an idea of world-destruction, Shakespeare found in Plutarch's life of Antony, and having allowed it to dilate and take colour in his own imagination, he transferred it to his play. Aboard Pompey's galley the masters of the earth hold hands and dance the Egyptian bacchanals, joining in the volleying chorus, "Cup us, till the world goes round!"; and Menas whispers his leader to bid him cut the cable, and fall to the throats of the triumvirs. A great painting by Orcagna shows a terrible figure, Death, armed with the scythe, and sweeping down through bright air, upon the glad and careless garden-party of noble and beautiful persons,—men and women who lean to one another, and caress their dogs and hawks, while they listen to the music of stringed instruments. In Shakespeare's scene of revelry, death seems to be more secretly, more intimately present, seems more surely to dominate life; though

* A word applied by Heine to Aristophanes—*Weltvernichtungsidee.*

it passes by, it passes, as it were, with an ironical smile at the security of the possessors of this world, and at the noisy insubstantial triumph of life, permitted for a while. If now Shakespeare be a satirist, his satire will not resemble the bright, airy mockery of fashions and affectations which made the early *Love's Labour's Lost* effective with youthful aristocratic patrons of the theatre. How great a distance has been measured since then! Shakespeare's satire will now be the deep or fierce complaint against the world, of a soul in its agony—the frenzied accusations of nature and of man uttered by Lear, or the Juvenalian satire of the Athenian misanthrope.

There is in every man of passionate genius a revolt against the insufficiency of the world, a revolt against the base facts of life. Most of us surrender to the world, sign a treaty of alliance with engagements of mutual service, and end by acquiescence. It is remarkable that Shakespeare's revolt against the world increased in energy and comprehensiveness, as he advanced in years. When he was thirty or five-and-thirty years of age, he found less in the world to arouse his indignation, than when he was forty. Neither by force or fraud, by bribe or menace, did the world subdue or gain over Shakespeare. If he attained serenity, it was by some procedure other than that of selfish or indolent acquiescence. No mood of egoistic *laissez faire* succeeded Shakespeare's mood of indignation.

Serenity Shakespeare did attain. Once again before the end, his mirth is bright and tender. When in some Warwickshire field, one breezy morning, as the daffodil began to peer, the poet conceived his Autolycus, there might seem to be almost a return of the light-heartedness of youth. But the same play that contains Autolycus, contains the grave and noble figure of Hermione. From its elevation and calm Shakespeare's heart can pass into the simple merriment of rustic festivity; he can enjoy the open-mouthed happiness of country clowns; he is delighted by the gay defiance of order and honesty which Autolycus, most charming of rogues, professes; he is touched and exquisitely thrilled by the pure and vivid joy of Perdita among her followers. Now that Shakespeare is most a householder he enters most into the pleasures of truantship.* And in like manner it is when he is most grave that he can smile most brightly, most tenderly. But one kind of laughter Shakespeare at this time found detestable—the laughter of an Antonio or a Sebastian, barren and forced laughter of narrow heads, and irreverent and loveless hearts. The sly knavery of Autolycus has nothing in it that is criminal; heaven is his accomplice. "If I had a mind to be honest, I see Fortune would not suffer me; she drops booties in my mouth." Whether Schiller's Franz Moor made many robbers may be doubtful. But certainly no person of spirit can read *A Winter's Tale* without feeling a dishonest and delightful itching of the fingers, an interest not wholly virtuous in his neighbour's bleaching-green, and an impatience to be off for once on an adventure of roving and rogueing with Autolycus.

* Readers of Mr Browning's "Fifine at the Fair" will associate an esoteric sense with the word "householder," and will remember his admirably bright and vigorous study of the causes of our love of truantship in the opening sections of that poem.

8

Shakespeare's Last Plays

In the foreging chapters we have been chiefly concerned with observing the growth of Shakespeare's mind and art. The essential prerequisite of such a study was a scheme of the chronological succession of Shakespeare's plays which could be accepted as trustworthy in the main. But for such a study it is fortunately not necessary that we should in every case determine how play followed play. It would for many reasons be important and interesting to ascertain the date at which each work of Shakespeare came into existence; but as a fact this has not been accomplished, and we may safely say that it never will be accomplished. To understand in all essentials the history of Shakespeare's character and Shakespeare's art we have obtained what is absolutely necessary, when we have made out the succession, not of Shakespeare's plays, but of Shakespeare's chief visions of truth, his most intense moments of inspiration, his greater discoveries about human life.

In the history of every artist, and of every man, there are periods of quickened existence, when spiritual discovery is made without an effort, and attainment becomes easy and almost involuntary. One does not seek for truth, but rather is sought for by truth, and found; one does not construct beautiful imaginings, but beauty itself haunts, and startles, and waylays. These periods may be arrived at through prolonged moral conflict and victory, or through some sudden revelation of joy, or through supreme anguish and renouncement. Such epochs of spiritual discovery lie behind the art of the artist, it may be immediately, or it may be remotely, and out of these it springs. Among many art-products some single work will perhaps give to an unique experience its highest, its absolute expression; and this whether produced at the moment or ten years afterwards, properly belongs to that crisis of which it is the outcome. Lyrical writers usually utter themselves nearly at the moment when they are smitten with the sharp stroke of joy, or of pain. Dramatic writers, for the purity and fidelity of whose work a certain aloofness from their individuality is needed, utter themselves more often not on the moment, but after an interval, during which self-possession and self-mastery have been attained.

Now, although we are not in all cases able to say confidently this play of Shakespeare preceded that, the order of his writings has been sufficiently determined to enable us to trace with confidence the succession of Shakespeare's epochs of spiritual alteration and development. Whether *Macbeth* preceded *Othello*, or *Othello Macbeth*, need not greatly concern us; the question is one chiefly of literary curiosity; we do not understand Shakespeare much the better when the question has been settled, than we did while the answer remained doubtful. Both plays belong, and they belong in a equal degree, to one and the same period in the history of Shakespeare's mind and art, to which period we can unquestionably assign its place. In the present chapter *Timon of Athens* is placed near *The Tempest*, although it is possible that a play, or two, or three plays in the precise chronological order may lie between them. They are placed near one another, because in *Timon of Athens* Shakespeare's mood of indignation with the world attains its highest, its ideal expression, while in *The Tempest* we find the ideal expression of the temper of mind which succeeded his mood of indignation,—the pathetic yet august serenity of Shakespeare's final period. For the purposes of such a study as this we may look upon *The Tempest* as Shakespeare's latest play. Perhaps it actually was such; perhaps *A Winter's Tale* or *Cymbeline*, or both, may have followed it in point of time. It does not matter greatly for the purposes of the present study, which preceded and which succeeded. These three plays, as we shall see, form a little group by themselves, but it is *The Tempest* which gives its most perfect expression to the spirit that breathes through these three plays which bring to an end the dramatic career of Shakespeare; and therefore for us it is Shakespeare's latest play.* We have been endeavouring, so to speak, to scan the metre of Shakespeare's life; to do this rightly, we must count rather by accents than by syllables; if we can find the last accented syllable, we have found the real close of the verse, although it may be an additional syllable or two follow, and enrich the verse with a dying fall. And so in the case of *Timon of Athens* it may actually lie in point of time at a considerable distance from those discoveries of evil in man's heart, which inspired the soliloquies of Hamlet, and the frenzied utterances of Lear; but in Timon indignation has attained its ideal expression; it is the decuman wave which sets shoreward from that infinite and stormy sea of human passion.

Timon of Athens, although deservedly one of the least popular of Shakespeare's plays, belongs to his best period, and was written by the poet with no half-hearted regard for his subject. Whether Shakespeare wrote his portion first, and left it unfinished to be completed by a later dramatist,—the conjecture of Mr Fleay; whether Shakespeare's play was cut down and altered for the stage, to please a public which demanded comedy and the conceits of clownage, either during the poet's life-time, or in the interval between his death and the appearance of the first Folio;† or whether Shakespeare worked upon the material

* Professor Ingram, in his paper "On the 'weak-endings' of Shakespeare," arranges the plays of the weak-ending period in the following order: *Antony and Cleopatra, Coriolanus, Pericles, Tempest, Cymbeline, Winter's Tale, Two Noble Kinsmen, Henry VIII.* From an aesthetic point of view *Antony and Cleopatra* and *Coriolanus* seem to me connected with the plays that immediately precede, not with those that follow them. Prof. Ingram is disposed to place *Macbeth* immediately before *Antony and Cleopatra.* I had independently arrived at the same opinion. Timon cannot be far off, and must, I think, come before *The Tempest.* Observe that *Pericles, Two Noble Kinsmen,* and *Henry VIII* are Shakespearian fragments. Thus *The Tempest, Winter's Tale,* and *Cymbeline* remain as the three *complete* plays which represent the final period of Shakespeare's authorship. I treat *Timon,* in this chapter, as earlier than these, but not a great deal earlier.

† See the laborious article by N. Delius "Ueber Shakespeare's *Timon of Athens,*" *Jahrbuch der Deutschen Shakespeare-Gesellschaft,* vol. ii, and

of a preceding writer (perhaps George Wilkins) as Mr Knight believed, and Delius, and Mr Spedding now maintain,—these are questions which do not essentially concern us.

With few exceptions those portions of the play in which Timon is the speaker, can have come from no other hand than that of Shakespeare. If such conjectures were allowed to possess any worth, one might venture to assert that by the time this play was written, Shakespeare had mastered the impulses within himself to mere rage against the evil that is in the world. The impression which the play leaves is that of Shakespeare's sanity. He could now so fully and fearlessly enter into Timon's mood, because he was now past all danger of Timon's malady. He had now learnt to strive with evil and to subdue it; he had now learnt to forgive. And therefore he could dare to utter that wrath against mankind to which he had assuredly been tempted, but to which he had never wholly yielded.

It would seem that about this period Shakespeare's mind was much occupied with the questions, In what temper are we

---

that by B. Tschischwitz "Timon von Athen. Ein kritischer Versuch," *Jahrbuch*, vol. iv. There is yet another and plausible theory, originated by Ulrici, and modified by Karl Elze. In the first Folio Timon ends upon p. 99. A vacant page (100) follows. Then immediately comes *Julius Caesar*, beginning not on p. 101, but on p. 109. Although there are irregularities in the pagination of the first Folio, such a gap between two plays does not occur elsewhere in the volume. Sheet ii is wanting. *Timon* ends with sheet hh: *Julius Caesar* begins with kk. Ulrici is of opinion that the printing of *Julius Caesar* was begun before that of *Timon* was finished, probably because the manuscript of *Timon* was imperfect, and the deficiencies could not be immediately supplied. Shakespeare's manuscript was not forthcoming; the play had to be made up from the scattered parts of the individual actors. These parts were marred by omissions, and by the introduction of passages not by Shakespeare. Karl Elze adds the conjecture that only the parts of the principal actors could be found. (The play seems not to have been popular, and perhaps it had not been represented for several years.) To complete the play the editors of the first Folio fell back, for minor parts, upon the old *Timon of Athens* (not much older perhaps than Shakespeare's play), which may have been the work of George Wilkins. Hence the incoherences and inconsistencies of the play as it exists at present. See the preface by Karl Elze to *Timon* in the German Shakespeare Society's edition of *Tieck's and Schlegel's Translation of Shakespeare*. For Mr Fleay's study of this play see "Transactions of the New Shakespeare Society."

to receive the injuries inflicted upon us by our fellow men? How are we to bear ourselves towards those that wrong us? How shall we secure our inward being from chaos amid the evils of the world? How shall we attain to the most just and noble attitude of soul in which life and the injuries of life may be confronted? Now, here, in *Timon* we see one way in which a man may make his response to the injuries of life; he may turn upon the world with a fruitless and suicidal rage. Shakespeare was interested in the history of Timon, not merely as a dramatic study, and not merely for the sake of moral edification, but because he recognised in the Athenian misanthrope one whom he had known, an intimate acquaintance, the Timon of Shakespeare's own breast. Shall we hesitate to admit that there was such a Timon in the breast of Shakespeare? We are accustomed to speak of Shakespeare's gentleness and Shakespeare's tolerance so foolishly, that we find it easier to conceive of Shakespeare as indulgent towards baseness and wickedness, than as feeling measureless rage and indignation against them—rage and indignation which would sometimes flash beyond their bounds, and strike at the whole wicked race of man. And it is certain that Shakespeare's delight in human character, his quick and penetrating sympathy with almost every variety of man, saved him from any persistent injustice towards the world. But it can hardly be doubted, that the creator of Hamlet, of Lear, of Timon, saw clearly, and felt deeply, that there is a darker side to the world and to the soul of man.

The Shakespeare invariably bright, gentle, and genial is the Shakespeare of a myth. The man actually discoverable behind the plays was a man tempted to passionate extremes, but of strenuous will, and whose highest self pronounced in favour of sanity. Therefore he resolved that he would set to rights his material life, and he did so. And again he resolved that he would bring into harmony with the highest facts and laws of the world his spiritual being; and that in his own high fashion he accomplished also. The plays impress us as a long study of self-control,—of self-control at one with self-surrender to the highest facts and laws of human life. Shakespeare set about attaining self-mastery, not of the petty, pedantic kind, which can be dictated by a director, or described in a manual, but large, powerful, luminous, and calm; and by sustained effort he succeeded in attaining this in the end. It is impossible to conceive that Shakespeare should have traversed life, and felt its insufficiencies, and injuries, and griefs, without incurring Timon's temptation,—the temptation to fierce and barren resentment. What man or woman, who has sought good things, and with whom life has not gone altogether smoothly and pleasantly, has not known, if not for days and weeks then for hours, if not for hours then for intense moments, a Timon within him, incapable for the while of making any compromise with the world, and fiercely abandoning it with cries of weak and passionate revolt? And when again such a man accepts life, and human society, it is not what it had been before. The music of his life is a little lowered throughout; the pegs are set down. Or what had been a nerve is changed to a sinew. Or he finds himself a little more indifferent to pain. Or now and then a pungent sentence escapes his lips, which is unintelligible to those who had only known his former self.

In the character of Timon, Shakespeare gained dramatic remoteness from his own personality. It would have been contrary to the whole habit of the dramatist's genius to have used one of his characters merely as a mask to conceal his visage, while he relieved himself with lyrical vehemence of the feelings that oppressed him. No; Shakespeare, when *Timon* was written, had attained self-possession, and could transfer himself with real disinterestedness into the person of the young Athenian favourite of fortune. This, in more than one instance, was Shakespeare's method,—having discovered some single central point of sympathy between his chief character and his past or present self, to secure freedom from all mere lyrical intensity by studying that one common element under conditions remote from those which had ever been proper or peculiar to himself.

Timon, in the opening scene, surrounded by the parasites of Athens, abandoned to a prodigality of heart and of hand, lives on terms of careless fellowship with all mankind and with himself. Like Lear, he is slenderly acquainted with his own heart, and he knows nothing of the hearts and the lives of the men about him. To him life's business is a summer mood. He moves in a dream,—a beneficent genius waited on by spirits, which the magic of his bounty has conjured around him. "We are born to do benefits; and what better or properer can we call our own than the riches of our friends? Oh, what a precious comfort 'tis to have so many, like brothers, commanding one another's fortunes!" Ventidius is imprisoned for debt, and sends a servant to beg for the sum of five talents. Timon, who has had no eye for the baseness of the man, exclaims:

> Noble Ventidius! Well;
> I am not of that feather to shake off
> My friend when he must need me. I do know him,
> A gentleman that well deserves a help:
> Which he shall have: I'll pay the debt and free him.

Timon is acquainted with the commonplaces about the deceitfulness of the world, and utters them, but in an unreal, insubstantial way of talking:

> Painting is welcome.
> The painting is almost the natural man;
> For since dishonour traffics with man's nature,
> He is but outside; these pencill'd figures are
> Even such as they give out. I like your work.

These words are not insincere, but they are altogether unreal and notional. And precisely because the goodness of Timon is so indiscriminating, so lax and liberal, it is not veritable goodness, which, as Shakespeare was well aware, has in it something of severity.* Precisely because Timon has not discovered evil in man's heart, he has made no genuine discovery of human goodness. He is altogether remote from the fact. His friends are summer swallows, who will fly away when the days grow cold. The one honest heart that he might have known—his steward's—is to him indistinguishable from the rest. His wealth has melted away, and he remains unaware that such is the case. The

* In Richardson's *Essays on Shakespeare's Dramatic Characters* (1786), the truth about Timon is brought out under a number of heads in a methodical and somewhat dry manner, but rightly and carefully.

steward presses the truth upon him, but Timon has no ears to hear it. The summer sea of happiness and universal benevolence, how shall it ever be ruffled?

Having never made discovery of human virtue the first incursion of veritable fact upon Timon, the first in his whole life, is that of the selfishness, ingratitude, and baseness of man. The entire dream-structure of his life topples, totters, and crashes down. The mirage of universal brotherhood among men vanishes, and he is left in the barren wastes of the world. And because Timon has lived carelessly, with relaxed moral fibre, now when calamity overtakes him, he is wanting in all capacity for patient endurance of the heart. He is "passion's slave":

> A pipe for Fortune's finger
> To sound what stop she please.

Shakespeare in an earlier play—that from which these words are borrowed—had pictured a man who had taken "Fortune's buffets and rewards with equal thanks." But the character of Horatio was not lax and self-indulgent; he was "more an antique Roman than a Dane." Timon is unable to accept his sorrow, and hold his nature strenuously under command until it can adjust itself to the altered state of things. He flings himself from an airy, unreal philanthropy into passionate hatred of men. He is a revolter from humanity. He foams at the mouth with imprecation. He shakes off the dust of Athens from his feet, and strives to maintain himself in isolation, the one protester in the world against the cruelty and selfishness and baseness of the race.

Here is one way of bearing a man's self towards the world which wrongs us. Nor is it devoid of a certain mistaken nobleness. There is at least something baser than the misanthropy of Timon—complacent acquiescence in the life of greed, of selfishness, of unrighteousness in the cowardly and lascivious Athens. Timon's rage proceeds in part at least from the natural goodness of Timon's heart. Misanthropy, as Ulrici has said, was an atmosphere of poison to him; he was therefore of necessity the victim of his annihilating rage against himself and all mankind. But one entrance into peace remained for Timon—death, and the oblivion of death. Thereupon the very "hem of the sea," as far from the world of men as may be, where the wave twice a-day effaces the print of human feet, and where no tear will be shed for him except the salt spray of the breaking billow, Timon will cease to be, and will attain everlasting forgetfulness. Gold he had become again possessed of, yellow and massy; but gold, without the human love of which he had dreamed, is to him worse than worthless,—it is the detestable corrupter of men. Power and influence he is offered again by the Athenian senate; but he cannot accept them among the proud wrong-doers, the loveless voluptuaries of the city. Better gnaw his root in solitude, and curse—yet better still to let sour words go by, and rest beneath the sands and the waves! The misanthropy of Timon was less a crime than a cruel disease, to which no one could be liable who did not possess a potential nobleness of nature. Neither his love was wise nor his hatred, but neither his love nor his hatred was altogether ignoble:

> Though thou abhorr'dst in us our human griefs,
> Scorn'dst our brains' flow and those our droplets which
> From niggard nature fall, yet rich conceit
> Taught thee to make vast Neptune weep for aye
> On thy low grave, on faults forgiven. Dead
> Is noble Timon; of whose memory
> Hereafter more.

The play of *Timon* contains a twofold contrast—First, the misanthropy of Timon is contrasted with that of Apemantus; and secondly, Timon's attitude towards those who have wronged him is contrasted with the bearing and conduct of Alcibiades. Apemantus serves as an interpreter and apologist of Timon. He has erected his natural churlishness into a philosophy and a creed. He snarls at the heels of humanity with a currish virulence, and yet is willing in currish fashion to pick up the scraps that fall. As Iago grows and puts forth his evil blossoms in an atmosphere of disbelief in beauty and virtue, which is death to Othello, so Apemantus finds it right and natural to hate mankind, and he does it with a zest and vulgar good-pleasure in hatred; while Timon hates, and is slain by hatred, because it was his need to love.

Gervinus has rightly noticed that Shakespeare in several of his dramas reflects his main plot in a secondary plot, making the latter serve to illustrate and illuminate the former. Thus the story of Gloucester and his unnatural Edmund is a secondary plot reflecting the story of Lear and his daughters: the thunder of that moral tempest rolls away with reverberations, which prolong and intensify its menace. In *Hamlet*, the position of Laertes, who had lost a father by foul means, and who hastens to revenge his death, repeats the position of the Danish prince himself. In *The Tempest*, the treasonable attempt of Caliban, Stephano, and Trinculo upon the life of Prospero, is by its wickedness and its folly a kind of parody upon the treason of Antonio and Sebastian against the King of Naples. Here, in *Timon of Athens*, the story of Alcibiades, so ill connected by external points of contact with that of the principal character, fulfils the same ethical and aesthetic purpose that the secondary plots fulfil in *Lear*, in *Hamlet*, and in *The Tempest*. This portion of the play, if not written by Shakespeare, was written either under Shakespeare's direction, or by one who had a certain comprehension of his method as an artist.

Alcibiades comes before the Athenian senate to plead on behalf of the life of a friend who had slain one who wronged his honour:

> With a noble fury and fair spirit,
> Seeing his reputation touched to death,
> He did oppose his foe.

It was precisely such plain loyalty of friendship as this shown by Alcibiades, which Timon had not found, and not finding which he had abandoned himself to desperation. The senators—whose words are excellent words, but wholly unreal—utter wise maxims about the patient bearing of injuries, and the unworthiness of revenge:

> He's truly valiant, that can wisely suffer
> The worst that man can breathe, and make his wrongs
> His outsides, to wear them like his raiment, carelessly,
> And ne'er prefer his injuries to his heart
> To bring it into danger.

But Alcibiades, who is of an active, practical, unideal character, is not able to discover wisdom in the suffering of evils which, by opposing, a man may end:

> Why do fond men expose themselves to battle,
> And not endure all threats? Sleep upon 't,
> And let the foes quietly cut their throats
> Without repugnancy?

Alcibiades, for daring the anger of the Senate, is sent into perpetual banishment. He, like Timon, is compelled to experience the ingratitude of his fellows. But Alcibiades has been living in the real world, and is able immediately to assign its place to this ingratitude and baseness in a world in which evil and good are mingled.

Although possessed of none of the potential nobleness of Timon, Alcibiades possesses one virtue,—that of perceiving such facts as lie within the range of his limited observation. He does not see the whole world, but he sees the positive limited half of it rightly in the main. He is less than Timon, and yet greater; for Timon miserably fails through want of the one gift which Alcibiades possessed. In like manner Hamlet had failed for want of the gift which Fortinbras possessed; and yet Hamlet's was beyond all measure a larger and rarer soul than that of the Prince of Norway. Alcibiades has, at least, not been living in a dream; he lays hold of the positive and coarser pleasures of life, and endures its positive, limited pains, definite misfortunes which lie within appreciable bounds. No absolute, ideal anguish like that of Timon can overwhelm him. Accordingly, instead of wasting himself in futile rage against mankind, Alcibiades resolves to set himself in active opposition to those who have wronged him. While Timon is lifting weak hands of indignation to the gods, Alcibiades advances against Athens with swords and drums. To him the Senate will bow with humble entreaties for grace. Timon had fiercely thrust away their advances, because he could not accept benefits or render service in a base world which was remote from the ideal he had dreamed. Alcibiades, who deals with the world as it is, will punish and will pardon. The rage of Timon had been barren; it is hushed at last under the sands and the wash of waves. But the positive opposition offered to evil by Alcibiades, though in kind of no ideal purity or virtue, bears fruit:

> Bring me to your city,
> And I will use the olive with my sword,
> Make war breed peace, make peace stint war, make each
> Prescribe to other as each other's leech.
> Let our drums strike.

The olive and the sword—punishment and pardon, these were the beneficent gifts which Athens really needed. These, and not the lax philanthropy, not the frustrate rage against mankind of Timon.

Yet the idealist Timon was infinitely interesting to the imagination of Shakespeare. The practical and limited character of Alcibiades was esteemed highly by him, but did not really interest him. In like manner Hamlet, who failed, interested Shakespeare; Fortinbras, who succeeded, seemed admirable to him, but in his presence Shakespeare's sympathies and imagination were not deeply moved. Can we miss the significance of such a fact as this? Can we doubt that the Hamlets and Timons of Shakespeare's plays represent the side of the dramatist's own character, in which lay his peculiar strength; and also his special danger and weakness. An Alcibiades, or a Fortinbras, represents that side of his character into which he threw himself for protection against the weakness of excess of passion, or excess of thought. It was the portion of his being which was more elaborated than the rest, and less spontaneous; and therefore he highly esteemed it, and loved it little. There is a poem by Shakespeare in which he expresses his admiration of the calm, self-possessed, successful man, upon whom nature bestows her gifts, because she is a good housewife, and knows that by such bestowal her gifts are husbanded; while the sensitive, the eager, the enthusiastic, who cannot possess themselves, squander the largess of the great giver of good things. But while Shakespeare thus expresses admiration, he remains remote and unmoved in the presence of such a practical, successful, unideal character. We discern that in his secret heart he knew there was a more excellent way. "The children of this world," Shakespeare would say, "are wiser in their generation than the children of light." Let us borrow from the children of this world the secret of their success. Yet we cannot go over to them; in spite of danger and in spite of weakness we remain the children of light:

> They who have power to hurt and will do none,
> That do not do the thing they most do show,
> Who, moving others, are themselves as stone,
> Unmoved, cold, and to temptation slow.
> They rightly do inherit heaven's graces
> And husband nature's riches from expense;
> They are the lords and owners of their faces,
> Others but stewards of their excellence.

Were there in the life of Shakespeare certain events which compelled him to a bitter yet precious gain of experience in the matter of the wrongs of man to man, and from which he procured instruction in the difficult art of bearing oneself justly towards one's wrongers? If the *Sonnets* of Shakespeare, written many years before the close of Shakespeare's career as dramatist, be autobiographical, we may perhaps discover the sorrow which first roused his heart and imagination to their long inquisition of evil and grief, and which, sinking down into his great soul, and remaining there until all bitterness had passed away, bore fruit in the most mature of Shakespeare's writings, distinguished as these are by serene pathetic strength and stern yet tender beauty.*

---

* I shall not enter into the controversy as to the interpretation of the Sonnets. The principal theories held with respect to them may be classified as follows: I. They are poems about an imaginary friendship and love; Dyce, Delius, H. Morley. II. They are partly imaginary, partly autobiographical; C. Knight, H. von Friesen, R. Simpson (On the Italian love-philosophy see Simpson's interesting *Philosophy of Shakespeare's Sonnets*, Trübner, 1868). III. They form a great allegory; Dr Barnstorff ("Schlüssel zu Shakespeare's Sonnetten," 1860. Mr W.H.=Mr William Himself!), Mr Heraud ("Shakespeare's Inner Life." The young friend=Ideal Manhood), Carl Karpf. IV. They are autobiographical; (a) Mr W.H.=Henry Wriothesley (the initials reversed), Earl of Southampton: Drake, Gervinus, Kreyssig, and others; (b) Mr W.H.=William Herbert, Earl of Pembroke: Bright, Boaden, A. Brown, Hallam, H. Brown. V. They were partly addressed to Southampton; other sonnets were written in his name to

The *Sonnets* of Shakespeare were probably written during those years when as dramatist he was engaged upon the substantial material of English history, and when he was accumulating those resources which were to make him a wealthy burgher of Stratford. This practical, successful man, who had now arrived at middle age, and was growing rich, who had never found delight, as Marlowe, Nash, Greene, and other wild livers had, in the flimsy idealism of knocking his head against the solid laws of the world, was yet not altogether that self-possessed, cheerful, prudent person, who has stood with some writers for the veritable Shakespeare. In the *Sonnets* we recognise three things—that Shakespeare was capable of measureless personal devotion; that he was tenderly sensitive, sensitive above all to every diminution or alteration of that love his heart so eagerly craved; and that when wronged, although he suffered anguish, he transcended his private injury, and learned to forgive. There are lovers of Shakespeare so jealous of his honour that they are unable to suppose that any grave moral flaw could have impaired the nobility of his life and manhood. Shakespeare, as he is discovered in his poems and his plays, appears rather to have been a man who by strenuous effort, and with the aid of the good powers of the world, was saved, so as by fire. Before

---

Elizabeth Vernon; other some, to Southampton in E. Vernon's name; and subsequently the Earl of Pembroke engaged Shakespeare to write sonnets on his behalf to the dark woman, Lady Rich. Of part of this theory the first suggestion was given by Mrs Jameson. It was elaborated by Mr Gerald Massey in the *Quarterly Review*, April 1864, and in his large volume *Shakespeare's Sonnets, and His Private Friends*. The peculiarity of Mr Henry Brown's interpretation ("The Sonnets of Shakespeare Solved," J.R. Smith, 1870) is, that he discovers in the sonnets an intention of Shakespeare to parody or jest at the fashionable love-poetry and love-philosophy of the day. See on this subject the articles by Delius and by H. von Friesen in *Shakespeare Jahrbücher*, vols. i and iv; the chapter "Shakespeare's episch-lyrische Gedichte und Sonnette" in H. von Friesen's "Altengand und William Shakespeare" (1874); and "Der Mythus von William Shakespeare," by N. Delius (Bonn, 1851), pp. 29-31. Critics whose minds are of the business-like, matter-of-fact, prosaic type cannot conceive how the poems could be autobiographical. Coleridge, on the other hand, found no difficulty in believing them to be such; and Wordsworth emphatically declares them to express Shakespeare's "own feelings in his own person."

Shakespeare zealots demand our attention to ingenious theories which help us to credit the immaculateness of Shakespeare's life, let them prove to us that his writings never offend. When they have shown that Shakespeare's poetry possesses the proud virginity of Milton's poetry, they may go on to show that Shakespeare's youth was devoted, like the youth of Milton, to an ideal of moral elevation and purity. When we have been convinced that the same moral and spiritual temper which gave rise to the "Comus" gave rise to the "Venus and Adonis," we shall think it probable that Shakespeare could have uttered the proud words about his unspotted life that Milton uttered.

Assuredly the inference from Shakespeare's writings is not that he held himself with virginal strength and pride remote from the blameful pleasures of the world. What no reader will find anywhere in the plays or poems of Shakespeare is a cold-blooded, hard, or selfish line; all is warm, sensitive, vital, radiant with delight, or a-thrill with pain. And what we may dare to affirm of Shakespeare's life is that whatever its sins may have been, they were not hard, selfish, deliberate, cold-blooded sins. The errors of his heart originated in his sensitiveness, in his imagination (not at first inured to the hardness of fidelity to the fact), in his quick consciousness of existence, and in the self-abandoning devotion of his heart. There are some noble lines by Chapman, in which he pictures to himself the life of great energy, enthusiasms, and passions, which for ever stands upon the edge of utmost danger, and yet for ever remains in absolute security:

> Give me the spirit that on this life's rough sea
> Loves to have his sails fill'd with a lusty wind
> Even till his sail-yards tremble, his masts crack,
> And his rapt ship run on her side so low
> That she drinks water, and her keel ploughs air;
> There is no danger to a man that knows
> What life and death is,—there's not any law
> Exceeds his knowledge; neither is it lawful
> That he should stoop to any other law.*

* Byron's *Conspiracy*, Act iii, Scene 1 (last lines).

Such a master-spirit, pressing forward under strained canvas, was Shakespeare. If the ship dipped and drank water, she rose again; and at length we behold her within view of her haven, sailing under a large, calm wind, not without tokens of stress of weather, but if battered, yet unbroken by the waves. It is to dull, lethargic natures that a moral accident is fatal, because they are tending nowhither, and lack energy and momentum to right themselves again. To say anything against decent, lethargic vices, and timid virtues, anything to the advantage of the strenuous life of bold action and eager emotion, which necessarily incurs risks, and sometimes suffers, is, we shall be told, "dangerous." Well, then, be it so; it is dangerous.

The Shakespeare whom we discern in the *Sonnets* had certainly not attained the broad mastery of life which the Stratford bust asserts to have been Shakespeare's in his closing years. Life had been found good by him who owned those lips, and whose spirit declares itself in the massive animation of the total outlook of that face.* When the greater number of these *Sonnets* were written Shakespeare could have understood Romeo; he could have understood Hamlet; he could not have conceived Duke Prospero. Under the joyous exterior of those days lay a craving, sensitive, unsatisfied heart, which had not entire possession of itself, which could misplace its affections, and resort to all those pathetic frauds, by which misplaced affections strive to conceal an error from themselves. The friend in whose personality Shakespeare found a source of measureless delight—high-born, beautiful, young, clever, accomplished, ardent—wronged him. The woman from whom Shakespeare for a time received a joyous quickening of his life, which was half pain—a woman of stained character, and the reverse of beautiful, but a strong nature, intellectual, a lover of art, and possessed of curious magnetic attraction, with her dark eyes which illuminated a pale face—wronged him also. Shakespeare bitterly felt the wrong—felt most bitterly the wrong which was least to be expected, that of his friend. It has been held to be an

* This is the more remarkable, because the original of the bust was almost certainly a mask taken after death; and the bust betrays the presence of physical death, over which however life triumphs.

additional baseness that Shakespeare could forgive, that he could rescue himself from indignant resentment, and adjust his nature to the altered circumstances. Possibly Shakespeare may not have subscribed to all the items in the code of honour; he may not have regarded as inviolable the prohibited degrees of forgiveness. He may have seen that the wrong done to him was human, natural, almost inevitable. He certainly saw that the chief wrong was not that done to him, but committed by his friend against his own better nature. Delivering his heart from the prepossessions of wounded personal feeling, and looking at the circumstances as they actually were, he may have found it very natural and necessary not to banish from his heart the man he loved. However this may have been, his own sanity and strength, and the purity of his work as artist depended on his ultimately delivering his soul from all bitterness. Besides, life was not exhausted. The ship righted itself, and went ploughing forward across a broad sea. Shakespeare found ever more and more in life to afford adequate sustenance for man's highest needs of intellect and of heart. Life became ever more encircled with presences of beauty, of goodness, and of terror; and Shakespeare's fortitude of heart increased. Nevertheless, such experiences as those recorded in the *Sonnets* could not pass out of his life, and in the imaginative recurrence of past moods might at any subsequent time become motives of his art. Passion had been purified; and at last the truth of things stood out clear and calm.*

The *Sonnets* tell more of Shakespeare's sensitiveness than of Shakespeare's strength. In the earlier poems of the collection, his delight in human beauty, intellect, grace, expresses itself with endless variation. Nothing seems to him more admirable than manhood. But this joy is controlled and saddened by a sense of the transitoriness of all things, the ruin of time, the inevitable progress of decay. The love expressed in the early

* All that refers in the above paragraph to the supposed facts which underlie the Sonnets, may be taken with reserve. Only, if this portion of "the mythus of Shakespeare" be no myth but a reality, the interpretation of events in their moral aspect given above is the one borne out by the sonnets and by Shakespeare's subsequent life.

Sonnets is love which has known no sorrow, no change, no wrong; it is an ecstasy which the sensitive heart is as yet unable to control:

> As an unperfect actor on the stage
> Who with his fear is put beside his part,
> Or some fierce thing replete with too much rage,
> Whose strength's abundance weakens his own heart,
> So I, for fear of trust, forget to say
> The perfect ceremony of love's rite,
> And in mine own love's strength seem to decay,
> O'ercharged with burden of mine own love's might.

The prudent and sober Shakespeare—was it he who bore this burden of too much love, he whose heart was made weak by the abundance of its strength? He cannot sleep: he lies awake, haunted in the darkness by the face that is dear to him. He falls into sudden moods of despondency, when his own gifts seem narrow and of little worth, when his poems, which yield him his keenest enjoyment, seem wretchedly remote from what he had dreamed, and in the midst of his depression he almost despises himself because he is depressed:

> Wishing me like to one more rich in hope,
> Featured like him, like him with friends possessed,
> Desiring this man's art, and that man's scope,
> With what I most enjoy contented least*

He weeps for the loss of precious friends, for "love's long-since-cancelled woe;" but out of all these clouds and damps the thought of one human soul, which he believes beautiful, can deliver him:

> Haply I think on thee, and then my state,
> Like to the lark at break of day arising
> From sullen earth, sings hymns at heaven's gate.

Then comes the bitter discovery,—a change in love that had seemed to be made for eternity; coldness, estrangement, wrongs upon both sides; and at the same time external trials and

* From its connection, we may infer that this last line refers to Shakespeare's poems and plays.

troubles arise, and the injurious life of actor and playwright—injurious to the delicate harmony and purity of the poet's nature—becomes more irksome:

> And almost thence my nature is subdued
> To what it works in, like the dyer's hand.

He pathetically begs, not now for love, but for pity. Yet at the worst, and through all suffering, he believes in love:

> Let me not to the marriage of true minds
> Admit impediments. Love is not love
> Which alters when it alteration finds.

It can accept its object even though imperfect, and still love on. It is not in the common acceptation of the word prudential—but the *infinite* prudence of the heart is indeed no other than love:

> It fears not Policy, that heretic
> Which works on leases of short-numbered hours,
> But all alone stands hugely politic,
> That it nor glows with heat, nor drowns with showers.

He has learnt his lesson; his romantic attachment, which attributed an impossible perfection to his friend, has become the stronger love which accepts his friend and knows the fact; knows the fact of frailty and imperfection; knows also the greater and infinitely precious fact of central and surviving loyalty and goodness; and this new love is better than the old, because more real:

> Oh benefit of ill! now I find true
> That better is by evil still made better;
> And ruined love, when it is built anew,
> Grows fairer than at first, more strong, far greater.

And thus he possesses his soul once more; he "returns to his content."

Such, briefly and imperfectly hinted, is the spirit of Shakespeare's *Sonnets*. A great living poet, who has dedicated to the subject of friendship one division of his collected works, has written these words:

> Recorders ages hence?
> Come, I will take you down underneath this impassive exterior,—
> I will tell you what to say of me;
> Publish my name, and hang up my picture as that of the tenderest lover.

And, elsewhere of these Calamus poems, the poems of tender and hardy friendship, he says:

> Here the frailest leaves of me, and yet my strongest-lasting:
> Here I shade and hide my thoughts—I myself do not expose them,
> And yet they expose me more than all my other poems.

These words of Whitman may be taken as a motto of the *Sonnets* of Shakespeare. In these poems Shakespeare has hid himself, and is exposed.

The plays belonging to Shakespeare's final period of authorship, which I shall consider, are three: *Cymbeline, The Winter's Tale,* and *The Tempest.** The position in which they were placed in the first Folio (whether it was the result of design or accident) is remarkable. The volume opens with *The Tempest;* it closes with *Cymbeline. The Winter's Tale* is the last of the comedies, which all lie between this play and *The Tempest.* The circumstance may have been a piece of accident; but if so, it was a lucky accident, which suggests that our first and our last impression of Shakespeare shall be that of Shakespeare in his period of large, serene wisdom, and that in the light of the clear and solemn vision of his closing years all his writings shall be read. Characteristics of versification and style, and the enlarged

* Mr Fleay at one time placed *Cymbeline* considerably earlier in the chronological succession of Shakespeare's plays (begun, 1605; finished, 1607-1608). See his article, "Who Wrote Our Old Plays?" in *Macmillan's Magazine,* September 1874. Professor Hertzberg, upon aesthetic grounds, and the evidence of metrical tests, confirms the view taken above, and assigns *Cymbeline* to the year 1611. In the percentage of feminine endings (on which verse-test Hertzberg chiefly relies for the determining of the dates of Shakespeare's plays), the difference between *Cymbeline, Winter's Tale,* and *The Tempest,* is less than two. Mr Fleay has recently adopted the date, 1609.

place given to scenic spectacle, indicate that these plays were produced much about the same time. But the ties of deepest kinship between them are spiritual. There is a certain romantic element in each.* They receive contributions from every portion of Shakespeare's genius, but all are mellowed, refined, made exquisite; they avoid the extremes of broad humour and of tragic intensity; they were written with less of passionate concentration than the plays which immediately precede them, but with more of a spirit of deep or exquisite recreation.

There are moments when Shakespeare was not wholly absorbed in his work as artist at this period; it is as if he were thinking of his own life, or of the fields and streams of Stratford, and still wrote on; it is as if the ties which bound him to his art were not severing with thrills of strong emotion, but were quietly growing slack. The soliloquy of Belarius, at the end of the third scene of the third act of *Cymbeline*, and that of Imogen when she discovers the headless body of Cloten, were written as if Shakespeare were now only moderately interested in certain portions of his dramatic work.† Such lines as the following, purporting to be part of a soliloquy, but being in fact an explanation addressed to the audience, could only have been written when the poet did not care to energize over the less interesting, but still necessary passages of his drama:

Belarius. O Cymbeline! heaven and my conscience knows
Thou didst unjustly banish me: whereon,

---

* The same remark applies to Shakespeare's part of *Pericles*, which belongs to this period.

† Gervinus, writing of *Antony and Cleopatra* (and he repeats the remark in the criticism of *Timon of Athens*), says, "It would appear as if Shakespeare, about the time between 1607-10, had had [...] intervals in which he wrote his poetry in a manner altogether more careless, whether we consider it from an aesthetic or an ethical point of view." *Shakespeare Commentaries*, vol. ii, p. 358. Gervinus attributes this carelessness to "the state of the poet's mind," p. 422. I see none of this alleged carelessness in *Antony and Cleopatra*, or in *Timon*. Both plays are written with intense and complete imaginative energy. Not so, however, with *Cymbeline* and *The Winter's Tale*. See on this subject some excellent remarks of Kreyssig. "Vorlesungen über Shakespeare" (ed. 1858), vol. iii, pp. 422-24.

At three and two years old, I stole these babes;
Thinking to bar thee of succession, as
Thou reft'st me of my lands. Euriphile,
Thou wast their nurse; they took thee for their
    mother,
And every day do honour to her grave:
Myself, Belarius, that am Morgan call'd,
They take for natural father.*

The impression that Shakespeare's interest in his art was less intense than previously it had been is confirmed by the circumstance that he now contributes portions to plays which are completed by other hands in an inferior manner. Into the subject of Pericles he entered with manifest delight; but he could be content to see his "Marina" wedged in between the rough and coarse work of another writer. In *The Two Noble Kinsmen* the degradation of Shakespeare's work by the unclean underplot of Fletcher is painful, and almost intolerable. And in *Henry VIII* all artistic and ethical unity is sacrificed to the vulgar demand for an occasional play and for a spectacle.

Yet it is not to be wondered at that Shakespeare now should feel delivered from the strong urge of imagination and feeling, and should write in a more pleasurable, more leisurely, and not so great a manner. The period of the tragedies was ended. In the tragedies Shakespeare had made his inquisition into the mystery of evil. He had studied those injuries of man to man which are irreparable. He had seen the innocent suffering with the guilty. Death came and removed the criminal and his victim from human sight, and we were left with solemn awe upon our hearts in presence of the insoluble problems of life. There lay Duncan, who had "borne his faculties so meek," who had been "so clear in his great office," foully done to death; there lay Cordelia lifeless in the arms of Lear; there, Desdemona, murmuring no word, upon the bed; there, Antony, the ruin of Cleopatra's magic; and last, Timon, most desperate fugitive from life, finding

* Professor Ingram suggests to me that the speech as written by Shakespeare ended immediately before these lines with the words, "The game is roused." These words are awkwardly repeated at the end of the speech, "The game is up."

his sole refuge under the oblivious and barren wave. At the same time that Shakespeare had shown the tragic mystery of human life, he had fortified the heart by showing that to suffer is not the supreme evil with man, and that loyalty and innocence, and self-sacrifice, and pure redeeming ardour, exist, and cannot be defeated. Now, in his last period of authorship, Shakespeare remained grave—how could it be otherwise?—but his severity was tempered and purified. He had less need of the crude doctrine of Stoicism, because the tonic of such wisdom as exists in Stoicism had been taken up, and absorbed into his blood.

Shakespeare still thought of the graver trials and tests which life applies to human character, of the wrongs which man inflicts on man; but his present temper demanded not a tragic issue,—it rather demanded an issue into joy or peace. The dissonance must be resolved into a harmony, clear and rapturous, or solemn and profound. And, accordingly, in each of these plays, *The Winter's Tale*, *Cymbeline*, *The Tempest*, while grievous errors of the heart are shown to us, and wrongs of man to man as cruel as those of the great tragedies, at the end there is a resolution of the dissonance, a reconciliation. This is the word which interprets Shakespeare's latest plays—reconciliation, "word over all, beautiful as the sky." It is not, as in the earlier comedies—*The Two Gentlemen of Verona*, *Much Ado about Nothing*, *As You Like It*, and others—a mere *dénouement*. The resolution of the discords in these latest plays is not a mere stage necessity, or a necessity of composition, resorted to by the dramatist to effect an ending of his play, and little interesting his imagination or his heart. Its significance here is ethical and spiritual; it is a moral necessity.

In *The Winter's Tale*, the jealousy of Leontes is not less, but more fierce and unjust than that of Othello. No Iago whispers poisonous suspicion in Leontes' ear. His wife is not untried, nor did she yield to him her heart with the sweet proneness of Desdemona:

> Three crabbed months had soured themselves to death
> Ere I could make thee open thy white hand,
> And clap thyself my love; then didst thou utter
> 'I am yours for ever.'

Hermione is suspected of sudden, and shameless dishonour, she who is a matron, the mother of Leontes' children, a woman of serious and sweet dignity of character, inured to a noble self-command, and frank only through the consciousness of invulnerable loyalty.* The passion of Leontes is not, like that of Othello, a terrible chaos of soul,—confusion and despair at the loss of what had been to him the fairest thing on earth; there is a gross personal resentment in the heart of Leontes, not sorrowful, judicial indignation; his passion is hideously grotesque, while that of Othello is pathetic.

The consequences of this jealous madness of Leontes are less calamitous than the ruin wrought by Othello's jealousy, because Hermione is courageous and collected, and possessed of a fortitude of heart which years of suffering are unable to subdue:

> There's some ill-planet reigns;
> I must be patient till the heavens look
> With an aspect more favourable. Good my lords,
> I am not prone to weeping, as our sex
> Commonly are; the want of which vain dew
> Perchance, shall dry your pities; but I have
> That honourable grief lodg'd here, which burns
> Worse than tears drown. Beseech you all, my lords,
> With thoughts so qualified as your charities
> Shall best instruct you, measure me; and so
> The king's will be performed!†

But although the wave of calamity is broken by the firm resistance offered by the fortitude of Hermione, it commits ravage enough to make it remembered. Upon the Queen comes a lifetime of solitude and pain. The hopeful son of Leontes and Hermione is done to death, and the infant Perdita is estranged from her kindred and her friends. But at length the heart of

---

* The contrast between *Othello* and *The Winter's Tale* has been noticed by Coleridge, and is admirably drawn out in detail by Gervinus and Kreyssig, to whose treatment of the subject the above paragraph is indebted.

† Mrs Jameson applies to the passion of Hermione, the fine saying of Madame de Stael, "Il pouvait y avoir des vagues majestueuses, et non de l'orage dans son coeur."

Leontes is instructed and purified by anguish and remorse. He has "performed a saint-like sorrow," redeemed his faults, paid down more penitence than done trespass:

> Whilst I remember
> Her and her virtues, I cannot forget
> My blemishes in them, and so still think of
> The wrong I did myself; which was so much
> That heirless it hath made my kingdom, and
> Destroy'd the sweet'st companion that e'er man
> Bred his hopes out of.

And Leontes is received back without reproach into the arms of his wife; she embraces him in silence, allowing the good pain of his repentance to effect its utmost work.

The sin of Posthumus had been less grievous; it had been half an error, and his restoration is proportionately more joyful. He too had learnt his own unworthiness, and learnt the measureless worth of Imogen. He will not render to the gods in atonement for his wrong less than his whole life:

> For Imogen's dear life take mine: and though
> 'Tis not so dear yet 'tis a life: you coin'd it:
> 'Tween man and man they weigh not every stamp;
> Though light, take pieces for the figure's sake;
> You rather mine, being yours; and so, great powers,
> If you will take this audit, take this life,
> And cancel these cold bonds.

It is not with silent forgiveness that Imogen receives back her husband; there are words of quick and exquisite mockery of joy. Posthumus had struck her to the ground, in her disguise as Lucius' page, because she had seemed to make light of his love and of his anguish. Imogen, with one word of playful reproach for this last error of her husband, as if that were all she had suffered at his hands, and a happy mocking challenge to him to be cruel again, has her arms round his neck, making the union of wife and husband perfect in a moment, forestalling all explanation, rendering forever needless the painful utterance of penitential sorrow:

Imo. Why did you throw your wedded lady from you?
Think that you are upon a rock, and now
Throw me again.

Post. Hang there like fruit, my soul,
Till the tree die! *

The wrong-doers of *The Tempest* are a group of persons of various degrees of criminality, from Prospero's perfidious brother, still active in plotting evil, to Alonzo, whose obligations to the Duke of Milan had been of a public or princely kind. Spiritual powers are in alliance with Prospero, and these, by terror and the awakening of remorse, prepare Alonzo for receiving the balm of Prospero's forgiveness. He looks upon his son as lost, and recognizes in his son's loss the punishment of his own guilt. "The powers delaying, not forgetting," have incensed the sea and shores against the sinful men; nothing can deliver them except "heart-sorrow, and a clear life ensuing." Goethe, in the opening of the second part of *Faust,* has represented the ministry of external nature fulfilling functions with reference to the human conscience precisely the reverse of those ascribed to it in *The Tempest.* Faust, escaped from the prison-scene and the madness of Margarete, is lying on a flowery grass-plot, weary, restless, striving to sleep. The Ariel of Goethe calls upon his attendant elvish spirits to prepare the soul of Faust for renewed energy by bathing him in the dew of Lethe's stream, by assuaging his pain, by driving back remorse:

Besäntftiget des Herzens grimmen Strauss;
Entfernt dea Vorwurfs glühend bittre Pfeile,
Sein Innres reinigt von erlebtem Graus.

To dismiss from his conscience the sense of the wrong he has done to a dead woman, is the initial step in the further education and development of Faust. Shakespeare's Ariel, breathing through the elements and the powers of nature, quickens the remorse of the king for a crime of twelve years since:

* The line "Think that you are upon a rock," is probably corrupt; no proposed emendation is satisfactory. The criticism of the play of *Cymbeline* in George Fletcher's *Studies of Shakespeare* (1847), may be mentioned as intelligent and appreciative.

O it is monstrous, monstrous!
Methought the billows spoke and told me of it;
The winds did sing it to me, and the thunder,
That deep and dreadful organ-pipe, pronounced
The name of Prosper: it did bass my trespass,
Therefore my son i' the ooze is bedded, and
I'll seek him deeper than e'er plummet sounded,
And with him there lie mudded.

The enemies of Prospero are now completely in his power. How shall he deal with them? They had perfidiously taken advantage of his unworldly and unpractical habits of life; they had thrust him away from his dukedom; they had exposed him with his three-years'-old daughter in a rotten boat to the mercy of the waves. Shall he not now avenge himself without remorse? What is Prospero's decision?

Though with their high wrongs I am struck to the quick,
Yet with my nobler reason 'gainst my fury
Do I take part; the rarer action is
In virtue than in vengeance; they being penitent,
The sole drift of my purpose doth extend
Not a frown further.

We have seen how Timon turned fiercely upon mankind, and hated the wicked race,—"I am Misanthropos and hate mankind." The wrongs inflicted upon Prospero were crueller and more base than those from which Timon suffered. But Prospero had not lived in a summer mood of lax and prodigal benevolence; he had lived severely, "all dedicated to closeness and the bettering of my mind." And out of the strong comes forth sweetness. In the play of *Cymbeline*, the wrong which Posthumus has suffered from the Italian Iachimo is only less than that which Othello endures at the hands of Iago. But Iachimo, unlike Iago, is unable to sustain the burden of his guilt, and sinks under it. In the closing scene of *Cymbeline*, that in which Posthumus is himself welcomed home to the heart of Imogen, Posthumus in his turn becomes the pardoner:

Kneel not to me;
The power that I have on you is to spare you;

The malice toward you to forgive you; live,
And deal with others better.

Hermione, Imogen, Prospero,—these are, as it were, names for gracious powers which extend forgiveness to men. From the first Hermione, whose clear-sightedness is equal to her courage, had perceived that her husband laboured under a delusion which was cruel and calamitous to himself. From the first she transcends all blind resentment, and has true pity for the man who wrongs her. But if she has fortitude for her own uses, she also is able to accept for her husband the inevitable pain which is needful to restore him to his better mind. She will not shorten the term of his suffering, because that suffering is beneficent. And at the last her silent embrace carries with it—and justly—a portion of that truth she had uttered long before:

How will this grieve you,
When you shall come to clearer knowledge, that
You thus have published me! Gentle my lord,
You scarce can right me throughly then to say
You did mistake.

The calm and complete comprehension of the fact is a possession painful yet precious to Hermione, and it lifts her above all vulgar confusion of heart or temper, and above all unjust resentment.

Imogen, who is the reverse of grave and massive in character, but who has an exquisite vivacity of feeling and of fancy, and a heart pure, quick, and ardent, passes from the swoon of her sudden anguish to a mood of bright and keen resentment, which is free from every trace of vindictive passion, and is indeed only pain disguised. And in like manner she forgives, not with self-possession and a broad, tranquil joy in the accomplished fact, but through a pure ardour, an exquisite eagerness of love and of delight. Prospero's forgiveness is solemn, judicial, and has in it something abstract and impersonal. He cannot wrong his own higher nature, he cannot wrong the nobler reason, by cherishing so unworthy a passion as the desire of vengeance. Sebastian and Antonio, from whose conscience no remorse has been elicited, are met by no comfortable pardon. They have received their lesson of failure and of pain, and may possibly be convinced of the good sense and prudence of honourable dealing, even if they cannot perceive its moral obligation. Alonzo, who is repentant, is solemnly pardoned. The forgiveness of Prospero is an embodiment of impartial wisdom and loving justice.

A portion of another play certainly belongs to this latest period of Shakespeare's authorship—a portion of *King Henry VIII.** Dr Johnson observed that the genius of Shakespeare comes in and goes out with Queen Katharine. What then chiefly interested the dramatist in this designed and partly accomplished *Henry VIII*? The presence of a noble sufferer,—one who was grievously wronged, and who by a plain loyalty to what is faithful and true, by a disinterestedness of soul, and enduring magnanimity, passes out of all passion and personal resentment into the reality of things, in which much indeed of pain remains, but no ignoble wrath or shallow bitterness of heart. Her earnest endeavour for the welfare of her English subjects is made with fearless and calm persistence in the face of Wolsey's opposition. It is integrity and freedom from self-regard set over against guile, and power, and pride. In her trial-scene the indignation of Katharine flashes forth against the Cardinal, but is an indignation which unswervingly progresses towards and penetrates into the truth.

* Karl Elze, in his article "Zu Heinrich VIII," (*Shakespeare Jahrbuch*, vol. ix), attempts to show, not successfully, I think, that the play was written in 1603, and "was set aside on account of Elizabeth's death, and kept there till Rowley brought out his '*When You See Me You Know Me;* or the famous Chronicle Historie of King Henrie the Eight,' in 1613. The Globe Company thereupon thought of their unused *Henry VIII*, put it into Fletcher's hands to alter, and then acted it." The portions of the play by Shakespeare are Act i, Scenes 1 and 2; Act ii, Scenes 3 and 4; Act iii, Scene 2 (in part Shakespeare); Act v, Scene 1. Roderick, in Edwards' "Canons of Criticism," (1765) noticed the peculiarity of the versification of this play. Mr Spedding and Mr Hickson (1850) independently arrived at identical results as to the division of parts between Fletcher and Shakespeare. Mr Fleay (1874) has confirmed the conclusions of Mr Spedding, (double-endings forming in this instance his chief test); Professor Ingram has further confirmed them by the weak-ending test, and Mr Furnivall by the stopt-line test.

When a man has attained some high and luminous tableland of joy or of renouncement, when he has really transcended self, or when some one of the everlasting, virtuous powers of the world,—duty or sacrifice, or the strength of anything higher than oneself—has assumed authority over him, forthwith a strange, pathetic, ideal light is shed over all beautiful things in the lower world which has been abandoned. We see the sunlight on our neighbour's field, while we are pre-occupied about the grain that is growing in our own. And when we have ceased to hug our souls to any material possession, we see the sunlight wherever it falls. In the last chapter of George Eliot's great novel, *Romola*, who has ascended into *her* clear and calm solitude of self-transcending duty, bends tenderly over the children of Tito, uttering in words made simple for their needs, the lore she has learnt from life, and seeing on their faces the light of strange, ideal beauty. In the latest plays of Shakespeare, the sympathetic reader can discern unmistakably a certain abandonment of the common joy of the world, a certain remoteness from the usual pleasures and sadnesses of life, and at the same time, all the more, this tender bending over those who are like children still absorbed in their individual joys and sorrows.

Over the beauty of youth and the love of youth, there is shed, in these plays of Shakespeare's final period, a clear yet tender luminousness, not elsewhere to be perceived in his writings. In his earlier plays, Shakespeare writes concerning young men and maidens, their loves, their mirth, their griefs, as one who is among them, who has a lively, personal interest in their concerns, who can make merry with them, treat them familiarly, and, if need be, can mock them into good sense. There is nothing in these early plays wonderful, strangely beautiful, pathetic about youth and its joys and sorrows. In the histories and tragedies, as was to be expected, more massive, broader, or more profound objects of interest engaged the poet's imagination. But in these latest plays, the beautiful pathetic light is always present. There are the sufferers, aged, experienced, tried—Queen Katharine, Prospero, Hermione. And over against these there are the children absorbed in their happy and exquisite egoism,—Perdita and Miranda, Florizel and Ferdinand, and the boys of old Belarius.

The same means to secure ideality for these figures, so young and beautiful, is in each case (instinctively perhaps rather than deliberately) resorted to. They are lost children,—princes or a princess, removed from the court, and its conventional surroundings, into some scene of rare, natural beauty. There are the lost princes—Arviragus and Guiderius, among the mountains of Wales, drinking the free air, and offering their salutations to the risen sun. There is Perdita, the shepherdess-princess, "queen of curds and cream," sharing with old and young her flowers, lovelier and more undying than those that Proserpina let fall from Dis's waggon. There is Miranda, (whose very name is significant of wonder), made up of beauty, and love, and womanly pity, neither courtly nor rustic, with the breeding of an island of enchantment, where Prospero is her tutor and protector, and Caliban her servant, and the Prince of Naples her lover. In each of these plays we can see Shakespeare, as it were, tenderly bending over the joys and sorrows of youth. We recognise this rather through the total characterization, and through a feeling and a presence, than through definite incident or statement. But some of this feeling escapes in the disinterested joy and admiration of old Belarius when he gazes at the princely youths, and in Camillo's loyalty to Florizel and Perdita; while it obtains more distinct expression in such a word as that which Prospero utters, when from a distance he watches with pleasure Miranda's zeal to relieve Ferdinand from his task of log-bearing: "Poor worm, thou art infected."*

It is not chiefly because Prospero is a great enchanter, now about to break his magic staff, to drown his book deeper than ever plummet sounded, to dismiss his airy spirits, and to return to the practical service of his Dukedom, that we identify Prospero in some measure with Shakespeare himself. It is rather because

* The same feeling appears in the lines which end Act iii, Scene 1:

Prospero. So glad of this as they I cannot be,
Who are surprised with all; but my rejoicing
At nothing can be more.

the temper of Prospero, the grave harmony of his character, his self-mastery, his calm validity of will, his sensitiveness to wrong, his unfaltering justice, and with these, a certain abandonment, a remoteness from the common joys and sorrows of the world, are characteristic of Shakespeare as discovered to us in all his latest plays. Prospero is a harmonious and fully developed *will.* In the earlier play of fairy enchantments, *A Midsummer Night's Dream*, the "human mortals," wander to and fro in a maze of error, misled by the mischievous frolic of Puck, the jester and clown of Fairyland. But here the spirits of the elements, and Caliban the gross genius of brute-matter,—needful for the service of life,—are brought under subjection to the human will of Prospero.*

What is more, Prospero has entered into complete possession of himself. Shakespeare has shown us his quick sense of injury, his intellectual impatience, his occasional moment of keen irritability, in order that we may be more deeply aware of his abiding strength and self-possession, and that we may perceive how these have been grafted upon a temperament, not impassive or unexcitable. And Prospero has reached not only the higher levels of moral attainment; he has also reached an altitude of thought from which he can survey the whole of human life, and see how small and yet how great it is. His heart is sensitive, he is profoundly touched by the joy of the children, with whom in the egoism of their love he passes for a thing of secondary interest; he is deeply moved by the perfidy of his brother. His brain is readily set a-work, and can with difficulty be checked from eager and excessive energizing; he is subject to the access of sudden and agitating thought. But Prospero masters his own sensitiveness, emotional and intellectual:

> We are such stuff
> As dreams are made on, and our little life
> Is rounded with a sleep. Sir, I am vexed;
> Bear with my weakness; my old brain is troubled:

* This point of contrast between *The Tempest* and *A Midsummer Night's Dream* is noticed by Mézières: "Shakespeare, ses Œuvres et ses Critiques," pp. 441-42.

Be not disturb'd with my infirmity;
If you be pleased, retire into my cell
And there repose; a turn or two I'll walk,
To still my beating mind.

"Such stuff as dreams are made on." Nevertheless, in this little life, in this dream, Prospero will maintain his dream rights and fulfil his dream duties. In the dream, he, a Duke, will accomplish Duke's work. Having idealized everything, Shakespeare left everything real. Bishop Berkeley's foot was no less able to set a pebble flying than was the lumbering foot of Dr Johnson. Nevertheless, no material substance intervened between the soul of Berkeley and the immediate presence of the play of Divine power.*

A thought which seems to run through the whole of *The Tempest*, appearing here and there like a coloured thread in some web, is the thought that the true freedom of man consists in service. Ariel, untouched by human feeling, is panting for his liberty; in the last words of Prospero are promised his enfranchisement and dismissal to the elements. Ariel reverences his great master, and serves him with bright alacrity; but he is bound by none of our human ties, strong and tender, and he will rejoice when Prospero is to him as though he never were.† To Caliban, a land-fish, with the duller elements of earth and water in his composition, but no portion of the higher elements,

* See a remarkable article on Goethe and Shakespeare by Professor Masson, reprinted among his collected Essays. On *The Tempest*, the reader may consult as an excellent summary of facts, the article "On the Origin of Shakespeare's Tempest": *Cornhill Magazine*, October 1872. It is founded upon Meissner's "Untersuchungen über Shakespeare's Sturm," (1872). See also Meissner's article in the *Jahrbuch der Deutschen Shakespeare-Gesellschaft*, vol. v. Jacob Ayrer's "Comedia von der schönen Sidea," will be found, with a translation, in Mr Albert Cohn's interesting volume *Shakespeare in Germany* (Asher, 1865).

† Ariel is promised his freedom after two days, Act i, Scene 2. Why two days? The time of the entire action of the *Tempest* is only three hours. What was to be the employment of Ariel during two days? To make the winds and seas favourable during the voyage to Naples. Prospero's island therefore was imagined by Shakespeare as within two days' quick sail of Naples.

air and fire, though he receives dim intimations of a higher world,—a musical humming, or a twangling, or a voice heard in sleep—to Caliban, service is slavery.* He hates to bear his logs; he fears the incomprehensible power of Prospero, and obeys, and curses. The great master has usurped the rights of the brute-power Caliban. And when Stephano and Trinculo appear, ridiculously impoverished specimens of humanity, with their shallow understandings and vulgar greeds, this poor earth-monster is possessed by a sudden *schwärmerei,* a fanaticism for liberty!

> 'Ban, 'ban, Ca'-Caliban,
> Has a new master; get a new man.
> Freedom, heyday! heyday, freedom! freedom! freedom, heyday freedom!

His new master also sings his impassioned hymn of liberty, the *Marseillaise* of the enchanted island:

> Flout 'em and scout 'em,
> And scout 'em and flout 'em;
> Thought is free.

The leaders of the revolution, escaped from the stench and foulness of the horse-pond, King Stephano and his prime minister Trinculo, like too many leaders of the people, bring to an end their great achievement on behalf of liberty by quarrelling over booty,—the trumpery which the providence of Prospero had placed in their way. Caliban, though scarce more truly wise or instructed than before, at least discovers his particular error of the day and hour:

> What a thrice-double ass
> Was I, to take this drunkard for a god,
> And worship this dull fool!

---

* The conception of Caliban, the "servant-monster," "plain fish and no doubt marketable," the "tortoise," "his fins like arms," with "a very ancient and fish-like smell," who gabbled until Prospero taught him language—this conception was in Shakespeare's mind when he wrote *Troilus and Cressida.* Thersites describes Ajax, (Act iii, Scene 3). "*He's grown a very land-fish, languageless, a monster.*"

It must be admitted that Shakespeare, if not, as Hartley Coleridge asserted, "a Tory and a gentleman," had within him some of the elements of English conservatism.

But while Ariel and Caliban, each in his own way, is impatient of service, the human actors, in whom we are chiefly interested, are entering into bonds—bonds of affection, bonds of duty, in which they find their truest freedom. Ferdinand and Miranda emulously contend in the task of bearing the burden which Prospero has imposed upon the prince:

I am in my condition
A prince, Miranda; I do think, a king:
I would, not so! and would no more endure
This wooden slavery than to suffer
The flesh-fly blow my mouth. Hear my soul speak:
The very instant that I saw you, did
My heart fly to your service; there resides,
To make me slave to it; and for your sake
Am I this patient log-man.

And Miranda speaks with the sacred candour from which spring the nobler manners of a world more real and glad than the world of convention and proprieties and pruderies:

Hence, bashful cunning!
And prompt me, plain and holy innocence!
I am your wife, if you will marry me;
If not, I'll die your maid: to be your fellow
Yon may deny me; but I'll be your servant
Whether you will or no.
Fer. My mistress, dearest;
And I thus humble ever.
Mir. My husband, then?
Fer. Ay, with a heart as willing
As bondage e'er of freedom.

In an earlier part of the play, this chord which runs through it had been playfully struck in the description of Gonzalo's imaginary commonwealth, in which man is to be enfranchised from all the laborious necessities of life. Here is the ideal of notional liberty, Shakespeare would say, and to attempt to realise it at once lands us in absurdities and self-contradictions:

For no kind of traffic
Would I admit: no name of magistrate;
Letters should not be known: riches, poverty,
And use of service none; contract, succession,
Bourn, bound of land, tilth, vineyard, none;
No use of metal, corn, or wine, or oil;
No occupation; all men idle, all,
And women too, but innocent and pure;
No sovereignty.
Seb. Yet he would be king on't.*

Finally, in the Epilogue, which was written perhaps by Shakespeare, perhaps by some one acquainted with his thoughts, Prospero in his character of a man, no longer a potent enchanter, petitions the spectators of the theatre for two things, pardon and freedom. It would be straining matters to discover in this Epilogue profound significances. And yet in its playfulness it curiously falls in with the moral purport of the whole. Prospero, the pardoner, implores pardon. Shakespeare was aware—whether such be the significance (aside—for the writer's mind) of this Epilogue or not—that no life is ever lived which does not need to receive as well as to render forgiveness. He knew that every energetic dealer with the world must seek a sincere and liberal pardon for many things. Forgiveness and freedom: these are keynotes of the play. When it was occupying the mind of Shakespeare, he was passing from his service as artist to his service as English country gentleman. Had his mind been dwelling on the question of how he should employ his new freedom, and had he been enforcing upon himself the truth that the highest freedom lies in the bonds of duty?†

---

* Act ii, Scene 1—The prolonged and dull joking of Sebastian in this scene cannot be meant by Shakespeare to be really bright and witty. It is meant to shew that the intellectual poverty of the conspirators is as great as their moral obliquity. They are monsters more ignoble than Caliban. Their laughter is "the crackling of thorns under a pot."

† Mr Furnivall, observing that in these later plays breaches of the family bond are dramatically studied, and the reconciliations are domestic

It remains to notice of *The Tempest* that it has had the quality, as a work of art, of setting its critics to work as if it were an allegory; and forthwith it baffles them, and seems to mock them for supposing that they had power to "pluck out the heart of its mystery." A curious and interesting chapter in the history of Shakespearian criticism might be written if the various interpretations were brought together of the allegorical significances of Prospero, of Miranda, of Ariel, of Caliban. Caliban, says Kreyssig, is the People. He is Understanding apart from Imagination, declares Professor Lowell. He is the primitive man abandoned to himself, declares M Mézières; Shakespeare would say to Utopian thinkers, predecessors of Jean Jacques Rousseau, "Your hero walks on four feet as well as on two." That Caliban is the missing link between man and brute (Shakespeare anticipating Darwinian theories), has been elaborately demonstrated by Daniel Wilson. Caliban is one of the powers of nature over which the scientific intellect obtains command, another critic assures us, and Prospero is the founder of the Inductive Philosophy. Caliban is the colony of Virginia. Caliban is the untutored early drama of Marlowe.* Such

---

reconciliations in *Cymbeline* and *A Winter's Tale*, suggests to me that they were a kind of confession on Shakespeare's part that he had inadequately felt the beauty and tenderness of the common relations of father and child, wife and husband; and that he was now quietly resolving to be gentle, and wholly just to his wife and his home. I cannot altogether make this view of the later plays my own, and leave it to the reader to accept and develop as he may be able.

* This last suggestion is that of M. Emile Montégut in the *Revue des Deux Mondes*. The following passage from Professor Lowell will compensate for its length by its ingenuity. "In *The Tempest* the scene is laid nowhere, or certainly in no country laid down on any map. Nowhere, then ? At once nowhere and anywhere,—for it is in the soul of man that still vexed island hung between the upper and the nether world, and liable to incursions from both [...]. Consider for a moment if ever the Imagination has been so embodied as in Prospero, the Fancy as in Ariel, the brute Understanding as in Caliban, who, the moment his poor wits are warmed with the glorious liquor of Stephano, plots rebellion against his natural lord, the higher Reason. Miranda is mere abstract Womanhood, as truly so before she sees Ferdinand as Eve before she was awakened to consciousness by the echo of her own nature coming back to her, the same, and yet not the same, from that of Adam. Ferdinand, again, is nothing more than Youth, compelled to drudge at something he despises,

allegorical interpretations, however ingenious, we cannot set much store by. But the significance of a work of art like the character of a man is not to be discovered solely by investigation of its inward essence. Its dynamical qualities, so to speak, must be considered as well as its statical. It must be viewed in action; the atmosphere it effuses, its influence upon the minds of men must be noted. And it is certainly remarkable that this, the last or almost the last of Shakespeare's plays, more than any other, has possessed this quality, of soliciting men to attempt the explanation of it, as of an enigma, and at the same time of baffling their enquiry.

If I were to allow my fancy to run out in play after such an attempted interpretation, I should describe Prospero as the man of genius, the great artist, lacking at first in practical gifts which lead to material success, and set adrift on the perilous sea of life, in which he finds his enchanted island, where he may

---

till the sacrifice of will, and abnegation of self, win him his ideal in Miranda. The subordinate personages are simply types: Sebastian and Antonio of weak character and evil ambition; Gonzalo, of average sense and honesty; Adrian and Francisco, of the walking gentlemen, who serve to fill up a world. They are not characters in the same sense with Iago, Falstaff, Shallow, or Leontius; and it is curious how every one of them loses his way in this enchanted island of life, all the victims of one illusion after another, except Prospero, whose ministers are purely ideal. The whole play, indeed, is a succession of illusions, winding up with those solemn words of the great enchanter, who had summoned to his service every shape of merriment or passion, every figure in the great tragi-comedy of life, and who was now bidding farewell to the scene of his triumphs. For in Prospero shall we not recognise the Artist himself:

> That did not better for his life provide
> Than public means which public manners breeds,
> Whence comes it that his name receives a brand—

who has forfeited a shining place in the world's eye by devotion to his art, and who, turned adrift on the ocean of life in the leaky carcass of a boat, has shipwrecked on that Fortunate Island (as men always do who find their true vocation) where he is absolute lord, making all the powers of Nature serve him, but with Ariel and Caliban as special ministers? Of whom else could he have been thinking when he says,

> Graves, at my command,
> Have waked their sleepers, oped, and let them forth,
> By my so potent art ?"

"Among my Books. Shakespeare Once More," pp. 191-92.

achieve his works of wonder. He bears with him Art in its infancy,—the marvellous child, Miranda. The grosser passions and appetites—Caliban—he subdues to his service:

> *Mir.* 'Tis a villain, sir,
> I do not love to look on.
> *Pros.* But as 'tis
> We cannot miss him.

and he partially informs this servant-monster with intellect and imagination; for Caliban has dim affinities with the higher world of spirits. But these grosser passions and appetites attempt to violate the purity of art. Caliban would seize upon Miranda and people the island with Calibans; therefore his servitude must be strict. And who is Ferdinand? Is he not, with his gallantry and his beauty, the young Fletcher, in conjunction with whom Shakespeare worked upon the two *Noble Kinsmen* and *Henry VIII*? Fletcher is conceived as a follower of the Shakespearian style and method in dramatic art; he had "eyed full many a lady with best regard," for several virtues had liked several women, but never any with whole-hearted devotion except Miranda. And to Ferdinand the old enchanter will entrust his daughter, "a third of his own life." But Shakespeare had perceived the weak point in Fletcher's genius—its want of hardness of fibre, of patient endurance, and of a sense of the solemnity and sanctity of the service of art. And therefore he finely hints to his friend that his winning of Miranda must not be too light and easy. It shall be Ferdinand's task to remove some thousands of logs, and pile them according to the strict injunction of Prospero. "Don't despise drudgery and dryasdust work, young poets," Shakespeare would seem to say, who had himself so carefully laboured over his English and Roman histories; "for Miranda's sake such drudgery may well seem light." Therefore, also, Prospero surrounds the marriage of Ferdinand to his daughter with a religious awe. Ferdinand must honour her as sacred, and win her by hard toil. But the work of the higher imagination is not drudgery,—it is swift and serviceable among all the elements, fire upon the topmast, the sea-nymph upon the sands, Ceres the goddess of earth, with harvest blessings, in the Masque. It is essentially Ariel, an airy spirit,—the imaginative genius of poetry but recently delivered in England from long slavery to Sycorax. Prospero's departure from the island is the abandoning by Shakespeare of the theatre, the scene of his marvellous works:

> Graves at my command
> Have waked their sleepers, oped, and let them forth,
> By my so potent art.

Henceforth Prospero is but a man; no longer a great enchanter. He returns to the dukedom he had lost, in Stratford upon Avon, and will pay no tribute henceforth to any Alonzo or Lucy of them all.*

Thus one may be permitted to play with the grave subject of *The Tempest*, and I ask no more credit for the interpretation here proposed than is given to any other equally innocent, if trifling, attempt to read the supposed allegory.

Shakespeare's work, however, will indeed not allow itself to be lightly treated. The prolonged study of any great interpreter of human life is a discipline. Our loyalty to Shakespeare must not lead us to assert that the discipline of Shakespeare will be suitable to every nature. He will deal rudely with heart, and will, and intellect, and lay hold of them in unexpected ways, and fashion his disciple, it may be, in a manner which at first is painful, and almost terrible. There are persons who, all through their lives, attain their highest strength only by virtue of the presence of certain metaphysical entities which rule their lives; and in the lives of almost all men there is a metaphysical period, when they need such supposed entities more than the real presences of those personal and social forces which surround them. For such persons, and during such a period, the discipline of Shakespeare will be unsuitable. He will seem precisely the reverse of what he actually is: he will seem careless about great facts and ideas; limited, restrictive, deficient in enthusiasms and imagination. To one who finds the highest poetry in Shelley, Shakespeare will always remain a kind of prose. Shakespeare is the poet of concrete things and real. True, but are not these informed with passion and with thought? A time not seldom comes when a man, abandoning abstractions and metaphysical

* Ulrici has recently expressed his opinion that a farewell to the theatre may be discovered in *The Tempest*; but he rightly places *Henry VIII*, later than *The Tempest*. *Shakespeare Jahrbuch*, vol. vi, p. 358.

entities, turns to the actual life of the world, and to the real men and women who surround him, for the sources of emotion, and thought, and action—a time when he strives to come into communion with the Unseen, not immediately, but through the revelation of the Seen. And then he finds the strength and sustenance with which Shakespeare has enriched the world.

"'The true question to ask,' says the Librarian of Congress, in a paper read before the Social Science Convention, at New York, October 1869, 'The true question to ask respecting a book, is, *Has it helped any human soul!*' This is the hint, statement, not only of the great Literatus, his book, but of every great Artist. It may be that all works of art are to be first tried by their art-qualities, their image-forming talent, and their dramatic, pictorial, plot-constructing, euphonious, and other talents. Then, whenever claiming to be first-class works, they are to be strictly and sternly tried by their foundation in, and radiation, in the highest sense, and always indirectly, of the ethic principles, and eligibility to free, arouse, dilate."*

What shall be said of Shakespeare's radiation through art of the ultimate truths of conscience and of conduct? What shall be said of his power of freeing, arousing, dilating? Something may be gathered out of the foregoing chapters in answer to these questions. But the answers remain insufficient. There is an admirable sentence by Emerson: "A good reader can in a sort, nestle into Plato's brain, and think from thence; but not into Shakespeare's. We are still out of doors."

We are still out of doors; and for the present let us cheerfully remain in the large, good space. Let us not attenuate Shakespeare to a theory. He is careful that we shall not thus lose our true reward; "The secrets of Nature have not more gift in taciturnity."† Shakespeare does not supply us with a doctrine, with an interpretation, with a revelation. What he brings to us, is this—to each one, courage, and energy, and strength, to dedicate himself and his work to that,—whatever it be,—which life has revealed to him as best, and highest, and most real.

---

* Whitman, *Democratic Vistas*, p. 67.

† *Troilus and Cressida*, Act iv, Scene 2.

Index